THE GENESIS OF
YOUNG OTTOMAN
THOUGHT

Modern Intellectual and Political History of the Middle East
Mehrzad Boroujerdi, *Series Editor*

THE GENESIS OF YOUNG OTTOMAN THOUGHT

A Study in the Modernization of Turkish Political Ideas

ŞERIF MARDIN

Syracuse University Press

First Syracuse University Press Edition 2000

00 01 02 03 04 05   6 5 4 3 2 1

Originally published in 1962 by Princeton University Press.

The paper used in this publication meets the minimum requirements
of American National Standard for Information Sciences—Permanence
of Paper for Printed Library Materials, ANSI Z39.48-1984. ∞™

Library of Congress Cataloging-in-Publication Data

Mardin, Serif.
The genesis of young Ottoman thought : a study in the modernization of Turkish
political ideas / by Serif Mardin.—1st Syracuse University Press ed.
p. cm. — (Modern intellectual and political history of the Middle East)
Originally published: Princeton, N.J. : Princeton University Press, 1962.
Includes bibliographical references (p.) and index.
ISBN 0-8156-2861-7 (pbk. : alk. paper)
1. Turkey—Intellectual life. 2. Turkey—Politics and government—19th century.   I.
Series.
DR557 .M3 2000
956.1'015—dc21   00-038779

Manufactured in the United States of America

·:9 CONTENTS 6:·

✥ PREFACE ✥

THIS book first appeared in 1962. It was the product of a suspicion that the story of the nineteenth-century reform movement in Turkey, which one could retrieve in the work of Turkish historians of the 1950s, provided us only with the thinnest surface of the process of change undergone by the Ottoman Empire. I suspected that the discourse of those historians deliberately blotted out items in the process of change which did not accord with the official republican storyline. A more generous supposition was that the distortion had not been deliberate but could have emerged as a result of the self-censorship, which, until recently, was an adjunct of the patriotic code of honor of Turkish republican intellectuals.

Outside Turkey too, a variant of this discourse was common. The expressed opinion of Bernard Lewis with regard to the era of the Tanzimat (1839–1876), for instance, consisted of a sanitizing of old Ottoman institutions on the way to the ultimate establishment of a secular republic.

Much way has been made since 1962 in studies of the Tanzimat but less in the study of the motivation of its first generation of libertarian constitutionalists. A number of doctoral dissertations in preparation will, I hope, further decode this issue. In the meantime the text still seems useful as an introduction to the Young Ottoman movement. It is now reprinted without change.

I am happy to take this opportunity to reiterate my gratitude to Professor Howard Reed, who made it possible for me to work on the manuscript and honor the memory of Professor Lewis Thomas who, at all times, encouraged its preparation.

PREFACE TO THE ORIGINAL EDITION

Two important methodological problems that confront anyone giving an account of Ottoman developments are those of transcription and of bibliographical systematization.

The following rules have been followed in the present work with regard to transcription:

Proper names of Ottoman-Turkish statesmen are spelled with the resources available in the modern Turkish alphabet in such a way as to approximate a transcription of their Arabic alphabet originals. Special diacritical signs devised for transcription systems are not used. Thus: "Ahmed" is used rather than the more current modern Turkish spelling "Ahmet"; "Midhat," rather than "Mithat"; "Subhi," rather than "Suphi."

The proper names of persons who were prominent in Ottoman cultural history but were not "Ottomans" are spelled as they are spelled in Turkey nowadays, with the *Encyclopaedia of Islam* transcription following in parentheses immediately after the first mention of the name in the text. Thus: Celaleddin-i Devvanî (Djalāl al-din al-Dawwānī).

Proper names of Arabic origin are spelled according to the *Encyclopaedia of Islam* transcription when used in an early Islamic context but, according to modern Turkish usage, in an Ottoman context. Thus: the caliph Abū Bakr, but Ebubekir Ratib Efendi (Ebübekir being optional in Turkish usage).

Entire phrases in Arabic often used for Turkish book titles, or *ḥadīth*, which are used by the Young Ottomans as titles for their articles are transcribed according to the *Encyclopaedia of Islam* transcription.

All other "Ottoman" words, with the exception of "*Hatt-ı Hümâyun*," are spelled as they appear in the following dictionary: Mustafa Nihat Özön, *Osmanlıca-Türkçe Sözlük* (Istanbul, 1955).

The sign ('), widely accepted in Turkish usage in words where the *ayn* still remains accentuated, is used throughout.

Insofar as the bibliography is concerned, the following principles were followed:

Whenever possible, dates of publication are ascertained by reference to the following work: Fehmi Ethem Karatay, *Istanbul Üniversitesi Kütüphanesi Türkçe Basmalar Kataloğu* (Istanbul, 1952), 2 vols. Otherwise, the following system was used:

When both the year and the month during which a certain work was published could be ascertained, only one A.D. date corresponding to the date of publication is given.

When the month could not be determined, the date of the Gregorian calendar corresponding to the first day of the Hicrî year is given.

When a book was published over a period of several years, the limit dates of the Gregorian calendar corresponding to these dates are mentioned. Thus: 1311-1314 Hicrî would be 1893-1897.

Whenever the date of publication was a Malî date (where the first ten months always correspond to a definite A.D. date) the two corresponding A.D. dates are given. Thus: 1326 Malî is A.D. 1910-1911.

After the first occurrence, "A.H." and "A.D." have been omitted from dates. The dates have been separated by a solidus (/), with the A.H. date first.

ꙮ ACKNOWLEDGMENTS ꙮ

THIS book owes much to a number of supporters and commentators at every phase of its preparation. While it is impossible to do justice to all, I should like to thank at least those who have been directly concerned with its writing.

I was first encouraged to take up Turkish modernization as a subject of a dissertation by Professor James T. Watkins III of the Department of Political Science of Stanford University. Many of the themes which are examined in the following pages will be familiar to those who had the fortune of witnessing the brilliant analysis given them—in the context of Western thought—by the late Professor Arnaud Leavelle of Stanford University. During my years of graduate work my friend John Holley, by his generosity, allowed me to concentrate on intellectual rather than physical labor. Professor Majid Khadduri provided me with the fundamentals of an understanding of Islamic culture. Professor Hilmi Ziya Ülken gave me a basic orientation in Turkish sources. Professor Halil Inalcık of the University of Ankara encouraged me to believe that my manuscript of a doctoral dissertation was worth being revised and expanded.

The Department of Oriental Studies at Princeton University, by providing me with an extended research associateship, gave me a unique opportunity to carry out this recommendation. Professor T. Cuyler Young, as the Chairman of the Department, and Professor Lewis V. Thomas, as director of Turkish studies, gave me the moral support which made it so agreeable to work in the Department. Both enabled me to see some of the problems which were being involved in the manuscript as work was progressing. Professor Thomas, by reading the manuscript undeterred by its original scheme of transliteration, and by suggestions as to the organization of the material afforded me expert advice. Sir Hamilton Gibb of the Center for Middle Eastern Studies of Harvard University made it possible for me to be in the United States at the time the manuscript was delivered to the Princeton University Press and thus enabled me to follow the first stages of its preparation for printing. Mrs. Jansen Dalby of the Department of Oriental Studies at Princeton University assured the typescript smooth sailing by allocating the resources of her office in a miraculously steady stream.

No words could express my sense of gratitude for the constant vigilance and editorial assistance of Miss R. Miriam Brokaw of Princeton University Press. Her refusal to be disturbed by some of the highly anarchical aspects of Turkish spelling and editing practices and her attempts to bring order into confusion are an indication of her systematizing patience.

My thanks are due to the Clarendon Press for permission to quote from *The Legacy of Islam* edited by T. W. Arnold and Alfred Guillaume; to the University Press of Cambridge for permission to quote from E. I. J. Rosenthal's *Political Thought in Medieval Islam: An Introductory Outline*; to Oxford University Press for permission to quote from H. A. R. Gibb and Harold Bowen's *Islamic Society and the West*, published under the auspices of the Royal Institute of International Affairs; to the Johns Hopkins Press for permission to quote from Majid Khadduri's *War and Peace in the Law of Islam*; and to the Middle East Institute for permission to quote H. A. R. Gibb's article on "Constitutional Organization," contained in *Law in the Middle East*, edited by Majid Khadduri and Herbert Liebesny.

THE GENESIS OF
YOUNG OTTOMAN
THOUGHT

❧ CHAPTER I ❧

Introduction

In Turkish, the word *Tanzimat* means "regulations," and is used to refer to a period of Turkish history (1839-1878) during which a considerable number of Western-inspired political and social reforms were carried out in the Ottoman Empire. To a modern Turk the term immediately conjures up the figure of Mustafa Reşid Paşa, the statesman who was instrumental in introducing these reforms into Turkey; it reminds one of the Europeanization of the army and the civil service, of the new officials wearing cutaway coats and fezzes instead of the flowing robes and turbans of their pre-Tanzimat predecessors. The term also brings to mind Fuad Paşa, the successor of Reşid, scattering witty epigrams in French at the lavish balls of the era and the growth of the institution of "mixed" secular courts of law in the empire.

The institutional transformations which took place in Turkey during the Tanzimat so impressed Western observers at the time that wide, although often superficial, coverage was given to this formal metamorphosis. The time, however, was not yet ripe, and the means at the disposal of the European observers not adequate to write a survey of the currents of thought that ran parallel to the reforms of the Tanzimat. The present study is an attempt to fill this gap. It endeavors to separate the strands that went into the political ideas of the Young Ottomans, a group of Turkish intellectuals who attained prominence during the late Tanzimat, in the years 1867-1878.

What is known about the Young Ottomans in contemporary Turkey cannot begin to compare, in wealth of detail or in accuracy of information, with what is known in England about seventeenth-century dissenters or in Western Europe as a whole about even more remote Medieval Conciliar controversies. Yet there is hardly a single area of modernization in

3

Turkey today, from the simplification of the written language to the idea of fundamental civil liberties, that does not take its roots in the pioneering work of the Young Ottomans. Paradoxically, any serious attempt to reinject Islam into the foundations of the Turkish state, were it to appear today, would also have to look back to their time. This is so because the Young Ottomans were at one and the same time the first men to make the ideas of the Enlightenment part of the intellectual equipment of the Turkish reading public and the first thinkers to try to work out a synthesis between these ideas and Islam.

For the mere sake of opening up a perspective of political modernization somewhat deeper than that provided by the thirty odd years of the Turkish Republic, there therefore exists a need for an account of the Young Ottoman movement. The specific reason, on the other hand, for which one is justified in saying that very little is known about them is that there exists only one work, in any language, that seriously attempts to unravel their history.[1] This is a Marxist analysis, the usefulness of which is limited by its attempts to establish a perfect correlation between the rise of the Young Ottoman movement and the economic changes that preceded their appearance. In other investigations which give the Young Ottomans peripheral attention the most elementary questions with regard to their activities have not been asked. It may be categorically stated, for example, that the Young Ottomans represented a form of political protest for which there had been no precedent in the Ottoman Empire. For the first time, an organized group of the Turkish intelligentsia was making use of the media of mass communication to voice extremely articulate criticisms of the government of the empire. The question thus arises as to how such a group could have emerged in the first place. No attempts have been made in these secondary works to solve such a riddle.

[1] Y. A. Petrosyan, *"Noviye Osmanii," I Borba za Konstitutsiu 1876 g. v Turtsii* (Moscow, 1958).

This absence of interest at points where interest should have concentrated points out the very real limitations of the methods heretofore used by Western students of Turkish reform. These studies constitute the bulk of the work that has been done on Turkish reform, but most of them have been carried on at the level of the sources most accessible to Westerners, i.e., they have been based on memoirs, diplomatic materials, and government documents. Thus the life and times of the "Great Elchi" Stratford Canning,[2] the impetus—real or imaginary—given to Turkish reform by representatives of the Western powers,[3] and the pressures exerted by these representatives to make Ottomans bow to their demands for reform are well-worn approaches to the "Westernization" of the Ottoman Empire. Even in works in which the Young Ottomans have been given some peripheral attention,[4] the formal, mechanical, and institutional aspects of reform have been attributed the greatest importance. Such avenues of research have the obvious disadvantage of not bringing into relief the stresses and strains, intellectual, social and cultural, which throughout the change were felt by the Ottomans themselves.

Turkish studies suffer from even more elementary defects. Of the two Turkish contributions which take up the Young Ottomans, the first, an autobiographical account by one of their members, sacrifices accuracy to the demands of purple prose,[5] while the second constitutes a monument to a type of antiquarian myopia which allows only for the collection of facts and precludes their organization into an intelligible whole.[6]

Thus there still remains the need of looking at the Young

[2] Harold Temperley, *England and the Near East: The Crimea* (London, Longmans, Green & Co., 1936).

[3] Frank Edgar Bailey, *British Policy and the Turkish Reform Movement: a Study in Anglo-Turkish Relations 1826-1853* (Cambridge, Mass., Harvard University Press, 1942).

[4] Ed[ouard] Engelhardt, *La Turquie et le Tanzimat* (Paris, Cotillon, 1880-1882).

[5] See below, Chapter II, note 1, for this work by Ebüzziya Tevfik.

[6] Midhat Cemal Kuntay, *Namık Kemal: Devrinin İnsanları ve Olayları Arasında* (Istanbul, Maarif Matbaası, 1944-1957), 2 vols. in 3 parts.

Ottoman movement from inside the Turkish chrysalis and of evolving a "physiology" of Turkish reforms. When this is undertaken, the Young Ottoman movement appears in its true perspective, viz., not as a *sui-generis* outcropping, but as the product of the many processes that had been at work in Ottoman society since the early nineteenth century.

It may be said, then, that the second aim of this study is to recapture and describe the process by which certain Western political concepts were introduced into Turkey even earlier than the last quarter of the nineteenth century and became part of the Turkish intellectual patrimony.

One of the most helpful ways of approaching such a problem seemed to lie in the concept of "operative ideals" developed by the late Lord Lindsay. According to Lord Lindsay, "political theory . . . is concerned with fact, but with fact of a peculiar kind. Its business is to understand the purposes or ideals actually operative in sustaining a political organization."[7] This study, taking its cue from Lord Lindsay's approach, tries to determine how these ideals changed in Turkey at a time when the institutional foundations of the modern state were being laid in that country.

Once this stand is taken, the study resolves itself into the investigation of three related but distinct problems, namely, the state of the operative political ideals in the Ottoman Empire at the beginning of the period under investigation, the influences to which these ideals were subjected, and the total change brought about by these influences.

The first one of these—the determination of the operative political ideals of Ottoman society in the middle of the nineteenth century—requires separate study because the subject has not yet been investigated. This is effected here by presenting a picture of the political ideals that motivated the architects

[7] A. D. Lindsay, *The Modern Democratic State* (London, Oxford University Press, 1943), I, 45. Lord Lindsay states that the political and social transformation of modern Turkey would constitute an interesting subject of study from this point of view (*ibid.*, p. 46).

of the Tanzimat. Those ideals were embodied in a reform policy that was initiated in the years during which the majority of the Young Ottomans were born. The reform ideals also set a "climate of opinion" which was still operative in official circles at the time the Young Ottomans became active.

While the political writings of the Young Ottomans undoubtedly reflect European influences, it is quite another matter to find out what, specifically, these influences were. Most of the thinkers of the early Tanzimat fail to indicate European mentorship, and their references to Western political thinkers are almost inexistent. The eclecticism of both groups presents a further challenge to anyone undertaking to disentangle their ideological pedigree. The present work tries to trace such influences to their source.

A special problem, in this connection, is that one has to determine whether the political ideology which the Young Ottomans contributed was the product of ubiquitous Western influences or whether these new ideas were generated by a complex background of more subtle, elusive and subterranean processes which laid the basis for changes in ideology.

It is probable that alterations in the structure of Turkish society and the establishment in the late eighteenth and early nineteenth century of new institutions were factors which prepared the ground for ideological permeation by the West. It is in this context that institutional history is of importance for the present study, which attempts to establish such links.

There is no better warning of the difficulties encountered in such an attempt to measure the relative role played by ideas and complex social changes in the development of a new political outlook than the definitive work of Daniel Mornet on the intellectual origins of the French Revolution.[8] What Mornet did, in effect, was to show that the influence of the *philosophes* and in particular that of Rousseau had not been so widespread as Taine had made it fashionable to believe.

---

[8] Daniel Mornet, *Les Origines Intellectuelles de la Révolution Française* (Paris, Armand Colin, 1933).

This was expressed in the rather upsetting statement that on the eve of 1789 not more than ten men who distinguished themselves among the revolutionaries had read the political works of Rousseau. Furthermore, Mornet showed that less specifically political ideas, such as the conception of a mechanistic system of nature and the general trend to think critically about problems of daily life, had a considerable share in leading to the revolutionary ideology. Even though identical issues may not arise in connection with the present study, and although the material that would be used in a Turkish equivalent of Mornet's study has not even been uncovered to date, his approach points to methodological refinements which cannot be overlooked with impunity. In particular, local Turkish developments which were only indirectly the product of Western influences must be brought in at all times to establish a meaningful picture of intellectual evolution.

It should be clear by now that the subject of this investigation is as much to gauge the rate of change of political beliefs in Turkey during the late Tanzimat as to test the internal consistency of any one of the systems of political thought developed by the Young Ottomans. This study therefore falls into two major divisions: the first, an account of the formation of Young Ottoman ideas; the second, an analysis of the political system of each of the Young Ottomans.

Up to the middle of the nineteenth century Turkey had remained outside the main stream of Western European intellectual development. Ottoman civilization was therefore deprived of the benefit of the political ideas that had gained currency in Europe during the Enlightenment. The political theory by which the rule of the Ottoman sultans was justified, for instance, identified political power with the vicarage of God. In the European political theory of the nineteenth century, on the other hand, the separation of secular and religious power was axiomatic. Thus the adaptation of Western European political ideas to suit the needs of the Ottoman Empire, which the Young Ottomans attempted, was bound to run into difficulties. This book is partly a survey of those difficulties.

We have yet to cover one of the problems enumerated above. That problem is one concerning the extent to which the ideas of the Young Ottomans produced in Turkey a changed conception of the state after the disbanding of their organization and the demise of the majority of their leaders. This task is not undertaken here and will constitute the subject of a subsequent work.

As no single important treatise on politics was published by the Young Ottomans, the sources that we have to rely on here are ones that are usually considered "occasional," such as newspaper collections and pamphlets. Neither are the figures which make up the Young Ottoman movement outstanding philosophers or scholars. Such men as Şinasi, Ali Suavi, and Ziya Paşa, who are taken up in the following pages, are no giants of political theory but belong to the category of *hommes de lettres*, a euphemism used by the French for the intellectual Jack-of-all-trades. Still, their thought is important insofar as it is the expression of the political beliefs of the earliest modern Turkish intelligentsia. Furthermore, the Islamic-scholastic side of the education of these men provided them with a discipline of mind which should not be underestimated; the political writings of Namık Kemal, for example, surpass in their compactness and clarity many more recent Turkish writings on politics.

The program of investigation outlined in the preceding pages is one which covers a wide area. In what follows, various portions of this area will be examined, one in each chapter. Every one of these sections, however, merely pinpoints an approach that may be adopted in studying the Young Ottoman movement. No part of this work claims to provide, in addition, analysis "in depth." The fondest hope that its writing can elicit is that the basic facets of Young Ottoman thought and action that are enumerated may be found to warrant more intensive research by future students of the movement.

The Young Ottomans

I. The Patriotic Alliance

IN THE summer of 1865 a picnic took place in the so-called Forest of Belgrade, a wooded valley lying behind the hills of the Bosphorus.[1] Attending it were six young men who had

---

[1] This version of the formation of the Patriotic Alliance, as this society was to be known, is based on the account of Ebüzziya Tevfik given in his *Origins of the Young Ottomans*, published as a serial in the daily *Yeni Tasvir-i Efkâr* in 1909. See Ebüzziya Tevfik, "Yeni Osmanlıların Sebeb-i Zuhuru," *Yeni Tasvir-i Efkâr*, May 13, 1909 to June 12, 1909; "Yeni Osmanlılar," *Yeni Tasvir-i Efkâr*, June 13, 1909 to June 25, 1909; "Yeni Osmanlılar Tarihi," *Yeni Tasvir-i Efkâr*, August 28, 1909 to January 8, 1911. Part of this work is available in modern Turkish script, having been transcribed in Latin characters. See G. A. Kuralay, "Yeni Osmanlılar Muharriri Ebüzziya," İstanbul Üniversitesi Türkoloji Enstitüsü, Tez 421, 1953 (unpublished B.A. paper, the Institute of Turcology, Faculty of Letters, University of Istanbul). Ebüzziya was one of the earliest members of the Alliance, but his account has been considered inaccurate and biased by some of his contemporaries. See İbnülemin Mahmut Kemal İnal, "Ayetullah Bey," in *Son Asır Türk Şairleri* (Istanbul, Orhaniye Matbaası, 1930-1942), pp. 149-151. According to the oral information gathered by one of the students of the movement, Midhat Cemal Kuntay, from the niece of Mehmed Bey, the Patriotic Alliance was founded by the following persons: Mustafa Fazıl Paşa, Mehmed Bey, Namık Kemal Bey, Nuri Bey, Ayetullah Bey, Reşad Bey, Agâh Efendi, and a "commoner" by the name of Pazarköylü Ahmed Ağa whose task it was to spread the ideas of the Alliance throughout the countryside. The fact that this latter person is also cited in some recently uncovered letters of Namık Kemal, while not mentioned in the account of Ebüzziya, casts further doubt on the accuracy of Ebüzziya's account. See Midhat Cemal Kuntay, *Namık Kemal: Devrinin İnsanları ve Olayları Arasında* (Istanbul, Maarif Matbaası, 1944-1957), I, 358. A variant of this account of the formation of the Patriotic Alliance has been given by the Turkish historian and statesman Cevdet Paşa, a contemporary of the movement. According to Cevdet Paşa, the catalytic agent in the formation of the Patriotic Alliance was the editorial office of the daily *Ceride-i Havadis*, where the poet Şinasi Efendi, Namık Kemal Bey, and other liberally inclined figures would gather for discussions. Cf. İnal, "Müşfik," p. 1020, where there are quoted unpublished portions of Cevdet Paşa's *Ma'ruzat*. Full treatment of the formation of the Alliance as well as of the Young Ottoman movement is to be found in only one other study, an article by the Turkish historian Abdurrahman Şeref. See Abdurrahman Şeref, "Yeni Osmanlılar ve Hürriyet," *Tarih Musahabeleri* (Istanbul, Matbaa-i Âmire, A.H. 1339/A.D. 1923-1924), pp. 172-182. According to Ismail Hikmet [Ertaylan]—see *Türk Edebiyatı*

decided to take action against what they considered to be catastrophic policies pursued by the Ottoman Government.

What united these young conspirators was a common knowledge of European civilization and an equal concern at the disintegration of the Ottoman Empire. Responsibility for the accelerated pace of the decline of the Sick Man of Europe was now laid by them at the door of a small group of statesmen headed by Âli Paşa and Fuad Paşa. These two men had, for some time, alternated in the offices of the Grand Vizierate and the Ministry of Foreign Affairs. They also held in their grip the formulation of the policies of the Porte. The appointment of ministers of state other than themselves had become their almost exclusive prerogative. They were thus accused of personal rule, of brewing wrong policies in an ivory tower, and of building an oligarchy of sycophants.

Almost all of the men present at the picnic had been working at one time or another in the Translation Bureau of the Porte, and most of them had thus been given the opportunity to acquaint themselves with European political systems as well as with the way the foreign policy of the empire was being conducted. They were a generation nurtured in the ways of

---

Tarihi, Ondokuzuncu Asır (Baku, Azer Neşir, 1925), I, 217—one of the few experts who has more than scratched the surface of the problem, the most truthful account of the activities of the group is to be found in the manuscript memoirs of Nuri Bey, one of the members of the Alliance. I have been unable to obtain this manuscript. Yet fragments of it which have appeared in print show the formation to have been quite different from what has been believed. Cf. Riza Tevfik, "Filozofa Göre Namık Kemal," in *Ölümünden Sonra Riza Tevfik* (ed. by Mustafa Ragıp Esatlı, Istanbul, Sinan Matbaası, n.d.), pp. 113-140. His manuscript clarifies the order of accession to the Alliance. Ziya Paşa, for example, is cited among the founders. Ali Suavi gives biased but important information about the origins of the Patriotic Alliance, the organization established by the Young Ottomans, in his memoirs in the *Ulûm*. See Ali Suavi, "Civan Türk Tarihi," *Ulûm* (undated, 1870), pp. 786-797, 896-932. (The collection of the *Ulûm* used by the author had only some of the title pages on which figure the exact date of publication of each number; location of the references, however, is possible because of consecutive paging.) This information, however, is too fragmentary to be used extensively at this date. The historian Jorga has no more to offer as a comment on the Young Ottomans than that they were "meistens verdorbene Osmanli." Jorga, *Geschichte des Osmanischen Reiches* (Gotha, Perthes, 1913), V, 537.

the West, thanks to the efforts of the very men they opposed. Âli and Fuad, their targets, had taken up the modernization of the Ottoman Empire where Reşid Paşa had left it. But just as Âli and Fuad had, in their time, opposed Reşid for being too mild a reformer, they in turn were now criticized by a new generation of political critics.

Leading the group of picnickers was one Mehmed Bey, who had received his education at the Ottoman school in Paris[2] and had returned well permeated with the ideas of constitutionalism and popular representation. Mehmed Bey had been able to kindle this reforming fire in the hearts of two younger friends, Nuri Bey and Reşad Bey. All three men were, at the time, employed in the Translation Bureau of the *Meclis-i Vâlâ*, an institution which was the direct lineal descendant of the *Meclis-i Vâlâ-yı Ahkâm-ı Adliye*, the first modern consultative governmental machinery established in 1837 by Mustafa Reşid Paşa.[3]

Among those present, second in importance after Mehmed Bey was Namık Kemal Bey, who had already acquired some fame as a poet in the literary circles of the capital. Shortly before, he had been entrusted with the publication of the *Tasvir-i Efkâr* by its preceding publisher, Şinasi Efendi, when Şinasi had to flee Turkey because of his involvement in a plot directed against Âli.[4]

A fifth member of the group, Ayetullah Bey, was the product of a household and an education most extraordinary in all respects. His father, Subhi Paşa, held court in his mansion in the midst of a continuous stream of men of learning and extended his hospitality to Eastern and Western scholars alike. It was unthinkable that an authority on any subject should

---

[2] See below, Chapter VII.

[3] For Mehmed Bey, see İnal, *Son Asır*, pp. 942-951; for Nuri, *ibid.*, pp. 1252-1261; for Reşad, Kuntay, *Namık Kemal*, I, 381-389. Detailed information on the governmental institutions mentioned will be found below, Chapter V.

[4] Ebüzziya Tevfik, "Yeni Osmanlılar," *Yeni Tasvir-i Efkâr*, 31 October 1909, p. 4.

go through Istanbul without visiting Subhi Paşa.[5] In such an
atmosphere, Ayetullah Bey had been given ample opportunity
to acquire a solid Western as well as Eastern culture. It was
this cultural background and, in particular, his admiration for
the achievements of Napoleon (an attitude the radical tenor
of which has been strikingly depicted in the case of Restoration
France) that made Ayetullah Bey join the ranks of the political opposition.[6]

The sixth member of the meeting was Refik Bey, the owner
of the short-lived periodical *Mir'at*, in which had appeared
Namık Kemal's translations from Montesquieu.[7]

That day those present decided to form a society whose aim
would be to change "absolute into constitutional rule" in the
empire.[8] This meant, in effect, to put an end to the preponderant influence of the ubiquitous Âli Paşa, who had also
antagonized the plotters by what they considered his lack of
nerve in his dealings with the European Great Powers.

The plotters were far from opposed to the monarchial
principle, yet they must have shared Kemal's estimate of the
ruling sultan, Abdülaziz, as a rather simple-minded prince
who had allowed himself to be cowed by Âli and as a potentate
whose traditionalism was overly naïve. There are indications[9]
that from the very beginning of their activities the conspirators

[5] See Haluk Y. Şehsuvaroğlu, "Sami Paşa Konağı," *Cumhuriyet* (Istanbul), August 24, 1951. For similar activities in the house of the protector
of the Young Ottomans, Yusuf Kâmil Paşa, see İbnülemin Mahmut Kemal
İnal, *Osmanlı Devrinde son Sadrıazamlar* (Istanbul, Maarif Matbaası, 1940-
1953), p. 235. For another center at the house of the patron of the Young
Ottomans, Mustafa Fazıl Paşa, see Osman Ergin, *Türkiyede Maarif Tarihi*
(Istanbul, Osmanbey Matbaası, 1939-1943), p. 316. For Subhi Paşa's biography, see Mehmed Süreyya, *Sicill-i Osmanî* (Istanbul, Matbaa-i Âmire,
1308-1311/1890-1894), III, 220 f.
[6] The psychological process whereby a desire for reform was associated
with an idealization of Napoleonic achievements has already been described
too well by Stendahl in his *Le Rouge et le Noir* to require that such a
connection be made.
[7] Kaplan, *Namık Kemal*, I, 50.
[8] Ebüzziya Tevfik, "Yeni Osmanlılar," *Yeni Tasvir-i Efkâr*, June 7,
1909, p. 3.
[9] Kuntay, *Namık Kemal*, I, 91-94.

were in touch with Prince Murad, the highly intelligent and cultivated nephew of Sultan Abdülaziz and heir to the throne, and that they looked hopefully to his eventual enthronement.

A retrospective glance at Turkish developments between 1856 and 1865 is necessary at this point, to get a better insight into the motivations and the aims of the young men who had assembled that day. When, in 1839, the semi-constitutional charter known as the *Hatt-ı Hümâyun* of Gülhane had been proclaimed, due to Reşid Paşa's efforts, one of Reşid Paşa's purposes in drafting it had been to establish the basis for the eventual creation of an Ottoman nation in which subjects would benefit from identical civil rights, automatically conferred with citizenship and not dependent on religious affiliation.[10] The Gülhane Rescript had promised that all Ottoman subjects would, thereafter, be treated on a basis of equality. Reşid Paşa, however, did not anticipate that specific demands to establish equality between Moslems and Christians would come very soon. Nor did he foresee that they would be as strong and explosive as they turned out to be. He lost sight of several developments which, although difficult to perceive in 1839, were to gain increasingly in momentum in the 1850's. In those years the more extensive commercial relations between Europe and the Ottoman Empire, the growth in missionary activities, the influence of the secular ideas of the Enlightenment on the Christian populations of the empire, the rising national and political consciousness of these same people, the growing interest taken by the European Great Powers in the protection of Christians in the empire—each raised a different problem in relation to the equality promised in the 1839 Rescript. Many of the regulations by which the Christian populations of the Ottoman Empire had abided for centuries now became galling restrictions which they hastened to shake off—and which the European powers were happy to

[10] For a doctoral dissertation which takes up this point see Halil İnalcık, *Tanzimat ve Bulgar Meselesi* (Ankara, Türk Tarih Kurumu Basımevi, 1940).

cooperate in eliminating. Each of the groups involved in this process thought of these restrictions in terms of its own interests. For the missionaries, the road block was the Ottoman custom of executing apostates; for the Christian population, which turned to the European Great Powers for succor, it was the ban on public manifestations of worship, the latitude allowed to administrators in granting permission to build new churches, the attribution of political authority to their religious leaders, the fact that, in lawsuits brought against Moslems, Christian testimony was not fully accepted, and that Christians were not appointed to offices of the state in proportion to their numbers and did not profit from the educational facilities introduced by the state since Reşid Paşa's reforms. The gist of this attitude was a demand by the non-Moslems that the entire population of the empire, without distinction of creed, be extended the privileges of the public services performed by the Ottoman state and the opportunities of employment provided by it. Yet traditionally the non-Moslem population of the empire had been granted special privileges so that these services might be performed by their own communities. The Ottoman statesmen were thus justified in believing that a surrender of these communal privileges should be the price paid for the establishment of an Ottoman nationality under which everyone would fully enjoy the benefits of state services as well as the equal protection of the laws. As matters turned out, these statesmen were never allowed an opportunity to carry out such ideas in practice, since they were under constant pressure from the Great Powers to grant at one and the same time equal rights of citizenship and special community privileges.

The point here was, of course, that European diplomats, even when they were not encouraging confusion in the assessment of the problems of the Ottoman Empire, were not themselves entirely aware that the legitimate grievances of the subject people of the Ottoman Empire were, since the beginning of the nineteenth century, inextricably entwined with the demands of an extra-rational nationalism. This second factor was to play an increasing role in Ottoman foreign affairs after the year 1856.

One additional pressure was generated by the foreign merchants residing in Istanbul, who were distressed by the lack of a precise commercial code to which they could have reference in disputes involving them with Moslems.

At the time of the Crimean War, Turkey's allies began to press the empire to carry out such reforms as would eliminate these disabilities. At first the idea of a guarantee of special rights to the Christians of the empire was seriously considered.[11] Eventually a plan was adopted which guaranteed these rights to all subjects, whether Christian or Moslem. These principles were embodied in a new Imperial Rescript, the *Hatt-ı Hümâyun* of February 18, 1856.[12] Since the *Hatt* was, in fact, the product of foreign interference in Ottoman affairs, a face-saving device was invented in that Article ix of the Treaty of Paris, to which the *Hatt* had been annexed, stipulated that the enforcement of the provisions contained in the *Hatt* was not to constitute a pretext for foreign interference. In fact, however, the powers did interfere in the affairs of the Ottoman Empire.[13] Thus, for example, when in 1860 the Christians of the Lebanon and the Moslem inhabitants of the area flew at each other's throats and the Porte did not intervene in time, French troops were sent into the Lebanon.

In general, the early 1860's were a time when the Ottoman Empire was beginning to feel the increasing tug of Balkan nationalism and when more and more its international relations were conducted under the surveillance of the Concert of Europe. The following are a few of the events which may be shown to have been directly responsible for the young conspirators' disgust with the Porte.

---

[11] F. Eichmann, *Die Reformen des Osmanischen Reiches* (Berlin, Nicolaische Buchhandlung, 1848), pp. 33, 34.

[12] Text in I. de Testa, *Recueil des Traités de la Porte Ottomane* (Paris, 1864-1911), V, 132-137.

[13] For an admission that this principle never worked and that the reforms of the 1860's were due to foreign pressures, see Testa, *Recueil*, VII, 349, 350.

Between 1859 and 1864 the vassal principalities of Moldavia and Walachia set out on an independent course, elected for themselves the same ruler, proclaimed a unitary constitution, and finally obtained autonomy.

In 1860 a revolt took place in Herzegovina which the Montenegrins soon joined. Two and a half years elapsed before this uprising could be controlled. When a treaty was finally signed between the Montenegrins and the Turks, the latter obtained the right to garrison blockhouses straddling the main Montenegrin highway. Yet these advantages were later given up by the Turks (March 1863).

In 1862 the Turkish garrison of Belgrade and the local population of the city clashed, with considerable losses on both sides. This matter was settled by an international conference which met in the Ottoman capital. The Turks then agreed to evacuate two of the six fortresses which they still occupied in Serbia.

Every one of these developments left a bitter taste in the mouth of the Turks. During the Lebanese crisis of 1860, for instance, Fuad Paşa, investigating the circumstances leading to the uprising, had the Turkish commanding general and two of his aides shot for not having stopped the encounter between Moslems and Druses in time. Many Turks were shocked by this severity, which they rightly attributed to a desire to placate European powers. Later a Christian was appointed governor of the Lebanon on the recommendation of the European powers—another blow to Ottoman pride.

The Rumanian developments had followed a dynamic of their own which was not to the liking of the European Great Powers, but this did not make them acceptable from the Ottoman point of view. In Bosnia the Ottoman army had not been able to rout much smaller forces; the advantages gained in the Montenegrin treaty had been relinquished by the Turks themselves.

Âli Paşa and Fuad Paşa had thus taken over the directing of Ottoman policies at an inauspicious time. Not the least of their troubles was that a smoldering resentment had been felt against the *Hatt-ı Hümâyun* of 1856 ever since its proclamation. As Cevdet Paşa points out, after the proclamation of this edict: "Many Moslems began to grumble: 'Today we lost our sacred national rights which our ancestors gained with their blood. While the Islamic nation used to be the ruling nation, it is now bereft of this sacred right. This is a day of tears and mourning for the Moslem brethren.' "[14]

In 1859 (September 17) a revolt called the Kuleli Revolt broke out in the capital. The leaders of the revolt were army officers and ulema who believed that the extent to which Fuad and Ali Paşa were ready to cooperate with the Great Powers and the corruption of the other ministers would lead Turkey to ruin. The revolt seems to have had as aim the assassination of the sultan, whose pro-Western inclinations were also considered nefarious. In short, it was a plot of zealots protesting against the extension of new privileges to the Christian populations and indignant at the loss of the empire's old prestige.[15]

In general, the gearing of Turkish reform to the wishes of the Christian populations of the empire made reform something lopsided in which the Moslem populations had no share. Yet reforms were as much needed to ease the lot of the Moslem-Ottomans as they were to make first-class citizens of the Christians. If the Christian was discriminated against in matters of public employment, the Moslem peasant was shouldering the incredible burden of a taxation system which kept him at starvation level. When an effort was made to relieve Christian disabilities, it was obvious that the suffering of Moslem-Ottoman subjects would stand out in greater relief than before.

[14] Ahmed Cevdet Paşa, *Tezâkir 1-12* (ed. by Cavit Baysun, Ankara, Türk Tarih Kurumu Basımevi, 1953), p. 68. *"Hukuk-u mukaddese-yi milliye"* is the term used by Cevdet.

[15] Uluğ Iğdemir, *Kuleli Vakası Hakkında bir Araştırma* (Ankara, Türk Tarih Kurumu Basımevi, 1937), p. 38. "Ulema" is the name used for the members of the *İlmiyye*, the "order" which was made up of doctors of Islamic law and also included teachers and the personnel officiating in mosques.

One of the advantages which the Christian-Ottoman communities had reaped from the proclamation of 1856 was that they were able to secularize what political power was allowed them in the settlement of intracommunity affairs. Under the old Ottoman system this power had been given to the leaders of the religious communities, the patriarchs. Now lay assemblies were formed which slowly took this power out of the hands of the patriarchs. The Armenian community even drafted a constitution for itself. The ideas of constitutionalism and popular representation thus gained a limited toe-hold in the empire among the Christians, just as they had been adopted in the newly emancipated territories of the empire.

The reverse was true with regard to Moslem Ottomans and to representation on an Ottoman-wide basis. Âli Paşa took a strong stand against any suggestions of constitutionalism or representative government. He believed that any movement aiming at the establishment of a national assembly should be curbed, since the latter, because of the multinational composition of the Ottoman Empire, would have led to the representation of those very elements which were bent on separation from the empire. As he expressed it: "The Ottoman Empire numbers twelve or fourteen nationalities, and unfortunately, as a result of the religious and racial hatreds which divide, above all, the Christian populations, each one of these nationalities does not as yet show great inclination to grant just and necessary concessions. If the representatives which they would nominate by way of elections were to be brought together today, such a national assembly would instantly give rise to all scandals imaginable."[16] Side by side with this attitude, Âli

---

[16] [Âli Paşa], *Réponse à son Altesse Moustafa Fazil Pacha au Sujet de sa Lettre au Sultan* (Paris, 1867), p. 24. In a memorandum delivered to the sultan in which he examined the need for reform, Âli Paşa's chain of reasoning was the following: In Europe no distinction was made any longer between holders of different beliefs; all individuals were equally entitled to freedom. (Notice the relation established between the granting of religious freedom and the guarantee of political rights.) On the other hand, a great many young Christian subjects of the Porte were being sent by their parents to Europe for study. These young men were infected with these ideas. The

Paşa felt that the populations of the empire, whether Christians or Moslems, were not "prepared" for constitutional rule.[17]

It is true that neither Fuad nor Âli Paşa was entirely indifferent to the problem of providing representative institutions for the Empire. Their approach to the creation of such institutions was to establish empire-wide intermediate bodies which, without providing for national representation, would at least allow local representative institutions to develop. By proclaiming the Law of the Organization of Provinces,[18] which allowed for an elected provincial council in each of the provinces of the empire, they hoped to prepare the Ottoman population for eventual self-government. On the other hand, they were convinced that the majority of the population was totally unfit to decide its own fate and they thought the Ottomans would acquire such qualifications only very gradually. It was Âli Paşa who had dismissed the mildly liberal poet Şinasi from the civil service and it was he who later was to draft the infamous *Nizamname-i Âli*, establishing arbitrary censorship over the press.

The picnic organized on that summer day in 1865 was, in fact, a reunion of all those who opposed the policies of Âli Paşa—a characterization of their goals that is just as useful in understanding the aims of the group as are their own, more abstract statements of principle.

It was decided, the day the picnic took place, to create a secret society which would be named the Patriotic Alliance

---

only way to counteract the resulting subversive tendencies was to put Christians on an equal footing with Moslems, which meant opening the civil service to them. In so doing, one had to be careful not to offend Moslem sensitivities and to work for the creation of Moslem administrative cadres. For this memorandum see Ali Fuad, *Rical-i Mühimme-i Siyasiye* (Istanbul, Yeni Matbaa, 1927), pp. 118-127, in particular p. 123. This document appears in [A.D. Mordtmann], *Stambul und das Moderne Türkenthum: Politische soziale und biographische Bilder von Einem Osmanen* (Leipzig: Dunker und Hunbolt, 1877), I, 75-90. Mordtmann was one of the tutors in Sami Paşa's house mentioned earlier in this chapter.

[17] [Âli Paşa], *Réponse*, p. 27.

[18] 7 Cemaziyülahir 1281/November 7, 1864, *Düstur*, Birinci Tertip (2nd ed., Istanbul, 1289-1299/1872-1882), I, 608.

("*İttifak-ı Hamiyyet*," in Turkish).[19] Ayetullah Bey had brought with him two books on the organization of the Carbonari,[20] the secret society which, in the beginning of the nineteenth century, had fought against the restoration in France and Italy. These books were to be used as guides in organizing the secret society.

No documents exist stating what the aims of the Patriotic Alliance were, nor is it possible to trace their ideology except as it may be inferred from later statements. The name "Patriotic Alliance" suggests an intellectual affiliation with earlier European revolutionary societies, such as the Tugendbund and the Giovine Italia. At least one author[21] has stated the search for such a connection to be misleading because the aims of the Patriotic Alliance were "medieval" in nature, thus at cross-purposes with the aims of its suggested forerunners.

There is no doubt, however, that the founding members of the Patriotic Alliance thought of themselves as aiming to follow the political lead of Europe, though their intense patriotism made them think of reform for Ottomans, by Ottomans, and along Islamic lines.

Insofar as Italy is concerned, there is evidence that Italian liberal movements were known and studied by them. In 1866 a man who was to become the patron of the founding members of the Patriotic Alliance, Mustafa Fazıl Paşa, set the king of Italy as an example for the sultan. Namık Kemal mentioned Garibaldi and Silvio Pellico in the same breath with Voltaire and Condorcet.[22] Mazzini, with his utterances to the effect that

[19] Kuntay, *Namık Kemal*, I, 18.

[20] Ebüzziya, "Yeni Osmanlılar," *Yeni Tasvir-i Efkâr*, June 7, 1909, p. 3.

[21] [Mordtmann], *Stambul*, I, 66.

[22] Kuntay, *Namık Kemal*, II, 485. Silvio Pellico (1789-1854) was an Italian nationalist whose activities, connected with those of the Italian Carbonari, led to his imprisonment in 1820 and his publication of a volume of memoirs, *Le Mie Prigioni* ("*My Prisons*"). This work, by pointing out the inhumanity with which political prisoners were treated, became a famous liberal text in the 1830's. The romantic liberal nationalism which was expressed in *My Prisons* was taken up by several theoreticians of the Risorgimento, such as Mazzini. The bible of Italian liberal nationalism, Gioberti's

a new epoch was dawning when the people would "replace the Church as the interpreters of God's word," was not far at all from the stand adopted by Namık Kemal.

Ali Suavi specifically states that "Young Spain, Young France, Young Italy"[23] were the organizations after which the secret society of 1865 had been modeled. He added that the European belief that the Ottoman Empire was in its death throes gave an additional reason to the founders to proclaim, by the inclusion of the word "Young" in the name of the society, the vitality of the empire. Suavi refers here to the term "Young Ottoman"—or "New Ottoman" when trans-

---

Il Primato Morale e Civile degli Italiani, was dedicated to Pellico. Cf. Georges Weill, *L'Eveil des Nationalités et le Mouvement Libéral 1815-1848* (Paris, Presses Universitaires de France, 1930), p. 416. In the middle of the nineteenth century Pellico was the man "who personified the alliance of patriotism and religion" (*ibid.*), a most important resemblance to the attitude assumed by the Young Ottomans. For Kemal's ideas regarding Pellico, see [Namık Kemal], " 'Mes Prisons' Tercümesi hakkında Kemalin mülâhazatı," *Mecmua-i Ebüzziya,* 21 Muharrem 1330/January 11, 1911, pp. 8-14. Another point of intellectual contact may be discerned in the writings of the intellectual mentor of the Young Ottomans, Şinasi, on the papal question. (See below, Chapter VIII.) Frederic Millingen, who was on the fringes of the Young Ottoman movement, states that he and Şinasi worked together in Paris and that he was asked by the latter to establish contact with Garibaldi. I take this information from Roderic Davison, "Reform in the Ottoman Empire 1856-1876" (unpublished Ph.D. dissertation, Harvard, 1942), p. 278, note 58, who quotes Millingen's *Les Anglais en Orient* (Paris, 1877), pp. 345-46.

As early as 1850 an English observer could state: "A protégé of Reshid Paşa [Şinasi?] confidently assured me that Turkey must gain independence [sic], power, greatness, that universal liberty and happiness were to come out pure and bright from the revolutionary cauldron, that civilization had taken a fresh start, or had a new birth at Paris in the month of February and that we should have soon a new and blessed world. The Turks of this school rejoiced at the news of Charles Albert having crossed the Mincio with an army of 40,000 men." Charles MacFarlane, *Turkey and Its Destiny* (London, John Murray, 1850), II, 671. For the influence in Istanbul of the Piedmontese minister Baron Tecco, see Marco Antonio Canini, *Vingt ans d'Exil* (Paris, Dramard-Baudry, 1868), p. 150.

[23] Ali Suavi, "Civan (sic) Türk Tarihi," *Ulûm,* 15 Zilkade 1286/February 16, 1870, p. 793. For the extremely general and somewhat misleading remarks of the orientalist Vambery on this subject—remarks which cannot be summarily dismissed because he states that he contributed articles to Young Ottoman publications and was very close to them during their exile—see Arminius Vambery, *Western Culture in Eastern Lands* (London, John Murray, 1909), pp. 321-323.

lated textually—by which these men became known at a later date.

As to the means the society planned to use in carrying its purposes to fruition, they are also difficult to ascertain. According to Ebüzziya, the members proposed to present a petition to the sultan exposing the misdeeds of Âli and Fuad Paşa. There are indications, however, that much less innocuous activities were planned. The organization of the Alliance by cells of seven, each responsible to a leader, and the secrecy of its membership (no member knew more than the names of seven other members) are signs which point in that direction. Eventually the leader of the Patriotic Alliance, Mehmed Bey,[24] was condemned to death for better reasons than having belonged to a political debating society intent on petitioning the sovereign. We know from the testimony of his daughter that once a week Mehmed Bey would don the loose robe of the *âlim* ("Doctor of Islamic Law") and go into the mosques and *medreses* to agitate for reform. It was this conspiratorial atmosphere which gave the Patriotic Alliance its special stamp. Ebüzziya admits that the Alliance was a "revolutionary" organization even though he denies that the members were intent on acts of terrorism.[25]

---

[24] Although we cannot establish with certainty what were the political ideals to which Mehmed Bey subscribed in 1865, we know what they were in 1870 from an article which appeared in the French Supplement of the *Inkilâb* (*Revolution*), the paper that he edited with Vasfi Paşa after his separation from the main body of the Young Ottomans. Despite the revolutionary emphasis, the link with the liberalism of the 1850's is visible, as when he stated: "In publishing a French bulletin our aim is to instruct republican Europe and America of the democratic tendencies of the Moslem Orient. . . . Brothers across the ocean, as well as across the desert, let us give one another our hand:

"Let us unite to conquer Liberty
Let us associate to arrive at equality
Let us cherish one another so that fraternity
might reign on earth."

Mehmed Bey, editorial, *La Révolution*, May 1, 1870, p. 1.

[25] "The discussions that day were concerned with the first steps to be taken so as to change absolute rule into constitutional rule, that is to say, with the

23

It is interesting to note, however, that between the years 1865 and 1867 other currents were working in Turkey in the same direction as that started by Mehmed Bey and his friends. Indeed, within a year of the creation of the Patriotic Alliance, two events occurred which revealed the nature of these parallel currents and also determined the fate of the members of the Patriotic Alliance.

One of these precipitating factors was the beginning of a serious insurrection on the Island of Crete, which once more raised the question of the viability of the Ottoman Empire. The second was the publication by a Turco-Egyptian paşa of a letter addressed to the sultan, demanding a constitutional reform—a crucial event in the shaping of the fortunes of the Patriotic Alliance.

An outbreak had already taken place in Crete in 1860 but now, in the first months of 1866, the diplomats accredited at the Porte expressed serious doubts as to whether the Cretan insurgents could be contained by the already harassed Turkish armies.[26]

The most impartial interpretations of this latest uprising, as well as of other separatist disturbances which had occurred earlier, was that the principle of nationality had become much more active among the Christian populations of the empire than had even been anticipated in drafting the Treaty of 1856 and the accompanying *Hatt-ı Hümâyun,* and that some change had to be brought in the civil and political status of the subject peoples of the empire to dampen their ardor. Another, more naïve explanation was that the Porte had failed to carry out the promises made to the Christian population of the empire in the Firman of 1856.

In 1867 specific proposals for reform were brought forth by France and Russia, purportedly to put an end to the recurrence of revolts and uprisings. The French plan was based on doing

---

organization of a revolutionary society." Ebüzziya, "Yeni Osmanlılar," *Yeni Tasvir-i Efkâr,* June 7, 1909, p. 3.

[26] Testa, *Recueuil,* VII, 403, Beust to Metternich, January 1, 1866.

away with all Christian disabilities but also on carrying out a wider program of reform for all Ottoman subjects than had hitherto materialized. It was hoped that these measures would be favorably received by both Moslems and Christians. Ideally, the move would have brought about the fusion of all people in the Ottoman Empire.[27]

The Russian plan, on the other hand, considered the splitting of the empire into autonomous regions administered by indigenous leaders elected by these populations.[28] In the case of Crete, the Russians advised outright annexation to Greece.

Pressure was put on the Porte by each side to adopt its proposals. The Cretan revolution kept the Porte busy for a long time. Expeditionary forces were sent to the island, but they met with little success. Eventually, in the winter of 1867-1868, Âli Paşa himself went to Crete. The inability of the Porte to deal with the Cretan insurrection caused bitter criticism among many people in the capital. The emotional ties with the island were strong; the history of its conquest had been one of the more colorful in the annals of Ottoman history. The plight of the Moslem population of the island, exposed to the depredations of local guerrilla bands, heaped injury on insult.

In later years the weakness of the Porte in handling the Cretan question was made the subject of one of the most famous and mordant of modern Turkish satirical poems, the "Zafernâme." This poem by Ziya Paşa,[29] the "elder statesman" of the Turkish reformists, shows to what heights of patriotic indignation the issue could incite Ottomans.

At the time of the crisis, two newspapers in the capital rushed to the defense of Ottoman Crete. One of these was the *Tasvir-i Efkâr* edited by Kemal; the other, the *Muhbir* whose chief editorial writer, Ali Suavi, had begun to cooperate with the Patriotic Alliance some time after its foundation. The

[27] *Ibid.*, pp. 418-428.   [28] *Ibid.*, pp. 446-455.
[29] For excerpts of the poem and a good commentary see E. J. W. Gibb, *A History of Ottoman Poetry* (London, Luzac, 1900-1909), v, 69 ff.

letter of the Ottoman press law of the time was more lenient than the existing press law in Turkey nowadays[30] but must have been enforced somewhat severely, since both the *Muhbir* and the *Tasvir-i Efkâr* were at first fairly cautious in their criticism of the government. The *Muhbir* first got considerable publicity in February 1867 when it organized a private collection for the Cretans who had been driven out of their homes by the guerrillas. This collection definitely displeased Âli Paşa.

Only in early March of 1867, however, did Ali Suavi abandon all prudence. On the eighth of March (2 Zilkade 1283) he came out with a flaming editorial in which he bitterly attacked the Porte's relinquishment of the fortress of Belgrade.[31] The next day the owner of the paper, Filip Efendi, received a curt note from the Ministry of Education to the effect that the *Muhbir* had been closed for one month. Filip Efendi had already printed the issue that bore the date of the third of Zilkade, and, under the legal obligation to print the notification sent him by the Ministry, he asked Namık Kemal to let the notice appear in the *Tasvir-i Efkâr* so that he would have at least partly complied with the law. One of the reasons for which he might have been loath to keep this last issue from the public was that it contained an excellent piece of journalism pointing out that Russia was behind the uprisings in the empire and that consequently its pressing for reforms was rank impertinence. It was also suggested that some remedy would be brought to this state of affairs if Ottoman statesmen were responsible to a "national assembly."[32]

[30] This was written in 1959 at a time when Turkish prisons were filling up with journalists.

[31] Up to that time the Turks had maintained a garrison in the fortress. The fortress was now handed over to the Serbs in return for the somewhat platonic promise that the Ottoman flag would continue to fly over the citadel in recognition of the sultan's *de jure* suzerainty. This was a diplomatic move which Âli Paşa wanted to conceal.

[32] *Muhbir,* 3 Zilkade 1283/March 9, 1867, p. 1. This article has been attributed to Ziya Paşa. Ali Suavi's reference to its printing—"the article was printed and published through my instrumentality"—"*benim marifetimle tab ve neşr olundu*"—is more ambiguous in Turkish than in the English translation. The article, both in terms of style and content, does not bear

Namık Kemal too had been quite circumspect at the beginning of the Cretan crisis. At first, the relations between the editorial offices of the *Tasvir-i Efkâr* and higher officialdom had been idyllic. A year before, Namık Kemal had been commended by Âli Paşa for an article on the disasters caused by frequent fires in the capital. Âli Paşa had closed his eyes to the remarks by which the article was prefaced—allusions to the virtues of freedom from foreign intervention.[33]

Under Kemal's editorship the *Tasvir-i Efkâr* had become the first Turkish newspaper to carry sophisticated analyses of foreign affairs and to go into such matters as the impact of new methods of warfare on the European balance of power.[34] It also took up more controversial matters, such as the mixing of foreign cabinets in Ottoman diplomatic affairs, but was not as yet aggressive in its treatment of the subject.[35] In the fall of 1866, however, Kemal wrote an article criticizing the impertinence of local Greeks in singing songs in their cafés that had as leitmotiv the extermination of the Turks.[36] The Ministry of Police had sent a rebuttal, asserting its vigilance in these matters, and this Kemal had had to print. But there the incident stopped.[37] This was only a straw in the wind.

When the crisis of the *Muhbir* arose, however, Kemal printed in the *Tasvir* both the order closing the *Muhbir* for one month and a protesting commentary by Filip Efendi. In the same issue he wrote an article on the Eastern question in which he protested against European interference in the Cretan question.[38] Three days later a new press ordinance was

---

the characteristics of Ali Suavi's pieces. See Ali Suavi, "Yeni Osmanlılar Tarihi," *Ulûm* (undated, 1870), p. 911.

[33] "Payitaht," *Tasvir-i Efkâr*, 3 Zilkade 1282, p. 1; Kuntay, *Namık Kemal*, I, 18.

[34] *Tasvir-i Efkâr*, 2 Rebiülahir 1283/August 14, 1866.

[35] "Girid meselesine dair," *Tasvir-i Efkâr*, 14 Cemaziyülevvel 1283/September 24, 1866.

[36] "Bir Mülâhaza," *Tasvir-i Efkâr*, 22 Cemaziyülevvel 1283/October 1, 1866.

[37] *Tasvir-i Efkâr*, 29 Cemaziyülevvel 1283/October 8, 1866.

[38] Namık Kemal, "Şark Meselesine dair bir Lâyihadır," *ibid.*, 4 Zilkade 1283/March 10, 1867.

proclaimed establishing strict censorship, Suavi was arrested, and the *Tasvir* was also closed for a month. Insofar as Kemal was concerned, this meant the end of his career as its editor, for while these developments were taking place another series of events had occurred which had already forced Namık Kemal to reveal his involvement with the political opposition, just as his stand on foreign policy had divulged what he thought about the government's conduct of foreign affairs.

Here again, a retrospective survey is necessary to understand Kemal's position. While unrest kept increasing in the capital in early 1867, the assertive figure of Prince Mustafa Fazıl Paşa began to give substance to the various protestations that were under way.

Mustafa Fazıl Paşa was a descendant of Mehmed Ali Paşa, the mutinous governor of Egypt who, early in the nineteenth century, had become practically the independent ruler of that province of the empire. Fazıl Paşa's life had been spent at the Porte. Most of his education was received at the bureaus of the Porte, where at the age of sixteen he had started his governmental career, being first appointed to the Bureau of the Grand Vizier.[39]

Except for a stay of four years in Egypt, his career had been that of an Ottoman state servant. He had risen fast to become Minister of Education in 1862, Minister of Finances in 1864, and had finally been appointed to the chairmanship of the Council of the Treasury (*"Meclis-i Hazain"*) when this body was established in October of 1865.[40]

Even though Fazıl Paşa's career was made in the Ottoman capital, his mind was not entirely occupied with his official duties, for Fazıl Paşa also had interests in Egypt. He was the brother of the khedive ("hereditary governor") of Egypt, Ismail Paşa. According to a rule of succession followed in Egypt as well as in the Ottoman Empire, Mustafa Fazıl

[39] Mehmet Zeki Pakalın, *Tanzimat Maliye Nazırları* (Istanbul, Kanaat Kitabevi [1940?]), II, 3-5.
[40] *Ibid.*

should have succeeded Ismail as khedive upon the latter's demise. However, Ismail had different plans and wanted to consolidate the khedivate in his own line of descent. For a long time Mustafa Fazıl Paşa had had an inkling that his brother would use all means in his power to reach his goal. In 1858, for instance, Fazıl's elder brother Ahmed, who was the heir at the time, died in a mysterious accident which it was believed Ismail had engineered.

The most serious crisis in the matter of succession occurred when in 1865 Khedive Ismail came to Istanbul to beg the sultan to change the Egyptian rule of succession. To gain this favor Ismail had relied on the fact that his mother and Sultan Abdülaziz's mother were sisters. He might also have suspected that the sultan himself was not averse to consolidating his own line of descent. That year, however, Fuad Paşa, then Grand Vizier, flatly refused Ismail Paşa's proposal.

The appointment, shortly thereafter, of Mustafa Fazıl Paşa to head the Council of the Treasury was an indication of Fuad's opposition to the sultan's scheme.

Just as the selection of Fazıl Paşa to fill this post was important, so too the creation of the new office which he was expected to fill was in itself a major event. It was an important step in a process which had been inaugurated in the second quarter of the nineteenth century—that of weaving a net of modern Ottoman institutions to provide adequate machinery for the administration of the Ottoman state. The particular function of the new council was to save the empire from financial disaster. Financial difficulties had indeed been dogging the administration of the empire from the earliest moments of Abdülaziz's accession to the throne. The consolidation of existing state indebtedness had brought only temporary relief and already, in 1865, payment of interest on the *consolidés* had been defaulted once. This sorry state of affairs was due, in part, to the huge expenditures of the sultan, who had not as yet been able to accustom himself to the idea of state funds as different from his personal *liste civile*. It was also due to the Porte's disregard for the niceties of public finance. Each of these two parties was convinced that the major blame could be placed on the other. Over and above these reciprocal recriminations was the irreducible fact that the Porte had been saddled with the almost insoluble problem of finding new and larger sources of revenue at a time when economic decline had already set in in the empire. It is also interesting that it should have been in this context of seeking measures to increase state revenue that one of the first references to the limitation of ministerial powers should have arisen.

The occasion was one of the earliest attempts by the Porte (in 1865) to secularize the religious endowments known as *Evkaf.* Such property was exempt from taxation and thus constituted an untouched source of revenue. Reporting developments with regard to this question from the Ottoman capital, a German correspondent stated at the time that "a section including almost the majority of the patriotic higher ulema" was willing to make certain concessions with respect to the secularization of the *Evkaf,*[41] provided a mechanism for the control of finances was established. It is quite probable that the ulema asked to be represented on the body which was to provide this mechanism.

The establishment of a Council of the Treasury was thus to meet an important need. Little did Fuad Paşa know, when he created this organ, that Mustafa Fazıl was to criticize Fuad's financial policy and present to the sultan a memorandum on the subject of the ineptitude of the Porte in financial matters. As soon as Fuad found out about this document, Mustafa Fazıl was dismissed from his post (4 Şevval 1282/February 7, 1866).[42] Then suddenly on April 4, 1866, Mustafa Fazıl was asked to leave the capital within twenty-four hours.[43] The reason for this brusque exile is not known, but it most proba-

[41] *Augsburger Allgemeine Zeitung*, October 31, 1865, p. 4927.
[42] Pakalın, *Tanzimat Maliye Nazırları*, p. 6; see also the (London) *Times*, March 1, 1866, p. 12.
[43] *Times*, April 6, 1866, p. 10.

bly involved some plot of Mustafa Fazıl against Fuad.[44] With Mustafa Fazıl out of the picture, the sultan finally had his way with his minister over the Egyptian succession. On May 27, 1866, a firman was proclaimed giving Ismail's direct descendants access to the khediviate.[45]

In Paris, where he had established residence, Mustafa Paşa lived in regal splendor, relying on the millions in exchange for which, it was reported, his royal brother had purchased all of his property in Egypt.[46] Late in 1866 the prince was negotiating with the Porte to be allowed to return to Turkey. Permission to return was finally granted him on December 20, but on condition that he stay out of Egypt and Istanbul. This amounted in reality to an outright refusal of the prince's request to be allowed to come back. Thus Fazıl girded his loins for another attack on Fuad.

Two developments which had taken place within the empire at this time had already stimulated the foreign-language press of the capital to take up the discussion of constitutionalism as a matter of routine news reporting. One of these was the proclamation, in November of 1866, of an Egyptian "constitution"—part of Ismail's modernist legerdemain—which was also discussed and praised by the *Tasvir-i Efkâr*.[47] The other was the favorable impression created by the speech with which Prince Charles of Hohenzollern had opened the Rumanian parliament in the fall of the same year. On this occasion the prince had firmly vowed to clean the Augean stables of Rumanian politics, and his enlightened attitude had impressed

---

[44] According to Mehmed Memduh, *Mir'at-ı Şuunat* (İzmir, Ahenk Matbaası, 1378/1910), p. 33, because of Mustafa Fazıl's attacks on Fuad.

[45] G. Douin, *Histoire du Règne du Khédive Ismail* (Rome, Istituto Polligraphico dello Stato, 1933), I, 214-217.

[46] David S. Landes, *Bankers and Pashas* (London, Heinemann, 1958), p. 212, note 1.

[47] See [Namık Kemal], "Şura-yı Nuvvab," *Tasvir-i Efkâr*, 29 Şaban 1283, in *Müntahabat-i Tasvir-i Efkâr* (ed. by Ebüzziya Tevfik, 3rd ed., Istanbul, Ebüzziya, 1311/1893-1894), p. 83. This work was used and the authorship of the article established in it by Ebüzziya found at a time when the collection of the *Tasvir* on which the author worked was no longer available.

newspaper-reading audiences in the Turkish capital. In the meantime, the Russian proposals for the establishment of autonomous regions in the empire had been presented to the Porte.

It was probably this favorable constellation, plus the news that Ismail's "Minister of Foreign Affairs," Nubar Paşa, was coming to Istanbul to negotiate new concessions, which made Mustafa Fazıl decide to make his bid in favor of Ottoman constitutionalism.

Early in February of 1867 the Paris _Journal des Débats_ printed a news item from its correspondent in Istanbul that Mustafa Fazıl Paşa, whose earlier representations before the sultan had been of no avail, was now taking upon himself the leadership of the reform movement in Turkey and, in particular, the direction of that section of the opposition known as "Young Turkey."[48] The prince, it was stated, expected to present to the sultan within a short time a project of reforms which would demand a complete rearrangement of the governmental machinery. On February 12, 1867, such a draft was, in fact, circulated in Istanbul by Halil Şerif Paşa, a cousin of Mustafa Fazıl, who was later to marry Fazıl's daughter.[49] Halil Şerif Paşa was a Turk whose father had emigrated to Egypt to serve as one of Mehmed Ali's captains. Halil himself, after having received a European education, had entered the diplomatic service of the Porte. He had been ambassador to St. Petersburg and was now back in the Ministry of Foreign Affairs in the capital.

The extent to which Halil's move was coordinated with the activities of Mustafa Fazıl is not completely clear but, as will be seen below, an understanding certainly existed. Halil strikes one throughout as having been more deeply imbued with the ideas of constitutionalism, and he was taken much more seriously by his contemporaries than was Mustafa Fazıl. Halil

[48] News item from Istanbul signed "F. David," _Journal des Débats_, February 5, 1867, pp. 1, 2.
[49] Engelhardt, _La Turquie et le Tanzimat_, I, 231-233.

Şerif Paşa's tactic was to take advantage of the pressure exerted by the Great Powers on the Porte to force it into an acceptance of his constitutionalist scheme. He thus tried to tailor his draft as much as possible on the French project of reforms earlier presented to the Porte. Consequently he got the support of the French ambassador, Bourrée. In this fashion the influence of Bourrée on the French-language newspapers of the capital, plus a liberal distribution of gratuities by Fazıl among the latter, combined with the critical situation facing the Porte and the immediate background of Egyptian and Rumanian constitutional steps resulted during the month of February 1867 in the outbreak of a vigorous constitutionalist campaign by the foreign press of the capital. Strangely enough, even the semi-official *La Turquie* did not shun a coolheaded, although not by any means unbiased, discussion of the comparative advantage of the existing system and constitutionalist rule. This might have been related to the real interest which, according to news reports, even official quarters were showing for a fundamental reorganization of the governmental machinery.[50] Most of the articles weighed the applicability of a constitutional system in the Ottoman Empire in quite general terms. The origins of the campaign went back, in fact, to the middle of January, at which time the first trial balloon had been launched by the *Courrier d'Orient.*

This newspaper was owned by a Frenchman by the name of Giampietry,[51] who, like many other persecuted liberals and political heretics, had established himself in Turkey. There are indications that Giampietry came to Turkey following the coup of Louis Napoleon. In the *Courrier,* which was widely read by the Turkish intelligentsia, Giampietry had for some time opposed the conservatism of its rival *La Turquie,* subsidized by the Porte. The project set forth by the *Courrier* was

[50] *Augsburger Allgemeine Zeitung,* February 20, 1867, p. 829.

[51] This correct spelling which is usually given as "Jean Pietry" may be found on two issues of the *Courrier* in the Clerbois collection of the University of California at Berkeley. I have been unable to locate a complete collection of this paper.

based on the "complete representation of the interests of all classes of society without distinction of race or religion."[52]

In this sense it was quite close to Halil Şerif Paşa's scheme, which was meant to give a voice to the people who made up the empire in determining governmental policy, and there is a possibility that the *Courrier*'s article might have been an early probe of Halil Şerif's.

There is little doubt, as later events were to confirm, that Giampietry was in direct contact with Mustafa Fazıl.

In the meantime, Mustafa Fazıl was not letting anyone forget that he was behind the constitutionalist effervescence. His *bon vivant* side made him vulnerable to ridicule and was indeed being exploited by European newspapers who depended on Russian rather than on Egyptian gold. The Belgian newspaper *Nord*, for instance, alleged that he was a fake more interested in advertising himself and his rights to the Egyptian throne than in reforming Turkey. This accusation was used by Fazıl Paşa as an opportunity to herald his leadership of Young Turkey in a widely publicized reply: "An article in the *Nord* of the first of February has only just been brought to my notice. The journals which have reported that I was engaged in founding a banking establishment are not satisfied with the denials with which this absurd story has met with from the good sense of the public before I took the trouble to contradict it through one of my secretaries. They still continue to publish variations of the same story on what they call my financial operations with the House of Messrs. Oppenheim. It is, however, essential that these newsmongers should know that at a time when the affairs of the Ottoman Empire are embarrassed, it is with these and not with my private affairs that I am occupied. It matters not whether a man is Musulman, Catholic, or Orthodox Greek to know that private interests should be postponed to the public good. It is sufficient to be a man of progress or a good patriot, which means one and the same thing. Such, at least, is the conviction of the great party of 'Young Turkey' of which I have the honor to be the representative.

"This party neither recognizes the resignation of fatalism nor gives way under disappointment. This means that the Cretan insurrection and yet the graver disasters with which we are threatened on many sides find it still resolute to complete these reforms which have ripened by reflection, experience, and suffering."[53]

This was followed by other communications in the same vein to European journals. Mustafa Fazıl's relations with the Patriotic Alliance are not entirely clear to this day, but it is to be noted that he did not claim in his letter to represent the Alliance but "the great party of 'Young Turkey.'" It can be surmised from this reference that, although self-appointed, Mustafa Fazıl Paşa considered himself the spokesman of a more diffuse and vague group than the Patriotic Alliance—a group known in Istanbul at that time as "La Jeune Turquie." Young Turkey was no organized society, but included all the men of importance in the capital who were earnestly interested in reform. Naturally it also included the members of the Patriotic Alliance.

While Mustafa Fazıl Paşa was engaged in replying to his detractors, the text of his letters had reached the capital and were printed in the *Muhbir* of February 8 and 10 (3 and 5 Şevval 1283).[54] On February 19, 1867, another of Âli Paşa's sycophants, De Launay, editor of the *Gazette du Levant*, took the party of Young Turkey to task and also attacked Mustafa Fazıl. This article, in turn, spurred Namık Kemal, by now one of the more important members of the Patriotic Alliance, to write an anonymous letter of protest to the editor of the

---

[53] *Levant Herald Daily Bulletin*, February 22, 1867. English translation, *Levant Herald*'s. For the Oppenheim mentioned here see Landes, *Bankers and Pashas*, pp. 111-120.

[54] There are indications that from the very beginning the *Muhbir* was subsidized by Mustafa Fazıl. See Ali Suavi, *Ulûm* (undated), p. 796.

Gazette. The letter, which was never posted and was only recently found among the correspondence of Namık Kemal, is one of the few documents which allows us to determine with greater precision the aims of Namık Kemal and his friends at that time. It also shows that Namık Kemal strove to defend the ideals of the party of Young Turkey as eagerly as we could have expected him to defend the ideals of the secret society which he could not mention, the Patriotic Alliance.[55] It is thus probable that the aims of both groups were quite similar.

Namık Kemal stated that the party of Young Turkey was not, as editor De Launay of the *Gazette* had stated, a constituted society. He pointed out that the party did not recognize the leadership of any individual, Fazıl Paşa included.[56] It consisted, according to him, of people "tied together by common ideas." Namık Kemal further rejected the idea set forth by De Launay that the party of Young Turkey was a new creation; he stated that the desire for reform had already given rise to several opposition parties in the preceding century. He described the party of Young Turkey as only having increased the number of "those who in our country have expressed this idea [the idea of reform] which is as old as the world itself."[57]

To the allegation of the *Gazette* that the party of Young Turkey discriminated against the Christian inhabitants of the empire—an accusation which De Launay based on the lack of reference to the special rights of the Christian population of the empire in Mustafa Fazıl's letters of protest to the *Nord*— Namık Kemal countered by protesting against the notion of "incarnating our ideas in his utterances [those of Mustafa Fazıl]" and by pointing out that the Christian population of

[55] For the text of this letter see Kuntay, *Namık Kemal*, I, 183-187, 290-291.

[56] This is corroborated by Suavi, who explains the heated discussions that preceded the acceptance of his leadership. From Suavi's account it would seem that this leadership was accepted by the time Kemal and Ziya escaped. See Ali Suavi, *Ulûm* (undated), p. 793.

[57] Kuntay, *Namık Kemal*, I, 291.

the empire, having been favored by the special protection of the Great Powers, had wrested more privileges for itself than had the Moslems. He added that the Christians did not shrink from leading a privileged life in a country which already had granted them equal status. Namık Kemal concluded: "This, then, is the true nature of the Jeune Turquie [in French in the original text]. Some members of this intellectual society having begun to direct the newspapers appearing in the Ottoman language, have brought about a mighty change in literature, which is the primary vehicle of progress. If, from now on, its true nature can be understood and it can profit, just as European journalism does, from the succor of the patrons of civilization, it is probable that it will accomplish great things for the fatherland."[58]

A few days after the attack of the *Gazette*, Namık Kemal reproduced Mustafa Fazıl Paşa's rebuttal to the *Nord* in the *Tasvir-i Efkâr*. Underneath it, as editor, he added the following cautious comment: "There is a section in this article which will appear to be of special importance to those who are thinking of the future of the nation [*"millet"*] and that is the mention which is made, that among those of the Ottomans who hold modern opinions, general interests are being preferred to particular interests. Those who hold these new opinions are labelled Young Turks [*"Türkistanın Erbab-ı Şebabı"*]. There is no doubt that at a time when Europe, accusing the Ottomans of being retrograde and stagnant, has taken certain official steps in connection with the settling of the Eastern Question, this favorable mention of the Young Turks might appear amazing in the West. This, however, is a matter to which we attribute great importance, for how can one possibly ignore one's great contemporaries? If there has been a partial progress in the field of science and in civilization [in Turkey], is not ninety per cent of it due to their efforts? True, these efforts are quite small compared to contemporary progress. But it should also sincerely be taken in consideration that

[58] *Ibid.*, p. 185.

our education is practically nil. One cannot get more out of individual work. In short, those who hold new opinions are the future salvation of the nation. It is our opinion that whatever is achieved by them, the chances of bettering the conditions of the fatherland will increase proportionally. It is for this reason that those who are cognizant of the state of affairs in the capital will never abandon hope in the well-being of the people regardless of the obstacles that are encountered by the Empire. Let the Europeans believe that the Ottoman Empire is on the way to the grave. We know that it is not in the midst of a cemetery but in its mother's womb."[59]

Two weeks later the *Tasvir-i Efkâr* was closed by order of Âli Paşa because of the article by Namık Kemal criticizing foreign intervention in the Cretan affair.

Mustafa Fazıl Paşa's campaign now culminated during the early days of March, which coincided with Namık Kemal's first days of enforced inactivity, in a letter to the sultan in which the fate of the Ottoman Empire was ascribed to an absence of constitutional machinery. A draft of a constitutional proposal is said to have accompanied the letter, which urged the sultan to take the lead in the constitutional-representative movement.[60]

The letter created a sensation in the capital. Although it is doubtful that it ever reached Abdülaziz, it was soon thereafter published in the daily *Liberté* (on March 24, 1867).[61] As

[59] Namık Kemal, "Mülâhaza," *Tasvir-i Efkâr*, 18 Şevval 1283/February 23, 1867.

[60] *Augsburger Allgemeine Zeitung*, March 20, 1867, p. 1292.

[61] On pp. 1, 2. The text appeared also as a brochure almost at the same time (*Journal des Débats*, March 26, 1867, p. 1; Auguste Vitu, "Le manifeste du Prince Mustapha," *L'Étendard*, March 25, 1867, p. 1). In fact, two brochures exist, published at that time—the first, *Lettre adressée à S. M. le Sultan par S. A. le Prince Mustapha-Fazil Pacha* (Paris, Imprimerie de C. Schiller, 1867); the second, the only copy which I have seen, at the École des Langues Orientales in Paris, *Lettre adressée à S. M. le Sultan par S. A. le Prince Mustapha-Fazil Pacha* (En turc, en français, en italien, en russe, en grec moderne, en turc, en caractères grecs et en caractères arméniens). The Turkish section begins: "translation of the petition presented by his highness Mustafa Fazıl Paşa, who is at present domiciled in Paris, to his imperial majesty. . . ." For doubts cast on Mustafa Fazıl Paşa's authorship,

early as March 8 Namık Kemal and his friends had obtained the text of the *Letter* and undertook to translate it for clandestine distribution.[62]

The task of translation was assigned to Namık Kemal's friend, Sadullah Bey (later Sadullah Paşa). The letter was thus duly translated and 50,000 copies were printed in the shop of the French printer Cayol and distributed in the capital.[63]

On March 17 Mustafa Fazıl Paşa, in Paris, was granted an audience by the emperor Napoleon and submitted his scheme to him.[64] At the same time Halil Şerif arrived in Paris, where the news circulated that he was to help Mustafa Fazıl to further his plans. Thus was substantiated the sympathetic approval by the French government of Halil Şerif's and Mustafa Fazıl's plans, as well as the link between the two men.

The ideas set forth by Mustafa Fazıl Paşa in his letter to the sultan have to be taken with some caution because there are indications that they were inspired by Émile de Girardin, the great French journalist and editor of the daily *Liberté*, with whom Mustafa Fazıl had established friendly relations in Paris. But there is no doubt that they created a sensation in the capital. As Ebüzziya states: "Up to that date, the few people who knew the ills that beset the body of the Empire had completely lost hope, considering these to be incurable. Public opinion consisted of the superficial conviction that

see below, Chapter IX. According to still other sources, a reprint of the letter published by the *Nord* was circulated clandestinely. See *Augsburger Allgemeine Zeitung*, April 2, 1867, p. 1503; *Neue Freie Presse*, April 4, 1867, p. 4; already in a dispatch dated March 23, the Istanbul correspondent of the *Indépendance Belge* spoke of "a brochure of Mustafa Fazıl Paşa published in the form of a letter to the Sultan," *Indépendance Belge*, April 7, 1867, p. 2, and in a dispatch dated March 17, the correspondent of the *Augsburger Allgemeine Zeitung* informed its readers that Mustafa Fazıl Paşa had forwarded a "message" to the sultan. *Augsburger Allgemeine Zeitung*, March 20, 1867, p. 1292.

[62] Ebüzziya, "Yeni Osmanlılar," *Yeni Tasvir-i Efkâr*, June 1, 1909, pp. 3, 4.

[63] Kuntay, *Namık Kemal*, I, 279-280, has a photographic facsimile of a copy of this tract.

[64] *Augsburger Allgemeine Zeitung*, March 20, 1867, p. 1287.

divine intervention would in time save the Empire. Mustafa Fazıl Paşa, however, diagnosed the sickness . . . and provided a remedy at the same time as he diagnosed the malady."[65]

It was indeed the basis of Mustafa Fazıl Paşa's influence that his letter popularized the idea, already accepted at the Porte, that arresting the decadence of the empire might be dependent on changes in political structure. The idea that such changes, over and above a streamlining of administration, involved a liberalization of the regime, however, was completely new and therein lay its explosive quality.

The party of Young Turkey, which had attained such public prominence as the result of all this correspondence, counter-correspondence, and tract distribution, was, as we have seen, the name by which for some years reformist elements had been known in Turkey. Mention of the term "Jeune Turquie" may be found as early as 1855 in Ubicini's *La Turquie Actuelle*. Even at that time, however, Ubicini found the term "Jeune Turquie" too ambiguous and proposed the distinction of "Jeune Turquie de Mahmoud" and "Jeune Turquie d'Abdul Medjid." By the first term Ubicini attempted to characterize the conservative-reformist trend. He stated that the second group, on the other hand, was so Europeanized that it would have been immaterial whether it had taken its ideas from the Koran or the Gospels, but that it believed in neither. He pointed out that this second clique under the leadership of Fuad Paşa, composed of the young men he had sent to be trained in European embassies, did not make the best possible impression in the capital.[66]

[65] Ebüzziya Tevfik, "Yeni Osmanlılar," *Yeni Tasvir-i Efkâr*, May 25 [*sic*, 24], 1909, p. 2.

[66] "Revenus en Turquie pour y occuper les emplois les plus importants du gouvernement et de l'administration, on dirait qu'ils recherchent moins ce qui convient à leur pays que ce qui peut accroitre leur renommée à l'étranger. Peu leur importe s'ils froissent ou non le sentiment religieux et national de Constantinople, pourvu que leurs noms soient cités avec éloge dans les journaux de Paris et de Londres. Ils croient pouvoir combattre le fanatisme par l'impiété. Ils ne s'aperçoivent pas qu'en choquant les idées reçues par le mépris evident des dogmes et des pratiques de la religion, l'inobservance de la loi, l'usage public du vin, l'adoption du costume européen, l'affecta-

Now, ten years after the publication of Ubicini's book, a third Young Turkey, the Young Turkey of the Patriotic Alliance, was combating the very tendencies of the over-Westernized Jeune Turquie of Abdul Medjid of which Ubicini spoke. One of the places in which this third Jeune Turquie had originated was the editorial office of the newly born Turkish press. A fourth Jeune Turquie was that which was limited to Halil Şerif and Mustafa Fazıl. Another place where criticism of Âli and Fuad Paşa arose was in the palace itself. Atıf Bey, Chief Private Secretary of the sultan, explains that around 1863 the palace Jeunes (*"jönler"*), composed of the poet Ziya Bey, who had started his career as secretary to the sultan (*"mabeyn kâtibi"*), and an employee of the naval yards by the name of Muhtar Bey, began to advise the sultan to select an active grand vizier and capable ministers.[67] In fact, Ziya had lost his post at the palace in 1861 due to his intrigues against Âli Paşa and had become the victim of the latter's wrath ever since that time.

It was therefore no great surprise that at the culmination of the crisis created by the *Muhbir* and *Tasvir-i Efkâr*, the Porte took action against Ziya (then still Ziya Bey) as well as against Kemal and Suavi. Suavi was given the most cavalier treatment and curtly told to take a trip to the Black Sea town of Kastamonu. The main reason for this severe action was that Ali Suavi was making the rounds of the coffeehouses of the capital (Ali Suavi's café audience composed of the "man in the street" made up a sixth type of Young Turkey), spread-

---

tion des manières françaises, dont s'indigne la gravit musulmane, ils ôtent tout crédit dans la nation et rendent impossible à l'avance tout le bien qu'ils pourraient faire." Ubicini, *La Turquie Actuelle* (Paris, Hachette, 1855), p. 163. The earliest reference to the term "Young Turk," spelled at that time without capital letters and referring to the young generation of the time, appears in the descriptions of an English traveler of the early nineteenth century who states that an admiration for the military was "pretty generally shared by the young Turks." See Charles MacFarlane, *Constantinople in 1828* (2nd ed., London, Saunders and Otley, 1829), II, 58.

[67] İnal, *Son Sadrıazamlar*, p. 70, quoting an unpublished manuscript of Atıf Bey. See also Memduh, *Mir'at-ı Şuunat*, p. 31; cf. *Augsburger Allgemeine Zeitung*, October 25, 1865, p. 4831.

ing the rumor that a massacre of Moslems by Christians was impending and that churches were being used as arsenals. Whether it was due to Suavi's agitation or was the result of spontaneous unrest, the disturbance so increased in the capital that two regiments were brought in as a precautionary measure.[68]

Much more lenient was the attitude of the government toward Kemal and Ziya. Kemal was appointed assistant governor of the province of Erzurum. Ziya was transferred from the Council of Judicial Ordinances to Cyprus (May 8, 1867).[69]

Both Namık Kemal and Ziya Paşa, who had a great many connections in the capital, tried to delay the authorities by providing an endless stream of excuses which, they hoped, would enable them to remain in Istanbul. Meanwhile, the news of their "appointments" had reached Mustafa Fazıl Paşa. Through Giampietry, the owner of the *Courrier d'Orient*, Fazıl Paşa sent word to all three men that he was ready to support them in their fight against Âli Paşa if they would come and work with him in Paris.[70] All three accepted, and within a few days they were smuggled outside the country. This was done with the help of French ambassador Bourrée through the good offices of Giampietry (May 17, 1867).[71]

Two days later the police raided a number of *medreses* and arrested two ulema who, although they were in close touch with the Young Ottomans do not seem to have been members of the Patriotic Alliance. These were Veliyüddin Efendi and Kemeraltılı Tahsin Efendi (not to be confused with Hoca Tahsin, who is discussed later in Chapter VII).[72]

Within two weeks there was a general arrest of the members

[68] *Augsburger Allgemeine Zeitung*, April 2, 1867, p. 1503.

[69] The government must have had an inkling of Ziya's connection with the Patriotic Alliance. Ziya Paşa is said to have stated that the Porte suspected him of having translated Mustafa Fazıl's letter. See Ali Suavi, *Ulûm*, 1870, p. 930.

[70] Ebüzziya, "Yeni Osmanlılar," *Yeni Tasvir-i Efkâr*, October 6, 1909, p. 6.

[71] *Ibid.*, p. 3.

[72] *Ibid*, June 3, 1909, p. 3; August 31, 1909, p. 4.

of the Patriotic Alliance.[73] This move on the part of the Imperial Police, which was not connected with the escape of Ziya, Kemal, and Suavi, was due to another development—the discovery of a plot engineered by Mehmed Bey who, infuriated by the recent turn of events, had planned a full-scale *coup d'etat*.

It is implied in Ebüzziya's account of the Young Ottomans that it was Ayetullah Bey who denounced the conspiracy.[74] Later Mehmed Bey, who had been able to escape from Turkey, was smuggled back in true romantic style, so as to find out whether the suspicion that Ayetullah Bey was a traitor had any basis in fact. Through the help of one of his Carbonari friends, Joseph Cabbaldini, Mehmed Bey, disguised as a laborer, stowed away aboard a ship. As soon as he set foot in Istanbul, he sought the house of Ayetullah Bey. Accosting Ayetullah Bey on the latter's way home, he threatened to kill him on the spot if he did not confess the truth. Ayetullah Bey protested his innocence and Mehmed Bey went back to the ship which had brought him. Once more, however, a denunciation was made to the police and a search was undertaken throughout the city for Mehmed Bey. This time there was no doubt as to who had betrayed him. The reason Ayetullah Bey seems to have suddenly decided to warn the government of Mehmed Bey's coup was that Mehmed Bey and the Alli-

[73] The *Indépendance Belge* of June 21, 1867, p. 3, gave full details about these arrests, which its Istanbul correspondent said took place on June 6. Subhi Bey (sic), Ayetullah Bey's father, "one of the most active members of the party in question," was said to be implicated. The same paper, June 25, 1867, p. 2, made the point that the rumor that an attempt had been planned on the life of the ministers was erroneous. However, shortly thereafter in Paris, Ziya made a statement denying that the people arrested figured "parmi les personnages marquans de la *Jeune Turquie*" and adding that he was waiting "avec une tranquillité sereine les prétendues révélations qui vont jaillir des prisons de Constantinople." *Journal des Débats*, editorial, June 19, 1867, p. 1.

[74] Ebüzziya, "Yeni Osmanlılar," *Yeni Tasvir-i Efkâr*, August 20, 1909 (p. 4) to August 25, 1909 (p. 4). In fact, what seems to have happened is that Ayetullah Bey decided to abstain from participating in the plot while his father Subhi Paşa gave the general alarm. See "İstanbuldan diğer tahrirat fi 26 Ramazan," *Hürriyet*, January 25, 1869, p. 5.

ance had evolved definite plans to use force in having their demands accepted.[75]

II. From the Patriotic Alliance to the Young Ottoman Society

Kemal and Ziya, who had met Suavi en route, arrived in Paris on May 31, 1867. They immediately repaired to the hotel of Mustafa Fazıl Paşa. The latter welcomed them and directed them to Şinasi, who found them rooms.

On August 10, 1867,[76] a group composed of Mustafa Fazıl, Ziya Bey, Namık Kemal Bey, Nuri, Suavi, Mehmed Bey, Reşad Bey, and Rifat Bey met in the mansion of the Paşa. Agâh Efendi was not unknown to the group, but he was a victim of guilt by association. He was an old collaborator of Şinasi and had been thrown out of his job in the Court of Accounts (*Divan-ı Muhasebat*) at the end of May 1867, whereupon he had followed Kemal and Ziya.[77] Rifat Bey, on the other hand, was a newcomer into the ranks of the reformers. At one time a son-in-law of the sultan and therefore made a paşa, he had been shorn of all attributes when his wife decided to divorce him. Being sent to Paris (a sop befitting a former *damad*), he decided that joining forces with the opposition was one way in which he could get even with the Palace.

It was decided that day that a new organization would be created which would adopt as its program the principles of reform mentioned in Mustafa Fazıl Paşa's letter to the sul-

[75] Compare Ebüzziya's protestations of innocence in "Yeni Osmanlılar," *Yeni Tasvir-i Efkâr*, June 9, 1909 to August 31, 1909, with Ayetullah's account in Inal, *Son Asır*, pp. 149-150. Ebüzziya does admit that the conspirators counted on the assistance of two men they had won over to their views, Mustafa Asım Paşa and Ömer Naili Paşa, who between themselves were responsible for law and order in the capital. Ebüzziya, "Yeni Osmanlılar," *Yeni Tasvir-i Efkâr*, June 8, 1909, p. 2.

[76] Ebüzziya, "Yeni Osmanlılar," *Yeni Tasvir-i Efkâr*, September 26, 1909, p. 4. Ebüzziya's account indicates that Fazıl Paşa had established contacts with the French Ministry of Foreign Affairs. This suggests that the French government, as pointed out earlier in this chapter, was not unaware of Mustafa Fazıl's schemes. *Ibid.*, September 15, 1909, p. 4.

[77] See Server İskit, *Hususî ilk Türkçe gazetemiz Tercüman-ı Ahval ve Agâh Efendi* (Ankara, Ulus, 1938), pp. 39, 40 (entry dated 26 Muharrem 1284).

tan.[78] Ziya Bey was placed at the head of this new group, called the New or Young Ottoman Society.[79] Ali Suavi was to proceed immediately to revive the *Muhbir*, which was to be the mouthpiece of the group.[80] The paper, however had to be published in London instead of Paris, because of the strict press regulations of the French.

The ensuing history of the publishing ventures of the Young Ottomans in Europe, though short, is nevertheless extremely complex. This was due as much to the real differences which underlay their superficially monolithic ideology as to the opportunistic nature of Mustafa Fazıl. The maneuvers carried on simultaneously by Mustafa Fazıl, Âli, and the khedive Ismail to defeat one another's purposes created an additional element of complication.

By the time the first issue of the new *Muhbir* appeared on August 31, 1867, two developments had already taken place which changed the picture as it had stood when Ziya and Kemal first arrived in Paris. Both had been precipitated by the state visit of Sultan Abdülaziz to Europe in July-August 1867, an unprecedented step for an Ottoman monarch.

First, Ziya Bey's conscience began to trouble him. Because of his long record of service to the sultan, Ziya constantly labored under the apprehension that his stand would be interpreted by the sultan as one of personal ingratitude. Thus when Abdülaziz arrived in London where Ziya had also gone because of troubles with the French authorities, he secretly presented the sultan with a petition wherein he clarified his stand vis-à-vis the monarch.

The second development was that Mustafa Fazıl patched up his differences with the Porte. During the sultan's stay in Paris, Fuad Paşa, who had accompanied the sultan, reached an

[78] The statutes of this society have been reported to have been published. See Engelhardt, *La Turquie*, I, 3. The date given for these statutes is April 30, 1867, a most improbable date in view of Ziya and Kemal's departure from Istanbul on May 17, 1867.

[79] *Levant Herald*, 4 Receb 1285/October 20, 1868, p. 2.

[80] Mithat Cemal Kuntay, *Sarıklı İhtilalci Ali Suavi* (Istanbul, Ahmet Halit, 1946), p. 41.

agreement with Mustafa Fazıl. Mustafa Fazıl immediately
called Kemal to Baden-Baden, where he explained the situation
to him, most probably, as a victory for the representative principle. Fazıl was going back to Turkey, but he had received
assurances that he would be allowed to prepare the groundwork
for the reforms that were close to his heart. This, at least, was
the interpretation that Kemal gave to Mustafa Fazıl's sudden
change of heart in a letter he wrote to his father.[81]

By the time the first few issues of the *Muhbir* were out,
Mustafa Fazıl was already in Istanbul. After he arrived there,
it became clear that the changes in the machinery of the government which were pledged by the government would not
go far. They amounted, in the end, to the refurbishing of
the already existing consultative machinery which had first
been established by Reşid Paşa in 1837. In 1867 this institution
was known as the *Meclis-i Vâlâ*, or Grand Council. This council was now to be separated into two. One of the resulting
bodies would have purely judicial functions and would serve
as a lay supreme court. The second, the Council of State,
was to be entrusted with the task of drafting laws and re-
viewing cases of administrative law. News of these preparations trickled to London and did not overly impress the editor
of the *Muhbir*, who made the acid comment that as long as
members of the law-drafting body were not *elected*, changes
would remain superficial.[82] The *Muhbir* also criticized the
principle of a lay supreme court and pointed out that none of
the resources of the Şeriat had been tapped in efforts at
modernization.[83]

This criticism was not to the liking of Mustafa Fazıl, who

[81] The text of this letter may be found in Kuntay, *Namık Kemal*, I, 325.
The same interpretation of Mustafa Fazıl's move was given by the Istanbul
correspondent of the *Augsburger Allgemeine Zeitung*, October 12, 1867,
p. 1559. This change of heart was already obvious in that Mustafa Fazıl
had accompanied the sultan all the way to Budapest on the latter's return
voyage. Ebüzziya Tevfik, "Yeni Osmanlılar," *Yeni Tasvir-i Efkâr*, September 26, 1909, p. 4.
[82] "Istanbuldan Tahrirat," *Muhbir*, October 26, 1867, p. 2.
[83] "İhtar," *ibid.*, September 7, 1867, p. 4.

wanted a more tactful opposition to the government. On the other hand, a stream of letters had begun to pour into the London headquarters of the Young Ottomans, to the effect that the arrival of Mustafa Fazıl had done little to change the political situation and that the sultan himself was preparing to change the rule of succession. Thereupon Ziya Paşa sent two letters on this subject to the capital, which were widely publicized.[84] Mustafa Fazıl replied by praising Ziya but still complaining of the "blundering" of the Muhbir.

Considerable confusion was created in the minds of the Young Ottomans exposed to these crosscurrents. To their consternation the Muhbir had, in fact, quite apart from the displeasure it had caused Mustafa Fazıl, turned out to be a rather sloppy product. Even though it made an earnest effort to explain the goals of the Young Ottomans, such as the establishment of a national representative body, the elimination of foreign interference in the domestic affairs of Turkey, the solution of the problem of reform along Ottoman and Islamic lines, it lacked the cutting edge of a sophisticated polemic and was too naïve for their taste. Suavi's egomania also seems to have caused considerable trouble.[85]

Kemal tried to make the best of this situation until March of 1868. At that date definite orders came from Mustafa Fazıl Paşa for Kemal to start another newspaper.[86] Thus in June of 1868 finally appeared the Hürriyet (June 29, 1868).

Mustafa Fazıl Paşa was no more satisfied with the Hürriyet than he had been with the Muhbir. The first issue of the new journal carried an article by Ziya Paşa lashing out at the Ottoman cabinet, and this was more than Mustafa Fazıl had asked for.[87]

Mustafa Fazıl Paşa's financial support of the Young Ottomans provides one of the important keys to the subsequent history of the Hürriyet. The exact nature of this aid, how-

[84] See Ziya Paşa, Veraset-i Saltanat-ı Seniye (Istanbul, n.p., 1326/1910).
[85] Kuntay, Namık Kemal, I, 485, for a letter of Kemal on this subject.
[86] Ibid., pp. 489, 490, for a letter of Kemal on the subject.
[87] Ibid., pp. 493, 494, for a letter of Kemal on the subject.

ever, is still obscure. Information available at present allows us to reconstruct only the following tentative picture of the complicated arrangements devised by Mustafa Fazıl before he left for Istanbul. In a bank in Paris or London Mustafa Fazıl had deposited 250,000 francs in Ziya's name.[88] Ziya, however, had not withdrawn any part of this sum a year after the departure of Mustafa Fazıl. The sum must, therefore, have been meant for use only in emergencies. The operating expenses of the *Hürriyet* and the salaries of the members of the editorial board, on the other hand, were paid every month. Mustafa Fazıl thus had a powerful monetary lever at his disposal in getting the Young Ottomans to conform to his wishes. These monthly contributions were channeled through Mustafa Fazıl's majordomo, Sakakini, to Rifat, who was in Paris. Since Rifat had sided with Mustafa Fazıl in finding the *Hürriyet's* criticism of the Porte extreme, this was a very congenial arrangement. At the beginning of August 1868 Rifat wrote a letter to the editor of the *Hürriyet* in which he criticized the article taking the Porte to task to which Mustafa Fazıl had raised objections. This letter was never printed and Rifat was so infuriated that he took this opportunity to stop payment to the Young Ottomans. It is not clear whether or not Rifat's move was instigated by Mustafa Fazıl.[89] At any rate, the breach between the Young Ottomans and Rifat never healed. Rifat categorically severed his relations with the group in a letter written five months later (January 22, 1869).[90]

Kemal quite rightly took this defection rather philosophically, with the comment that Rifat had joined the ranks of the Young Ottomans only as a steppingstone to the hand of

[88] Information about these financial arrangements may be found in Ebüzziya, "Yeni Osmanlılar," *Yeni Tasvir-i Efkâr*, September 27, September 30, and October 1, 1909, p. 4 in all issues.

[89] Compare Ebüzziya's account in Ebüzziya Tevfik, "Yeni Osmanlılar Tarihi," *Yeni Tasvir-i Efkâr*, November 15-16, 1909, p. 4, with Namık Kemal's letter in Kuntay, *Namık Kemal*, I, 403-406.

[90] A rather muddled statement of his stand appeared in pamphlet form at that date. This pamphlet is reproduced in Ebüzziya Tevfik, "Yeni Osmanlılar Tarihi," *Yeni Tasvir-i Efkâr*, November 18, 1909, p. 4.

Mustafa Fazıl's daughter. According to Kemal, it was Rifat's failure to attain this primary goal which resulted in his estrangement from the Young Ottoman cause. Kemal did not, however, adopt such a detached attitude toward Mustafa Fazıl's persistent demands that he stop publishing the *Hürriyet* and dissociate himself from Ziya. The latter, at first the leader of the Young Ottoman group by reason of seniority, had now fallen out of favor with Mustafa Fazıl because of his outspoken criticism of Âli. Gradually the prince's contributions became smaller. Kemal could not meet publishing costs.[91] Mustafa Fazıl, however, was unable to make a clean break with the Young Ottomans, because the latter were in possession of several documents bearing his signature in which his relations to the Young Ottomans and to the *Muhbir* were laid out quite plainly.[92]

It is not surprising that under these circumstances the most fiery of the Young Ottomans, Mehmed Bey, should have become so disillusioned with the Young Ottomans as to abandon the *Hürriyet* group and begin the publication in Paris of a periodical of his own, the *İttihad*. It is reported that in this journal there appeared articles in Turkish, Greek, Armenian, and Arabic. In so doing, Mehmed Bey wanted to show the truly pluralistic nature of his scheme of reform for the Ottoman Empire. Later, in Geneva, he published the *İnkilâb*, the most radical of Young Ottoman publications, of which only a few issues appeared.

Another less tangible but still cumulative malaise had for some time been sapping the morale of the Young Ottomans. This feeling is best described by Nuri Bey, who states:

"After having remained in London for a while, Mehmed Bey returned to Paris with Reşad Bey, thus leaving Namık Kemal alone in London. Since the old bonds existing between

[91] See in particular Namık Kemal's letter to his father dated August 5, 1868, in Kuntay, *Namık Kemal*, I, 493-495.
[92] For a letter of Namık Kemal, see *ibid.*, pp. 443, 565.

the associates while they were in Paris were dissolving, the first enthusiasm began to wane.

"First of all, let me speak of myself. As my ignorance was beginning to decrease and my eyes to open, thanks to my dogged efforts at study, I began to experience a complete change in ideas. By uncovering the fact that a country could not be changed through the sole desire to do so of three or four people, I began to have grave doubts as to the ultimate success of our movement. Even though I was eager to fancy myself a student who had come to Paris for his studies, and though I desired to act accordingly, having discovered the impossibility of reaching truth without education, I noticed that great obstacles were in my way. My friends were going to misunderstand me; they would say that I was fickle and had no perseverance. This thought sapped all my courage. How-ever, I could not any more find the same pleasure in sharing the ideas of my friends and I could not keep from being assailed by grave doubts about the extent to which our discussions and talks were of use.

"Mehmed Bey considered that the complete establishment of freedom in our country would only be possible in terms of a movement coming from the nation. Ziya Bey considered a close cooperation with the Sultan to be the best device for attaining our goals and getting to power. Agâh Efendi considered that it was necessary to infiltrate into the government to carry out our goals. As to Kemal Bey, since he held the conviction that 'The Ottoman tribe has never demanded more than what has been granted to it by the Ottoman Dynasty, its rulers. Whenever the ruler is against it, nothing can be done in our country,' this type of thinking led him to believe that there was no way to succeed other than bringing to the throne a well-intentioned ruler who, realizing the necessities of the time, would carry out the reforms which would put new life into the state.

"Insofar as Rifat was concerned, similar to the mathematicians who cannot think of anything except in terms of mathematics, he could not control his desire to apply the dicta of jurisprudence with which his mind was taken and therefore could not resist the temptation of proclaiming the necessity for every one of the actions undertaken towards the materialization of our aims, to fit legal standards. But just as he did not define what he meant by this, he did not consider any ideas except his own to be reasonable.

"Reşad Bey, while feeling that we were stuck in a problem without issue, did not pass opinion on this personally, and considered the best way out was to bury himself in study.

"Let us now come to Suavi. The highly eccentric conduct of Suavi, added to his immorality and the fact that this was known to all of us, made us handle him in a way that would preclude his engaging into activities that would show us in a wrong light."[93]

Finally, the return of Mustafa Fazıl Paşa and the obvious ambiguity of his relations with the exiles had aroused the suspicions of the newspaper-reading public in the capital. Although the *Hürriyet* was regularly smuggled into Turkey and widely distributed, the concurrent collaboration of its patron with the Imperial Government robbed its criticism of any sting for those who were acquainted with the *Hürriyet's* background of intrigues. The uninitiated, on the other hand, could do no more than puzzle at the Paşa's presence in Turkey.

Ironically enough, while the *Hürriyet* was in these straits, two prospective donors appeared whom the Young Ottomans had only known as enemies to that date. The first of these was Âli Paşa. The Porte approached the *Hürriyet* with an offer to buy 2000 subscriptions, on condition that the *Hürriyet* modify its approach.

Kemal's friends, Nuri and Reşad, decided that they could deceive the Porte into believing that for the sake of such a contribution they would betray their ideals. Furthermore, they felt no loyalty to Mustafa Fazıl who, to ensure that Ziya Paşa

[93] Ertaylan, *Türk Edebiyatı Tarihi, Ondokuzuncu Asır*, I, 218 f., quoting Nuri's manuscript mentioned in note 1 at the beginning of this chapter.

would stop writing his highly personal articles against Ottoman ministers, was ready to split the Young Ottoman group.
The plan was to write one article favoring the Porte but to
continue to attack it after the subscription money had been
received on the strength of the article in favor. Kemal was
convinced that this was the best solution of their problem and
the article was duly written.[94]

At the same time Kemal was indignant at the absurdity of
the situation into which he had been forced. He wrote his
father to plead with Mustafa Fazıl to desist from his childish
demands that Kemal disassociate himself from Ziya, for this
would have meant his disassociation from the majority of the
Young Ottomans who had become anti-Fazıl. This, in turn,
would have meant stopping the publication of the *Hürriyet*.
Kemal was outraged even at the thought of such a prospect.
But Kemal's pleas were not successful, and the subscription
scheme also fell through.

A second "angel" now appeared who was also interested in
keeping the *Hürriyet* alive; this was the khedive Ismail. The
khedive had quarreled with Âli Paşa and now found the
Hürriyet to be a good platform for anti-Âli propaganda. This
time it was Ziya Paşa who was inclined to think of accepting
the khedive's contribution.

An extraordinary editorial policy now ensued whereby, on
one hand, Ziya Paşa in his articles lashed at Âli Paşa, in return
for the khedive's gratuities, without, however, explicitly taking
up the defense of the khedive; on the other hand, Kemal, who
disagreed with Ziya's stand, carried on a polemic against the
khedive in pages of the same journal.[95]

Due to the contributions of the khedive, Ziya was able to

[94] "Yaşasın Sultan Aziz Han, Aferin Bab-ı Âli" ("Long live Sultan
Abdülaziz, Bravo to the Porte!"), *Hürriyet*, December 21, 1868, p. 1. For
a letter of Kemal see Kuntay, *Namık Kemal*, I, 443.

[95] This is a paraphrase of Kemal's own description, *ibid.*, p. 442. Professor Abdülkadir Karahan of the University of Istanbul has recently found in
the British Museum letters exchanged between Ziya and an intermediary of
the khedive which clarify these arrangements.

eke out a living in London. This state of affairs continued until
the summer of 1869, when once again the Egyptian question
took a new turn and Mustafa Fazıl succeeded in separating
Kemal from Ziya.

In the spring of that year the khedive Ismail had embarked
on two undertakings, both of which were most distasteful to
the Porte. The first of these was a campaign of self-advertise-
ment aimed at demonstrating the extent of the khedive's Europeanization. The official reason for Ismail's visit was that of
extending to European sovereigns invitations to attend the
opening of the Suez Canal, but Ismail was using this opportunity to show that Egypt was far enough ahead on the road
to civilization to be given its place in the community of nations.
The second of Ismail's aims, related to the first, was to establish a few precedents to strengthen a prospective claim to
wider independence from Turkey. Such actions, undertaken
in the name of the Egyptian principality, as preparations to
float the third Egyptian loan in seven years and orders for
armaments from European arms manufacturers, were meant
by the khedive as tests that would show how far he could go
in freeing himself completely from Turkish tutelage. During
his trip the khedive's aide, Nubar Paşa, had made rather short
shrift of Ottoman plenipotentiaries accredited in the various
European capitals which he had visited and had humiliated
several of them in matters of protocol by insisting on taking
precedence over them. The resulting displeasure of the Porte
was so great and Âli Paşa so infuriated by khedivial conduct
that Ismail's dismissal seems to have been seriously considered.
Fazıl Paşa's hopes that he would be appointed in his brother's
stead were once more aroused.

The account of the developments that followed as given by
Ebüzziya does not fully agree with information which is
found in Kemal's own letters. Most pervasive again, however,
are financial questions, with the two princely brothers vying
with each other in the use of monetary inducements and deter-
rents. The khedive struck first and in July of 1869 an attempt

was made to bribe Kemal through the khedive's expert on such delicate missions, the Polish *émigré*, Felâtun Paşa. Felâtun Paşa, having contacted Kemal, was unceremoniously ejected by the latter from the hotel room in which the interview had occurred. At this juncture some really important news with regard to his political future must have reached Mustafa Fazıl, who was vacationing in Hamburg. Having "broken the bank" at the local casino, he was engaged in spending the 600,000 francs he had won when he suddenly left for Istanbul, where he arrived at the end of July 1869. Two days after his arrival he was appointed minister without portfolio.[96] Then in mid-August his agent Sakakini arrived in Ostend, where Ziya and Kemal were vacationing, with a request from Fazıl that the publication of the *Hürriyet* should, once and for all, be suspended. This time Kemal, despairing, gave up, but Ziya flew into a towering rage, sent back to Mustafa Fazıl the 250,000 francs left as emergency funds, and retired to Geneva. He also declared to Sakakini that the printing press of the *Hürriyet*, established in the name of the Young Ottoman, Agâh Efendi, would continue to serve the ends of the Young Ottoman Society. Thus, after having overseen the printing of a series of three articles which he had written, Kemal handed the administration of the press over to Agâh on September 6, 1869.

According to Ebüzziya,[97] Ziya was approached in Geneva by the emissaries of the khedive and provided with more extensive support than he had received up to that time. Some such arrangement must have taken place for Ziya to have been able to go on publishing the *Hürriyet* singlehandedly, beginning with the issue of September 13, 1869. The fact that the *Hürriyet* was now transformed into an exclusively anti-Âli polemical sheet certainly also points in that direction.[98]

[96] Douin, *Histoire*, II, 316-326.

[97] Ebüzziya Tevfik, "Yeni Osmanlılar Tarihi," *Yeni Tasvir-i Efkâr*, December 14, 1909, p. 4.

[98] Kuntay, *Namık Kemal*, I, 442.

The degree of elasticity that was demanded of an editorial policy which at one and the same time had to appeal to readers in Istanbul (thus to be critical of Ismail, who was greatly disliked), but also had to serve Ismail's ends (thus implying that in some respects Ismail was really not at fault) and concurrently to lash at the Porte was not beyond the polemical talent of Ziya.

In the Ottoman capital too Ismail was victorious. The plan for his deposition had not been looked upon with favor by the European powers, but Ismail secured his position well without any outside help. He spent extraordinary sums making friends in the immediate entourage of the sultan and thus was able to influence the latter in his favor. By December of 1870 Mustafa Fazıl's hopes of being made khedive had completely faded.

By January 1870 Namık Kemal was emphatically requesting that the *Hürriyet* print the news of his dissociation with it. When this was not done, he printed and distributed a notice of the complete severance of all his ties with the *Hürriyet*. The reason for this was clear—under khedivial patronage the *Hürriyet* no longer served the cause of Young Ottoman reform.[99]

As editor, however, Ziya Paşa immediately got into complications. In February of 1870 the British authorities started a lawsuit against him for having published in the *Hürriyet* an article by Suavi advocating the assassination of Âli Paşa.[100] Ziya, fearing the penalties incurred under British law for such an offense, fled to Switzerland, where the next issue of the *Hürriyet* appeared in April of 1870. A definite shift in attitude, due to Ziya's editorship, could now be seen: the Geneva issues of the newspaper were increasingly concerned with defending the sultan against Mehmed Bey's new publication, the

[99] Facsimile, *ibid.*, p. 445. For Ziya's negotiations with Ismail see *ibid.*, II, 1-91. Ali Suavi states that the Young Ottomans who were true to their ideals decided to "expel" the prince from the organization (*Ulûm*, undated, pp. 836-841).

[100] *Hürriyet*, December 20, 1869, p. 3.

Inkilâb,[101] where the first attempts were made to elaborate a theory of revolutionary action.

Namık Kemal, even after his resignation from the *Hürriyet*, remained in London, supervising a printing of the Koran—a venture in which Mustafa Fazıl had engaged.[102] Upon having been promised that he could safely return, Namık Kemal left London for Istanbul.[103] Once back in the capital, Mustafa Fazıl Paşa after repeated requests succeeded in having Kemal call on Âli Paşa.[104] Kemal had promised Âli that he would not resume his journalistic writings upon his return and, indeed, only published a few short humorous pieces in the weekly humor magazine, the *Diyojen*.[105] Thus the first phase of the Young Ottoman venture came to an end. Mehmed, Nuri, and Reşad were later to join forces in Paris, where all three served as volunteers with the Republican forces during the Commune.

III. Later Developments

In September 1871 Âli Paşa died and the uncle of Mehmed Bey, Mahmud Nedim Paşa, was made Grand Vizier. Upon the general amnesty granted by Mahmud Nedim, the remainder of the Young Ottomans arrived in Istanbul. From this time on, more than ever before, the Young Ottoman movement is associated with the activities of Kemal, with the other members more or less following his lead. Under Mahmud Nedim Paşa's rule, Kemal attempted to bring out a newspaper which would have been called *İstiklâl* ("Independence"). But since he had been the owner of a newspaper which had been closed, the existing press law did not allow him to own a newspaper. The Young Ottomans, therefore,

---

101 Kuntay, *Namık Kemal*, I, 446. I was able to see only the French supplement of this publication entitled *La Révolution: Organe de la Démocratie Musulmane*, No. 1, May 1, 1870.

102 Kuntay, *Namık Kemal*, I, 495.

103 He left London on November 25, 1870.

104 Kuntay, *Namık Kemal*, II, 98, 99, note 6.

105 The *Diyojen* was published by Kemal's friend, an exponent of liberal ideas, Theodor Kasap. For information about the latter see İhsan Sungu, "Teodor (sic) Kasap," *Aylık Ansiklopedi*, I, 126, 127.

decided to rent the name of a newspaper which was appearing under the name of *İbret*.

The publication of the *İbret* had been made possible, again, by the generosity of Mustafa Fazıl Paşa. The prince had purchased the printing plant of the *Tasvir-i Efkâr* in the fall of 1871 when, within a week of Âli Paşa's death, Şinasi succumbed to an illness which had been undermining his health for years. Mustafa Fazıl Paşa had then turned the press over to the two Young Ottomans who were already in the capital in the fall of 1871. One of these was Kemal; the other was Ebüzziya Tevfik, the author of the only extant history of the Young Ottoman movement. Ebüzziya was a former colleague of Kemal from the days of the Patriotic Alliance and had taken over the *Tasvir-i Efkâr* following Kemal's flight. The *Tasvir*, however, had not been published very long by Ebüzziya, whose main occupation was that of a secretary at the Council of State. When, soon after the purchase of Şinasi's press, Ebüzziya was dismissed from the governmental post he held, Fazıl Paşa's gift indeed proved a godsend.

The dismissal of Ebüzziya had a special significance in relation to the goals which at an earlier time the Young Ottomans had set themselves. It was a sign that, with the demise of Fuad Paşa in 1869 and the disappearance from the political scene of Âli Paşa, all paths had not as yet been cleared for them. In fact, upon their return the exiles were to find that the ideas they had championed were meeting with more invidious obstacles than those at one time thrown up by Âli and Fuad. On the one hand, they discovered that there existed an influential group of superreactionaries who were not at all convinced of the excellence of their synthesis between East and West. On the other hand, they found that the "tyranny" of ministers of which they had complained was more entrenched and pervasive a force than they had thought possible.

Ebüzziya's loss of his job was the consequence of a head-on encounter with the first force, i.e., religious reaction. This was a first portent that the facts of Ottoman society were somewhat different from what the Young Ottomans had imagined them to be. Namık Kemal's second clash with bureaucratic authoritarianism which came somewhat later was, in turn, a harsher warning of the realities of political life. It is indeed an irony of fate, and no doubt must have struck Kemal as such, that when this clash occurred and Kemal was asked for the second time in his life to leave Istanbul for having criticized the government, it should have been Midhat Paşa, then Grand Vizier—the very same Midhat Paşa whom the Young Ottomans had praised both in the *Muhbir* and the *Hürriyet* as *the* ideal statesman—who insisted that Kemal conform to this demand.

The reason for Ebüzziya's loss of his job in 1871 is, in itself, quite instructive as to the competing currents of thought that were at work in the Ottoman Empire at the time. Following Mahmud Nedim Paşa's appointment to the grand vizierate, the presidency of the Council of State had been given to Namık Paşa. The latter had been known as a man of broad liberal views and had, for a while, served as the Ottoman ambassador to the Court of St. James. Namık Kemal had also praised him in the *Hürriyet* as an able and honest statesman. Lately, however, Namık Paşa had come under the influence of a *Halveti* mystic group and had decided that his earlier admiration of things European had been mistaken.[106] One of

106 Ebüzziya mentions the influence on Namık Paşa of a *Halveti* group whose founder was Ibrahim Kuşadalı. See Ebüzziya Tevfik, "Yeni Osmanlılar Tarihi," *Yeni Tasvir-i Efkâr*, October 5, 1909. Kuşadalı had died in 1845-1846, but his disciples seem to have retained considerable influence. Kuşadalı's circle provides us with an interesting illustration of the contradictory directions in which such mystical teachings could work. Among his disciples were Ali Âli and Müşfik, the chief editorial writers of the *Ceride-i Havadis* (see below, Chapter IV) and men who were precursors of the Young Ottomans in establishing a nucleus of the discontented intelligentsia. Another disciple of Kuşadalı was Şeyh Osman Şems, who imparted his mystical insight to Kemal and seems to have influenced Kemal's conception of individual freedom. (See below, Chapter X.) In the case of Namık Paşa, Kuşadalı's influence showed in the form of neopuritanism. For Kuşadalı, see Bursalı Mehmed Tahir, *Osmanlı Müellifleri* (Istanbul, Matbaa-i Âmire, 1333/1914-1915), I, 151; İnal, *Son Asır*, pp. 97, 1022, 1976. The *Halvetiye*

the first steps he had taken to mend his ways was to announce that in the future the employees of the Council of State were to interrupt their work at prayer time and assemble in a room which Namık Paşa had had converted into a chapel. The Paşa was to act as a prayer leader. Ebüzziya and some of his friends failed to appear at prayer time and were thereupon dismissed.

Ebüzziya thus decided to make a living by publishing books. His guess that an audience of potential book readers existed in Istanbul proved to be right and he made a handsome profit on the sale of his first two publications. The first of these was a drama entitled *Ecel ve Kaza* ("Fate and Fatality"), a patriotic piece which Ebüzziya himself states to have been the first work of its kind in Turkey.[107]

The second work was a biography of Saladin by Namık Kemal. Both brochures were completely sold out within a short time. Neither was the enthusiasm for the booklet on the life and times of Saladin, the Islamic hero, entirely fortuitous. The idea of a renaissance of the Islamic people was in the air and had even had repercussions among the Young Ottomans. The latter now began to work out a more extensive theory of the political unification of Islamic people.

The origin of this reappraisal went back to the new pattern assumed by the European balance of power following the Franco-Prussian War. As a result of its defeat, France had lost its preponderant position in the Middle East. On the other hand, in the Ottoman area Russia had been strengthened by the war, and Balkan nationalist and separatist movements began more and more to take their cue from the Russian Pan-Slavists. For some time, this had worried the Young Ottomans,

---

was one of the oldest orders with definitely ascetic practices. See John P. Brown, *The Dervishes or Oriental Spiritualism* (ed. by H. A. Rose, London, Oxford University Press, 1927), p. 288. For Namık Paşa's influence, see Benoit Brunswik, *La Succession au Trône de Turquie* (Paris, Amyot, 1872), pp. 49, 50.

[107] Ebüzziya Tevfik, "Yeni Osmanlılar Tarihi," *Yeni Tasvir-i Efkâr*, October 6, 1909. Unless otherwise indicated, my account of the Young Ottomans' fortunes between 1870 and 1876 is based entirely on Ebüzziya's serial.

who were also aware of the extent of the Russian cultural penetration into the Balkans.[108]

In Germany too a Pan-German movement was taking shape. Conversely, as Engelhardt well describes it, a feeling arose in the Ottoman Empire, both in official circles and among the out-and-out opponents of Westernization, that this was the time for the Ottoman Empire to escape the tutelage of the Western Powers.[109] There occurred an ingathering of hitherto centrifugal forces. The common focus was the desire to free the Ottoman Empire of its inferior position in its relations with Western Powers. From this to the idea of a bond uniting all Moslems was only a step. This step was taken when the Young Ottomans "invented" Pan-Islamism.[110]

Already, in their articles in the *Hürriyet*, the Young Ottomans had stated that it had been the aim of the Ottoman sultans, at the time of the expansion of the Ottoman Empire, to establish such a union of all Islamic people.[111] In another context, the noncommittal attitude of the Porte toward Central Asian khans who were pleading for Ottoman support against

[108] "Mesele-yi Şarkiyenin Bugünkü Hali," *Muhbir*, September 7, 1867, p. 2.

[109] Engelhardt, *La Turquie et le Tanzimat*, II, 89-91.

[110] See Kaplan, *Namık Kemal*, p. 80. Nuri Bey explained the attitude of the Young Ottomans as follows: "Against this kind of European union, we are obliged to secure our own country's political and military union," *ibid*. For a sample of the Young Ottomans' new approach see Namık Kemal's article on Islamic union, "İttihad-ı İslam," *İbret*, June 27, 1827, in Mustafa Nihat Özön, *Namık Kemal ve İbret Gazetesi* (Istanbul, Remzi Kitabevi, 1938), p. 74. The specific form that this union was to assume was that of a tightening of bonds with those of the provinces of the Ottoman Empire, such as Egypt and Tunis, which for some time now had been hanging to the mother country only by the most tenuous of threads (Nuri, "Teşyid-i Revabıt," *İbret*, June 20, 1872). The developments that had precipitated the new interest for a tighter-knit Islamic community were the success that the Germans had obtained in their own efforts at union and the spread of the Pan-Slav idea. On the other hand, Kemal also realized that the new advances in communications provided the *means* of cementing such national clusters. As he stated: "Twenty years ago, the fact that there were Moslems in Kaşgar was not known. Now, public opinion tries to obtain union with them. This inclination resembles an overpowering flood which will not be stopped by any obstacle placed in its way" (Namık Kemal, "Meylan-ı Âlem," *İbret*, July 6, 1872, in Özön, *Namık Kemal*, p. 91).

[111] [Ziya Paşa?], "Mülâhaza," *Hürriyet*, November 9, 1868, p. 1.

Russia had been criticized by the *Hürriyet* as a shameful re-
treat at a time when Moslem brethren were crying for help.[112]

Thus an amorphous proto-Pan-Islamism had for some time
been implicit in the Young Ottoman position. Now, after their
return to Turkey, the *İbret* specifically took up for discussion
the idea of an Islamic union.[113]

It is important to keep in mind at this juncture that the
Young Ottomans had little in common with the more reactionary groups who thought of Islamic union in terms of a
preparation for a splendid holy war to end all holy wars. The
Young Ottomans' lack of aggressive proclivities, their emphasis on self-improvement through the adoption of selected
features of Western life, the purely defensive stand involved
in their demands that Western slights on Ottoman sovereignty
cease—all these were features of their ideology which carried
through into their writings in the *İbret*.[114] It was true, however, that men of all shades of opinion in the capital were in a
mood to enjoy the history of Saladin's prowesses.

Another result of the Franco-Prussian War had been the
displacement of France by Germany as the most successful
embodiment of Western civilization. Kemal's new admiration
for Prussia may be followed in a "paper" which Âli Paşa had

[112] Editorial, *Hürriyet*, May 10, 1869, p. 1.

[113] Namık Kemal was also corresponding at the time with Léon Cahun,
the French author whose works of historical fiction about the Turks of
Central Asia were to influence Turkish intellectuals in the first years of the
twentieth century. See Kuntay, *Namık Kemal*, I, 1, p. 530. In 1867 at the
time when Mustafa Fazıl Paşa's *Lettre* had appeared in *Liberté*, Léon
Cahun had been contributing articles on the Ottoman Empire to this newspaper in which he stated that the problem of "liberty" was the core of
Turkish ills (*Liberté*, June 10, 1867, p. 1) and in which he described the
arrests of June 1867 (*Liberté*, June 22, 1867, p. 2). Kemal probably was in
touch with Cahun while he was in Paris.

[114] The *İbret*, for example, was most enthusiastic about the society for
the propagandizing of Islam established by Tahsin Efendi (see below, Chapter VII). It stated that to find a principle of Islamic union in the "pages
of books" was a better way of going about this task than by the use of the
sword. See Namık Kemal, "İttihad-ı İslam," *İbret*, June 27, 1872, in Özön,
Namık Kemal, p. 78. This moderation stands out particularly when it is
compared with the more extreme *Basiret*, see Mordtmann, *Stambul*, I, 147,
351; II, 240-244.

convinced him to prepare after his return to Istanbul.[115] Âli had been curious regarding Kemal's opinion of Prussian successes. Interestingly enough, in the memorandum which he delivered, Kemal gave as his estimate for the reasons for Prussian superiority the extent of their technical advances. In this, and in the importance granted in Germany to practical training, he thought lay the reasons for which the Ottoman Empire would have to look up to Germany in the future, rather than to France or England. Kemal's concern with the technical apparatus of progress is also reflected in the majority of the articles he wrote for the *Ibret*.

The final ingredient that gave the *Ibret* its stamp was the great disappointment of the Young Ottomans with the government of Mahmud Nedim. This was caused, in turn, by the incredible disorganization of the governmental machine under Mahmud Nedim's rule. Mostly interested in keeping possible rivals out of sight, Mehmed Bey's uncle had begun to shift ministers, governors, and generals at a breath-taking pace and was unable to attend to the slightest governmental routine.[116] Consequently the *Ibret* took over, as a critic of the government, where the *Hürriyet* had left off. Again, it was the khedive Ismail who was to cause the activities of the Young Ottomans to come to a standstill.

When, in May of 1872, the *Ibret* first appeared, the khedive had been on his yearly visit to the Ottoman capital. He believed that with Âli Paşa out of the way it would not be difficult to cut away a few more of the ties of vassalage that bound Egypt to the Ottoman Empire. He was ready to pay dearly for any achievements in this respect. During Ismail's visit there appeared in the columns of the daily *Hakayik ül-Vekayi*

[115] The text of this report may be found in [Namık Kemal], "Kemal beyin bir mütalaa-i siyasiyesi," *Mecmua-i Ebüzziya*, 1 Muharrem 1298/ December 4, 1880, pp. 225-231.

[116] On Mahmud Nedim's earlier life and his rivalry with Fuad, see Cevdet Paşa, "Maruzat" *T.T.E.M.* (1926), XVI, 168, 169. On his policy of dismissal, Mordtmann, *Stambul*, I, 117, 118, and Ali Efendi, *Istanbulda Yarım Asırlık Vekai-i Mühimme* (Istanbul, Matbaa-i Hüseyin ve Enver, 1325/1909-1910), p. 30.

a running commentary of his doings which, to the exasperated Young Ottomans, seemed of utmost servility and which, in fact, was quite fawning. This was the result of Ismail's generosity with its editor. The *İbret* thereupon took the *Hakayik ül-Vekayi* to task several times in a row. The *İbret* also incurred official displeasure by giving a day-by-day pinprick account of Midhat Paşa's voyage back to the capital. Midhat had been recalled from the governorship of Baghdad and was returning to Istanbul before proceeding to a new post, but Mahmud Nedim shuddered at the thought of having a serious rival in Istanbul.

At first the incursions of the *İbret* into such dangerous chronicling drew only a mild rebuke for discourtesy to Ismail. Ismail, as usual, went his own way in trying to settle the matter and had recourse to his usual glittering, if unimaginative, monetary argument. He proposed a bribe to Kemal. His emissary, however, was again shown the door. Ismail had better luck with Hurşid Bey, who headed the press section of the Ministry of Education. Thus in mid-June the *İbret* was suspended for a duration of four months.

The Young Ottomans were not entirely surprised when, on opening a pro-government daily a few days later, they saw that they had been appointed to administrative posts in various parts of the empire. The same day Mehmed Bey announced that his uncle Mahmud Nedim was genuinely sorry that the Young Ottomans were receiving such harsh treatment but that he had been obliged to give in to an order from the Palace. This excuse is not entirely implausible, for Ismail had just endeared himself to the sultan by a gift of hundreds of rare African birds. Mahmud Nedim had asked his nephew to reassure the Young Ottomans that he was as close to them as ever. A visit by Nuri, Reşad, Kemal, and Ebüzziya to the grand vizier was of no use; Mahmud Nedim declared to the young men that he never could have found better administrators. An interview with Rüşdü Paşa made the four companions realize that even Ottoman statesmen whom they trusted considered them a nuisance. This realization prompted Nuri and Reşad to accept their appointments. At least, they thought, as administrators they could try to improve the country from a position of personal strength.

As for Kemal, he devised a way of delaying his departure from the capital. The usual procedure was that an administrator, on receiving an appointment in one of the provinces, put up collateral provided by money-lenders as security toward the repayment to the central administration of the taxes to be collected. The latter were then repaid when the actual tax-collecting had begun. Kemal, on principle, refused to enter into an arrangement which he thought was humiliating to the sultan's subjects. He also used this excuse to delay the procedure of his appointment.

By that time Midhat Paşa had arrived in the capital and Kemal served as an intermediary between the Ottoman heir, Prince Murad, and Midhat. Nothing came out of these contacts, Midhat having refused to discuss what had all the earmarks of a conspiracy to depose Abdülaziz. A few days later Midhat had succeeded in having himself appointed grand vizier through the simpler tactic of asking an audience from the sovereign (July 31, 1872).

What should have been a complete change in the fortunes of the Young Ottomans, however, provided no more than cold comfort for them. Midhat Paşa insisted that Kemal, who had antagonized all too many people at the Porte, leave for his post in Gelibolu. The grand vizier personally stood as the guarantor required for his appointment. As for Ebüzziya, he was free to act as he pleased, since the position to which he had been appointed while Mahmud Nedim was in power had been created by Mahmud and was abolished upon his fall from power. On the twenty-sixth of September 1872 Kemal left for Gelibolu. Ebüzziya accompanied him and after a short stay returned to Istanbul. Fifteen days later Midhat Paşa was dismissed and Rüşdü Paşa was appointed in his stead.

Ebüzziya had decided that he would devote himself to publishing, regardless of the obstacles that he would encounter. Back in Istanbul he bought the rights of a newssheet which had stopped publication, the *Hadika*, and transformed it into an organ of political criticism. When the four-month period for which the *İbret* had been suspended came to an end, somewhat shortened by an act of imperial mercy, Ebüzziya resumed the publication of the *İbret*. Namık Kemal sent articles to both journals. Kemal was finally able to get himself dismissed and returned to Istanbul on December 20, 1872. He once again assumed entire responsibility for the *İbret*. Both Kemal and Ziya were also using the columns of a humorous weekly, the *Diyojen*, to needle the government. Neither fun-making nor criticism endeared the Young Ottomans to Rüşdü Paşa. On January 13, 1873, the *Diyojen* was suspended for an unlimited time. Ebüzziya continued his attacks in the *Hadika*, but at the end of January Rüşdü Paşa found a pretext to close it too.

The occasion was a memorable one, even if Rüşdü Paşa did not realize it at the time. The incident he seized on was the first recorded instance of labor agitation to have occurred in the Ottoman Empire. This had been caused by arrears in the payment of navalyard workers. A march on the Ministry of the Navy had been organized by the hungry workers to present a petition to the Minister. Soldiers had refused to disperse the workers and the minister himself had escaped under a hail of stones. The crowd had then proceeded to the Grand Vizierate. There they had found the gate doors locked. As a last resort the workers had come to Ebüzziya's printing plant and requested that he publish their petition. Ebüzziya had agreed to this. The *Hadika* was thereupon suspended on January 23, 1873. On this occasion, however, Namık Kemal, whose articles dealing with such abstractions as "progress" and "civilization" were thought to be less dangerous than those of the *Hadika*, was not bothered. Kemal thus failed to rush to Ebüzziya's defense in the *İbret*—an attitude which Ebüzziya mentions as the only one he ever had to criticize throughout their long association.

Within two days Ebüzziya was again busy looking up influential friends to register the name of another newspaper. He was successful in getting permission to publish one entitled *Cüzdan*. The man who granted the permission to Ebüzziya was Halil Şerif Paşa. After 1867 Halil Şerif had receded into the background of Turkish constitutionalism, but as Turkish ambassador to Vienna he had maintained close relations with the Young Ottomans. Namık Kemal had been his guest for some time while Kemal was on his way back to Istanbul. In the fall of 1872 Halil Şerif, as Minister of Foreign Affairs, had been preparing a plan for a federal constitution for the Ottoman Empire which had been wrecked by the pressures brought to bear on the Grand Vizier Rüşdü Paşa by Russian Ambassador Ignatyeff.[117] Halil Şerif was not unwilling, therefore, to embarrass his ministerial colleague by increasing the number of liberal publications.

The *Cüzdan* came out at a time when even nonpolitical articles were beginning to be closely scanned. Thus an article on Darwin which appeared in the periodical *Dağarcık*, published by Ahmed Midhat, had led the Ministry of Education to circularize a note among editors asking them to be cautious in selecting suitable subject matter for articles. Ebüzziya thereupon printed an announcement in the *İbret* on the day the *Cüzdan* was offered for sale, implying that every article contained in it violated the instructions of the Ministry of Education. The result was that the *Cüzdan* was sold out the very day it appeared. By the time government agents came to seize the issue only 200 copies were left at the printing plant.

The event which precipitated the third exile of the Young Ottomans, however, was somewhat unexpected. Sometime in March of 1873 Nuri Bey had returned to Istanbul. In cooperation with Kemal and under the sponsorship of Halil Şerif Paşa he had started a theatrical arts society so as to build up a solid "Ottoman drama" repertoire for the small theater started by one Güllü Agop. The theater in its Western form

[117] Davison, "Reform in the Ottoman Empire," p. 384.

was an innovation in Turkey and after Şinasi's and Ahmed Vefik Paşa's efforts to introduce the genre in Turkey it was beginning to appeal to Turkish audiences. The Güllü Agop Theater had begun by giving Ebüzziya's *Fate and Fatality*; later, on April 1, 1873, a play written by Kemal was performed. The subject of the play was the defense by the Turks of the fortress of Silistria during the Turko-Russian War. Patterned on patriotic French plays of the period but colored by a romanticism which had gone out of fashion in Europe, it was, indeed, quite effective on a Turkish audience. The direct appeal to the spectator's emotions—an outstanding technical advantage of the Western theater over its stylized, Turkish equivalent—had an immediate effect. The whole theater rocked with shouts of "Long live Kemal!"[118]

It would seem from the evidence that has been gathered that this outburst of patriotism particularly upset the government because Namık Kemal was in touch with many people who were known to be plotting the overthrow of Sultan Abdülaziz and his replacement by his nephew Murad. Under these circumstances evidence of widespread support for Kemal among the elite meant an increase in the potential danger represented by Prince Murad.

Immediately thereafter (April 5, 1873) the *İbret* was suspended and Namık Kemal, Ebüzziya Tevfik, Ahmed Midhat, Nuri, and a young *âlim*, Bereketzâde Ismail Hakkı, who had been in close touch with Kemal were one by one incarcerated at the Ministry of Police in the capital. All these men were then sent into exile: Kemal to Cyprus, Ebüzziya and Ahmed Midhat to Rhodes, Nuri and Bereketzâde to Acre.

Namık Kemal remained under house arrest in Cyprus for more than two and a half years. Fortunately for him, in 1876 Sultan Abdülaziz was deposed. The conspiracy to depose the sultan had been engineered by such eminent politicians as Midhat Paşa and Rüşdü Paşa and such outstanding military leaders as Hüseyin Avni Paşa and Süleyman Paşa. Great hopes

[118] Özön, *Namık Kemal*, pp. 208-211.

were raised by what was supposedly a triumph of liberal forces. It was at this point that Ziya Paşa's figure reemerges from the political limbo in which it had been floating since 1870. Important things had happened to Ziya too, but his relations with Kemal had become progressively cooler in the years 1870-1876. Before the deposition of the sultan, upon Mahmud Nedim's appointment Ziya Paşa had hurried back to Turkey. Mahmud Nedim was a personal friend of his and provided Ziya with a governmental position.[119] Ziya's close relations with the Palace also made things easier for him. Immediately upon his return he wrote several (unpublicized) elegiac poems in praise of the sultan. He was not any more in the awkward position of having to prove the extent of his attachment to the House of Osman while at the same time lambasting the Ottoman Porte.

However, Ziya was soon at odds with Mahmud Nedim. The clash occurred on the occasion of the renewal of a railroad building concession. This contract had already considerably enriched the Austrian entrepreneur, Baron Hirsch. The agreement was now coming up for extension to a committee on which, among others, sat the Minister of Foreign Affairs Savfet Paşa, Mahmud Nedim, and—Ziya. Both Savfet and Mahmud Nedim wanted Ziya to initial the renewal without giving him time to examine the text of the document closely. Ziya refused and tendered his resignation. Ziya's close connections with the Palace, however, enabled him to feel no misgivings with regard to Mahmud Nedim, to live in comparative ease, and even to get a post on the Council of State.

While Kemal was languishing on Cyprus, Ziya succeeded in having an anthology of Ottoman verse published. This work, the *Harabat*, gave rise to one of the most famous controversies of Ottoman literary history, for Kemal in his exile tore it to shreds in a devastating critique, widely circulated in the capital

---

[119] For Ziya Paşa see İsmail Hikmet [Ertaylan], *Ziya Paşa: Hayatı, Eserleri* (Istanbul, Kanaat Kütüphanesi, 1932), p. 54 *et seq.*; Kuntay, *Namık Kemal*, II, 1, 410, 411.

in manuscript form.[120] Kemal's criticism, acid, competent, and merciless, was that many of the men represented in the anthology had no original talent, that they were mostly followers of the old school and of the type of literature which the Young Ottomans had earlier criticized as overloaded and empty. He was also shocked by the discovery of a series of Ziya's odes to the Sultan, whose existence he had never suspected.[121]

Thus by 1876 the relations between the two men could not have been worse. It is to the credit of Ziya Paşa that, under such circumstances, he should have taken the initiative immediately following the deposition of Abdülaziz to petition the Grand Vizier Rüşdü Paşa for Kemal's release. Rüşdü Paşa would have been quite content to forget about Kemal, but Ziya was also on good terms with Murad. In the last days of Abdülaziz's reign Ziya had finally turned against his imperial ruler and had served as an intermediary between Midhat and Murad. He consequently had been appointed First Secretary of the Palace and therefore wielded some power and got his way.

Some time before the coup one other Young Ottoman had already been released under somewhat different circumstances. This was Ahmed Midhat, who had been pardoned by the ubiquitous Rüşdü Paşa, back in power once more. An article of Ahmed Midhat's from his place of exile to the periodical *Kırkambar*, published in his absence by his brother, had pleased Rüşdü Paşa. Ahmed Midhat had therefore been contacted and asked to work for the Porte—an invitation he had accepted. The article which had so pleased Rüşdü Paşa was a defense of Islam against Christianity.[122]

In general, as Kemal's uncle, Mahir Bey, pointed out to his nephew in a letter written at the time when Kemal was still

---

[120] Gibb, *History of Ottoman Poetry*, V, 78, 79. The *Harabat* was published at the end of 1876, see p. 83.

[121] See Süleyman Nazif, *İki Dost* (Istanbul, Kanaat Kütüphanesi, 1925), pp. 37-39; Gibb, *Ottoman Poetry*, V, 84, 85, for the dates on which these works were published in the *Mecmua-i Ebüzziya*.

[122] Kuntay, *Namık Kemal*, II, 1, 418.

in exile, pamphlets and articles taking up the defense of Islam were becoming increasingly fashionable. This was only one of the outward signs of a greater restlessness among the conservative elements of the capital, an uneasiness which inevitably took some of its more violent expressions from the thousands of softas, or students of theology. Some time before the coup Rüşdü Paşa and Midhat Paşa had taken advantage of this mood to get the softas to demonstrate in front of the palace gates for the dismissal of Mahmud Nedim. This tactic was completely successful. Now Rüşdü Paşa was trying to ride and control the crest which had brought him to power by taking over the manufacture of pro-Islamic propaganda. The collective pro-Islamic drive was so powerful that it affected even the prisoners, despite the distance that separated them from the capital. Thus, in addition to Ahmed Midhat, Bereketzâde İsmail Hakkı had written, in prison, a work describing the feats of Islamic heroes in Syria.[123]

Although Kemal had a tendency to dismiss this Islamic revivalism as the work of a few cranks, he did not approve of the more extreme and anti-Western cast that it was taking. The essentially different problem which he had in mind with regard to Eastern versus Western beliefs was quite clearly demonstrated in his own contribution to the defense of Islam—his "Rebuttal to Renan." In this work, written in the 1880's, Kemal's remarks were not directed against Christianity but against materialistic atheism. To Rüşdü Paşa's practical, if less refined mind, however, Ahmed Midhat and his defense of Islamic values were an asset.

In June 1876 Kemal, Nuri, and Hakkı returned to Istanbul. One of the first signs of a genuine change in the political atmosphere was the use by the new sultan in his first proclamation of words such as the "fatherland" and "liberty." Both of these were Young Ottoman expressions par excellence.

Upon the enthronement of Murad, a Grand Council of Notables assembled (June 8, 1876)[124] at the official residence

---

[123] *Ibid.*, pp. 475, 477.   [124] *Ibid.*, p. 713.

of the Şeyh ül-Islam to discuss constitutional reform. This was a gathering of those leaders of the community who, the Young Ottomans had stated, would, if convened, provide at least a rudimentary form of representation. As to a more elaborate national assembly, Midhat Paşa had already discussed his own plan for one with the British ambassador in the winter of 1875.[125] According to Süleyman Paşa, who was a member of this council, only two of those present at the meeting—Halil Şerif Paşa and himself—made outright and firm demands that a representative assembly be established immediately. Midhat, it seems, did no more than commend Süleyman Paşa, after the session was over, for his zeal in defending the principle of representation. Here, of course, the coolness in Midhat's relations with Süleyman, whom he later deprecatingly described as a "military paşa," and Süleyman's dislike for Midhat have to be taken into consideration.[126]

Süleyman Paşa's report does, however, confirm the great cautiousness of Midhat Paşa—a trait which the Young Ottomans also criticized. At a time when Rüşdü Paşa was still grand vizier, Midhat Paşa had no intention of antagonizing a man who, though he wanted control over the machinery of the state, could not by any stretch of the imagination be described as an ardent constitutionalist. Nor was Midhat in a hurry to attract the criticism of those who were adamantly opposed to a constitution. The latter were in a majority in the Council of Notables.

As for the Young Ottomans, at first they were not directly involved in these activities. Namık Kemal had not as yet received any governmental appointment. Ziya Paşa, on the other hand, had been dismissed from his post as First Secretary of the Palace because both Midhat and Rüşdü were afraid that he would there form the nucleus of a "third force," taking its

---

[125] See Henry Elliot, "The Death of Abdul-Aziz and of Turkish Reform," *The Nineteenth Century* (1888), XXIII, 279.

[126] See *Süleyman Paşa Muhakemesi* (ed. by Süleyman Paşa Zâde Sami, Istanbul, Matbaa-i Ebüzziya, 1328/1910), pp. 46, 47.

power from the person of the new sultan. He was later appointed Undersecretary in the Ministry of Education.[127]

It is quite probable that the suicide of Sultan Abdülaziz, caused by the shabby treatment he had received after his deposition, was an event which upset the Young Ottomans considerably. A new development soon added a complication to an already confused picture: as days went by, it was realized that Sultan Murad, in whom such great hopes had been placed, was mentally unbalanced and unfit to reign. This fact caused great consternation because the candidate to the throne, Murad's brother Abdülhamid, was distrusted both by the Porte and by intellectuals. The ministers knew that he was deceitful and cunning, and they suspected that his rule would mean a return to imperial control over the affairs of the state. Midhat Paşa, who knew the prince best, was delegated to speak to him and wring specific promises from him, among which were the writing of a constitution and the establishment of a national assembly. The nomination of Ziya and Kemal to the key posts of palace secretaries has also usually been stated to have been one of these demands, but recent evidence has thrown doubt on this part of Midhat's bargaining points.[128]

The importance that the drafting of a basic charter acquired as soon as Abdülhamid's candidacy to the throne became a possibility is apt to be overlooked. What had happened was that the restoration of imperial authority had once again become a primary danger. The earlier emphasis which had been placed on representation was thus shifted to the eliciting of a document which would restrict the sultan's power. From Abdülhamid's point of view, the greatest danger was that the rift, which separated constitutionalists like Midhat from advo-

[127] Kuntay, *Namık Kemal*, II, 1, 719; Ahmed Hamdi Tanpınar, *XIX ncu Asır Türk Edebiyatı Tarihi* (2nd ed., Istanbul, İbrahim Horoz, 1955), p. 286.

[128] See the information given to Kuntay by the Young Ottoman Nuri Bey. Nuri, having been breastfed by the same nurse as the sultan, had the dubious distinction of being Abdülhamid's "milk brother." According to him, Kemal refused the sultan's offer to become his First Secretary. Kuntay, *Namık Kemal*, II, 2, 17.

cates of a supremacy of ministers like Rüşdü, would heal. The sultan therefore adopted the tactic of appearing to back the constitutionalists. This explains why, in the first days of his reign, he encouraged the establishment of a constitutional committee although his first edict upon his accession to the throne (September 10, 1876) made only the vaguest mention of an "assembly" and emasculated the text prepared for him by the Porte. The change made by the sultan in the text of his speech won him the heart of the anticonstitutionalists. His advocacy of a constitutional committee created the impression that he was not entirely lost to the constitutionalist cause. Every one of the groups involved in this struggle thus was led to believe that the sultan was not entirely beyond salvation. When they saw through his designs, it was already too late.

The constitutional committee was organized on October 8, 1876 (19 Ramazan 1293).[129] A subcommittee was established to draft the text of a new constitution. Ziya was nominated chairman of the subcommittee. On November 2 Kemal was appointed to the Council of State and a few days later to sit on the constitutional subcommittee.[130]

A first draft of the constitution was presented to the sultan at the end of November. He was not satisfied with it and sent it back to the Council of Ministers. While the latter were discussing possible ways of amending the first draft, the sultan sent word that he desired to have an article included which would give him the power to expel from Turkey any "undesirable elements." The Council of Ministers did modify this draft as requested by the sultan. Namık Kemal, however, tried to forestall their changes by forwarding a series of petitions to the sultan in which he attempted to argue that it was not the

[129] See Bekir Sıtkı Baykal, "93 Meşrutiyeti," *Belleten* (Jan.-Apr. 1942) VI, 56.

[130] Kuntay, *Namık Kemal*, II, 75-85, 56, 17. These developments as presented here still need considerable clarification and the chronological sequence suggested above is only tentative.

original text but the amended version which restricted the sultan's powers. What Kemal was hoping to achieve was to save the first few articles of the draft constitution, taken out during the amending process in the Council of Ministers. These articles defined the powers of the monarch and therefore set limits to his authority. That Kemal was also earnestly worried about the possibility of a resurgence of the hegemony of the Porte is clear. He was unable to subordinate this fear entirely to the more urgent one of autocratic rule. These representations of Kemal were of no avail. The document was not amended any further.

On December 20 the Sultan dismissed Rüşdü Paşa and brought Midhat Paşa to the grand vizierate. Abdülhamid had seized on a temporary setback of Rüşdü Paşa to get rid of him. The latter's downfall had been caused by developments on the international scene. Since June of 1876 insurrections in the Balkans had been followed by a war against Montenegro and Serbia. The Ottoman army was waging a victorious war against Serbia when an ultimatum had come from the Russians to stop the offensive and to establish an international conference to discuss the situation. Rüşdü Paşa had given in, and his prestige in the capital had fallen considerably.

Although he thus strengthened Midhat's hand, the sultan still tried to postpone as much as possible the enactment of the constitution. A final effort was made by his allies to put back the date of its proclamation. Midhat Paşa was adamant, and on December 3, 1876 (7 Zilhice 1293), the Imperial Firman whereby the sultan proclaimed the constitution was sent to the Porte.

The sultan, however, was not the only opponent of the constitution. At the end of October 1876 a group of Mahmud Nedim's supporters, led by high-ranking ulema, some of whom had sat on the Council of Notables, had tried to arouse the population of Istanbul against the drafting of such a document. These men were immediately sent off into exile, but similar anti-Western and anti-constitutional groups were at work in the capital.[131]

Although the actions of the forces of reaction spurred Kemal to write a series of articles in defense of the constitution, reactionary elements did not seem to him to constitute the main danger. To the Young Ottomans and to Midhat the main danger was that no constitution would be forthcoming, or that, if it were, the sultan would not observe it. As early as October of 1876 they seem to have been working to destroy the sultan's control over the Ottoman army by appealing directly to the individuals who made up the army. In Midhat Paşa's mansion the headquarters of a charitable society was established. The purpose of this society was ostensibly to provide clothes for soldiers in Bosnia. Garments purchased with the funds collected were taken to the front by the agents of this Military Donations Society and distributed to soldiers. With each gift came a letter thanking the soldier in the name of the fatherland for his sacrifices and implying that these were not in vain since he was fighting for national independence and political freedom.[132] The style was reminiscent of the speeches given to the French revolutionary army of 1792. The real relation, however, was with later revolutionary ideas, as subsequent developments were to show.

The Donations Society had been sponsored by Midhat Paşa, Ziya, and Kemal.[133] Although Süleyman Paşa himself denies

[131] For a text of an order of Mehmed Rüşdü forbidding the public discussion of reform see Staatsarchiv, III, No. 5775. For the conspiracy of ulema, Kuntay, Namık Kemal, II, 2, 84. On the other hand, some of the âlims are reported to have adopted a strictly neutral attitude. When Abdülhamid, for instance, tried to obtain from them a categorical firman against the constitution, he was unsuccessful. See Memduh Paşa, Esvat-ı Sudur (Izmir, Vilayet Matbaası, 1333/1914), p. 89. Controversy among the ulema sitting on the constitutional committee raged around the Koranic dictum with regard to the obligation of the ruler to consult with the community; Koran (Bell), III, 153. The point at issue was whether this had reference both to Moslems and Christians; Kuntay, Namık Kemal, II, 2, 130. At least one âlim, Esad Efendi, had published a pamphlet stating that the people had the right to depose a tyrannical ruler. Ibid., p. 59, note 14.

[132] For a copy of such a letter see Süleyman Paşa Muhakemesi, p. 66.

[133] Ibid.; Nazım Paşa, "Bir Devrin Tarihi," Cumhuriyet, February 14, 1939, p. 2.

it, according to some accounts he also was a member of this
society.[134] What is beyond doubt is that during the crucial
December days when the sultan was trying to stall the proclamation of the constitution, the Donation Society's headquarters
were slowly transformed into an organizational center for the
establishment of a national guard, a militia made up of volunteers. Süleyman Paşa admits that he translated the regulations
of the French national guard to serve as a guide to the formation of these citizens' battalions. Streets were now filled with
these representatives of the nation in arms in their new uni-
forms. Units were commanded by idealistic young sons of the
the best families in the capital. Although these battalions were
theoretically meant to be sent to the front, there is no doubt
that the sum total of these activities greatly alarmed the
sultan, since it amounted to an attempt to subvert the armed
forces and establish a corps whose loyalties would be to
Midhat and Kemal. This was proven when attempts to impress men of the militia into regular formations were vocifer-
ously resisted.[135]

On February 5, 1877, Midhat Paşa was dismissed and sent
outside Turkey in accordance with article 113 of the constitution. Soon thereafter, among the papers of a student at the
military academy who had been in close touch with Kemal, a
document was found outlining a plan for the deposition of
Abdülhamid. The caliphate was to have been taken away from
the Ottoman dynasty and the emir of Mecca, Şerîf Abd ul-
Muttalib (Sharīf 'Abd al-Muṭṭalib), brought to the throne.
This document caused considerable anxiety at the palace.
Within a few days Namık Kemal was imprisoned and put on
trial for attempting to dethrone the sultan. The court, presided
over by Kemal's former patron Abdüllatif Subhi Paşa, exonerated Kemal, but he nevertheless remained in jail. Finally he
was exiled to Midilli (Mytilene). The sultan had thought it

[134] Nazım Paşa, *loc.cit.*
[135] From the diary of the commanding general of the palace guards
("Mabeyn Feriki"), Said Paşa. Kuntay, *Namık Kemal*, II, 2, 167, note 7.

fitting on this occasion to make up for the troubles he had caused Kemal by taking care of his traveling expenses and by giving him the generous monthly stipend of fifty liras.[136] Ziya Paşa was placed out of the way by being appointed to the governorship of Syria.

From his exile in Midilli Kemal tried, by corresponding with acquaintances in the Ottoman Assembly, to continue to be politically influential. But these activities too came to an end when the Assembly was suspended by Abdülhamid. Later Kemal was placed at the head of the administration of the island. He was then successively transferred to Rhodes and to Sakız (Chios), each time in an administrative capacity. He died in Sakız on December 2, 1888.

Ziya Paşa, harassed by the enemies that he had made, died a broken man as governor of Adana in 1881. Agâh, who had returned from Europe in 1872, was given a governmental post before Abdülhamid himself seized the Ottoman governmental machinery, but was also exiled to Ankara in 1877. This was due to Abdülhamid's conviction that he had a hand in organizing the protest of the softas in 1876.[137] This accusation, however, does not fit in at all with what we know of Agâh's character. The issue is still unsolved. In 1886 Agâh was pardoned and sent as minister to Athens, where he died in 1886.

Nuri Bey had been appointed to a governmental post as early as 1876 because of his relation to Abdülhamid. He remained in state service until 1906, the date of his death. Reşad died as a Paşa in 1910. Mustafa Fazıl Paşa had broken with the Young Ottomans sometime in 1873-1874, and he died shortly thereafter, at the beginning of December 1875.[138] Ali Suavi had remained in Europe up to October of 1876.[139] On his return he was made the director of the newly established

[136] *Ibid.*, p. 267.

[137] For this protest see Ahmed Rasim, *İstibdattan Hakimiyet-i Milliyeye* (Istanbul, Vatan Matbaasi, 1923-1924), I, 121, 122.

[138] For Reşad see İnal, *Son Asır*, p. 408, note 1; for Agâh see *Sicill-i Osmanî*, I, 393; for Mustafa Fazıl, *ibid.*, IV, 481.

[139] See Kuntay, *Sarıklı İhtilalci*, p. 82, note 1, quoting a letter of the poet Abdülhak Hâmid.

(1868) lyceum of Galatasaray, but was dismissed shortly thereafter. His end came during an unsuccessful coup that he had organized in May of 1878 to bring Murad back to the throne.[140]

Thus the Young Ottoman movement came to an end.

Epilogue

To extract even the beginning of a meaning from the often puzzling turns that the Young Ottoman movement took, one has to analyze its activities from the vantage point of the paradox inherent in its formation. This paradox consisted in that men with such a diversity of backgrounds, and in many ways such dissimilar ideals, should have fought, even for a short time, for a common cause.

Among the Young Ottomans existed at least four categories of reformers. Of these, Mehmed Bey, Halil Şerif, and Mustafa Fazıl represented those most attuned to the liberal ideal of progress through emancipation from all remnants of a bygone age. They were the most universal, the closest to starting from the basic postulate of the brotherhood of humanity. It is unfortunate that Mustafa Fazıl should also have been the most malleable, the most ready to set his principles aside for personal advantage. The remark attributed to Agâh Efendi that he always knew the Young Ottoman movement would not last long since it was hard to picture a prince so persistent in retaining all his privileges leading a group of revolutionaries also points to an important truth: Mustafa Fazıl was not really in touch with the grassroots ferment that lay behind Young Ottoman activities. Mustafa Fazıl Paşa's proposals were an attempt at unification which attempted to take its strength from an appeal to the "people," the latter in reality consisting of an ideal, limited electorate. These "peo-

[140] For the establishment of the *lycée* see İhsan Sungu, "Galatasaray Lisesinin Kuruluşu," *Belleten* (1944), VIII, 315-347. For Ali Suavi's coup, İsmail Hakkı Uzunçarşılı, "Ali Suavi ve Çırağan Sarayı Vak'ası," *Belleten* (1944), VIII, 71-116.

ple," whether Moslems or Christians, had already decided against such rational solutions of their problems and had begun to go their separate ways.

The second category of reformer among the Young Ottomans was that represented by Kemal. Kemal too was immersed in the stream of liberal Western ideas, but for him "liberty" and "the nation" were key ideals. Kemal had the advantage of being an ideologist, of having taken quite effortlessly to the manipulation of symbols—something that was missing in Halil Şerif. Kemal also had that liking for abstractions which was characteristic of so many nineteenth-century political image makers. Unaware of the substratum of irrationality underlying human conduct, confident that the granting of a representative assembly would dispel the various separatisms that had been wrecking the empire, he was an advocate of reason in the solution of political problems. At the same time, however, Kemal was the romantic bard of ancient Ottoman achievements. Thus by the strongly emotional content of his own writings he kept Ottoman audiences spellbound.

At another level too Kemal was nearer to "the people" than Mustafa Fazıl or Halil Şerif. He was in close touch with the great social ferment that was silently at work in the Ottoman Empire because of the disintegration of the traditional framework of Ottoman society. He could feel the bewilderment of those who were left stranded, materially and spiritually, by these changes.

In Ali Suavi this last aspect of Kemal's character was exaggerated to the point of making him a caricature of Kemal. Ali Suavi was perhaps the only real representative of "the people" among the Young Ottomans. He expressed the hostility of the small man of the capital for a type of Westernization of which the lower middle class had collected only fringe benefits, but which had aroused its eagerness to share in the material blessings of progress.

Ziya Paşa was a man of the palace whose basic quarrel was with the ministers of the Porte and whose ideological contribution to the Young Ottoman movement was not very great, although here again he was affected by an ideological malaise.

What caused a meeting of these divergent attitudes and beliefs was a common dislike among the Young Ottomans for the rule of Âli and Fuad Paşa, a belief that by constitutional and representative government more could be done than these Ottoman statesmen had achieved. Why, then, did such a feeling arise at this time? The concomitant growth of a journalistic movement with the protestations of the Young Ottomans would seem to point in the direction of a change in the pattern of social communications which should be studied in conjunction with the increase in Western influences. But more evidence will have to be accumulated before such a theory can be substantiated for Turkey. The consequence, for the Young Ottomans, of this basic dissimilarity which they learned to understand with time was that they encountered a series of disillusionments in the brief years during which they worked together. These exhausted the momentum of the Young Ottoman movement quite soon. Their permanent contribution, on the other hand, was the establishment of a climate of opinion wherein discussions centered around such conceptions as that of "liberty" and "the fatherland" became widespread and gained increased momentum despite Abdülhamid's censorship. This was no mean intellectual legacy.

In such a detailed study as this one the differences that split the Young Ottoman movement through the middle have a tendency to linger in one's memory because of their sheer colorfulness. There thus exists a danger of losing sight of the dedication and basic intellectual toughness which it took to face repeated exile and imprisonment in the pursuit of ideals. This latter point has not been stressed here because it has been overstressed in Turkish literature. It is only fair to state that the Young Ottomans were human but that they had courageous and generous natures. The example they set by their actions was at least as important in galvanizing the opponents of Abdülhamid to action as was their intellectual legacy.

CHAPTER III

The Islamic Intellectual Heritage of the Young Ottomans

IN THE writings in which they expounded their political ideals, the Young Ottomans rely, to a large extent, on the vocabulary of Islamic political theory. Such, for example, is their use of the words *adalet* (*'adl*—"justice" in Arabic), *biat* (*bai'a*—"contract of investiture"), *icma'-i ümmet* (*idjmā'* and *umma*—"consensus of the community"), *meşveret* (*mashwarā*—"consultation"). The meaning of these terms has to be understood before the theories of the Young Ottomans can be evaluated. By the same token, it is necessary to determine whether the Young Ottomans left intact or modified the meaning of the classical Islamic terminology they were using. As a prelude to the studies of their ideas, therefore, these words have to be reintroduced into their original context and a survey made of Islamic political theory. Unfortunately, neither is this operation by itself sufficient to place Young Ottoman political thought in perspective. This is so because these reformers could have drawn not from *one* but from *several* Islamic political theories: they had available to them the political theology of the Koranic exegetes, the political philosophy of the Islamic political philosophers, the practical counsels of which the Islamic "Mirrors for Princes" were made, and the Turko-Iranian-Mongolian theory of secular legislation and state supremacy.

Of these four Islamic streams, the Young Ottomans drew their arguments almost exclusively from political theology and relied for illustrations on the idealized picture of Islamic government provided by traditionalist writers. The reason they adopted such a stand may be found in a common characteristic of a number of Islamic modernist movements during the nineteenth century, namely, purism, the attempt to go

81

back to the original "unspoilt" sources of Islam. A similar stand is seen as early as the eighteenth century in the puritanism of the Wahhabis, although to call the latter modernist in any other respects is impossible. The same purism does reappear, however, in the ideas of the Egyptian reformer Muhammed 'Abdu. Among the Young Ottomans, this idea takes the form of a belief that the political theory of the Koran and its interpreters provides the strongest guarantee of individual freedom.

The historical antecedents of this stand and the reasons for which the Young Ottomans did indeed have a point in this respect—although not a very strong one in view of the stage of history at which they were advancing it—will be investigated below.

In only two instances have I been able to locate a Young Ottoman reference to the political *philosophers* of Islam which is of substantive interest and which consists in more than an enumeration of the "great figures" of Islam. One is a passage in one of Kemal's writings in which he mentions the political philosophers Nasreddin-i Tûsî (Naṣīr al-Dīn al-Ṭūsī), İbn Sina (İbn Sīnā), and Hüseyin Vaız Kâşifi (Ḥusain Wā'iz Kāshifī), the popularizer of the doctrines of the jurist Devvanî (al-Dawwānī).[1] The second reference is to a spiritual heir of Devvanî.[2] The contributions of these men to Islamic philosophy and the relations between their ideas is thus investigated in detail in the following pages. Such a detailed investigation is necessary, for, although the Young Ottomans did not subscribe to these ideas, their foes, the defenders of state authority and supremacy, seem to have been inspired by them for centuries.

I. Political Theology

A. NOMOCRACY

The system of government which was the product of the

---

[1] Fevziye Abdullah Tansel, "Namık Kemal'in Hukukî Fikirleri," *Türk Hukuk Tarihi Dergisi* (1944), I, 57.

[2] See below, p. 99.

teachings of Muhammed has, in one instance, been described as a "nomocracy," this term being used to denote that in Islam the law precedes the state and constitutes the principle guiding social cohesion.[3]

Indeed, this terminology points out one of the more salient characteristics of both the political theory of Islam and the practice followed in Islamic states, for the Koran, the law laid down by God, was the ultimate source according to which was to be determined the political organization of the believers. In it were expounded the principles of the law that was to govern the Moslem community, the system of taxation that was to apply to the believers, and the militancy that was expected of the Moslems.

In theory, therefore, "Islam is the direct government of Allāh, the rule of God, whose eyes are upon his people. The principle of unity and order which in other societies is called *civitas*, *polis*, capital, in Islam is personified by Allāh: Allāh is the name of the supreme power acting in the common interest. Thus the public treasury is the 'treasury of Allāh,' the Army is the 'army of Allāh,' even public functionaries are 'the employees of Allāh.' "[4]

Three consequences of importance for political theory follow from such a basic assumption. The first is that in Islam political obligation is founded not on a lay theory of ethics but on the religious dicta of the Koran. It is because of this aspect of Islamic political theory that in Islam the idea of a contract of society is conceived in a much narrower frame than it was in the Greek, Roman, medieval Christian, and modern Western world. Secondly, in many respects the Islamic conception of natural law differs not only from that of the Enlightenment philosophers but from medieval Christian conceptions. Finally, in Islam the possibilities for evolving a

[3] Majid Khadduri, *War and Peace in the Law of Islam* (Baltimore, Johns Hopkins Press, 1955), p. 16.
[4] David de Santillana, "Law and Society," in *The Legacy of Islam* (Eds., T. W. Arnold and Alfred Guillaume, London, Oxford University Press, 1931), p. 286.

theory of politics as a self-contained process with its own inner dynamic are very much restricted (for a consistent and ultra-orthodox believer, completely ruled out). One corollary of this last political theorem is that a political theory which is philosophical rather than theological in nature immediately becomes suspect to the orthodox.

Let us now examine the first two points mentioned and then introduce as much of a glimpse of the practice of the Islamic state as modifies or clarifies these principles.

B. POLITICAL OBLIGATION

In Islam political authority is a divinely established category. This goes back to the following verse of the Koran: "O ye who believe, obey God and obey the Apostle and those among you invested with authority."[5]

It follows from the above statement that a principle of authority is established in Islam which transcends the particular authority of the Prophet; there are others who have to be heeded in addition to the Prophet—those vested with authority. The Islamic conception of the contract of society is one which is derived from the same fundamental stand.

A modern scholar has stated the Koranic theory of contract to be the following: "The world was at first created to be inhabited not by one, but by a variety of peoples, each endowed with its own divine order . . . which constituted a covenant between Him and that people. . . . But these peoples, one after the other, have broken their covenant and distorted the teachings of their Prophets. . . . It became necessary, accordingly, to make a last effort and Allah decided to send Muhammed, the last of his prophets. . . .

"It follows, accordingly, that Muhammed's mission might be regarded as an evidence of Allah's desire to renew his covenant (or covenants) with mankind and that those who responded to Muhammed's call became God's true believers. . . . Thus the foundation of Islamic social polity was

[5] *Koran*, VII, 2; VIII, 20; Bell, I, 137, 164.

made on the basis of a compact of agreement, being understood that this agreement was by no means one between two equals. *It was rather a compact of submission, which reflects the nature of Allah's covenant with man.*"[6]

Insofar as the *practice*—as opposed to the *theory*—of government in the earliest Islamic states is concerned, the developments which took place up to the tenth century resulted in the elaboration, by the Koranic exegetes, of a theory somewhat more complicated than that found in the Koran.

The prophet Muhammed himself had concentrated the three powers of government in his hands. As the self-appointed leader of the believers and as the organizer of the activities of his followers in regard to the spreading of Islam, he held the executive power. As the promulgator of the divine and unchangeable legislation, he held the legislative power. As the settler of the disputes that had arisen within his fold, he also exercised the judicial function. After the death of Muhammed, the Koran having been once laid down and being the word of God which could not be changed or altered, the legislative function came to an end. His successors, therefore, held only two of these powers—the executive and the judicial. With time, however, an interpretive function was gradually vested "in the body of 'Ulema or students of the spiritual legacy of Muḥammad."[7]

The successors of the prophet were called caliphs (from the Arabic _khalīfa_, "successor"). The classical doctrine of the caliphate, which was to determine once and for all the relations between sovereign and subject, was formulated at the time of the Abbasid Caliphate in the eighth century. During this period the right of the doctors of Islamic law to interpret the law laid down by the Prophet was also subject to the encroachments of the Arabic rulers, who were bent on the centralization

[6] Khadduri, *War and Peace*, pp. 7, 8, 9 (my italics in quotation).
[7] H. A. R. Gibb and Harold Bowen, *Islamic Society and the West: A Study of the Impact of Western Civilization on Moslem Culture in the Near East*, I, *Islamic Society in the Eighteenth Century* (London, Oxford University Press, 1951), I, p. 26.

of their empire and who did not want to be thwarted in their designs by this class from which the judges were drawn.[8] The basic theory of government developed by these doctors of Islamic law had, therefore, "the character of an apologia for the *status quo nunc*."[9]

It is only in a detailed investigation of the Moslem conception of natural law, however, that the purely *philosophical* limitations which tied these jurists hand and foot may be fully appreciated. It is also in the course of such a survey that the full extent of their courage in transcending the additional, *practical* limitations under which they were laboring is uncovered.

C. THE ISLAMIC VIEW OF NATURAL LAW

One of the most important conceptions that had been set forth by the medieval exponents of natural law in the West— and one around which gravitated many of the philosophical discussions relating to natural law—was the distinction made between natural law as the will of the divinity and natural law as an order of things existing independently of the will of the divinity and which the divinity itself left alone. This conception, which was taken over by St. Thomas Aquinas as the distinction between *natura naturata* and *natura naturans*,[10] had its origin in the Aristotelian problem of the efficient cause. The problem may be stated as follows: Aristotle affirmed that the universe had always existed, but he did not tackle the problem

[8] *Ibid.*, p. 27.

[9] *Ibid.*, p. 27. Although the ruler is held to be elected, the electors are not the body of the people but a small group of qualified electors. See D. B. MacDonald, "Idjma'," *Encyclopaedia of Islam*, II, 448.

[10] "Nature Naturante et Nature Naturée," *Vocabulaire Technique et Critique de la Philosophie* (ed., André Lalande, Paris, Presses Universitaires de France, 1951), p. 673. "La nature naturante est Dieu en tant que créateur et principe de toute action, la nature naturée est l'ensemble des êtres et des lois qu'il a créés." See also St. Thomas Aquinas, *Summa Theologica*, Prima Secundae, question 85, article 6. St. Thomas took this distinction verbatim from Ibn Gabirol (Avicebron) who, though a Jew, was working in the tradition of Islamic philosophy. See J. M. Ramirez, O.P., *De hominis beatudine* (Salamanca, 1942); what is interesting, however, is that it had little influence on the thought of the jurists.

of the originator of the order of nature. With the rise of Christianity and then of Islam, however, the problem of the originator of the order of nature was automatically solved by the creeds. It was God who had created the order of nature. Yet the important question remained whether God had created an order of nature moving "towards self-fulfillment"[11] or whether He was manifesting His own will in each individual event taking place in the order of nature. Was the movement of every particle of the universe motivated by the will of God to move it at that very instance, or did the hand of God set the universe in motion once and for all just as it would wind a clock? It is characteristic of the Western conception of the order of nature and the conception of natural law based on it that, as far back as St. Thomas, there can be found ideas of an independent automatism of eternal matter subservient, of course, to the will of God but possessing its own peculiar inner logic.[12]

Thus even St. Thomas provided the ultimate basis for a belief in the autonomy of nature and the secularization of natural law. For, if natural law was part of the unchangeable order of things, a fundamental change, such as the elimination of God as the ultimate power enthroned over this order, need not change the order itself.

Indeed, this conception of natural law was one which went back farther than St. Thomas. Underlying the ancient Greek as well as Roman definition of natural law was the concept that law was, as phrased by Cicero, the product "not of opinion" but of "a certain innate force."[13] This "certain innate force" had been called *physis* by Aristotle and stood, in his scheme, in contrast to *nomos*, the name he gave to positive or conventional justice. The whole conception was a part of the

[11] Ewart Lewis, *Medieval Political Ideas* (London, Routledge and Kegan Paul, 1954), p. 12.

[12] See George H. Sabine, *A History of Political Theory* (New York, Henry Holt, 1937), p. 252.

[13] Lewis, *Medieval Political Ideas*, p. 7: quoting Cicero, *Rhetoric*, Book 2, Chapter 53.

Greek idea of nature, of a world of self-moving things. It could be found as far back as Heraclitus in the idea of a common natural source of laws and physical motion and reappeared as one of the elements of the Stoic fusion of law with the general cosmic law governing the universe. In this latter synthesis, the moral imperative of natural law, which had also existed from time immemorial, became one with the physical imperative of natural regularities, i.e., "The Stoics like their later counterparts, linked together the starry heavens and the moral law within: the law that preserved the stars from doing wrong was also the role of duty."[14]

There was only a short step from the fusion of moral with physical law to the idea that nature in general, i.e., animals as well as humans, were subject to natural law. This step was taken by Ulpian, who defined law as that "which nature has taught all living animals."[15] The earlier formulation of the same idea, Gaius' idea of *ius gentium* in which moral law rather than physical law was taken as a starting point of natural law, also lived on.[16]

In short, the conception of natural law had two connotations in the West. It meant (*a*) those principles that are inherently reasonable and right and (*b*) those principles which result from the physical imperative of natural regularities. Both of these approaches found parallels in medieval controversies regarding natural law. The first was reflected in the dispute between the nominalists and the realists as to whether law is binding because it is reasonable or because it is a command of God.[17] The second was reflected in the idea of a law of nature which unfolded by itself without the active interference of God.

[14] Basil Willey, *The Eighteenth Century Background* (New York, Columbia University Press, 1940), p. 14.

[15] Lewis, *Medieval Political Ideas*, p. 8.

[16] See A. P. D. D'Entrèves, *Natural Law* (London, Hutchison, 1951), p. 25.

[17] For a study of the controversy between the realists and the nominalists, see Otto Gierke, *Political Theories of the Middle Age* (trans. with intro. by Frederick William Maitland, Cambridge, The University Press, 1951), pp. 172-173.

In the Islamic creed the question of an order of nature independent of the will of God was solved along lines diametrically opposed to that of the Thomistic solution. The issue raised ticklish metaphysical problems which orthodox Islamic thinkers evaded by denying the validity of a metaphysic outside God. For them, "secular" metaphysics and philosophy had failed in not providing a synthetic view of the universe. The theologians pointed out that in Aristotle's universe the order of nature and the creator were disassociated from each other. It was held, on the other hand, that the most valid conception of the universe was that of a current of being emanating from an inexhaustible source, God, which spread over everything outside God.

In view of this stand, Islamic natural law could not be conceived of as anything but the revealed law of God and as the immanence of God in nature. Natural regularities were the very sign of the presence of God, and a proof of this immanence was the fact of miracles worked by God. The fundamental opposition of Islamic theologians to the idea of an autonomy of nature may be gathered from the outcry raised when the Islamic philosopher Ibn Rüşd (Ibn Rushd) attempted to adopt a stand by which he allowed for the concept of a self-moving nature. It is also characteristic that the ideas of his opponent and detractor Gazalî (al-Ghazālī) were much more widely accepted in Islam at large than were his own.

Insofar as the principle of inherent reasonableness is concerned, in Islam the law of the universe, which is also the law of God, could not be apprehended by the mere use of reason. Even Ibn Haldun (Ibn Khaldūn), one of the greatest Islamic thinkers, who, by the use of a cyclical theory of history, made an attempt to introduce the idea of the regularity of social occurrences into Islamic thought, spoke of the uses of reason in politics with the greatest caution.[18]

18 "That state whose law is based on rational statescraft and its principles, but lacks the supervision of the Revealed Law, is likewise, blamatory, since

A further consequence of the Islamic conception of natural law is, therefore, that the European controversy between the nominalists and the realists as to whether natural law is binding because it is reasonable or because it is the command of God is hardly relevant.

Paradoxically, while in Islam the will of God may at any moment disrupt the order of nature,[19] the law of the Koran itself is extremely inelastic. True, there are recognized sources of the law "subsidiary" to the Koran, such as the *Sünnet* (*sunna*—"the practice of the prophet Muhammed") the *Ícma'* (*idjmā'*—"consensus of the Islamic community"), and the agreement of the jurists on a principle deduced from the above-mentioned sources. Nevertheless, the divine origin of the Koran acted as a brake on the speculative activities of the jurists with regard to the creation of a doctrine of natural law. The possibility, always present in the Christian approach to natural law, of giving a new twist to the doctrine of natural law, a process which can be witnessed as early as the Middle Ages, was considerably restricted in orthodox Islamic theory because natural law was a law which was written and unchangeable and because natural law was identical with the law of the land.

In addition, natural law had a religio-ethical substratum in Islam and could not, therefore, be identified as in the West with an impersonal and fixed order of things, a fate which

---

it is the product of speculation without the light of God. For the Lawgiver knows best the interest of man in all that relates to the other world which is concealed from them. The principles of rational government aim solely at apparent and worldly interests, whereas the object of the Lawgiver is men's salvation in the hereafter." Ibn Khaldūn, *al-Mukaddima*, Book 3, Chapter 25, omitting the Koranic citations by which the argument is supported. Quoted by H. A. R. Gibb, "Constitutional Organization," *Law in the Middle East*, I, *Origin and Development of Islamic Law* (eds. Majid Khadduri and Herbert J. Liebesny, Washington, D.C., The Middle East Institute, 1955), p. 13.

[19] For a complete study of this question in Islam see *Averroes' Tahafut al-Tahafut* ("*The Incoherence of Incoherence*"), (trans. and notes by Simon van den Bergh, Oxford University Press, 1954), 2 vols.

befell the European theories of natural law under the influence of Newtonian ideas. It could not be transformed into a conception of a natural law identical with the order of physical regularities, as happened in the physiocratic conception of natural law or in that of d'Holbach.

In short, the possibilities that were provided by the Western conception of the autonomy and essential rationality of nature and natural law, which in Europe led to the investigation of the natural and self-evident rights inherent in nature, were considerably restricted in the body of doctrine available to the orthodox thinkers of Islam.

Yet, within the limitations set by the Islamic principle of the immanence of God, the jurists of Islam devised three escape hatches: a theory of representation which introduced a temporal element into the political theory of Islam, a conception of natural rights which came close to medieval Western theories of natural rights, and, finally, a method of gauging legitimacy that was a timid step in the direction of an embryonic theory of resistance.

This is how the first development took place. Following the death of the prophet Muhammed, the selection of a political leader to succeed him became an urgent political problem. The successor chosen was one of his companions, Abū Bakr. Since Abū Bakr came to power by the consensus of the companions of the Prophet, it was held that he was *elected* to his office. Moreover, since the allegiance of the companions of the Prophet had been given to Abū Bakr in person, this transaction was interpreted to be a "contract" entered into by the leader and the community of Islamic believers and was in symbolic form for each of the succeeding caliphs.

"The election of a successor to Muhammad by leading Moslems had obviously introduced the 'popular' factor in the selection of the executive head of government. A new contract seems, therefore, to have been added to the first; a contract between the Moslem community on the one hand and the caliph who was enthroned for the purpose of enforcing the divine law on the other."[20]

Consequently, "this principle of an elected ruler governing according to law is central in the Sunni ["orthodox"] Islamic doctrines of the state and sovereignty and may be found in every text book of the Holy Law."[21]

On the other hand, the theory of natural rights was developed by the following chain of reasoning:[22] Man, argued the jurists, has been placed since time immemorial in the situation of a slave in his dealings with God. Indeed, the first agreement arrived at between man and God was one which related to man's acceptance of his condition of slavery vis-à-vis God. This may be gathered from the following verse of the Koran: "When thy Lord took from the children of Adam, from their loins, their posterity and made them testify as to themselves: 'Am not I your Lord?' and they said: 'Yea, we testify'—lest ye should say on the day of the resurrection: 'Of this we have been neglectful. . . .' "[23]

Yet, paradoxically, this primeval obligation which man has assumed toward God is also the basis of man's absolute liberty in this world, for men are free to observe or to violate the terms of this agreement. Furthermore, this agreement has conferred on man the free use of the things of this world and thus places him in a situation superior to that of all other creatures. Thus while he is an *object* of imprescriptible rights

---

[20] Khadduri, *War and Peace*, p. 11.

[21] Bernard A. Lewis, "The Concept of an Islamic Republic," *Die Welt des Islams*, NS (1955), IV, 7.

[22] The following account is based on the introduction by Leon Ostrorog to his translation of the works of the Islamic jurist el-Māwārdi: Conte Leon Ostrorog, *El-Ahkam Es-Soulthaniya* (Paris, Ernest Leroux, 1910), 2 vols. This introduction is based, in turn, on the Turkish editions of three textbooks of Islamic jurisprudence which had a wide circulation in the Ottoman Empire: (1) The Kashf ul-Asrār of Abū'l-Ḥasan 'Ali b. Muhammad b. Ḥusayn al-Bazdawī (1009-1089), Istanbul, 1308/1890. (2) The Mir'at al-uṣūl of Molla Muḥammad bin Farāmurz (d. 1480), Istanbul, 1308/1890. (3) The al-Mawāḳif of 'Adud al-din al-Iʿdjī (1281-1355), Istanbul, 1292/1875.

[23] *The Koran*, Sura VII, verse 171; Bell, I, 154.

on the part of God, man is the *subject* of imprescriptible rights vis-à-vis the world. In consequence of his theologically recognized position as a master of the external world, man has been granted a free and inviolable juridical personality (*"zimma"*). Every man is thus the possessor, in terms of his relations with other men, of a free and inviolable juridical personality which is the physical counterpart of the metaphysical obligation he has undertaken toward God. While, on the one hand, he is the possessor of a subjective freedom of choice, he is also the recipient of an objective freedom stemming from the inviolability of his juridical personality (*"ḥurrīya"*) and possesses the right of the free use of the material objects of the world (*" ʿibāha"*). Since these liberties are the result of an agreement, one could almost say a contract, with God, no human being can ever curtail the liberty of another Moslem. However, this liberty can be curtailed wherever there are explicit statements to this effect in the Koran. Such, for example, is the institution of property which sets a barrier to the immeasurable appetites of man. Such, also, is the institution of trusteeship (*"wilāya"*) which confers on an individual the right to decide for another.

Finally, the following were the means by which the jurists developed the embryo of a theory of resistance: By analogy with the case of trusteeship, Moslem jurists generally interpreted the Koranic principle of authority with which the ruler is invested as being of the order of that exercised by the trustee in a "general trust"; it was thus implied that the community is entrusted to the leader. The leader may, however, *delegate* this authority to his aides (*"tawkīl"*). We shall later see how in the nineteenth century this last concept became of central importance in political theory. These various limitations, such as the institution of trusteeship, which restrict the liberty of man, have to be understood, however, in a very particular sense in Islamic theory. Since they have a religious origin, they are not merely convenient political devices but rather categories which have a divine origin and are preordained. Similar to the Platonic categories, they exist independently of their terrestrial manifestations.

Whether a concrete case falls within the pale of any one of these categories is dependent on the appearance of what has been called "apparent occasions," i.e., "the facts of the case." Thus, to ascertain whether a *de facto* ruler is really the human being invested with authority to which reference is made in the aforementioned quotation from the Koran, there is necessary a strict examination of the signs that show that the ruler is the rightful one meant by the Word. This is why the enumeration of the qualities of the ruler plays such a considerable role in the treatises of the Islamic jurists dealing with the state. It is in the determination of these "apparent occasions" that the skill of the doctors of Islam was given free rein, and it is as the result of the gap thus provided that they were able to exert their influence. It should be noted that these means were not sufficient in themselves for the enunciation of a doctrine of natural rights, but the latitude which the doctors of law were given in the interpretation of "the facts of the case" provided them with the opportunity of opposing the exercise of an authority which they would consider unjustified.

II. The Political Theory of the Philosophers

What has been described to this point is the thought of the orthodox jurists of Islam and the background of Islamic practice which underpinned it. Side by side with the orthodox theory, however, had been developing a tradition of political thought which was greatly influenced by secular theories of the state, although the limitations placed by Islam on completely free metaphysical or philosophical speculation also impressed on these latter theories a characteristically Islamic stamp.

This secular current of Islamic political theory was the product of the speculations of the Falāsifa, the Islamic philosophers. One recent student has characterized the latter as students of Platonic political philosophy and the products of their thought as commentaries on Plato's political treatises.[24] Among them may be cited such thinkers as Farabi (Al-Fārābî), İbn Sina (Ibn Sīnā), and Devvanî (al-Dawwānî). Some of these philosophers, such as Devvanî, were also jurists and thus tried to achieve a synthesis between *political theology* and *political philosophy*. But in general, and before the more cutting edges were taken out of philosophical thought by such synthesizers, the position of the Falāsifa was sometimes dangerously close to heresy. Their ideas were considered subversive if not sacrilegious.

This is quite understandable in view of the real changes that the Falāsifa brought to what we have entitled the "political theology" of Islam. Farabi, for example, although paying lip service to the theological polity established by the Koran, considered man's natural propensities as *zoon politikon* ("*ḥayawān madanî*") to be the basis of society. He also held political science to be the science that "inquires into the human actions and habits necessary for the attainment of perfection."[25]

Farabi's follower, İbn Sina, tried to achieve a synthesis between the idea of a divinely ordained political system and that of a secular kingship and succeeded in linking "the ideal state of Islam with the ideal state of Plato's philosopher-king."[26]

The process by which this synthesis was gradually refined, adopted in this new form by Ottoman statesmen, and eventually made into a theoretical justification of Ottoman governmental practices is a fascinating subject which has not been investigated to date. It is therefore useful to go in somewhat greater detail into this development.

A. THE THEORY OF ERKÂN-I ERBAA

Two of the more fundamental deviations of İbn Sina's political theory from that of the orthodox jurists were that

---

[24] E. I. J. Rosenthal, *Political Thought in Medieval Islam: An Introductory Outline* (Cambridge, University Press, 1958), pp. 113-114.

[25] *Ibid.*, p. 126.

[26] *Ibid.*, p. 144.

(*a*) he accepted as an element of government "laws laid down by human authority to secure material well-being,"[27] and that (*b*) he took for granted, but also considered essential, the presence of functionally differentiated "orders" in the realm. As Rosenthal points out: "[Ibn Sina] assigns to the lawgiver (*sānin*) the primary task of ordering the life of society organized in the state, by dividing the citizens (as Plato had done) into three estates: the rulers, the artisans and the guardians. Each group is administered by a master (*"ra'īs"*) who, in turn, appoints masters of lesser authority over smaller units. We are reminded of Al-Fārābī's division, based on Aristotle, into rulers and ruled in hierarchical order from the first ruler over secondary rulers who partly rule and are ruled, down to those who only accept rule, the masses. Every citizen executes his alloted task, so that there is not one person who does not benefit the state by his work. . . .

"Next he stresses the need for capital in order to guarantee the general welfare and, in particular, to provide for the guardians. It is to be made up of taxes, fines and legal booty (*fay'*). This last, a concept peculiar to the Islamic state, is to be used equitably in the general interest (*maṣālih mushtaraka*)."[28]

This fundamental aspect of Ibn Sina's theory was not new for the Islamic world. As early as the ninth century, Arabic "mirrors" included closely apparented descriptions of social stratification. Ibn Sina's theory differs from similar earlier descriptions, however, in being more detailed and more rigid. The emphasis on the administration of each group by a leader, for example, is new. The origins of this rigidity are probably due to a direct connection between Ibn Sina's theories and earlier Sassanian conceptions which had constituted the fountainhead of theories of stratification in the first place.[29] As has

[27] *Ibid.*, p. 145. [28] *Ibid.*, p. 152.
[29] For early Arab precedents see Gustave E. von Grünebaum, *Medieval Islam* (2nd ed., Chicago, University of Chicago Press, 1953), p. 171. For Sassanian origins, *op.cit.*, p. 202.

been explained by one author, who described the historical process whereby these earlier ideas—and the practices they underpinned—were amalgamated into the Islamic synthesis: "In contrast to the ordinary run of converted Persians who had sought and found identification with Arab society . . . wide strata of the Persian nobility had succeeded, upon adopting Islam, in maintaining their landed property, their social standing, their political influence—all this while keeping within their own traditional class hierarchy. With their inclusion in the leading stratum of the 'Abbâsid capital two social systems came to coexist at court: the Arab-Muslim, which relegated the non-Arabs to the bottom of the ladder, and the Iranian, which classed people according to profession rather than descent."[30]

Ibn Sina's Central Asian origins might well be a clue to the importance he accorded to functionally differentiated social orders. Certainly, pre-Ottoman Turks seem to have been won over to this type of explanation. Thus, toward the end of the eleventh century, some fifty years after Ibn Sina's death, his theory appears almost simultaneously in three "mirrors" which, if not all "Turkish," did, however, all become Ottoman political classics. These were: the *Siyasetnâme* of the Selçuk vizier Nizam ül-Mülk[31] (1092); the *Kutadgu Bilik* (1070)[32]; and the *Kabus Nâme* (1082).[33]

In the *Kabus Nâme*, the whole theory of capital as guaranteeing general welfare, of the guardians as protectors of the capital producers, and of the ruler ruling over the latter through justice is expressed in synoptical form as follows: "Make it your constant endeavor to improve cultivation and to govern well, for understand this truth, *good government is*

---

[30] *Ibid.*   [31] *Ibid.*

[32] See Otto Alberts, "Der Dichter des Uigurisch-Türkischem Dialekt geschriebenen Kutadgu Bilig (1069-1070 P. Chr.) ein Schuler des Avicenna," *Archiv für Philosophie: Archiv für Geschichte der Philosophie* (1910), VII, 326.

[33] *A Mirror for Princes*, The Qabus Nama by Kai Ka'us Ibn Iskandar, Prince of Gurgan (trans. and intro. by Ruben Levy, New York, Dutton, 1951).

secured by armed troops, armed troops are maintained with gold, gold is acquired through cultivation and cultivation sustained through payment of what is due to the peasantry, by just dealing and fairness: be just and equitable therefore."[34]

In this statement the number of "estates" mentioned has settled around three, but more often in later "mirrors" four orders are mentioned. One of the first works of this type is the manual of administration of the İlhanid vizier and philosopher Nasreddin-i Tûsî[35] (Naṣr al-Dīn al-Ṭūsī, 1201-1274). What is interesting here is that Tûsî tries to describe İlhanid administrative practices, as distinguished from earlier idealizations of governmental arrangements. This is again a reminder that what we face is not only a theory of government, but, to a certain extent, a description of social and political relations as they actually existed.[36]

The secular strains of Tûsî's theory, whatever their origin, were not lost to the Ottoman world. The channel through which they were transmitted to the Ottoman Empire were the works of the jurist Celaleddin-i Devvanî (Djalāl al-Dīn al-Dawwānî, 1427-1501). In the works of Devvanî the theory of the four orders takes the following new form: "Corresponding to the four elements of the physical temperament there are four classes, which together make up and preserve the equity of the body politic, 'the political temperament.' The first are the men of knowledge . . . and this class is composed of doctors of theology and law, judges, secretaries, fiscal officials, geometricians, astronomers, physicians and poets who guarantee the maintenance of religion and the world. Next come the warriors and defenders. The combination of pen and sword ensures stability and guarantees public welfare. The third

---

[34] *Ibid.*, p. 213 (my italics in quotation).

[35] See Şerefeddin Yaltkaya, "İlhaniler devri idarî teşkilâtına dair Nasîr-ed-dîni Tûsî'nin bir eseri," *Türk Hukuk ve İktisat Tarihi Mecmuası* (1939), II, 6-16.

[36] This may be gathered also from the shifts in the classes included among the four orders. A study of these differences could establish a picture of the actual social power wielded by members of the "orders" at different times.

class consists of traders, artisans and craftsmen who provide for the needs of all. Last come the farmers who produce our food. Only the equilibrium and mutual help of these four classes secures political life."[37]

This concatenation of political principles appears again and again in the works of Ottoman statesmen on politics. It may be found in such chronologically widely separated productions as the political works of Kâtib Çelebi,[38] the political treatise of Hasan Kâfi (known as Ak Hisarî) entitled *Usul ül-Hikem* (*Usūl al-ḥikam fi niẓām al-ʿālam*, 1595-1596),[39] the counsels of viziers and governors of Sarı Mehmed Paşa,[40] and the writings of the Tanzimat statesman Akif Paşa.[41] The technical name used for the temporal elements (the military aristocracy, soldiers, property, and the subjects) which made up this synthesis was *erkân-ı erbaa* (the four orders). In its most sophisticated version, in which a place is also found for the Şeriat, this theory appears in the conclusion of the *Ahlâk-ı Alaî* (*Akhlāk-ı ʿAlaʾī*), a treatise on ethics by the seventeenth-century Turkish jurist Kınalızâde. It is here stated in graphic form as follows:

Namık Kemal was exposed to Kınalızâde's doctrines and praised his work highly. He added, however, that he found the *Ahlâk-ı Alaî* too dry and forbidding. This accusation of a failure to appeal to one's emotions gives us another insight into the psychological function fulfilled by "political theology" in the elaboration of Young Ottoman political theories.[42]

[37] Rosenthal, *Political Thought*, p. 220.

[38] For the section of Kâtib Çelebi's *Dustur ül-Amel*, containing these ideas, see F. Behrnhauer, "Hâği Chalfa's Dustûruʾlʾamal; Ein Beitrag zur Osmanischen Finanzgeschichte," XI, 119, *ZDMG* (1857).

[39] See French trans. by Garcin de Tassy in *Journal Asiatique* (1824), IV, 219-220.

[40] See *Ottoman Statecraft: The Book of Counsels for Viziers and Governors, Naṣāʾiḥ ül-vüzera veʾl-ümera* of Sarı Meḥmed Pasha the Defterdâr (trans., introd., and notes by Walter L. Wright, Princeton, Princeton University Press, 1935), p. 119, 176.

[41] See Ihsan Sungu, "Mahmud II nin İzzet Molla ve Asâkir-i Mansure Hakkında bir Hattı," *Tarih Vesikaları* (October 1941), I, 176. See below, Chapter v, for Akif Paşa.

[42] Kaplan, *Namık Kemal*, p. 141. For one instance in which Kemal used the expression "circle of Justice" see Namık Kemal, "Wa-shāwirhum fī ʾl-ʾamr," *Hürriyet*, 20 July 1868, p. 1.

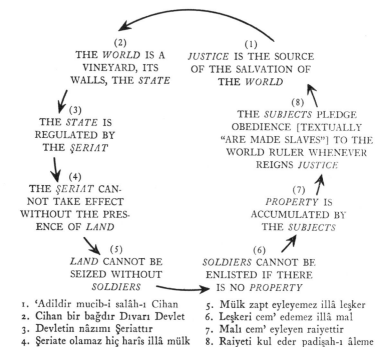

(2)
THE *WORLD* IS A
VINEYARD, ITS
WALLS, THE *STATE*

(1)
JUSTICE IS THE SOURCE
OF THE SALVATION OF
THE *WORLD*

(3)
THE *STATE* IS
REGULATED BY
THE *ŞERIAT*

(8)
THE *SUBJECTS* PLEDGE
OBEDIENCE [TEXTUALLY
"ARE MADE SLAVES"] TO THE
WORLD RULER WHENEVER
REIGNS *JUSTICE*

(4)
THE *ŞERIAT* CAN-
NOT TAKE EFFECT
WITHOUT THE PRES-
ENCE OF *LAND*

(7)
PROPERTY IS
ACCUMULATED BY
THE *SUBJECTS*

(5)
LAND CANNOT BE
SEIZED WITHOUT
SOLDIERS

(6)
SOLDIERS CANNOT BE
ENLISTED IF THERE
IS NO *PROPERTY*

1. 'Adildir mucib-i salâh-ı Cihan
2. Cihan bir bağdır Dıvarı Devlet
3. Devletin nâzımı Şeriattır
4. Şeriate olamaz hiç harîs illâ mülk

5. Mülk zapt eyleyemez illâ leşker
6. Leşkeri cem' edemez illâ mal
7. Malı cem' eyleyen raiyettir
8. Raiyeti kul eder padişah-ı âleme adil

B. JUSTICE AND THE PHILOSOPHER-KING

One aspect of Kınalızâde's statement strikes a note one does not encounter in Tûsî: the Şeriat has again a primary part to play in the political process. In fact, this was a contribution of Devvanî's which Kınalızâde had incorporated in his own book. Thus a passage which in Tûsî ran:

"The governor is a person endowed with divine support ... in order to perfect individual men and to arrange ⟨and bring about⟩ the ⟨general⟩ welfare. Philosophers call this person 'king absolutely speaking' and call his ordinances, the art of government. The modern ⟨philosophers⟩ call him imam and his function the imamate. Plato calls him 'world ruler' and Aristotle 'statesman' ... that is the man who watches over the affairs of the city state. ..."[43]

[43] Rosenthal, *Political Thought*, p. 216, quoting Tûsî.

became in Devvanî:

"The lawgiver is a person endowed with divine inspiration and revelation . . . to establish regulations governing man's duties to God . . . and his social relations . . . for the good order of this life and the next. . . . The ancient philosophers call him a lawgiver . . . while the moderns call him a prophet."[44]

And this second passage was taken over almost verbatim by Kınalızâde.

Thus, through Devvanî's and then Kınalızâde's works, the means of identifying the sultan with the philosopher-king became available. This synthesis was fairly long-lived. As long as the basic consideration prevailed that nothing was worse than anarchy, and as long as institutionalized methods of opposition to the existing political machine did not exist, it proved an adequate political model. In failing to take notice of the actual or subterranean opposition to the established political powers, however, this final synthesis failed even at the time it was conceived. For both Devvanî and Kınalızâde, by assigning the highest place in their scheme to the Şeriat, did not keep up with the realities of the political life of their time. In particular, the *Ahlâk-ı Alaî* did not reflect the overwhelming importance that secular lawmaking had come to assume by the time it was composed (the seventeenth century). It relegated to the background the fact that the sultan did proclaim edicts which had the force of law, the fact that the bulk of the "constitutional law" of the empire was extra-Şer'i law. Kınalızâde's smooth synthesis only served to disguise a certain antagonism between what has been characterized as the "ruling institution" in the Ottoman Empire and the ulema, between

---

[44] *Ibid.*, p. 215, quoting Devvanî. For an outdated translation of Devvanî which still remains the only one see [Djalāl ad-Dīn al-Dawwānī], *Practical Philosophy of the Muhammadan People* (trans. by W. Thompson, London, Allen, 1839).

the sultan, the executive officers of his household, and his government on one hand and the ulema on the other.[45]

C. SECULAR VS. RELIGIOUS LAWS

There were two facets to the attacks of the ulema against the secular lawmaking power of the Ottoman sultan. The ulema themselves always kept these two facets confused because it was to their advantage, and the Young Ottomans, who in the nineteenth century took up the argument of the ulema, often used the same smoke screen. It is important, therefore, to disentangle these two different aspects of the "clerical" protestations.

The background for secular lawmaking by kings had been set by the Islamic conception of " *'Urf.*" This theory stated that where the Şeriat did not provide a solution to existing problems, the measuring rods of "necessity" and "reason" could be used to enact regulations with the force of law.[46] Some advantage was taken of this theory in early Islamic states. In 1058 Tuğrul Bey, a Selçuk Turk whose Turkish "palace mayor" predecessors had for some time held the real power in the Abbasid Caliphate, had the ruling caliph transfer sovereignty over all Islamic lands to himself.

When Tuğrul Bey's successor created the Selçuk state, Turko-Iranian governmental practices began to prevail. Among these was the secularization of public law. As a matter of form only, the ultimate infallibility of the Şeriat in all matters, public and private, was still acknowledged.[47]

It is in the thirteenth century that developments occurred which made it possible for the ulema to equate the use of secular law with the most tyrannical of absolutistic practices. These developments were due to the invasion of the Middle East by the Mongols.

[45] Gibb and Bowen, *Islamic Society*, I, 1, 32.
[46] For developments in the Ottoman Empire see H. İnalcık, "Osmanlı Hukukuna Giriş," *Ankara Üniversitesi Siyasal Bilgiler Fakültesi Dergisi* (June 1958), XIII, 102-126.
[47] *Ibid.*, p. 105.

The Mongols too regulated their social life by means of secular law. For example, upon being proclaimed Çingiz Han ("emperor of the world"), the Mongolian ruler Temuçin had proclaimed his basic code of laws or *"Yasa"* (1206), which was to apply throughout his empire. But the Mongols also had a theory of unquestioned and complete allegiance to the will of the ruler which, in the extreme form in which they practiced it, was not common to the Turks. The Mongols so overwhelmed the Middle East militarily and were so successful in asserting their rule throughout a sizable portion of Islamic countries that their methods of government—which were also thought to account in part for their success—were believed to be a model of efficiency. Absolutism, *à la Mongole*, set the fashion, and thus the Islamic conception of " *'Urf*," the Turkish practice of secular lawmaking, and absolute rule were indiscriminately grouped together under the same heading. One consequence of this was that secular legislation suffered from guilt by association.[48]

Long after the end of the Mongol invasions the ulema continued to identify secular lawmaking with absolutism, and they had no trouble in pointing to the existence of secular laws in the Ottoman Empire: the Ottoman sultans, in consonance with age-old Turkish practices, had taken upon themselves the legislation of what amounted, eventually, to entire codes of law which were extra-Şer'i. Permanent and uniform guides for the administration of the empire were thus compiled and codes of criminal law also drafted.[49]

A body of public law was thereby created, known by the

[48] For the *'Urfi* theory of the Sultan's powers see R. Levy, " *'Urf*," *Encyclopaedia of Islam* IV: 1031, Reuben Levy, *The Social Structure of Islam* (Cambridge, University Press, 1957), p. 261. For the fashion which the Mongols set in politics see *Kānūnnāme-i Sultānī ber Müceb-i Örf-i Osmānī: II Mehmet ve II Bayezit Devirlerine Ait Yasakname ve Kanun-nameler* (eds., Dr. Robert Anhegger and Dr. Halil İnalcık, Ankara, Türk Tarih Kurumu Basımevi, 1956), Introduction, p. xvi, note 27; p. 14. For the Yasa see George Vernadsky, "Cengiz Han Yasası," *Türk Hukuk Tarihi* (Ankara, 1949), I, 106-132.

[49] İnalcık, "Osmanlı Hukukuna Giriş," p. 122.

name of *kanun* (the name for each individual codification being *kanunnâme* or *yasaknâme*), and only matters that had reference to private law such as inheritance, marriage, and torts were left to the ulema to decide in the light of the divine law or Şeriat.[50]

The fact that the sultan arrogated to himself the right to make law in this fashion was one which the ulema could never swallow and gave rise to a smoldering resentment against the imperial prerogative. In addition, the validity of a secular law's resting ultimately on the will of the sultan was a concept which the less sophisticated ulema were at a loss to understand, since they had been taught that no law was above divine law. This may be gathered from successive edicts of the *Şeyhülis-lâm* (head of the ulema), instructing teachers of the religious law to make their students realize that, in the course of their professional life, they would meet with cases where they could not apply the measuring rod of the Şeriat.[51]

Thus the ulema, though they achieved increasing control of part of the machinery of the state in the fifteenth and sixteenth centuries, could still stand up in the nineteenth century as the upholders of religious principle against bureaucratic expediency and as the defenders of the "rights" of their Islamic brethren.

We shall later witness how, when the time came for the Young Ottomans to enunciate their theories of government, they, adopting the line of attack of the ulema, heaped the onus of all that was despotic or autocratic in Ottoman governmental practices of the past on "Mongolian" accretions without specifying whether by "Mongolian" they meant the Ottoman tradition of having to submit to the personal commands of the Grand Vizier without a possibility of appeal or the presence in the state of a code of administrative law which competed with the Şeriat.

[50] Ömer Lûtfi Barkan, "Kanun-Nâme," *Islâm Ansiklopedisi* (1952), VI, 191.
[51] Barkan, "Kanun-Nâme," p. 191.

In conclusion, it might be said that the Islamic past laid little ground for the permeation of Turks by European political philosophy, but that the politico-ethical commands of the Şeriat provided one possible point of contact with the political theory of the West, insofar as Western theory also disguised, even in its most rationalistic form, certain religio-ethical convictions about the inviolability of the human person.

Specifically, the opposition of the ulema to the imperial prerogative of lawmaking explains the process by which, for many Young Ottomans, the establishment of a constitutional system in Turkey was equated with a return to the rule of law as embodied in the practice of the Şeriat.[52]

None of the elements in the political *Weltanschauung* to which the Young Ottomans became heirs may be fully appreciated if they are not set into the general framework of deep, genuine and all-pervasive concern for the welfare of the Islamic community. This feeling was translated, following the Ottoman ascendance in the Islamic world, into a profound and sincere devotion to the Ottoman state. Such a willingness to sacrifice one's own interests to that of the state, expressed

[52] The prestige that the ulema acquired in the heyday of the Ottoman Empire because of the high ethical and intellectual standards that prevailed among them has been well described by the historian Hammer. The reasons for which their prestige lingered so long after the disappearance of these qualities among them may also be gathered from the same passage:

"De toutes les institutions Ottomanes la plus éxemplaire est sans contredit celle fondée par le Sultan Mohammed II, et perfectionnée par le Sultan Souleiman Ier qui a eu pour objet d'etablir la hiérarchie des Oulémas. Cette communauté aristocratique tout à la fois enseignante et magistrale, qui établit dans l'état un sorte de corps législatif forma dès lors un utile contrepoids au pouvoir militaire et imposa une certaine retenue aux dérèglements du despotisme même.

"Ce ne fut point une noblesse territoriale mais une aggrégation de mérites fondés sur la science de la loi, une aristocratie de théologiens et de jurisconsultes, de juges et de professeurs, dont la fermeté et la haute science contribuèrent principalement à preserver le vaisseau de l'état des orages suscités tantôt par le despotisme, tantôt par l'anarchie, deux fléaux qui si fréquemment menacèrent de le submerger."

J. de Hammer [von Hammer-Purgstall], *Histoire de l'Empire Ottoman depuis son Origine jusqu'a nos jours* (trans. by Hellert, Paris, Bellizard-Barthès, Dufour et Lowell, 1835-1843), XVII (1841), XL, XLI.

in the extremely common saying, "Allah din-ü devlete zeval vermesin" ("God protect religion and the state") was the obverse facet of the tradition of obeisance and the absence in Islam of a widely accepted theory of justified resistance. Among modern Western students of the Ottoman Empire for whom the high value of political and social dissent is axiomatic, this ability of the individual to identify his own aim with that of the state has not been given the impartial and objective treatment it deserves,[53] but the evolution of Young Ottoman thought makes little sense if it is ignored.

[53] For the beginnings of such an attempt from a slightly different point of view see Hellmut Ritter, "Irrational Solidarity Groups: A Socio-psychological study in connection with Ibn Haldun," *Oriens* (1948), I, 1-44. But the "solidarity group" that coalesced into the Ottoman Empire had very special characteristics and traditions at its basis as demonstrated by Paul Wittek in *The Rise of the Ottoman Empire* (London, Luzac, 1938), especially pp. 37-43.

❧ CHAPTER IV ❧

Turkish Political Elites in the
Nineteenth Century

THE most widely accepted theory purporting to explain the attitude assumed by Namık Kemal and his collaborators toward the government of the Ottoman Empire in the 1860's is one which attributes their criticism to the "tyranny" then existing in Turkey. This explanation has one disadvantage in that it does not dwell on the specific nature of the abuses against which the Young Ottomans were protesting. True, the age-old authoritarian basis of the empire and the tradition of subservience to the state bring to mind as a possible explanation of Young Ottoman discontent the misuse of the imperial prerogative, irresponsibility, or even tyranny on the part of the sultan. At first sight too the facts seem to substantiate this charge. In the last years of the reign of Sultan Abdülmecid (from 1854 to 1861), the Ottoman Empire had obtained several large loans from Europe, which were paid only by entering into other and larger debts. The increasing autonomy of formerly subject territories gave physical proof of the empire's decline.

Toward the end of his life the sultan had lapsed into a life of debauchery which undermined his already weak health and eventually caused his death. A similar process was repeated during the reign of his successor Abdülaziz (from 1861 to 1876) who, at the time he stepped on the throne, was hailed as the man who would put the empire together again but who did not fulfill these expectations. Abdülaziz spent money lavishly on the construction of palaces and on other personal "hobbies." These excesses weighed heavily on the taxpayers, whose burdens were increased to defray the expenses incurred by the sultans.[1]

[1] Frederick Millingen, *La Turquie sous le Règne d'Abdul Aziz* (*1862-1867*), (Paris, Librairie Internationale, 1868), p. 361.

The natural expectation of an observer would therefore be that the "tyranny" of which the Young Ottomans were complaining in most of their writings was due to the conduct of the sultan. It is thus quite surprising to find out that the attacks of the Young Ottomans were rarely directed at the sultan's person and never against the institution of the monarchy. Toward the sultanate the Young Ottomans always showed the deepest respect.[2] "Up to the present," stated Namık Kemal, "the sultan has never refused to do anything which has been required of him which would be of profit for the people."[3] The target of Young Ottoman criticism was not the monarchy but the Porte, and in particular the two pillars of the Ottoman administration of the time—Fuad and Âli Paşa, who are remembered in Turkey as "good men," modernizers of the empire, and statesmen who laid the foundations of modern Turkish administration.[4] Also, in for attacks were Âli and Fuad's "*ministrable*" colleagues and the narrow circle of statesmen who gravitated around these figures and monopolized the higher offices of state. What at first sight seems a peculiar fixation of the Young Ottomans, however, becomes intelligible the moment we realize that Sultan Abdülaziz had little or almost no hand in the preparation of the day-to-day policy of the Ottoman Empire. With regard to the determination of state policy, he was a virtual prisoner of Fuad and Âli.[5] In fact, the ultimate result of this hegemony of the Porte was that the sultan was deposed, in 1876, by the very successors

[2] A. Vambery, "Freiheitliche Bestrebungen im Moslimischen Asien," *Deutsche Rundschau* (October, 1893), LXXII, 65.

[3] Namık Kemal, "Usûl-ü meşverete dair geçen numaralarda münderiç mektupların beşincisi," *Hürriyet*, October 19, 1868, p. 7.

[4] T[ürk] T[arih] T[edris] Cemiyeti, *Tarih III. Yeni ve Yakın Zamanlar* (Ankara, Maarif Matbaası, 1941), p. 248.

[5] Sultan Abdülmecid was found one day knocking his head against the walls of his palace crying for God to deliver him from the hands of Reşid Paşa. Abdurrahman Şeref, *Tarih Musahabeleri*, p. 106. For an exposé of the feuds between Abdülaziz and Fuad see also Ahmed Saib, *Vak'a-yı Sultan Abdülaziz* (2nd ed., Cairo, Hindiye Matbaası, 1326/1908), p. 32. Fuad was avenging himself for the fate suffered by his father İzzet Molla, who had been exiled twice because he had dared advise Sultan Mahmud. See below, Chapter v.

of Âli and Fuad. Even though the statesmen who in 1876
carried out the coup were enemies of Âli and supposedly
friendly to Young Ottoman ideas, what is interesting is that
they carried to its logical end the monopolizing of political
power that characterized Âli's policies. Thus, of all the processes of transformation going on at the time in the empire,
the emancipation and rise to power of the higher bureaucrats
seems to have been the strongest, as it was also the most pervasive.[6] What had happened was that the earlier alliance between the sultan and the bureaucrats against the Janissaries
had begun to disintegrate after the elimination of the Janissary
corps in 1826. Beginning with the reign of Mahmud II (from
1808 to 1839), modernization, which the sultan desired because it promised a strengthening of the army and an increase
in the centralized control of the state, had become too complex
a goal for the sultan to control and the power necessary to
enforce the modernist and reformist drive was transferred to
the bureaucracy. After Mahmud, both the machinery of reform established by the sultan and the very protection accorded
to such reformist ministers as Reşid Paşa had made Mahmud's
imperial successors mere onlookers on the political scene. Conversely, during the reign of Abdülmecid and Abdülaziz there
had risen to power a new bureaucratic elite which arrogated
to itself the political power that Selim III (1789-1807) and
Mahmud had been able to concentrate in their own hands
for a short time.[7]

---

[6] The plotters were Mütercim Rüşdü Paşa, Hüseyin Avni Paşa, Midhat
Paşa, and Süleyman Paşa. Sultan Abdülaziz's position has been described in
Abdurrahman Şeref, *Tarih Musahabeleri*, p. 106 ff. Frederick Millingen,
La Turqiue, pp. 286-319, 322, 325. For the deposition of Sultan Abdülaziz
see Comte E. de Kératry, *Mourad V, Prince, Sultan, Prisonnier d'Etat, 1840-
1878, d'après des Témoins de sa Vie* (Paris, E. Dentu, 1878); Halûk
Şehsuvaroğlu, *Sultan Aziz: Hususî, siyasî hayatı, devri ve ölümü* (İstanbul,
Hilmi Kitabevi, 1949); İsmail Hakkı Uzunçarşılı, "Sultan Abdülaziz
vak'asına dair vak'anüvis Lûtfi Efendinin bir Risalesi," *Belleten* (1943),
VII, 349-373; Süleyman Hüsnü Paşa, *Hiss-i İnkılâb Yahut Sultan Abdülazizin Hal'i ile Sultan Murad-ı Hâmisin Cülûsu* (İstanbul, Tanin Matbaası,
1326/1910).

[7] See below, Chapter v, for a description of this process.

The general pattern of this process of elite formation which was repeated throughout the Middle East in the nineteenth and twentieth centuries has been described as follows: "The imposition of Western administration and law has introduced a fresh complication both in the structure and the ideology of the Muslim society. By stabilizing at a given moment a transitory situation . . . modernism . . . brought to a sudden stop the circulation of authority and placed it in the hands of the fortunate few who happened to be in possession of it at that juncture. . . . It is not always realized that this crystallization of authority had a marked effect in changing the nature of the relations between those who possessed it and those over whom it was exercised. . . . This creation of vested interests came about not by the minor revolutions of the Islamic society itself, but as the result of the sudden imposition of alien ideas."[8]

In fact, the process was a little more complex than this description allows, for in it were encapsulated two distinct developments. First, as one historian has stated, "the status of servants of the government changed from that of slaves to the sultan to that of servants of the state."[9] This happened during the reign of Mahmud.

But even more important than this emancipation was a second change, i.e., the offensive smugness and self-assertiveness of the new government elite. This self-assurance replaced the earlier belief, held most strongly by Ottoman bureaucrats themselves, that "the neck of a servant of the sultan is thinner than a hair's breadth." Now the bureaucrats of the Tanzimat believed that they were the only people who could reestablish the "old Ottoman glory," which seems to have been the

---

[8] H. A. R. Gibb, "Social Reactions in the Muslim World," *Journal of the Royal Central Asian Society* (October, 1934), XXI, 548.

[9] Dr. Georg Rosen, *Geschichte der Türkei von dem Siege der Reform im Jahre 1826 bis zum Pariser Traktat vom Jahre 1856* (Leipzig, Hirzel, 1866), I, 302. For earlier developments see Engelhardt, *La Turquie et le Tanzimat*, I, 28 f.

ultimate goal of all Ottoman Turks. Insofar as they were justified in holding the belief that their services were indispensable, Gibb's above-mentioned description of the rise to power of Middle Eastern elites because of "new ideas" is indeed quite accurate.

The process had already begun in the last years of the reign of Mahmud. Already Reşid Paşa's attitude toward his imperial master, one which showed only in his contacts with foreigners, was that the sultan was basically incapable of leading a reform movement. As Reşid Paşa himself had stated to Palmerston, "If the new institutions, which Sultan Mahmud has sometimes espoused, have, at times, encountered difficulties . . . its cause must only be attributed to the sovereign's arrogance."[10] And again, "He [the Sultan] had no knowledge whatsoever of the skills needed in administering the affairs [of state]. . . . His mind lacked discrimination. To flatter his pride and his vanity was to assure oneself of his approbation."[11] Reşid Paşa implied, of course, that he, Reşid, was quite well versed in "administering the affairs" of the empire.

Âli and Fuad Paşa elaborated on this attitude and Âli Paşa fostered the new idea that a small elite should take upon itself the administration of matters of state. The historian Cevdet Paşa, who occupied more than one government post during the successive premierships of Âli Paşa, relates the words of the latter, spoken at a private meeting, to the effect that "the Lord has entrusted the well-being of the state to five or six people. These should govern the fate of the state."[12] Cevdet Paşa explains how his silence on this occasion was correctly interpreted as disapproval of this theory and adds that while

[10] Bailey, *British Policy and the Turkish Reform Movement*, pp. 271, 272.
[11] *Ibid.*
[12] Ebul'ülâ Mardin, *Medenî Hukuk Cephesinden Ahmet Cevdet Paşa 1822-1895* (İstanbul, Cumhuriyet Matbaası, 1946), p. 10, note 8, quoting an unpublished portion of Cevdet's *Tezâkir*, folio 4, p. 18. For almost the same conception as held by Hüseyin Avni Paşa, one of the generals who deposed Abdülaziz, see Ahmed Saib, *Tarih-i Sultan Murad-ı Hâmis* (2nd ed., Cairo, Matbaa-i Hindiye, n.d.), p. 164.

Fuad Paşa "was not as despotically inclined as Âli Paşa, he also held similar opinions."[13]

Accounts of the rise of this new Turkish elite, which was quite conscious of the eminent role that history had called on it to play, may be found in several of the works written by contemporary European observers. The most fiery of these are the memoirs of Frederick Millingen, a man well acquainted with the intimate lives of the Turkish statesmen of the Tanzimat, who also bore a deep grudge against Fuad Paşa.[14] The power of the sultan, Millingen stated, was more than counterbalanced by "the preponderant influence of the bureaucrats of the sublime Porte." He added: "These *kiatibs* form a powerful corporation which, possessing the advantages of a relatively superior erudition and versed in the routine of administration, has easily been able to usurp and conserve a preponderance over the other bodies of the state. Its political attributions extend to all branches of administration and thanks to it, this corps has acquired a limitless power and influence. It is from the corps of bureaucrats that emerge ordinarily the great Efendis, the chiefs of bureaux, imperial commissioners, governors, ambassadors, ministers, etc. Not content with the legitimate exercise of their power in the ministries which constitute their domain and in the sphere of their attributions, these *kiatibs* have seized power by spreading their ramifications and meddling in the smallest details of governmental organization."[15]

The new bureaucrats seem to have taken advantage of their position to play the role of minor despots even in their relations with the ulema, whose influence as a group had been so deeply feared in earlier times.[16] So that the remark of

[13] Mardin, *Medeni Hukuk Cephesinden*, p. 10, note 8.

[14] Millingen was the son of Dr. Millingen, Byron's physician. His mother's second husband was Kıbrıslı Mehmed Emin Paşa, grand vizier for a short time in the 1860's, whose stepson Millingen thus became. For the life of Millingen and his relation with the Porte see Davison, "Reform in the Ottoman Empire 1856-1876," p. 133 *et seq.*

[15] Millingen, *La Turquie*, p. 255.

[16] *Ibid.*, p. 257.

Engelhardt that the first show of discontentment against the imperial power—the "Zealot" coup, known in Turkish history as the Kuleli Revolt (1859)—was due to the distaste felt throughout the country for this new governmental elite does not come as a surprise. Engelhardt states that "feelings ran high in particular against that sort of oligarchy which, since the beginning of the reign of Abdülmecid, surrounded the throne and made of a sovereign who lacked both experience and will the instrument of its intrigues and so to speak the unconscious accomplice of its dilapidations. A revolutionary breath went through the army, spread among the Ulemas and in the highest ranks of the administration."[17]

Many Turks joined in the chorus of protestations directed against the uncontrolled actions of the new Ottoman elite. It would seem that one key to the majority of the political writings of Namık Kemal—certainly to those he composed during his three years of voluntary exile—is an unrelenting hatred of the graft and oppression of the new bureaucracy and the small group of "experts" led by Âli Paşa.

In one instance, for example, in one of Kemal's writings an imaginary peasant was made to wonder at the number of palaces one came across in the capital. The peasant indicated that there were several sovereigns. The answer provided by Namık Kemal was the following: "Yes, there exists more than one sovereign, but one of them is called the Padişah ['sovereign'], he is the true sovereign. The others have now become partners in his rule although they have not yet been able to take his title away. At present they are called ministers."[18]

[17] Engelhardt, *La Turquie et le Tanzimat*, I, 158.
[18] Namık Kemal, "Idare-i Hâzıranın Hulâsa-i Âsarı," *Hürriyet*, December 28, 1868, p. 6. For Ziya Paşa's ideas see his *Letter* to the Polish newspaper *Dziemik Poynanski* in the *London Times*, December 31, 1867, p. 8. "The origin of the mischief is the peculiar form of government, unlike any that exists in other despotic states. Unlimited as is the power of the Porte, it is not vested in the Sultan but in a handful of dignitaries. . . . Those dignitaries form a set of statesmen who, for a period of 25 years, have alternately relieved each other in office."
The Young Ottomans' antipathy for the men who filled the highest offices of the state and especially for the grand vizier had deep historical roots. For

Namık Kemal devoted considerable space to such subjects as the reforming of government service and to the techniques by which these new "upper" bureaucrats could be held in check.[19] The curtailment of liberty which he associated with the rise of this new class he described as follows: "In old times a temporary tyranny could be instituted by the use of imperial edicts, later an order, a paper signed by the minister of interior, still later, the will of the police commissioner or even of a police sergeant became sufficient to put out the fires of an innocent hearth, to destroy an entire family."[20]

The fact that Namık Kemal himself traced his ancestry back to a well-established family which had been important

---

a long time the grand viziers had been part and parcel of the *Enderun-u Hümâyun*, i.e., the imperial court. As such they had a career which was characteristic of the members of the so-called Ruling Institution, the governing elite attached by ties of personal absolute allegiance to the sultan. Ideally, they would have been Christians converted to Islam in their early childhood and then educated for statesmanship, later rising to the highest offices of the Ottoman "executive." This staffing of key posts had not been accepted with equanimity either by the mass of the Turkish population or by the lower bureaucracy. The masses seem to have resented the disdain for "Turks" that obtained at the *Enderun* and which appeared in such expressions that were used in court circles as "Etrak-ı bî-idrak" ("senseless Turks"). The members of the bureaucracy and the less important ulema were incensed by the attitude of the members of the *Enderun* that they were above ordinary (Şer'i) justice.

As the system of staffing the Ruling Institution with converts broke down, the office of grand vizier did lose its "foreign" cast, but as it had been the focus of suspicions for a long time the Young Ottomans could still make it the center of their anticosmopolitan and anticorruptionist drive. For the attitudes of the Devşirme toward Turks see İsmail Hakkı Uzunçarşılı, *Osmanlı Devleti Teşkilâtında Kapukulu Ocakları: I Acemi Ocağı ve Yeniçeri Ocağı* (Ankara, Türk Tarih Kurumu Basımevi, 1943), pp. 140-141. For the analysis by the Young Ottoman Ali Suavi of the privileged status of the members of the Ruling Institution see Ali Suavi, untitled article, *Ulûm* (undated [1870]), p. 1000.

[19] Kemal had detailed projects for the establishment of specialized training for officials and their promotion on the basis of merit. Not the least interesting of his proposals was his conviction that an effort should be made to recruit candidates for state employment in the provinces. See Namık Kemal, "Memur," *İbret*, October 8, 1872, in *Külliyat-ı Kemal: Makalât-ı Siyasiye ve Edebiye* (ed. by Ali Ekrem [Bulayır], Istanbul, Selanik Matbaası, 1328/1910), pp. 135-148.

[20] Unpublished letter of Namık Kemal. Quoted by Süleyman Nazif, *Namık Kemal*, p. 44.

before the reforms but which had later declined both in terms of personal fortune and of position—very probably due to the fact that it had not been able to adapt itself to the new demands for Europeanized statesmen—points to the subconscious motivations which might have roused a deep hostility toward the new bureaucratic pedants, whose pomposity Namık Kemal constantly ridiculed.[21]

But the accusations leveled by the Young Ottomans against the statesmen of the Tanzimat did not come only under the heading of "tyranny." In addition, these statesmen were charged with having adopted the most superficial parts of European culture, those aspects which the Young Ottomans considered immoral. One of their complaints, for example, was that Westernization had been understood by Fuad Paşa and his imitators as equivalent to "the establishment of theaters, frequenting ballrooms, being liberal about the infidelities of one's wife and using European toilets."[22] Again, Namık Kemal stated that he rejected a Europeanization which consisted of letting women walk around décolleté.[23]

All these were jabs at the fashionable circles presided over by Fuad Paşa, where Western social manners and amenities had been widely adopted. One final reproach made by the Young Ottomans to the statesmen of the school of Âli Paşa was that the latter had forgotten about the great opportunities afforded by the "unfathomable sea of the Şeriat."[24]

[21] Editorial, *Hürriyet*, November 2, 1868, p. 2. Namık Kemal traced his ancestry to Grand Vizier Topal Osman Paşa, the victor of the war waged against Nadir Şah in Persia. His grandfather, Şemseddin Bey, was the master of ceremonies of Selim III; the father of Namık Kemal, Mustafa Asım Bey, was the court astronomer or rather "astrologist," a position which put him in the ranks of the non-European "old-fashioned" elite. Theodor Menzel, "Kemal," *Encyclopedia of Islam*, ıı, 847-851. On Namık Kemal's pride in the achievements of his ancestors cf. Rıza Tevfik, in Esatlı, *Ölümünden Sonra Rıza Tevfik*, p. 116.

[22] Ziya Paşa, "Yeni Osmanlılardan bir Zat Tarafından Matbaamıza Göderilip Derc Olunan Hâtıralar," *Hürriyet*, April 5, 1869, p. 7.

[23] Namık Kemal, "Fırkamız meydana çıktı çıkalı," *Hürriyet*, September 7, 1868, p. 7.

[24] Ziya Paşa, "Yeni Osmanlılardan bir Zat," *Hürriyet*, April 5, 1869, p. 6.

It is true that the new Turkish elite was, by earlier standards, quite blunt and merciless in enforcing the political, social,
and intellectual Westernization of Turkey. In this respect they
were continuing a trend begun by Reşid Paşa. Reşid Paşa himself had been so far inclined to Westernization that he had
considered the salvation of Turkey to lie in what he called
"the way of civilization."[25] The new elite took over this
Western-mindedness of Reşid Paşa and carried it even farther.
These men, for example, were the first members of the Masonic lodges that were established in Turkey by foreigners.[26]
However the strongest evidence of their pro-Western orientation may be seen in the favorable attitude that they adopted
toward the creation of lay courts and the adoption of codes of
law modeled on European codes.[27] It is indeed extraordinary
that when the project for the creation of such courts—which
had been suggested by Western powers—was being discussed
at the Porte, there should have existed a group of statesmen
who were not averse to the suggestions of the French ambassador, Bourrée, of having the entire French civil code translated into Turkish and used as a Turkish civil code.[28]

The dichotomy between the attitude of the suave and
Europeanized statesman of the Tanzimat[29] and the cultural

[25] In the original document in which he mentioned this idea, Reşid Paşa
used a phonetic transcription in Turkish of the French "civilization." See
Reşat Kaynar, *Mustafa Reşit Paşa ve Tanzimat* (Ankara, Türk Tarih
Kurumu Basımevi, 1954), p. 69.

[26] According to Ebüzziya, the first Masonic lodge was created in Turkey
by the British ambassador, Sir Henry Bulwer, in 1857. Not to be outdone,
the French ambassador had created a rival lodge the following year. This
lodge which had the name of "Union d'Orient" included among its members
Âli Paşa, Fuad Paşa, Mustafa Fazıl Paşa, Reşid Paşa, Süleyman Paşa,
Edhem Paşa, Münif Paşa. See Ebüzziya Tevfik, "Farmasonluk," *Mecmua-i
Ebüzziya*, 18 Cemaziyülahir 1329, pp. 683-686.

[27] The commercial code of 1850 was copied almost literally from the commercial laws of France. Ubicini, *Letters on Turkey*, I, 166. Provincial
administration was based on the system developed in France during the
reign of Louis XVI. Editorial, *La Turquie* (Istanbul), January 9, 1867.

[28] See Mardin, *Medenî Hukuk Cephesinden Ahmet Cevdet Paşa*, p. 88 *et
seq.* On the advisory status granted to a French jurist and the intention of the
Porte to take over sections of the Code Napoleon see *Levant Herald* (Istanbul), May 1, 1869, p. 2.

[29] Jorga, *Geschichte*, v, 419.

and religious puritanism of the Young Ottomans shows that the Young Ottomans, who have been represented as the inheritors of a Western-oriented tradition introduced by their intellectual mentor Şinasi,[30] had, in fact, more complex intellectual antecedents. Âli Paşa, the sworn enemy of Şinasi, was intellectually closer to him than the Young Ottomans were ever to be. Mustafa Fazıl Paşa, even though he combatted Âli Paşa, should be placed in the same cultural locus. All three men were devoid of the self-consciousness which is found among the Young Ottomans. They did not try to compare Islam with the West; they felt Islam was above such comparisons. On the other hand, in Namık Kemal, Ali Suavi, and Ziya Paşa we encounter a type of conduct which is conspicuous by the amount of energy it devoted to the defense of parochial values. It is because Şinasi realized this difference that he chose to steer clear of the Young Ottomans in Paris. Thus within a few years of Ottoman political development were compressed the typically eighteenth-century attitude of Şinasi, convinced of the eventual triumph of reason, and the typically modern reaction of Kemal, introducing a militancy and a cult of national values that was to become the hallmark of twentieth-century nationalism.

Yet it should not be forgotten that Namık Kemal's demands centering around the reestablishment of Ottoman practices such as the rule of religious law were based on a perfectly cogent argument. One of the primary results of the political developments in the Ottoman Empire in the nineteenth century had been the separation of religious criteria from the practice of government.[31] This separation occurred almost in-

[30] For this approach to the Young Ottomans see Tanpınar, *XIXncu Asır*, pp. 194-196.

[31] Cf. Roderic H. Davison, "Turkish Attitudes Concerning Christian-Muslim Equality in the Nineteenth Century," *The American Historical Review* (July 1954), 59:844. See also Engelhardt, *La Turquie*, I, 37, who speaks of this aspect as "a revolution." Insofar as public instruction is concerned, one author points out that, by the creation in 1846 of a Ministry of Education, "the secularization of instruction became an accomplished fact."

sensibly. It began with the establishment of institutions (both civil and military) where efficiency was the primary goal and where not even a pretense was made of creating an ideology that would clothe these institutions. Thus in the Ottoman state created during the Tanzimat there was no possibility of an ultimate reference to something more exalted or less pedestrian than the paper-pushing routine of the bureaus of the Porte or the mere "physical" strengthening of the state. Whether in the process of carrying out the Westernization of Turkey and the streamlining of governmental and administrative practice there arose injustices was immaterial to Tanzimat statesmen like Âli Paşa. The empire had to be saved first. This kind of attitude, however, resulted in an ideological vacuum, for the Tanzimat statesmen contributed nothing to replace the Şeriat as a measuring rod of good and evil in politics. They did not realize the implications of the creation of such an ideological vacuum. They were Europeanized to the extent of accepting Islam as a "private" religion. The least that can be said about this attitude is that they were shortsighted, for they dealt with a religion that was conceived of as invading every crevice of the citizen's actions, a religion about which an Islamic mystic, Gazalî (al-Ghazālī), had complained that it prescribed to the smallest detail of everyday life.[32] By creating political institutions which were not dependent on the impetus or control of religious law the Tanzimat statesmen created a disequilibrium in Ottoman society.[33]

M. Belin, "De l'Instruction Publique et du Mouvement Intellectuel en Orient," Le Contemporain (1866), XI, 218. See also below, Chapter VII.

[32] H. J. Lammens, S.J., L'Islam, Croyances et Institutions (Beyrouth, Imprimerie Catholique, 1926), p. 124.

[33] The best exposition of this problem is one given by a modern scholar who has examined the relevance of the problem for the Turkey of Atatürk:

"The crucial matter is, perhaps, that the Turks, in rejecting the Shari'ah, think of themselves as having discarded only the equivalent of what in Western civilization might be thought of as ecclesiastical positive law. They do not think of having abandoned the equivalent of what is embodied in Western tradition as the concept of natural law. If there is no transcendent justice in the universe to which man's conscience can appeal, against the

It was this impossibility of having reference to an ultimate ethical-political code against which Namık Kemal protested. This is what he objected to when he pointed to the heresy of instituting lay tribunals. This is the meaning of the profound shock which he expressed in connection with the speech pronounced by Sultan Abdülaziz on the occasion of the opening of the Council of State of the Ottoman Empire in 1868. This was a liberal measure and Namık Kemal agreed that the sultan should take advantage of this creation of new institutions to herald the fact to Europe. But there was nothing in this speech, according to Kemal, which contradicted the bases of religious law. Why, then, complained Kemal, was there no reference in this speech to the guidance afforded by religious law in political matters? "If," continued Kemal, "the purpose is to imply that up to this day the people in the Ottoman Empire were the slaves of the sultan, who, out of the goodness of his heart, confirmed their liberty, this is something to which we can never agree, because, according to our beliefs, the rights of the people, just like divine justice, are immutable."[34]

One interesting aspect of the chain of events which led to the formation of the Turkish bureaucracy and the reaction engendered by these bureaucrats is that it does duplicate developments which occurred in the West. For one, it parallels the history of constitutionalism in Europe, which developed "as a system of controls imposed upon a vigorous bureaucracy."[35]

---

empirical actions and even the laws of a society, that man and that society are precarious in the extreme. . . .

". . . But with what, if anything, have they replaced the principles on which the Shari'ah is based? . . . Our reference is to the ultimate principles, of man's rights and duties as related to the very structure of the Universe. . . .

"If the members of the Grand National Assembly have replaced the Shari'ah with a foreign code because it seemed to them good, what is to keep them tomorrow from replacing this by fascist laws, if it seemed to them, as a ruling group, profitable?" W. C. Smith, *Islam in Modern History* (Princeton, Princeton University Press, 1957), pp. 196, 197.

[34] Namık Kemal, "al Ḥaḳḳ Ya'lū wa-lā Yu'lā 'alayhı," *Hürriyet*, June 29, 1868, p. 3.

[35] Carl J. Friedrich, *Constitutional Government and Democracy. Theory and Practice in Europe and America* (Boston, Gum and Co., 1950), p. 57.

Insofar as Turkey is concerned, one of the first references to constitutionalism made by an Ottoman was also inspired by this problem. In an opuscle published in 1869, a Polish *émigré* who had been converted to Islam and had been granted the title of Paşa stated, "Our constitution . . . has not and shall not have any other goal than the replacement of the exclusive action of the bureaucrats by one exerted in concert with a national institution."[36]

Secondly, the case of the bureaucratic elite which developed in Turkey as the result of the Tanzimat reforms also presents a similarity with that of modern technocracies and the problems raised by the latter. Since the beginning of this century a number of studies have tried to indicate the essentially undemocratic nature of modern technological elites or of entrenched bureaucracies or of an excessive delegation of powers,[37] and these studies have described the fashion in which the elites tend to arrogate to themselves the right to decide lines of policy which are too technical to be understood or controlled by the electorate or even their representatives. In the case under study, a similar movement was taking place in Turkey. The new bureaucratic intelligentsia of Turkey often went ahead with schemes which it dubbed Europeanization and which its control of Western languages and exclusive contacts with the West made it impossible for the traditional Ottoman elite to question. For the latter had already agreed, after the bitter military defeats suffered at the beginning of the nineteenth century, that Europeanization would be of the greatest profit to the state. But the public servants to whom this task was entrusted were now in the position of being able to justify every one of their moves with the rationalization that it was necessary for Turkey. Their knowledge of Western

[36] Mustafa Djelaleddine, *Les Turcs Anciens et Modernes* (Constantinople, Imprimerie du Courrier d'Orient, 1869), p. 209.

[37] Lord Hewart of Bury, *The New Despotism* (London, Ernest Benn, 1929); Ludwig von Mises, *La Bureaucratie* (trans. Florin et Barbier, Paris, Medicis, 1946); H. J. Laski, "Bureaucracy," *Encyclopedia of Social Sciences* (1935), III, 70-73.

languages, on the other hand, gave them a weapon which in many respects was similar to that held by the specialized technocrats of our age. The indications are that they used this privileged position with little regard for the population at large and that they felt superior to all other classes in the empire.

Finally, it is also quite true that on *political* as well as social and cultural grounds the Young Ottomans were justified in accusing the new elite of being tyrannous. For the policies of Âli and Fuad Paşa were what could be called typically Metter-nichian policies. For them, the word "liberty" carried with it the disadvantage of implying that the various parts of the empire were at liberty to secede from the mother country. The peculiar bitterness of the attacks of the Young Ottomans, however, resulted from the fact that they also accused these statesmen of being traitors to their culture.

None of the explanations listed in the foregoing exposé provided cogent reasons for which the protests against the higher bureaucrats of ministerial rank should have originated among the bureaucrats themselves, for Ziya and Kemal both had been government employees. Kemal had spent most of his life up to 1867 in government service and Ziya was still a civil servant at the time. Nor are we better informed than we were at the beginning of this study as to why such ulema as Ali Suavi should have joined forces with them. Somehow the European inclinations of the Tanzimat statesmen seem to be an insufficient explanation of this estrangement from the government of the students of Islamic tradition. Finally we still have to provide a reason for the many sympathizers the Young Ottomans found among the military. At least one way of unraveling the factors at play in bringing about this triple alliance of bureaucrats, ulema, and soldiers is to investigate the sociological elements hiding behind their triple protest, in which case it is found that the same developments which pushed the bureaucratic elite of the Tanzimat upward pressed downward on the low-ranking bureaucrats, on the majority of the ulema, and on the army as a whole.

Two main causes for the indignation of the bureaucrats proper may be singled out. First, within the ranks of the Ottoman state servants a deep chasm had formed separating the functionaries who came from families which had been able to maintain their status for one or more generations from those who depended only on their own ability for advancement. The mechanism by which this dichotomy, already apparent in the administration of the Ottoman Empire in the eighteenth century, had been transmitted to the Turkey of the Tanzimat, on the other hand, was the following: After 1839 the government abandoned the practice of sequestrating the fortunes of high-ranking government employees and reverting the money to the treasury at their death.[38] Consequently, many of the great bureaucrats of Reşid Paşa's time had been able to amass considerable wealth. Thus, just as the Tanzimat "brought to a sudden stop the circulation of authority," it had also frozen the circulation of wealth. The sons of the lucky beneficiaries of this new state of affairs commanded privileges which put them ahead of other employees of the state. As Franz von Werner, a contemporary critic of the Porte, stated: "The world of Ottoman state servants constitutes a closed society. . . . The Bureaucracy is not anymore primarily recruited as in earlier times from the entire Empire but much more from narrower circles of civil service families to which the Christians bring a sizeable contingent. . . . The son of the government employee naturally steps again into the service of the state. Entrance and success are made easier through the connections of the father."[39]

---

[38] The most fundamental step in this direction had already been taken by Mahmud on June 30, 1826, immediately following the destruction of the Janissaries. As time went by, however, and the sultan began to distrust his bureaucratic advisors this firman became inoperative in fact. See Général Antoine Andreossy, *Constantinople et le Bosphore de Thrace* (Paris, Duprat, 1841), p. 69; for a complete survey, see M. Cavid Baysun, "Musâdere," *Islâm Ansiklopedisi* (1959), VIII, 669-673.

[39] Murad Efendi [Franz von Werner], *Turkishe Skizzen* (2nd ed., Leip-

A specific example of how this process worked, not so much in the elevation to office of the rich as in the denial of opportunities to the poor, may be seen in the case of instruction in Persian. Fluency in this language, an important qualification for advancement, could be gained only if one possessed private income, since instruction in Persian was not provided at the free public lectures in the mosques and private tutoring was the only way to acquire the skill.[40] Reşid Paşa had attempted to deal with this problem by appointing Persian teachers to the Porte who were on hand for free instruction. He also established a preparatory school for future bureaucrats, based on selection according to merit, but here too young boys from eminent families were allowed to graduate without too much brain-racking.

It is significant, in the light of the foregoing, that Namık Kemal should have come from a family which was financially destitute and that Ziya Paşa should have received his schooling in the section of the school for bureaucrats which accepted boys from families that could not afford to pay for their sons' education. In general, the Young Ottomans often used the term *bey zâde* ("son of bey") or *kibar zâde* ("son of a refined person") in a derogatory fashion to characterize the young fops of their time, mostly sons of ministers who relied on their parents' position or fortune to rise in a governmental career.

A second factor of importance with respect to the social origins of the Young Ottoman movement is related to their

---

zig, Verlag der Durr'schen Buchhandlung, 1878), p. 67. The process seems to have been more complex than Werner assumes. Insofar as the *Divan-ı Hümâyun Kalemi*, i.e., the Bureau of the Grand Vizierate, is concerned, for instance, higher employees were paid by being given a *zeamet* ("non-hereditary grant of state land"). With time these passed on to the descendants of the holders of office who were nominated to the same bureau. This seems to have occurred *before* the Tanzimat. It was aggravated in the 1850's and 1860's by the fact that the nominees failed to appear at their jobs. Namık Kemal, "Hariciye Nezareti," *Hürriyet*, April 26, 1869.

[40] *Tarih-i Lütfi* (Istanbul, various publishers, 1290-1328/1873-1911), 8 vols., IV, 115.

position as intellectuals. Why, of all the bureaucrats affected, should those with an intellectual bent have led the protest? The first, obvious, and rational, but superficial, answer is that they possessed the tools for engaging in such a revolt. Here again, the facts are much more complex than the misleading, a posteriori rationalistic appraisal.

In the nineteenth century there began to appear with increasing frequency in Turkish literary circles a type of intellectual already well known in Europe. This type was the *literateur* of humble origins and modest means but of unlimited ambitions. To describe the intellectual climate which these men brought with them is difficult, but it amounts, in essence, to a "rise in the level of expectations." The change in outlook can be observed among some of the lesser known, but in the long run socially more effective, Turkish minor poets who traditionally occupied jobs as government employees and whose views were transmitted to the Young Ottomans.

Because of the permanent occupancy of executive positions by the higher bureaucrats and their sycophants, the middle and lower echelons of Ottoman state service were, with some noticeable exceptions, cluttered with men possessing literary talent but unable to rise to the highest ranks in the normal course of a governmental career. This restriction of opportunities provided these men with a justified source of complaint. Indeed, many employees of the Porte witnessed the ineptitude of superiors to whose higher and better-paid jobs they could never expect to be promoted. The reason it is difficult to resolve the resulting indignation into its component parts is that, while these employees of the state had reasons for complaining, beginning with the 1850's and 1860's these complaints were being expressed with a vehemence that had little relation to the actual plight of these men. Yet the real despair felt by many of the figures who were caught in the social mechanism of the Tanzimat is evidenced in their natural progression from anger to alcoholism to loss of health to

death. The immediate example that comes to mind is that of
Ziya Paşa who was only saved from alcoholism induced by
some of his older poet-bureaucrat cronies through the intervention of the grand vizier Edhem Paşa. The term "rise in
the level of expectations" thus seems most useful to describe
this psychological climate. The reasons for this despondency
are still obscure but might have arisen from an awareness of
the value of communication in the modern world. The "middle grade" bureaucrats knew that as repositories of the skills
of communication their importance had increased, but this was
the very moment when the development of a new elite less-
ened their opportunities for advancement. The trend in the
early nineteenth century to grant to all literate persons the
title of Efendi,[41] formerly restricted to the ulema—a superficial change from which state functionaries had benefited—was
being given the lie by the reality of shrinking opportunities.

A typical example of the *homme de lettres* in question may
be found in the case of the poet Savfet Efendi. Savfet started
his career as a servant of Hatif Efendi, the chief accountant
of the palace. Because of some verses of his which he presented
to Husrev Paşa, the reorganizer of the Turkish army at the
time of Mahmud, he was noticed by Lebib Efendi, the accountant of the Imperial Arsenal. He was taken into the latter
bureau and in 1843 was promoted to a bureau of the Porte.
He then rose quite regularly in rank until his retirement, but
never attained the executive level.

Although in his youth Savfet went so far as to attend some
of the courses in Persian offered by the Beşiktaş Society (a
gathering of encyclopedists which is discussed later),[42] what
is significant is that he was not an advocate of Westernization
for Turkey. His reactions to the pro-European writings of the
diplomat Mustafa Sami, whose *Avrupa Risalesi* ("*European*

[41] Orhan F. Köprülü, "Efendi," *Islâm Ansiklopedisi* (1946), IV, 132.
[42] Cevdet Paşa, *Tarih-i Cevdet* (2nd ed., Istanbul, Matbaa-i Osmaniye,
1309/1891-1892), 12 vols., XII, 184. For the Beşiktaş Society see below,
Chapter VII.

Journal") eulogizing the European way of life appeared in 1840, were deeply scornful.[43]

What Savfet is remembered for nowadays is his satirical poem *Béranger*, in which he compared the lowly position of the Ottoman man of letters with that of his European counterparts, and contrasted the respect that European aristocrats showed for the remains of the French poet Béranger with the indignities he, Savfet, suffered at the hands of Turkish authorities for debts outstanding to a grocer.

It is no coincidence that the poem *Béranger* has survived Savfet's other literary productions, for the piece has the bite of a class grievance even though the occasion for its composition was rather petty. A career similar to that of Savfet is that of the poet Ali Âli Efendi. Ali Âli Efendi carried the rancor which he stated to be the product of the government's lack of recognition for his talents into the editorial offices of the *Ceride-i Havadis*, the first privately owned Turkish newspaper.[44]

Ali Âli's literary productions also show the mark of the grudge he bore against "the system." It is during his editorship of the *Ceride* that Victor Hugo's *Les Misérables* was serialized, and the one book that he edited, *Hançerli Hanım* (*"The Lady with the Dagger"*), is about a man who prefers the love of a slave to that of a *grande dame*. The plot, it is true, was one composed by a storyteller of the time of Murad IV, but it cannot be entirely a coincidence that it was chosen by Âli for publication in book form.[45]

Similar too are the careers of the poet Hafız Müşfik Efendi and Nüzhet Efendi, both members of the staff of the *Ceride-i Havadis*. Müşfik was the son of a slave merchant who worked his way through the bureaus of the Porte. He resigned when his pending appointment to the bureau of the Undersecretary

[43] İnal, *Son Asır*, p. 1648.

[44] *Ibid.*, p. 103. For the influence of the *Ceride-i Havadis*, see below, Chapter VIII.

[45] See Mustafa Nihat Özön, *Türkçede Roman* (Istanbul, Remzi, n.d.), pp. 97 ff., for the text of this story.

for Foreign Affairs—a post which carried considerable prestige—failed to materialize. What had happened was that Âli Paşa had appointed his own son-in-law, who had little qualification for the job, to Müşfik's hoped-for post. Âli Paşa must often have repented his action, for according to the historian Cevdet Paşa it was Müşfik who first made the editorial offices of the *Ceride-i Havadis* into a gathering place for the discontented young bureaucratic intelligentsia of the capital and thus laid the groundwork for the Jeune Turquie. Both Müşfik and Ali Âli were close friends of Ziya Paşa.[46]

If the swift rise of a new elite accompanied by a restriction of opportunities provides an explanation of the dynamics of Young Ottoman protest, their alliance with the ulema can be explained in terms of a similar loss of status incurred by these pillars of Islam. This loss of status was caused by three developments: the secularization of the machinery of the state, the secularization of the judiciary, and the secularization of education. The third of these factors will be investigated in detail in the next chapter; the second was already touched upon above; thus the investigation of the first remains to be taken up here.

Of these three policies the secularization of the machinery of the state had been the first to be undertaken. After 1839 the local judges or *kadıs* had soon been deprived of such administrative functions as they exercised under the old regime.[47] Administrative functions were thus made a monopoly of the bureaucrats. This new monopoly was reflected in the use of a new word for administrative positions—*menasıb-ı mülkiye* ("administrative posts") which replaced the earlier term of *menasıb-ı kalemiye*, a much less differentiated term

---

[46] This information is quoted by İnal from Cevdet Paşa's "Mâruzat" without any reference to the page or place of publication. İnal, *Son Asır*, p. 1020. This passage could not be located in the published portions of the "Mâruzat." See [Cevdet Paşa], "Cevdet Paşanın Mâruzatı," *TTEM* (January 1924) XIV, 52 to *TTEM* (July 1927), XVI, 220 and therefore must be part of the unpublished portions of the memoirs.

[47] Osman Nuri [Ergin], *Mecelle-i Umûr-u Belediye* (Istanbul: Matbaa-i Osmaniye, 1922), p. 273.

used in a much wider sense for all "clerks."[48] The process was so strange for old Ottomans of all classes that it baffled many of the onlookers. As a contemporary Turkish observer stated: "I can understand [such a concept as that of] the military: they are trained in military schools. I can also understand [such a concept as that of] the ulema: they are trained in religious schools, but I can't understand the concept of an administrative official. What do you think they are?"[49]

The change was doubly distasteful to the ulema, whose job opportunities had shrunk and who resented the influx of bureaucrats into positions which had formerly been manned by them.

In the 1870's in an anonymous pamphlet an *âlim* expressed his opinion on the matter by denying that the new administrators had any competence in carrying out the tasks they were assigned and stated: "These men are not clerks but ignoramuses [textually not people who write but people who spoil or erase: *musannif değil, muharrif . . .*]. Only those that come from the ranks of the ulema deserve to be called clerks. An understanding of science ['*ilm*': there is a play here on the word *âlim*, the singular of ulema, which textually means 'a student of science' but was the term used to describe 'a doctor of Islamic law'] is acquired only through years of study and exertion in the *medrese* [religious schools]. These men are just ordinary scribes. They are men whose drunken souls have seized on the present opportunity and been spellbound by the spoils afforded by the state. And the gold which they are allotted every month and which they steal whenever they find the opportunity, provides that glitter of their countenance which impresses millions of imbeciles."[50]

This type of complaint is quite close to that expressed by the

[48] The first use of the word may be traced to 1836 at which date Pertev Paşa introduced the term "Umur-u Mülkiye Nazırı," for the Minister of the Interior. See Lûtfi, *Tarih*, v, 29 f. Also below, Chapter v.

[49] Sami Paşa Zâde Hüseyin Bey, "Yeni Osmanlılar," *Hadisat-ı Hukukiye ve Tarihiyye: Kısm-ı Tarihî*, II, 18 (May 1, 1341-May 14, 1925).

[50] Mehmet Kaplan, "*Tanzîr-i Telemak*," [İstanbul Universitesi] *Edebiyat Fakültesi Türk Dili ve Edebiyati Dergisi* (1948), III, 1-20.

Young Ottoman Ali Suavi, himself a preacher, i.e., an *âlim* at the level of those who suffered the most because they did not have the qualification or the influence to sit as judges in Şer'i courts. Suavi accused the Tanzimat statesmen of having actively conspired to cause the downfall of the ulema.[51] That the new elite was wary of the latter is quite clear from the testimony of Millingen, who states: "The corps of the Ulemas, an ecclesiastical legislature, the ancient power and the prestige of which have tumbled in the face of the progress of scepticism, this corps itself has had to lower its head to the ascendancy of the Porte. There is no law, not even the Koran, the aegis of which can protect the judges and the ulema. Always, by the tribunals sits some emissary representing the Porte in view of having the orders and the whims of a *kiatib* carried out."[52]

The plight of the ulema was not made easier by the favoritism which was shown in making appointments to what places were left for them to fill. Here again, the practice of granting diplomas of "doctor in Islamic law" ("*ru'us*") to young men who had the influence required to be appointed but did not possess the qualifications for the office went back to the eighteenth century, but favoritism became particularly galling when opportunities in general for a career as an *âlim* were restricted. Namık Kemal voiced this complaint in the *Hürriyet*: "In fact, if a candidate to the diploma, having given himself to study for fifteen to twenty years, and having waited endlessly for the announcement of a *ru'us* examination—which like comets appear only every fifteen years—is faced with the sight of a diploma hanging on the neck of the new born son of so and so, and if ignoramuses and scum who could not even qualify as his pupils obtain titles and offices—all this while he is plunged in poverty and misery—why should he thereafter take the pains to increase his knowledge?"[53]

[51] Ali Suavi, "Mevt ül-Ulema," *Muhbir*, January 10, 1868, p. 4.
[52] Millingen, *La Turquie*, p. 257; cf. Jorga, *Geschichte*, v, 565.
[53] Namık Kemal, "Devlet-i Aliyeye bais-i tenezzül olan maarifin esbab-ı

Those who suffered most from this combination of circumstances were the lesser ulema, from whose rank came both the Young Ottoman *âlim* Ali Suavi and such sympathizers as Hoca Tahsin, Sarıyerli Sadık Efendi, and Veliyüddin Efendi. This also explains why Mehmed Bey found that to don the outfit of an *âlim* and try to create a stir among the "mosque ministers," the lower ulema, was a most effective technique of propaganda. On the other hand, ulema who were able to gear themselves to the new system kept outside the circle of political critics. Thus Cevdet Paşa, who at an early age had begun to work directly under Reşid Paşa, was not a protester, although he shared the Young Ottoman's misgivings about the fate of the doctors of Islamic law. At a more modest level an example of integration is provided by the *âlim* Süleymaniyeli Kâmil Efendi, who was the tutor and companion of Mehmed Bey while the latter was studying at the Ottoman School in Paris. Kâmil Efendi studied law in Paris and on his return found employment in the Imperial Customs, where he remained until his death in 1905.[54]

Finally, there were at least three reasons for which the Young Ottomans could find allies among the military: First, the demands of the military for efficiency in carrying out reforms, as analyzed in Chapter v. Secondly, the army was not anchored down by tradition or vested interests, since it had been created anew after the destruction of the Janissaries. The young men of the 1850's who became the leaders of the 1870's were outsiders to the existing Ottoman "establishment." This was the result of a deliberate policy of cutting off the new army from any traditionalistic roots. Other characteristics of the new army, such as low social status, worked in the same direction. A British student of Turkish life in the first half of the nineteenth century spoke, for example, of the college of military surgeons as "all . . . taken from the very poor classes: I was

---

tedennisi," *Hürriyet*, August 3, 1868, p. 2. Also, "Türkistanın esbab-ı tedennisi," *Hürriyet*, July 27, 1868, p. 2.

[54] İnal, *Son Asır*, p. 942, note 3.

told that the Turks were one and all of the lowest grade, the sons of boatmen, horse-keepers, petty dealers, bazaar porters and the like, and that no Turk of the high or even middle class ever sent his son to the College."[55] The third factor was that the hegemony of the bureaucrats had been achieved at the expense of the military, who had been pushed into the background after 1826. A most striking and accurate description of this process has been given by Franz von Werner, a diplomat accredited to the Porte at the time: "The era between the introduction of reforms and the death of Âli Paşa marks the high point of its [i.e., the bureaucracy's] influence. In fact after the destruction of the Janissary corps it was a part of the internal policy of the Ottoman power-wielders to equate the military spirit with a survival of Janissary defiance and so the army was forced into the shadow by the bureaucracy. In opposition to the fundamental theocratic-military principles regulating the Ottoman world the Efendi gained precedence over the Bey, the bureau over the military camp. The increased transactions with the Great Powers and the higher significance of the latter made the Cabinet of the Minister of Foreign Affairs the center of gravity of the administration. . . . Whereupon came into being an almost omnipotent Patriciate of the Pen."[56]

The sociological forces which drove the Young Ottomans to action may thus be said to be twofold: On one hand the increment of the process of disintegration was the transmission to the Turkey of the Tanzimat of what corruption had crept into the Ottoman administration by the end of the eighteenth century. But only when this was compounded by an unsettling of the economy of the Ottoman Empire as well as by a

[55] Charles MacFarlane, *Turkey and its Destiny* (London, John Murray, 1850), II, 266.

[56] Murad Efendi, *Türkische Skizzen*, p. 65. Millingen states with regard to the Army: "Ils la surveillent sans cesse d'une manière toute spéciale; un kiatib choisi parmi eux avec le titre de conseiller, siège constamment à côté du ministre de la guerre, du ministre de la marine et des commandants des armées." Millingen, *La Turquie*, p. 255.

stopping in the circulation of elites and the emergence of a new "patriciate" did the movement of protest crystallize. In this chapter we have examined that aspect of the Young Ottoman movement which was concerned with the emergence of a new elite; toward the end of the next chapter we shall try to examine how the commercial policies of the Tanzimat created the basis of social and economic disorganization which made some of them, such as Ziya Paşa and Ali Suavi, feel even more bitter toward the Porte than Namık Kemal.

·:9 CHAPTER V 6:·

The Young Ottomans and the Ottoman Past

THE Young Ottomans considered themselves reformers whose
task it was to arrest the process of Ottoman decline. To find
political remedies that would eradicate the causes of this decline they took up the study of the Ottoman past and made
ample use of historical situations to build up their arguments.
Together with *interest* in the past, however, came *involvement*
with it, for the Young Ottomans were quite enmeshed in what
they were studying, in the sense that they cherished certain
values which they associated with the Ottoman way of life.
Their historical reconstructions were therefore seldom completely accurate. Nevertheless, many of their arguments with
regard to the process of Ottoman decay, if somewhat biased,
were not fundamentally incorrect. One such belief, for example, was that when the Janissaries were annihilated in 1826
no constituted social corps was left in the body politic to
counterbalance the power and the influence of the bureaucrats
of the Porte.[1]

The Young Ottomans also held that the Janissaries had for
a long time satisfactorily performed the function of expressing
popular grievances. Similar conceptions of the Janissaries as
having provided a safety valve are encountered in the writings
of more than one student of Turkish reforms.[2] The amount
of truth this theory contains must be properly assessed if we
are to understand why the Young Ottomans gave it such importance. Once this is done, Young Ottoman theories become
understandable, and considerable light is shed on the reasons
for which they relied on what might strike us as rather unusual
interpretations of Ottoman history.

Just as they thought highly of the Janissaries, the Young

[1] Namık Kemal, "Hubb ul-Watan min al-imān," *Hürriyet*, June 29,
1868, p. 1. Ali Suavi, "La Verité," *Muhbir*, November 7, 1867, p. 1.
[2] See below, footnote 111.

Ottomans praised such Ottoman governmental practices as that of consulting with eminent men before taking important political decisions (*"usul-ü meşveret"*). This method, they stated, was a Turkish forerunner of European parliamentary practice which had developed independent of European advances and prepared Ottomans for parliamentary rule.[3] They also claimed that, instead of taking advantage of this background, the statesmen of their time had stifled these institutions. Here again the convictions of the Young Ottomans have to be placed in the context of Ottoman development to appreciate the extent to which they were correct in their assessment, the extent to which, although mistaken, they still sincerely believed these practices to have existed, and the extent to which they were falling back on Ottoman customs to disguise the new political conceptions they wanted to introduce under the cloak of accepted usage.

Finally, although they respected the architect of the Tanzimat, Mustafa Reşid Paşa, for his accomplishments, the Young Ottomans felt quite uneasy about the direction which the reforms of the Tanzimat had taken since his death and found the seeds of these displeasing developments in the fundamental attitude assumed by Reşid Paşa toward reforms. Here again the issue has to be placed in the context of actual developments. All three of these Young Ottoman beliefs that need to be clarified have to do with the dynamic of the Ottoman reform movement, and a survey of Turkish modernization in the eighteenth and nineteenth centuries is necessary before we can take up the Young Ottoman ideas for analysis.

I. Ottoman Reforms to 1829

At the core of the process of Ottoman modernization lay a problem of military policy: continued military defeats and losses of territory stimulated the Ottomans to look for the

---

[3] Namık Kemal. See the series known as "Usul-ü meşveret," *Hürriyet*, September 14, 1868, p. 5; September 21, 1868, p. 6; September 29, 1868, p. 5; October 12, 1868, p. 7; October 19, 1868, p. 6.

factors underlying Western military superiority. As early as the seventeenth century Ottoman statesmen had become aware that the administration of the empire left a great deal to be desired.[4]

Nevertheless, it is only in the eighteenth century and in relation to military reform that the connection was established once and for all between *reform* and *Europeanization*. Two ensuing aspects of the attempts to modernize the Ottoman Empire should be kept in mind.

First, the shock experienced by the Ottomans when they realized the empire was declining, and especially the trauma caused by the continuous reverses which they suffered in the late eighteenth century, was a very severe and painful one. This was so because the ideology of conquest was part of a religious belief—the belief in war as a means of propagating Islam; because, in addition, territorial expansion had played such an important part in the founding of the Ottoman Empire; finally, because losses of territory meant losses of revenue at a time when Ottoman statesmen were also highly concerned with the process of economic decline and fiscal inefficiency. The horrified realization of Ottoman regression constituted the motive force behind all Ottoman reform movements and eventually provided the impetus that drove the Young Ottomans to act.

Concurrently with the bitter realization of Western superiority, the conviction began to take shape progressively that it was necessary to abandon the earlier conception of reform as a reaffirmation and reinstatement of the earliest and "purest" Ottoman practices. Nobody was quite sure as to when the Ottoman government had functioned in its "pure" state, but it certainly was an ideal that reformists kept in their minds for a long time. Even after the first quarter of the nineteenth

---

[4] For the attempted reforms of Osman II (1618-1622), Hammer, *Histoire de l'Empire Ottoman*, VIII, 302-303; for later developments [Koçu Bey], "Kogábeg's Abhandlungen über den Verfall des Osmanischen Staatsgebaudes seit Sultan Suleiman dem Grossen" (trans. by W. F. A. Bernhauer), XV, 272-332, ZDMG (1861).

century, when it was no longer possible to press very convincingly for a return to the ideal of old Ottoman order, the idea did not lose its attractiveness and also found echoes among the Young Ottomans.

Because modernization meant changes in the practices of the Ottoman state and because it involved the relinquishment of the idealized picture of these practices, it was a process full of protests, reappraisals, convulsions, and revolutions. Not the least of the influences that made this historical evolution such a trying one was a struggle for power hidden behind it. In this struggle the Ottoman bureaucracy, which supported first indigenous and then Western-oriented reform, was pitted against other influence groups in the empire, i.e., the Janissaries, the ulema, and eventually the sultan himself. This last stage occurred in the years immediately preceding the formation of the Young Ottoman movement.

The story of this struggle has not, as yet, been told. There is no thorough study of the rise of Turkish bureaucracy in the eighteenth century, nor is there a study of the continuity between the bureaucracy of the eighteenth century and that of the Tanzimat. A brief survey of the earliest systematic attempts at reform does enable us, however, to trace a pattern of alignments which are repeated in every movement of this type up to the destruction of the Janissaries. This pattern lingers on into the nineteenth century and reappears in a subdued and modified form in the years immediately preceding the formation of the Patriotic Alliance.[5]

The reform movement of which we shall attempt a schematic case study is that of Nevşehirli İbrahim Paşa, an Ottoman grand vizier who was in power in the last years of the reign of Ahmed III (1703-1730).

The fact that İbrahim Paşa had a hand in carrying out the first military reforms of the Ottoman Empire is not generally

[5] The plot of the military and the ulema to unseat Reşid Paşa in August 1840, the anti-Western agitation preceding the outbreak of the Crimean War, and the so-called "Kuleli" coup of 1859 are examples of this continuity.

known. Yet it was during his grand vizierate that one of the first-known documents elaborating the reasons for Western superiority, couched in the form of a dialogue between a foreign officer and a Turk, was presented to the sultan.[6] It was during his vizierate too that the first proposals to modify Ottoman military practice in accordance with Western European methods of training and warfare were made by the French Huguenot Rochefort. The adoption of this plan was seriously considered by İbrahim Paşa.[7]

Rochefort's proposals were being made at a time when İbrahim Paşa was encouraging other contacts with the West. In 1720 he advised Sultan Ahmed III to send an envoy to France. An Ottoman dignitary was thereupon dispatched to Versailles. This plenipotentiary, Yirmi Sekiz Mehmed Çelebi by name (Mehmed Çelebi "the 28th" is the nearest English equivalent), was instructed by the vizier to study French "methods of government and education and report on those that would be applicable to the Ottoman Empire."[8]

One of the results of Yirmi Sekiz Mehmed Çelebi's mission to France was the institution by his son, Yirmi Sekiz Çelebi Mehmed Efendi Zâde Said Ağa (later Efendi), of the first Ottoman printing press in 1726,[9] with the collaboration of the Hungarian convert Ibrahim Müteferrika.

The firman in which permission was granted to establish

[6] Faik Reşit Unat, "Ahmet III devrine ait bir Islahat Takriri," *Tarih Vesikaları* (1941), I, 107-121.

[7] These proposals are described in the letter of an informant in the pay of the Austrian internuncio at the Porte. See Hammer, *Histoire de l'Empire Ottoman*, xv, 348-356. Rochefort's proposals were threefold, first a group of Huguenots were to be given asylum by the Porte and settled in Moldavia and Walachia. These settlers would then introduce into the Ottoman Empire "arts, sciences and manufactures" (Hammer, xv, 351), thus obviating the need for Ottomans to buy textiles and silk materials in Europe. Finally a corps of engineers would have been created who would have staffed a school for training Ottoman engineers. The French ambassador successfully blocked the adoption of Rochefort's plans.

[8] Enver Ziya Karal, *Osmanlı Tarihi*, v: *Nizam-ı Cedit ve Tanzimat Devirleri 1789-1856* (Ankara, Türk Tarih Kurumu Basımevi, 1947), p. 58.

[9] Selim Nüzhet [Gerçek], *Türk Matbaacılığı* (Istanbul: Ebüzziya, 1928), p. 40. Comments by Gibb and Bowen, *Islamic Society*, I, 2, 153-154, are misleading.

this press specifically granted permission to print books on "history, medicine, philosophical sciences, astronomy and geography."[10] In 1727-1728 (1140 A.H.) military training on new European lines was begun and the regulations pertaining to it were written by Müteferrika.[11]

At the time, the relations between Turkish court circles and the Court of Versailles were quite cordial and did not consist only of official contacts. During İbrahim Paşa's vizierate it became fashionable in the Ottoman capital to copy European manners. Even the European tulip craze spread to Istanbul, and therefore the reign of Ahmed III has been known by Turks as the "Era of Tulips." This is how a Turkish historian has described the period: "In the Era of Tulips an extraordinary closeness was established between the Turks and Westerners and especially between the Turks and the French. Envoys who were sent to Paris and Vienna, thanks to the incisive mind of Ibrahim Paşa and owing to political necessity, attempted to herald the achievements of European civilization once they had returned to their country. This is why the Era of Tulips became a brilliant era of awakening for the Turks. This was the first stage of the appearance of European civilization in the East."[12]

Yet even in those times there was evidence that Westernization would encounter strong resistance in Turkey. Yirmi Sekiz Çelebi did not like to display his knowledge of French, many precautions had to be taken to make the establishment of the printing press appear to be a new method to facilitate the training of doctors of Islamic law, and Ahmed III was obliged to abdicate as the result of a revolt of Janissaries, while his

[10] A. Refik, *Hicrî On Ikinci Asırda İstanbul Hayatı (1100-1200)* (Istanbul, Devlet Matbaası, 1930), pp. 90, 91, has the text of this firman.

[11] Mehmed Esad, *Mir'at-ı Mühendishane-i Berri-i Hümâyun* (Istanbul, Karabet, 1316/1898-1899), pp. 5, 6.

[12] Ahmet Refik, *Lâle Devri* (5th ed., Istanbul, Hilmi Kitaphanesi, 1932), p. 199; see also Albert Vandal, *Une Ambassade Française en Orient sous Louis XV, la Mission du Marquis de Villeneuve 1728-1741* (2nd ed., Paris, Plon, 1887).

Westernizing vizier was executed and his body paraded through town.

In this case the primary antireformist impetus came from Janissaries who were feeling, in terms of irregular pay, the effects of the general economic decline of the country. Allied with the Janissaries were the poorer classes of the capital. In revolting, the Janissaries expressed social grievances but also their disgust with the luxurious life led by Ottoman officials and specially with the Western forms that this luxury had taken. The common people of the capital did not see any connection between the appreciation of tulips and the answering of their daily problems.

What is significant here is that the original modernizing impetus which led to the revolt came from the grand vizier. Later developments were to show that this was no coincidence. Indeed, a gradual transformation seems to have occurred in the Ottoman Empire beginning with the eighteenth century which placed the grand viziers and the higher bureaucrats of the empire in the position of reformists. Since the reign of Murad III (1575-1595) "the Sultan as an actual governing power had passed from the scene,"[13] and the conduct of the affairs of the state had been concentrated into the hands of the grand vizier and indirectly into those of his adjuncts, the Secretary for Foreign Affairs ("*Reis ül-Küttab*"), the Secretary of the Interior ("*Kâhya bey*"), the Undersecretaries of State ("*Tezkereci*," "*Mektubcu*," "*Kâhya Kâtibi*," "*Beylikçi*," "*Âmedi*"), and a variable number of chanceries which grew to twenty-four at the beginning of the nineteenth century. Of these, the Secretaryship of Foreign Affairs, the Secretaryship of the Interior, and the Undersecretaryships of State made up an executive complex under the direction of the Grand Vizier which is usually referred to as the Porte.[14]

Concurrently with the increased importance assumed by the Porte, the "men of the pen" ("*ehl-i kalem*"), or bureau-

[13] *Ottoman Statecraft*, p. 32.
[14] Gibb and Bowen, *Islamic Society*, I, 113, 117-127.

crats of all ranks employed at the Porte, rose in status. In earlier times the term "men of the pen" had been used to refer to learned men in general and under this title were included both doctors of Islamic law and heads of chanceries and their staffs.[15] Later, however, the term began to denote only the Ottoman secular bureaucracy[16] who now took over state functions which the ulema no longer satisfactorily performed. The reason given by the historian Cevdet Paşa for the increasing influence wielded by the "men of the pen" is that the knowledge of governmental affairs became limited to this group.[17] At the same time, the doctors of Islamic law lost their standing as men learned in the affairs of the state. This, in turn, seems to have been due to two factors: first, a command over facts and figures became increasingly important in the conduct of the affairs of the state; secondly, as the constitutional law of the empire became more complex from the rapid multiplication of edicts and as its foreign relations became more vital, bureaucrats with a knowledge of the latest developments acquired an advantage over the ulema. An

[15] For the origins of this term see Joseph von Hammer-Purgstall, *Des Osmanischen Reichs Staatsverfassung und Staatsverwaltung* (Vienna, Camesinaschen Buchhandlung, 1815), p. 110 ff; Mouradjea d'Ohsson, *Tableau Général de l'Empire Ottoman* (Paris, 1788-1824), VII, 191-196; Ismail Hakkı Uzunçarşılı *Osmanlı Imparatorluğunda Merkez ve Bahriye Teşkilâtı* (Ankara, Türk Tarih Kurumu Basımevi, 1948), pp. 39-110, 360, 361; Gibb and Bowen, *Islamic Society*, I, 1, p. 127. See also "Principes de Sagesse touchant l'art de gouverner: Usul al-Hikam fi nizam al-Alam Par Rizwan-ben-abd'oul-mannan-Ac-hissari," trans. by Garcin de Tassy, *Journal Asiatique* (April 1824), IV, 217. For earlier statements confirming the above see Yaltkaya, "İlhanlılar Devri İdarî Teşkilâtına Dair," p. 10, where the ulema are enumerated first among the "people of the pen"; see also W. F. A. Bernhauer, "Hâg'î Chalfa's Dustûru'l-'amel: ein Beitrag zur Osmanischen Finanzgeschichte," *ZDMG* (1857), XI, 120, in which the ulema are still considered the repositories of all types of sciences both religious and secular; also Gibb and Bowen, *Islamic Society*, I, 1, 45.

[16] Hammer, *Histoire*, XVII, 39 f. Hammer was describing the situation at the end of the eighteenth century, but a subtle change may already be discerned in a text of the beginning of the eighteenth century where reference is had to *aklam* (i.e., bureau) rather than *ehl-i kalem*. See *Ottoman Statecraft*, pp. 94, 96. In the same work the proliferation of bureaucratic offices also comes out. See *ibid.*, p. 95, Gibb and Bowen, *Islamic Society*, I, 1, p. 127.

[17] Cevdet, *Tarih*, V, 107 f.

interesting example of the prestige that accrued to the bureaucrats as repositories of skills of communication—as opposed
to those of interpretation vested in the ulema—is reported by
Hammer in connection with the nomination of the historian
Vasıf to head one of the chanceries of the Porte: "Lorsqu'il
arriva de Rousdjouk à Schumma, Wassif Efendi, depuis peu
de retour de sa captivité vint lui offrir ses homages, Mouhsin-
zâde [the Grand Vizier Muhsinzâde] qui le connaissait pour
réunir à une haute capacité un style facile et élégant, l'éleva
à la dignité de khodja [executive member of any chancery]
du diwan imperial. En lui rendant son brevet, il ne lui dit
pas suivant l'usage, 'Tu es nommé khodja,' c'est à dire seigneur
du diwan, mais seulement, 'Nous t'avons nommé écrivain,'
indiquant ainsi que dans l'origine, les seigneurs du diwan
n'étaient autre chose que des écrivains experts à manier la
plume."[18]

The somewhat distorted fashion in which this development
was reported in Young Ottoman writings was that they attributed the ineffectiveness and ignorance of the ulema of their
time to the fact that, beginning with Ahmed III, religious
sciences were neglected while "poetry" and secular pursuits
in general were given greater importance.[19]

There were also other related factors which made for the
rise of bureaucrats. First, there had been a polarization in the
corps of the ulema which resulted in the estrangement from
each other of "lower" and "higher" ulema,[20] with the first
remaining in contact with the people and assuming the functions of "leaders of prayers,"[21] while the second ensconced
themselves in higher governmental positions such as lucrative

---

[18] Hammer, *Histoire*, XVI, 305. The title of *Hoca*, or *Hâce* (spelled
"*hodja*" by Hammer), carried the connotation of being one of the ulema.
Hammer, *op.cit.*, XVII, 198, 199.

[19] Namık Kemal, "Devlet-i Aliyyeye Bais-i Tenezzül Olan Maarifin
Esbab-ı Tedennisi," *Hürriyet*, August 3, 1868, p. 2.

[20] Cevdet Paşa, *Tarih*, V, 107.

[21] Gibb and Bowen, *Islamic Society*, I, 2; 95, uses the term "mosque
ministers."

judgeships which they farmed out to others. There was considerable bad feeling between these two groups.[22]

The higher ulema had become completely corrupt and ignorant, even in matters of religion. Yet the lower ulema still had considerable prestige among the people, while the higher ulema occupied, as judicial officers, governmental positions that by themselves carried great weight.

What happened in a movement of modernization such as that carried out by İbrahim Paşa was that the lower ulema immediately aligned themselves with the Janissaries and the populace, while the higher ulema, at first neutral, seem to have joined the revolt only when they realized it would be successful. Thus in the outburst of 1730 the "leaders of prayer" played a prominent role.[23] In the nineteenth century the clerical allies of the Young Ottomans were to consist of such lower ulema, prayer leaders, and preachers.

A final point of interest with regard to Turkish reform of the type first carried out in Damad İbrahim Paşa's time is its ultimate continuity despite momentary setbacks. It is only the assumption of an unabated interest in the highest governmental circles for à la franga reform that can explain the continuity of the Ottoman policy of periodically dispatching envoys to Europe with specific instructions to report the latest European developments on all levels—governmental, social, economic, and in respect to arts and crafts.[24] Between 1720 and 1838 exactly *forty* such reports on the state of European affairs and advances were presented to the Porte, notwithstanding the many antireformist outbursts that occurred in the same period. The latest in this series of reports—the one by Sadık Rifat Paşa (1838)—will be shown[25] to contain the theory of the Tanzimat reforms.[26] It is also interesting to notice in this

[22] Cevdet Paşa, *Tarih*, v, 107.

[23] Hammer, *Histoire*, XIV, 238.

[24] For a late prototype of such instructions, see Karal, *Selim III* (1946), pp. 198-202.

[25] See below, Chapter VI.

[26] For a list of these reports see Faik Reşit Unat, "Şehdi Osman Efendi Sefaretnamesi," *Tarih Vesikaları* (June 1941), I, 67-69.

connection that all great Turkish reformers between 1720 and 1839 held at one time the post of Secretary for Foreign Affairs (*"Reis ül-Küttab"*).

Military reforms had their ups and downs in the years following the revolt of 1730, but what is remarkable here too is that the thread of Westernization was picked up within two years of the uprising. In 1732 the Marquis de Bonneval was entrusted with the formation of an artillery corps and for a long time played an important part as a counselor on foreign affairs to the Porte.[27]

The same year there was published the first Turkish book taking up systematically the analysis of Western superiority— Ibrahim Müteferrika's *Usul ül-hikem fı nizam ül-ümem.*[28] This was also the first work which contained information on European governments—the earliest hint that something might be learned from the West in this respect.

In 1734 on the advice of Bonneval a school of mathematics (*"Hendesehane"*) was opened in the capital to train military engineers. Later this school was disbanded, but in 1759 the students who had been instructed at the then-defunct school were brought together again by Grand Vizier Ragıb Paşa, who tried to keep the school out of the limelight so that the experiment might succeed.[29] During his grand vizierate Ragıb Paşa also drafted the son-in-law of the French ambassador to the Porte, the Baron de Tott, to carry out some of his public works.

While Ragıb Paşa's efforts to revive the engineering school seem not to have borne any fruit, the training of troops on the European model was again taken up by Grand Vizier Muhsinzâde in 1773. This time a corps of Turkish light artillery was finally established (1774) with de Tott's cooperation.[30] Once more these attempts slackened when de Tott left in 1776,[31] but here again the thread was picked up by Grand

[27] Hammer, *Histoire*, XIV, 268.
[28] Selim Nüzhet, *Türk Matbaacılığı*, pp. 62, 63.
[29] Mehmed Esad, *Mir'at-ı Mühendishane*, p. 7.
[30] Hammer, *Histoire*, XVI, 378.
[31] Karal, *Osmanlı Tarihi*, V, 61.

Vizier Halil Hâmid Paşa (1782-1785) (who also rose to the grand vizierate from the bureaus of the Porte and the Ministry of Foreign Affairs).[32]

Halil Hâmid Paşa reinstated the engineering school (1784) and relied on Prussian as well as French advisors to set up plans for reorganizing the military. Thus he laid the groundwork for the reforms of Selim III (1789-1807). Halil Hâmid Paşa's work came to an end when he was destituted and executed in the wake of his attempt to bring Selim III to the throne. In this case again only a short time elapsed before the reforming activities were once more undertaken under the aegis of Sultan Selim.

Selim is usually considered the most important reformer of the eighteenth century, but this was so in great part because he took advantage of the groundwork laid by earlier viziers. While still heir to the throne, Selim had begun a correspondence with Louis XVI with regard to the type of reform that would be most suitable for Turkey.[33] He also secretly sent a personal envoy to the French court. It appears from this correspondence that here again the organizing force which channeled Selim's good intentions was the mentorship of Ebubekir Ratib Efendi, who was Undersecretary of State for Foreign Affairs at the time he began working with Selim. The earliest theory of reform that appears in the memoranda of Ebubekir Ratib to Selim is that of a recasting of Ottoman military practices. Ebubekir Ratib Efendi stated it as "reform in consonance with the practice of my ancestors." In 1791, however, after a mission to Vienna during which he investigated the Austrian army and administration, Ratib Efendi changed his opinion and came out for the adoption by the Ottoman Empire of the most important European military techniques.[34]

[32] Ismail Hakkı Uzunçarşılı "Sadrazam [sic] Halil Hâmid Paşa," *Türkiyat Mecmuası* (1936), V, 226, 233.

[33] Ismail Hakkı Uzuncarşılıoğlu, "Selim III' ün Veliaht iken Fransa Kıralı Lui XVI ile Muhabereleri," *Belleten* (April 1938), II, 191-246.

[34] Karal, *Selim III* (1946), p. 40.

A year later, in 1792, Selim III asked state officials to report to him on the state of the Ottoman Empire and to suggest measures for reform. Twenty-two statesmen handed in projects for military and, to a much smaller extent, financial and administrative reorganization; among these men were an adviser to the Ottoman army by the name of Bertrand and the Chevalier d'Ohsson, a local Christian attached to the Swedish embassy. On this occasion, again, it was the *Reis ül-Küttab* Raşid Efendi who drafted the most radical Turkish proposal for the reform of the army.[35]

Beginning with the appointment of Ratib Efendi to the post of Secretary for Foreign Affairs (May 1795), foreign military specialists were called in in great numbers and new military formations[36] on the European model (*"Nizam-ı Cedid"*) were established.[37] Administrative reorganization did not go beyond measures to better the system of taxation. But at least one treatise describing these attempts was published in French to advertise to the world the changes brought about during Selim's reign.[38]

Selim was deposed (1807) by substantially the same type of cabal that had caused the uprising of 1730 and was succeeded by the reactionaries' choice, his brother Mustafa IV. Hardly had a year gone by when a group of heads of chanceries led by the Minister of Foreign Affairs were able to escape from Janissary field headquarters[39] and find asylum in the army of the commanding general of the Danube province, Bayraktar or Alemdar Mustafa Paşa. These officials, known in Turkish history by the name of Rusçuk Yârânı

[35] *Ibid.*; Karal, "Nizam-ı Cedide Dair Lâyihalar," *Tarih Vesikaları* (1941), I, 414-425; (1942), II, 104-111, 342-351, 424-432.

[36] Karal, *Selim III* (1946), p. 73.

[37] Franz Babinger, "Nizam-ı Djedid," *Encyclopedia of Islam*, III, 936; Karal, *Selim III*, throughout. The term *"Nizam-ı Cedid"* ("new order") had been used as early as 1696 by Grand Vizier Köprülü Fazıl Mustafa Paşa to characterize his attempted administrative reforms. Ali Suavi considered the latter the first young Ottoman; see Ali Suavi, *Ulûm* (1870), p. 789.

[38] See Mahmoud Rayf [sic] Efendi, *Tableau des Nouveaux Règlements de l'Empire Ottoman* (Constantinople, Nouvelle Imprimerie du Génie, 1798).

[39] Cevdet, *Tarih*, VIII, 213.

("the comrades of Rusçuk") were able to organize a counter-revolution, depose Mustafa IV, and bring to the throne Mahmud, a nephew of Selim. (Selim himself had perished in the counteruprising.[40])

Although Bayraktar was given the grand vizierate because he held the military power, the Rusçuk Yârânı took the administration of the state into their hands. Bayraktar himself acknowledged that he was a military figurehead used by the bureaucrats to get power.[41]

As soon as they regained power, the conspirators quickly disposed of their ulema enemies, plus at least one higher bureaucrat who had cooperated with Mustafa IV. This they did with the specific intent of disguising the real nature of the liquidation they were conducting.[42]

Again within a year the reactivation of the program of training for new military formations on the European model led to another revolt of Janissaries and the suicide of Bayraktar Mustafa Paşa. The tragic circumstances under which the reigning Mahmud II had been brought to the throne led him to act with great caution under the circumstances, and while he gave in to the Janissaries at the time and fell under the influence of antireformist elements for a while, he eventually became convinced that the Janissary formations should be abolished. This was carried out in 1826; the Janissaries having attempted to revolt again were given no quarter and were almost exterminated. What remained of the corps was scattered in the provinces. It became a criminal offense to pronounce the name Janissary and the religious order of Bektaşi associated with the Janissaries was also banned.

With the elimination of the Janissaries, the first stage of Turkish modernization, which was primarily, although not

[40] Karal, *Osmanlı Tarihi*, v, pp. 91-93.
[41] Ismail Hakkı Uzunçarşılı, *Meşhur Rumeli Ayanlarından Tirsinikli Ismail, Yıllık Oğlu Süleyman Ağalar ve Alemdar Mustafa Paşa* (Istanbul, Maarif Matbaası, 1942), pp. 148, 149.
[42] Tahsin Öz, "Selim III, Mustafa IV ve Mahmut II zamanlarına ait birkaç vesika," *Tarih Vesikaları* (June 1941), I, 21.

exclusively, a matter of military reforms, came to an end. Increasingly, thereafter, Turkish reformist activities have to do with the streamlining of Ottoman government.[43]

Yet again, a link exists between the era of Selim and the reforms of Mahmud, in that both sultans were relying on the same group of bureaucrats to carry out reforms. Another link between the reigns of Selim and Mahmud was evidenced in that both sultans showed a strong desire to eliminate whatever disorder and anarchy had crept into the administration of the empire—a wish which quite naturally took the form of a desire to breathe a new fire into the monarchical institution. Selim was not, as he is often made to appear, a man of mild disposition, but was an ambitious prince who was impatient to step into the place of his brother, Abdülhamid; he engaged in conspiracies to this end while he was heir apparent. He was also a strong-willed monarch who did not spare the threats that he would condemn his own son to death were he to fail in carrying out his orders.[44]

But what had been a quality which the bureaucrats of the Porte welcomed in Selim was transmitted to his nephew Mahmud as a desire to reestablish at all costs the hegemony of the sultan. Mahmud eventually antagonized the statesmen on whose cooperation he depended because he tried to impose his own will in all important policy decisions. We shall see later how the increasing dependence of the state on bureaucrats, combined with the sultan's own capriciousness, hastened the process by which the higher employees of the Ottoman state were progressively taking over the elaboration of policy. The beginning of the reign of Mahmud, however, was an era of cooperation between the sultan and the bureaucrats who had brought Mahmud to the throne. The first fruits of this

[43] Many Ottomans, however, were not quite able to undertake the mental leap from military to governmental reform. Typical in this respect is the attitude of Husrev Paşa, who carried through Mahmud's military reforms but who could not become reconciled to further reforms.

[44] Karal, *Selim III* (1946), p. 115, quoting Cevdet Paşa, *Tarih*, IV, 291. Many of the imperial firmans (edicts) in Karal's work bear out this attitude.

cooperation was the signature of the *Sened-i Ittifak* or Pledge of Agreement (or Alliance). This document was aimed at curbing the powers of the local dynasties, or *Âyan*, and the entire transaction was directed by the officials who had organized Alemdar's counterrevolt and now were in control of the state.[45] The *Sened-i Ittifak*, far from being a Magna Carta, was one of the first steps toward the transformation of the Ottoman Empire into a modern centralized state.[46]

In the early years of his reign Mahmud, who was just as interested in regaining his empire as his bureaucrats were in streamlining it, successfully engaged in other consolidating activities. He recovered taxes which were no longer being collected from local administrators because of the weakness of the metropolis; regained control over the hereditary *paşalıks* of Trabzon, Erzurum, and Van; broke the power of the Karamanian dynasty; reduced various local feudal lords in Anatolia and Rumelia; restored his authority over Izmir, Sakız, Chios, the Dardanelles, Cyprus, Morea, and Vidin; and reasserted his authority over the undisciplined Janissaries of Salonika.[47]

These drives to regain control over the empire required a hand of iron, which the sultan happened to have, but which did not always endear him to his subjects. In the case of the suppression of the *Âyans*, for example, a contemporary witness stated: "Simultaneously with the deliberate and cautious undermining of the Janissary power, means equally specious . . . were employed to restrict or destroy the power of distant pashas, and of the âyans. . . . The exposure of these operations of years would present a piece of almost unparalleled craft and cruelty; but they were successful, and the

[45] Uzunçarşılı, *Alemdar Mustafa Paşa*, pp. 138, 140.

[46] Although the document itself amounted to a recognition of the independence of *Âyans* insofar as it did rely on their assistance, the historian Cevdet Paşa quite clearly indicates that this was a temporary compromise due to the weakness of the central powers. Cevdet, *Tarih*, IX, 6, 278-280.

[47] Howard A. Reed, "The Destruction of the Janissaries by Mahmud II in June 1826," unpublished Ph.D. dissertation, Princeton, 1951, pp. 21-24.

losses of the inhabitants of remote provinces who had been happy and prosperous in proportion to the stability and independence of their local governors, . . . did not interfere with the satisfaction of Mahmood, or the plans of his counsellor, who, from the course of his study and associations, had been led to consider the government of France, where the destruction of the ancient nobility, and the drunken liberty of the people, had paved the way to a military despotism—the unchecked will of one—as the most perfect government of Europe. . . ."[48]

A theoretical counterpart of these attempts of the sultan to pull his empire together was the active fostering of the idea of complete obeisance to the sultan. Mahmud ordered his *Şeyhülislâm* to write a book in which the theory of imperial fiat would be stated uncompromisingly. The result was a collection of twenty-five traditions of the Prophet with regard to the absolute necessity to obey rulers. This constitutes Mahmud's contribution to political philosophy.[49]

A key date with regard to the sultan's attitude seems to have been that of the unsuccessful Russian war of 1828, in which the sultan engaged despite the advice of some of his statesmen. It was only then that Mahmud realized that military reforms in the empire were not sufficient and that reestablishing "normalcy" was also inadequate. It is at this time that the beginning of serious structural reforms in the state may be observed.

II. Governmental Reform in Mahmud's Time

The first move that the sultan undertook was to eliminate a number of palace offices, both to cut expenses and because they no longer had any use.[50]

[48] MacFarlane, *Constantinople in 1828*, II, 110. See Davison, "Reform," pp. 185-186, for favorable comments on the *derebey* system.

[49] Yasincizâde Abdülvehhab, *Hulāsat el-burhān fī 'ita'at el-Sultan* (Istanbul, 1247/1831); also, Engelhardt, *La Turquie et le Tanzimat*, I, 17.

[50] A complete description of these moves is given in Hammer, *Histoire*, XVII, 191-192.

The sultan was careful not to antagonize the ulema by directly challenging them or changing their status.[51] At one time, in the 1830's, an attempt was made to downgrade them in the protocol of the state, but ulema displeasure caused the rule to be rescinded.[52]

What was done, however, was to grant more extensive privileges to the employees of the Porte. Thus the rise to power of the bureaucracy was accelerated.

Immediately following the abolition of the Janissary order, a uniform was set for the employees of the Porte.[53] In 1832 offices of the state were reorganized to fit four principal categories.[54] On the same date government by fiat came to an end, i.e., the imperial practice of embodying unilateral policy decisions in *hatts* drafted by the sultan himself was discontinued.[55] State functionaries who had rendered outstanding services were granted a decoration, the *Nişan-ı İftihar*, and it was made hereditary.[56]

Offices staffed by state functionaries increased, while the number of positions filled by the ulema remained constant or even declined.[57] This latter situation arose whenever one of the departments under the jurisdiction of the *Şeyhülislâm* was amalgamated into a department of the Porte,[58] as new ministers were established whose duties encroached on the functions performed by the ulema,[59] or as a result of placing under the supervision of the state sources of income which formerly had been at the disposal of the ulema.[60]

The position of the employees of the Porte was reinforced by the elimination of the system under which appointments

[51] Hammer, *Histoire*, XVII, 180.
[52] See Lûtfi, *Tarih*, v, 25 (1251/1835-1836).
[53] *Ibid.*, III, 148 (1245/1829-1830).
[54] *Ibid.*, IV, 114 (1248).
[55] See İ. H. Uzunçarşılı, "Hatt-ı Humâyûn," *Islâm Ansiklopedisi* (1950), v, 374.
[56] Lûtfi, *Tarih*, IV, 140.
[57] *Ibid.*, 126. For trends in the year 1839, see p. 66.
[58] *Ibid.*, v, 124 (1254).
[59] *Ibid.*, v, 3 (1251).   [60] *Ibid.*, v, 124 (1254).

were only held for one year at a time[61] and by granting them regular salaries.[62]

New governmental institutions on Western lines were created,[63] such as the *Official Gazette* ("*Takvim-i Vekayi*"), which had to be staffed by more and better bureaucrats; a postal system was put into operation;[64] a police system was organized.[65] Entirely new ministries, such as the Ministry of Finance, were established.[66]

In a document written in 1829 the Secretary for Foreign Affairs, Pertev Efendi, enunciated a theory of government in which, of the four fundamental "orders" making up the state, he did not fear to give precedence to the "men of the sword" and the "men of the pen," while he did not even bother to mention the ulema.[67]

As to the new forms that the exercise of political power took during the reign of Mahmud, the most outstanding step here was the establishment, at the end of his reign, of a new machinery of government whereby the day-by-day control of policies by the grand vizier and other ministers was now institutionalized. It was to be expected that with a ruler such as Mahmud this would not come about easily. Here again the crucial developments occurred after 1829.

It had been a well-established principle of Ottoman government that political decisions of great weight were taken "in council,"[68] i.e., in the presence and with the advice of state dignitaries including the highest ulema. For reasons which are still obscure, this system had fallen into disuse by the eighteenth century. Halil Hâmid Paşa and Selim III had both tried to restore the old system without success.[69] Mahmud, in the first years of his reign, relied on the advice of a narrow circle of anti-Westerners such as Halet Efendi; but later, when

---

[61] *Ibid.*, p. 154.   [62] *Ibid.*, p. 152.   [63] *Ibid.*, III, 145, 157.
[64] *Ibid.*, IV, 126.   [65] *Ibid.*, p. 165.   [66] *Ibid.*, V, 113.
[67] İhsan Sungu, "Mahmut II 'nin İzzet Molla ve Asakir-i Mansure Hakkında bir Hattı," *Tarih Vesikaları* (October 1941), I, 176.
[68] Karal, *Selim III* (1946), pp. 148-150.
[69] Cevdet, *Tarih*, III, 16, 38; cf. Karal, *Selim III* (1946), pp. 149-156.

he found they misled him, he got rid of them. From the destruction of the Janissary order to 1830 he relied on his own judgment, but the experience of the Turco-Russian War chastened him somewhat. It is not entirely clear whether the information is correct that in 1835 an embryonic *Council of Ministers* ("*Meclis-i Hass*") was organized which met twice a week at the Sublime Porte under the presidency of the grand vizier.[70] But what is quite clear is that in 1836 an Imperial Council on Military Affairs was established, that reforms other than military reforms were discussed in this council, and that eventually the Porte imposed its own view that a separate council for the discussion of governmental reform had to be created.[71] On the other hand, with the increase in the volume of international affairs, the sultan began to rely increasingly on the young men who were being nurtured in the bureau of the Undersecretary of State for Foreign Affairs ("*Âmedci*"). One of these young men was Mustafa Reşid Paşa. It is due to his advice that in 1837 two governmental institutions were finally established to provide permanent consultation with Ottoman ministers.[72]

Of these two bodies, one, the *Dâr-ı Şûrâ-yı Bâb-ı Âli* was to be the institutionalized form of the Council of Ministers; while the second, the *Meclis-i Vâlâ-yı Ahkâm-ı Adliye* ("Supreme Council of Judicial Ordinances"), was a more specialized governmental organ where the decisions arrived at during discussions were to be embodied in laws and presented to the sultan for approval.[73] The *Dâr-ı Şûrâ-yı Bâb-ı Âli* was to be duplicated at the provincial level in the form of appointive local councils, and these provincial organizations were to

[70] A. Heidborn, *Manuel de Droit Public et Administratif de L'Empire Ottoman* (Leipzig, C. W. Stern, 1908), I, 151, note 28; cf. Lûtfi, *Tarih*, V, 70, 71. The source quoted by Heidborn, i.e., Abdurrahman Şeref, *Tarih-i Devlet-i Osmaniye* (Istanbul, Karabet Matbaası, 1315-1318/1897-1901), 2 vols., II, 379, 381, mentions the date 1838 and not 1835.

[71] Lûtfi, *Tarih*, V, 178, 179.

[72] See Kaynar, *Mustafa Reşit Paşa*, pp. 99-128.

[73] Osman Ergin, "Asırlar boyunca Imparatorluğu idare eden Bâb-ı Âli," *Tarih Dünyası* (August 1950), I, 394; Lûtfi, *Tarih*, V, 178, 179; Kaynar, *Mustafa Reşit Paşa*, p. 198.

correspond with the mother body and suggest reforms that were needed.[74] It was decided at the time these institutions were established that the sovereign would come every year to the *Meclis-i Vâlâ-yı Ahkâm-ı Adliye* and on that occasion make a speech quite similar to the European "speech from the throne" characterizing European parliamentary monarchies. Important state matters and accomplishments of the preceding year would be covered at the same time.[75]

Because of the innovation represented by this creation of new institutions, historians have usually chosen to bring out only one aspect of this reform—that which in modern terminology would be called the "democratic" aspect. Such, for example, is the interpretation of the official chronicler of the Ottoman Empire, Lûtfi Efendi, who pointed out that at a time when the need for reform justified Sultan Mahmud in establishing autocratic rule, the latter had realized the advantages of the "legitimate method of constitutionalism," had established two "constitutional bodies," and had made it a rule that no regulations regarding "the state and the people" were to be carried out unless passed by these two bodies.[76]

Taken in the general context of Ottoman reform, the true nature of these bodies emerges without difficulty: both were established to facilitate the administrative streamlining of the empire. Reşid Paşa's attempts to exclude from the Council of Judicial Ordinances men who could not "divest themselves from the manners and customs with which the old generation was impregnated" shows the extent of the modernist approach which lay behind their establishment.[77]

---

[74] Lûtfi, *Tarih*, v, 179.

[75] Kaynar, *Mustafa Reşit Paşa*, pp. 210-214.

[76] Lûtfi, *Tarih*, v, 106. Lûtfi Efendi was the official chronicler of the empire from 1886 onward and was on close terms with Sultan Abdülhamid II (reign. 1876-1909). His praise of members of the royal family should thus be taken with a grain of salt, but it is interesting to note that Lûtfi Efendi chose to point out the "democratic" aspects of the Turkish reform movement to a sultan who was a thoroughgoing autocrat himself.

[77] Kaynar, *Mustafa Reşit Paşa*, p. 105, quoting an unpublished document in Reşid's handwriting. The allusion might be to Husrev Paşa, who wanted the reforms to stop at the military stage.

Although, in a communication sent to the sultan, Reşid Paşa himself established a parallel between these institutions and European parliaments, he never mentioned the idea of popular sovereignty and specifically stated that, while members of similar bodies in Europe were elected, under the Ottoman monarchy they could only be appointed. This was quite a logical appraisal of a system under which sovereignty had been held in trust for God by the sultan.

While Reşid Paşa could not have reference to the idea of popular sovereignty, the new bodies *could* be rationalized as consultative assemblies made up of experts without doing violence to Islamic ideas, since there existed in Islam a theory of the delegation of the sovereign's power to his ministers.

Meanwhile, changes continued. In March of 1838, with the appointment of Grand Vizier Mehmed Emin Rauf Paşa, the title of prime minister was used for the first time. The title of grand vizier was restored within a year, but the change was significant.

The sultan, in turn, could go so far as to state in the firman in which he established the title of prime minister that, since most of the affairs of the state were being handled by ministers, no need was felt any more for a grand vizier. He added that, as an additional distinction but not as a mark of having granted special powers, he would confer the title of prime minister on any of the ministers of state whom he thought was fit to lead his colleagues.[78] This "collegial" theory of government was quite new for the Ottoman Empire, since the grand vizier had, up to that point, been the absolute delegate (*"Vekil-i mutlak"*) of the sultan.

The culmination of all these moves was the proclamation by Mahmud's successor, Abdülmecid, of a rescript bearing the character of a semiconstitutional charter, the *Hatt-ı Hümâ-*

[78] Lûtfi, *Tarih*, v, 113, 114; cf. Okandan, "Amme Hukukumuzda Tanzimat Devri," *Tanzimat* I: *Yüzüncü Yıldönümü Münasebetile* (ed. by Maarif Vekâleti, Istanbul, Maarif Matbaası, 1940), pp. 102-104.

yun of Gülhane, for which the groundwork had been prepared during Mahmud's reign.[79]

III. The Immediate Origins of the Hatt-ı Hümâyun of Gülhane

When, on November 3, 1839, Mustafa Reşid Paşa, then Foreign Minister, walked up to a podium in the middle of the Imperial Park of Gülhane and read to the dignitaries of the Porte and the foreign diplomats summoned for the occasion the Imperial Charter known as the *Hatt-ı Hümâyun* of Gülhane, all those present realized that an important step had been taken in the direction of the modernization of the Ottoman Empire.

The reaction in Europe was prompt and enthusiastic. To many Europeans it seemed the sultan was suddenly falling in with the contemporary inclination of formerly wicked monarchs to grant their people a constitution. This undoubtedly was, in their opinion, "a good thing" and represented no mean achievement in the direction of Westernization.[80]

Even the more delayed responses were flattering. Auguste Comte decided, after having taken stock of this unexpected development for a few years, that the Ottoman Empire was the political and social laboratory of which he had dreamed. Here was a country where the Religion of Humanity could become the guiding beacon of governmental action for, he stated, Islam did not stand in the way of a complete remodel-

---

[79] See "Das Conseil d'utilité publique in Konstantinopel," *Augsburger Allgemeine Zeitung, Beilage* No. 317 (1839), pp. 2479-2482, for one of these preparatory steps. Even in 1838 a scheme of reform was being considered having as goals: (1) just taxation, (2) the elimination of forced labor contribution (*"angarya"*) and forced seizure, as well as (3) the establishment of the principle of equality before the law. Cavid Baysun, "Mustafa Reşit Paşa," *Tanzimat*, p. 731; Kaynar, *Mustafa Reşit*, p. 99. For the text of the rescript see Belin, "Charte des Turcs," Series 3, *Journal Asiatique* (January 1840), IX, 5-29. Jean Deny has a useful summary of various editions of the charter in his obituary of Kraelitz-Greifenhorst, *Journal Asiatique* (April-June 1933), vol. 222, 357-360.

[80] Bailey, *British Policy*, p. 192, note 44; Sabri Esat Siyavuşgil, "Tanzimatın Fransız Efkâr-ı Umumiyesinde Uyandırdığı Akisler," *Tanzimat*, pp. 750-753.

ing of society, and the rulers of the Ottoman Empire had shown that they believed in "energetic" reforms.[81]

This assessment of Comte was, in reality, somewhat of an understatement. Sultan Mahmud II, who had died three months before the rescript was proclaimed, had indeed been as absolutistic a reformer as could be found. He had had only a withering contempt, which expressed itself in very concrete and severe measures, for the obstacles that stood in his way, whether human or institutional. This character of the ruler, on the other hand, was not without having influenced the preparation of the *hatt*, which aimed primarily at curbing such imperial caprice in the conduct of the affairs of the state. In other words, the proclamation read in the park of Gülhane, in which the promise to respect "life, honor, and property" held such a prominent place, was not really, as many a European's wishful thinking would have had it, a fundamental statement of individual liberties. The *hatt* was the equivalent of a European constitutional charter only insofar as it promised that henceforth, in the Ottoman Empire, government would be based on principles which eliminated arbitrary rule, but it was only incidentally a "bill of rights." Some of the more experienced observers of Turkish affairs did, at the time, realize this,[82] and even Prince Metternich did not feel loath to congratulate the successor of Mahmud, the adolescent Sultan Abdülmecid, for affixing the imperial seal to the rescript.[83]

Reşid Paşa himself, two years after the proclamation, protested against the suspicion, which he stated the *hatt* had

[81] Auguste Comte, "A son Excéllence Reschid Pacha, ancien grand visir [sic] de l'Empire Ottoman," *Système de Politique Positive ou Traité de Sociologie Instituant la Religion de l'Humanité* (Paris, Carillan-Goeury et Dalmont, 1853), III, xlvii-xlix.

[82] See Bailey, *British Policy*, pp. 198, note 69, 199, 200. For the similarity in points of view between the British and the Austrians, *ibid.*, p. 193, note 46.

[83] [Clemens Prince Metternich], "Sur les Réformes d'Abdul Medjid en Turquie," *Memoires, Documents et Ecrits Divers laissés par le Prince Metternich, Chancellier de Cour et d'Etat* (ed. by Prince Richard Metternich, Paris, Plon, 1883), V, 378-386.

sometimes raised, of "connivance with European constitutionalism." He stated that education was by no means so widespread in Turkey as to make constitutionalism possible, and he spoke of the principal dispositions of the document as "only intended to introduce a complete security of the life, property and honor of individuals and regulate the internal and military expenditures of the Porte."[84]

If the charter of Gülhane had been primarily prepared as an instrument to make the Ottoman state function with greater efficiency and to eliminate the wastefulness of uncontrolled imperial fiat, a special aspect of this purpose was that the charter was aimed at giving more extensive powers than they had hitherto wielded to the Ottoman "men of the pen," the bureaucrats of the Porte who, as the state machinery was gradually streamlined, had become progressively indispensable.[85] This aspect of the *hatt* may be better understood by determining, with greater accuracy than has been done to date, whose "life, property and honor" it was meant to protect and what, precisely, its author, Mustafa Reşid Paşa, had in mind in drafting such a document. Upon examination, it will be seen that a most important component of Reşid's intentions was to make the Ottoman state officials benefit from the protection of organic laws which the sultan himself would pledge to observe. In Reşid's own words he desired to benefit from the advantages of "*une système immuablement établi.*"[86]

What Reşid desired to safeguard with such a "*système*" is alluded to by a contemporary observer of the Turkish scene. The latter states that, after the destruction of the Janissaries and the defeat of the antireformist element in the empire, "the men who had floated to the surface of the wreck of the

---

[84] Nicholas Milev, "Réchid Pacha et la Réforme Ottomane," *Zeitschrift für Osteuropaische Geschichte* (1912), II, 388.

[85] The governmental bodies established in 1837 were also the institutional expression of the idea that in carrying out the business of the state it was imperative to rely on a fairly wide group of experts at the ministerial and under-secretary level. Thus the "men of the pen" were finally accorded an official recognition of the primacy of the services they rendered.

[86] Bailey, *British Policy*, p. 271.

orthodox Turkish party were in general needy, unillustrated by descent" and therefore set out to "acquire wealth to gain influence and make partisans in default of which they would be mere bubbles on a troubled sea."[87]

Reşid Paşa probably remembered in this connection the number of wealthy men who for no other reason than that they possessed the means to defray the cost of Mahmud's reforms had been summarily arrested, dispossessed, and sometimes even executed during Mahmud's reign.[88]

There is no doubt that for some time before the proclamation of the Gülhane Rescript, while Mahmud was still alive, Reşid had been greatly perturbed by the heavy-handed fashion in which the monarch had carried out his reforms, that he believed that because of the sultan's uncontrolled actions the full benefit of reform had not been reaped during his reign.

In an interview with Palmerston, a few months before the passing of the rescript and immediately following Mahmud's death, Reşid Paşa explained to the British statesman that he had been especially revolted by the cruel treatment meted out by his imperial master to those of his ministers who happened to incur the sultan's displeasure. Among such highly placed bureaucrats who had met an unenviable fate, Reşid Paşa mentioned his former patron and mentor, Pertev Paşa.[89] Indeed, at the time the above interview was taking place, the memory

[87] Sir Adolphus Slade, *Turkey and the Crimean War* (London, Smith and Elder, 1867), p. 31 f. Almost the same wording is used in Ziya Paşa's "Hâtıra-i Evveliye," *Hürriyet*, March 8, 1869, page 6.

[88] As attested by the Austrian internuncio to the Porte in a contemporary dispatch to Metternich: "Jamais l'arbitraire n'avait été porté a un tel excès que sous le règne du Sultan défunt. Quand à la propriété, le Sultan en disposait sans égards ni scrupules, dépouillant les uns au profit des autres. Les concussions des fonctionnaires publics devenaient plus fortes à mesure que l'on se croyait moins sûr de conserver ce que l'on avait acquis, chacun cherchant du moins a sauver quelques épargnes faites a la dérobée pour se mettre a l'abri des événements et se garantir contre les coups du sort." Baron Sturmer to Metternich, November 6, 1839. Cited by Milev, "Réchid Pacha et la Réforme Ottomane," p. 383.

[89] For the text of this interview see Bailey, *British Policy*, Appendix III, 271-276.

of the tragic rivalry between Akif Paşa and Pertev Paşa, exacerbated by the part the sultan had chosen to play in it, was still fresh in the minds of the employees of the Sublime Porte.

In the conflict for power and influence between these two highly gifted statesmen, Pertev had been able, at first, to draw the sultan to his side. This had happened in 1836. At the time Akif was Secretary for Foreign Affairs[90] and had been greatly embarrassed by the histrionics of Ponsonby, the British ambassador to the Porte. A British citizen, while hunting in the vicinity of Istanbul, had been imprisoned for wounding a Turkish boy. The crude threats of Ponsonby to bring down the Ottoman Empire about Akif's head if he did not immediately liberate this subject of Her Majesty, placed Akif in a difficult situation. Finally he had to give in. The Englishman, a Mr. Churchill, was freed, awarded an indemnity, and presented with a diamond-studded imperial decoration. Akif Paşa, however, was dismissed for this loss of face. His rival Pertev thereupon stepped into his shoes. Some time later Akif's star had again prevailed. This time Akif succeeded in so thoroughly discrediting Pertev that the latter was exiled by the sultan to Edirne, and then this punishment, being deemed too lenient, was followed within a matter of hours by his condemnation to death. Immediately thereafter the sultan repented his hasty decision, but—alas—the sentence had already been carried out when the order for its revocation arrived in Edirne. Akif was dismissed shortly thereafter.

Pertev was the last politician to be executed by the traditional method of the bowstring, and though his rival, Akif, was later pursued by the avenging Reşid Paşa, it was for reasons connected with the neglect of Akif's official duties and the sentence was passed by one of the administrative tribunals

[90] The whole incident is related by Akif Paşa in his *Tabsıra.* See Arthur Alric, *Un Diplomate Ottoman en 1836 (Affaire Churchill)*, Traduction Annotée de l' "Eclaircissement" (Tebsireh) d'Akif-Pacha (Paris, Ernest Leroux, 1892).

established after the proclamation of the Gülhane Rescript.[91]

Pertev is one of the figures in Turkish history probably most misunderstood in the West, for he was labeled a "reactionary" by Western publicists. This reputation of Pertev's was due to his strong measures against Christian minorities.[92] With regard to the streamlining of the Ottoman state, however, Pertev was not a reactionary; on the contrary, he was the final link leading to Reşid in a chain of Secretaries for Foreign Affairs who had reform at heart. After Selim's death, in his position as Undersecretary for Foreign Affairs, in his own handwriting Pertev had drafted the Charter of Alliance.[93]

Such modernization of the administration as was necessary to give the metropolis a better grasp over the empire had been the fruit of his labors. On his advice the grand vizierate had been reorganized, the office of Assistant to the grand vizier ("*Sadaret Kethüdalığı*") recast into a Ministry of the Interior ("*Umur-u Mülkiye Nezareti*")[94] and a permanent secretary-general ("*Müsteşar*") appointed for the first time in an Ottoman ministry.

It is only by mentioning the name of the man who had taught Pertev the art of statesmanship, however, that the whole pattern in the transmission of reformist attitudes

[91] Akif Paşa's biography may be found in Alric, *Un Diplomate Ottoman*, pp. ii-iv; see also Ibnülemin Mahmud Kemal İnal, *Son Asır*, pp. 80-89; Gibb, *Ottoman Poetry*, IV, 322-335. For Pertev Paşa, the above source and also İnal, pp. 1312-1324.

[92] M. A. Ubicini, *Letters on Turkey* (trans. by Lady Easthope, London, John Murray, 1856), II, 113; Franz Babinger, "Pertev," *Encyclopedia of Islam* (1936), IV, 1066. A somewhat fairer description is given by Slade, *Turkey and the Crimean War*, p. 16.

[93] See above, p. 148; for Pertev's role see Alric, *Un Diplomate Ottoman*, pp. 124-125; also below, Chapter VI.

[94] This was considered by Akif Paşa to constitute in itself a slap to the Sultan since it implied that the machinery of the state was not meant only to carry out his will. See İnal, *Son Asır*, p. 82. When Akif Paşa replaced Pertev in September 1837, the term was changed to that of *Umur-u Dahiliye Nazırı*. See Abdurrahman Şeref, *Tarih-i Devlet-i Osmaniye*, II, p. 383. Lûtfi, *Tarih*, V, 29; for the text of the firmans reorganizing these offices see "Extrait du *Moniteur Ottoman* du 21 Zilcadi 1251 de l'hégire," *Journal Asiatique*, Series III, II, 78:83 (July 1836); also *Moniteur Ottoman*, April 23, 1836.

throughout the first three decades of the nineteenth century becomes entirely clear. This man, Galib Paşa, was the "man of the pen" and Secretary for Foreign Affairs who, having escaped from Janissary field headquarters, had instigated the counterrevolution of Alemdar Mustafa Paşa and later had advised Sultan Mahmud as to the steps to be followed in the destruction of the Janissaries.[95]

Thus from Galib to Pertev to Reşid (and, as we shall see, to Reşid's colleague Rifat) runs a continuous stream of reformist policy which had been espoused by "men of the pen" since the end of the eighteenth century.

In the bureaucratic circles of the Ottoman capital the memory of Pertev's death sentence, carried out in 1837, was still vivid in 1839. There is no doubt that the incident deeply affected Reşid Paşa.

This was not the only dismissal that had taken on the proportions of a scandal during Mahmud's reign. Another government official, Keçecizâde İzzet Molla, a man of great culture and considerable political acumen, had been curtly dismissed and exiled in 1828 on the eve of the war with Russia because he had petitioned the sultan not to have recourse to war and to try to settle the matters outstanding between the two countries by negotiation. The war party having won the sultan over to their side, Keçecizâde was sent away.[96] Here again it was Galib Paşa whose influence was instrumental in the eventual reinstatement of İzzet.

That such fallings-out of favor, to which in earlier times officials had submitted with comparative docility, could now become *causes célèbres* was in itself an indication that the

[95] See Orhan F. Köprülü, "Galib Paşa," *Islâm Ansiklopedisi* (1947), IV, 710-714. Pertev had written the draft of the firman abolishing the Janissaries. See Reed, "The Destruction of the Janissaries," p. 240.

[96] Sungu, "Mahmud II nin . . . bir hattı," throughout; İnal, *Son Asır*, pp. 723-746; Abdurrahman Şeref, *Tarih Musahabeleri*, p. 69. İzzet Molla's exile bears directly on the history of the Young Ottomans. İzzet's son, Fuad Paşa, tried to take his father's revenge by whittling the imperial prerogative. Probably because İzzet had not as yet given in to European ways as much as his son, the Young Ottomans admired him as a "patriot." See Gibb, *Ottoman Poetry*, IV, 311.

bureaucratic apparatus of the Porte was gaining an ascendance which it had not possessed in the past. All signs indicate, in fact, that in the case of İzzet Molla, as well as that of Pertev, the "wielders of the pen" had created through their control of literature and communications in general a potent image of imperial caprice where a century before, faced by a similar situation, they would simply have rationalized the sultan's action. Reşid Paşa's lack of respect for the sultan on occasions when he knew he was not being overheard by Turkish ears was characteristic of this new emancipation of the servants of the Porte and indicative of their aspirations.[97]

Already for some time before the death of Mahmud, Mustafa Reşid had tried to convince the sultan to proclaim a charter on the lines of the Gülhane Rescript, but he had failed because of the opposition of Akif Paşa. The latter was well aware of the consequences of such a move on the imperial prerogative and warned the sultan that, by giving in, his imperial powers would be shorn to the benefit of others.[98]

The events which made up the backdrop of the proclamation of the charter thus support the contention that the *hatt*, while concerned with the rejuvenation of the empire and the protection of the rights of "all" its subjects (as the document was phrased), was aimed in particular at the emancipation of the officials of the Porte.[99]

The beginning of the era of reforms in Turkey is usually dated from the proclamation of the Charter of Gülhane.

Between 1839 and 1867 a number of institutional changes were made continuing those begun at the time of Mahmud and in many ways fulfilling the promises of the charter. These are the best-known aspect of the Tanzimat era, and therefore

[97] Bailey, *British Policy*, p. 272.

[98] Lûtfi, *Tarih*, VII, 390, note 2.

[99] Milev, "Rechid Pacha," p. 384. This thesis is not new; the Bulgarian historian Milev attributes its first formulation to another Bulgarian historian, Rakowsky. Milev does not give us Rakowsky's argument and himself only fleetingly mentions this aspect of the charter.

a short enumeration of these transformations will be sufficient here.[100]

In 1840 a code of penal laws was promulgated. In 1845 an assembly of provincial delegates was gathered in the capital to impress them with the seriousness of the reform program. In 1847 modern secular criminal tribunals were established. In 1850 a secular code of commerce based on European practice was promulgated. In 1840, 1854, 1861, and 1868 the governmental mechanism first created by the establishment of the Meclis-i Vâlâ was recast. In 1856 an Ottoman bank was established. Between 1845 and 1868 education was almost completely secularized. After 1856 new regulations regarding the Christian subjects of the empire were made. In 1861 a secular code of commercial procedure was adopted. In 1864 a new law for provincial administration was put into effect. In 1867 foreigners were granted the right to own property. In 1868 a new *lycée* was established where teaching was to be in French. Progressive steps were taken to secularize pious foundations throughout these years.

The Young Ottomans expressed strong reservations with regard to the Charter of Gülhane and the era of reforms it initiated. Namık Kemal considered it at best a missed opportunity and at worst a concession granted to Western states to elicit their aid at a time when the empire was threatened by its Egyptian vassal Mehmed Ali Paşa.[101] What Kemal was referring to was the fact that the document had indeed been meant to show the European powers that the empire was earnestly concerned with the protection of its Christian subjects.

Another reason for which the Young Ottomans objected to

---

[100] For a listing of these changes, see J. H. Kramer's "Tanẓīmāt," *Encyclopedia of Islam*, IV, 659.

[101] "While on the surface it, the Tanzimat Rescript, gives the impression that it was made to guarantee everybody's life, property and honor, in reality it had been proclaimed with the purpose of strengthening the state [i.e., protect it from foreign intervention]." Namık Kemal, "Tanzimat," *İbret*, 4 Ramazan 1289. Reproduced in its entirety in Reşat Kaynar, *Mustafa Reşit Paşa*, p. 195. Cf., however, Namık Kemal, "Al-Hak ya'lu wa lā yu'la 'aleyhi," *Hürriyet*, June 20, 1868, p. 2, where the "tongue in cheek" attitude of Kemal is obvious.

the Gülhane Rescript was that it provided for the perpetuation of reform without clearly limiting it by the principles of the Şeriat. According to them, Reşid Paşa had thereby opened the way for the "tyranny" of his successors. A further criticism of the Young Ottomans was that the institutions created to implement the charter after 1839 were modelled on Western institutions at a time when Ottomans were completely unfamiliar with the body of Western culture and thought underpinning these institutions. This, stated the Young Ottomans, caused complete confusion and chaos among government employees, the great majority of whom did not even grasp what the new regulations were about and therefore were not able to implement them.[102]

In particular, the Young Ottomans criticized the many changes in the structure of provincial administration and central government which had begun to be carried out soon after 1839 and which had resulted in extensive changes in the quarter century that separated the proclamation of the Rescript from the rise of the Patriotic Alliance. They extended their criticism even farther back to include Mahmud's policy of suppressing the provincial gentry which had preceded these changes and made them possible, the elimination of the Janissaries without an equivalent counterweight to the administration, and the impersonal harshness which had accompanied the Tanzimat reforms. They pointed out that the new method[103] of government by councils had, in reality, been used to provide sinecures; that the governmental bodies that became heirs to the *Meclis-i Vâlâ* had, in fact, served the same purpose; that the standards of the ulema had purposely been neglected as a result of the control of the pious foundations by the state (1838 onward); that the changes brought to the judiciary, such as the establishment of new secular "mixed" tribunals (1840 onward) and the writing of new codes of law (1840

[102] Namık Kemal, " 'Inna'llāha ya'mur bi'l 'adl wa'l-iḥsān." *Hürriyet*, January 18, 1869, p. 3.
[103] Ziya Paşa, "Istanbuldan . . . fi 2 Şaban," *Hürriyet*, November 30, 1868, p. 5.

onward) of Western inspiration, had created confusion. They added that this had diminished rather than increased the means of redress available to individuals.[104] They criticized the inhumanity of the new police organization.[105] They wrote that the heavy burden of taxation shouldered by the peasants had worsened after the Tanzimat.[106] They complained about the economic exploitation of the empire by foreigners and put the blame for the ruin of Turkish manufactures on the new commercial policies introduced after 1839.[107]

None of these complaints were devoid of foundation and all had been voiced by European visitors who had come to Turkey in the quarter century that preceded the rise of Young Ottoman protests. In the year the Janissaries were destroyed, the French geographer Fontanier had already sympathized with the apprehension with which the people of Istanbul had watched the total extinction of this corps.[108]

Sir Adolphus Slade, who had served as an advisor to the Turkish navy, vividly described the evils of centralization.[109] Both Slade and the British traveler MacFarlane lambasted the elimination of the provincial gentry.[110] Both associated the elimination of these elements with the rise of unchecked brigandage throughout Anatolia.[111]

[104] Namık Kemal, "Devlet-i Aliyyeyi," *Hürriyet*, August 24, 1868, p. 1.

[105] "Zaptiye İdaresi Hakkında," *Hürriyet*, August 17, 1868, p. 4.

[106] Namık Kemal [?], "İdare-i Hâzıranın Hulâsa-i Âsarı," *Hürriyet*, December 28, 1868, p. 6.

[107] Editorial, *Hürriyet*, August 10, 1868, p. 1.

[108] "The people as a whole regretted the Janissaries; they felt, as if by instinct, that their sole dike against absolute power had been overthrown, that their liberty had been destroyed, while it would be a long time before they might exchange it for the benefits of civilization." Victor Fontanier, *Voyage en Orient entrepris par l'ordre du government français de l'année 1821 à l'année 1829* (Paris, 1829), I, 322; Slade, *Turkey and the Crimean War*, p. 31. For others who held similar views with respect to the Janissaries see A. D. Mordtmann, *Stambul und das moderne Turkenthum*, I, 134. A. Slade, *Records of Travels in Greece and Turkey ... 1829-1831* (London, Saunders and Otley, 1833), I, 306-319.

[109] Slade, *Turkey and the Crimean War*, p. 39 ff.

[110] MacFarlane, *Turkey and Its Destiny*, II, pp. 38-39; Slade, *Turkey and the Crimean War*, p. 11.

[111] Slade, *Turkey and the Crimean War*, p. 29; MacFarlane, *Turkey and Its Destiny*, I, 397 ff.

Complaints echoing the Young Ottoman protest against the failure of the Tanzimat statements to reform the farming out of taxes may be found in almost any of the Western books on Turkey written after the Tanzimat. MacFarlane also concurred on another subject of Young Ottoman criticism—the administration of pious endowment revenues ("vakıf revenues") by the state.[112]

With regard to the process of economic exploitation to which the Young Ottomans referred, Slade stated in 1876: "Ambassadors under the new *régime* how much soever [sic] disagreeing on some points have cordially agreed with each other in enforcing the commercial legislation founded on treaties applicable to bygone days, which has made Turkey virtually a colony after the old colonial fashion, bound to admit the product of every European state without *reciprocity* at a uniform low rate of duty reduced lower by partial tariffs and by a system of smuggling from which she is not allowed to protect herself."[113]

That the Turkish population of Anatolia, already retrogressing for some time, had declined as a result of a combination of these factors was again a fact that was well known.

The one Young Ottoman contention that was quite unrealistic was that the Ottoman method of government by council had been eliminated by the men of the Tanzimat.[114]

Although the materials to prove such a point conclusively would take a long time to collect, the overall impression

[112] ". . . the reformers who are uprooting religion, and a respect for it in every direction, have virtually destroyed the security which the mosque, and the mosque alone, could give to any landed property; they have destroyed the independence of the Turkish Church—if I may so call it; they have laid their greedy hands upon nearly all the *vakoufs* of the empire, and are undertaking to provide out of the common state treasury, for the subsistence of the Ulema, Mollahs and college or medresseh students, to keep up the mosques and the medressehs, to repair the bridges, Khans, &c., and to do, governmentally, that which the administrators of the *vakouf* had done or ought to have done. Hence, with very few exceptions, we see the heads of the mosques and medressehs in abject poverty; the rabble students in rags. . . ." MacFarlane, *Turkey and Its Destiny*, I, 396 f.

[113] Slade, *Turkey and the Crimean War*, p. 50.

[114] See above, Chapter IV.

gained from a study of Young Ottoman writings is that one of the major roots of their protests originated in the spectacle of the ruin of Ottoman trade associations and guilds. These had gradually lost power as the result of the decline of the Turkish "manufacturing industry," as Ubicini named it.[115] The latter, in turn, was a victim of European manufacturing and in particular of British textiles. This process had deep repercussions in Ottoman society because manufacturing and trading, with its appendage of guild organizations, had for a long time constituted the truly central part of Ottoman city life.[116] A "typical Ottoman citizen" was more likely to be a member of a guild than part of the administrative machine. This economic backdrop has not been studied up to this time because of the convenient fiction, sedulously fostered by those who prefer clichés to the study of facts, that economic activity in the Ottoman Empire was the monopoly of the non-Moslem while the Moslem preferred war or administration as an occupation. That Turkish manufacturing activity was circumscribed by primitive methods is true, that it did not play a role in Ottoman society could not be more mistaken. What is usually referred to as the "comprador" type of economic exploitation did not fully develop until the Crimean war. As Ziya Paşa pointed out[117] there were a class of Turkish-Ottoman traders at the beginning of the century, called *Hayriye Tüccarı* who had eagerly sought the same commercial privileges as had been granted to foreign traders, known as *Avrupa Tüccarı*, and who for a time had tried to compete with the latter.[118] By the 1860's these *Hayriye Tüccarı* had all but disappeared.

The destruction of the Ottoman economy created a pool of unemployed who flocked into state employment. It also swelled the ranks of the theological students. The latter thus

[115] Ubicini, *Letters on Turkey*, I, 339-341.

[116] For examples of guild influence see Münir Aktepe, *Patrona İsyanı* (1730), (Istanbul, Edebiyat Fakültesi Basımevi, 1958), pp. 23-40, 134.

[117] Ziya Paşa, "Hâtıra," *Hürriyet*, May 3, 1869, pp. 7-8.

[118] For this term see: Osman Nuri [Ergin], *Mecelle-i Umûr-u Belediye* (Istanbul, Matbaa-i Osmaniye, 1338/1922), p. 680.

became an increasingly unruly element. It is in this light that the protectionist policies of the Young Ottomans became intelligible, and that their criticism of the economic privileges accorded to foreigners can be understood. In a wider context, the tentative hypothesis which comes to mind that in the Ottoman Empire there had existed at the beginning of the nineteenth century a potential bourgeoisie the growth of which the earlier industrial development of Europe had checked, and the corollary of this hypothesis that the bureaucracy was led to assume the role which the bourgeoisie would otherwise have played as the midwife of an opposition to the existing powers, still need to be investigated in detail. What little information there is on the subject substantiates such a theory. Such an approach also explains many of the vagaries of Turkish political development during the time of the Young Ottomans and even in later times.

·9 CHAPTER VI &·

Sadık Rifat Paşa: the Introduction of New Ideas at the Governmental Level

THE view of the Gülhane Rescript that was advanced in the preceding chapter was derived from a reconstruction of the events just prior to its proclamation. The interests of its sponsors in a policy of reform were thereby uncovered. This method does not tell us much, however, about the new "operative ideals" that came with the Tanzimat. The latter are difficult to establish for the simple reason that the architects of the Tanzimat have left no explicit theoretical justification of their own actions.

Some information about the nature of the changes of this order involved in the Tanzimat may be gathered from a study of the *text* of the Gülhane Rescript. At least two important aspects of the "operative ideals" embodied in it provide an inkling of what these "ideals" might have been. For one, the engagement taken by the sultan in the charter to observe its terms was the first overt expression of a renewed decline of the imperial prerogative. Secondly, the wording of the charter showed a secular approach to the problems of government which had never before been overtly proclaimed. To understand the importance of this novel approach a retrospective survey of certain developments in this field of "ideals" in Mahmud's time is necessary.

A preliminary question inevitably arises as to what the repercussions of the French Revolution had been in the Ottoman Empire. The answer is: almost nil in the sense of an immediate, direct transmission of ideas. Thus the thesis contained in the one competent study of these trends[1] that "Turkish-speak-

---

[1] Bernard Lewis, "The Impact of the French Revolution on Turkey: Some Notes on the Transmission of Ideas," *Journal of World History* (January 1953), I, 105-125. Professor Lewis' thesis is that "the French

ing Frenchmen and French-speaking Turks formed a new society in the capital, in which the ideas of the times were freely discussed and the enthusiastic optimism of revolutionary France found a ready response among a new generation of Turks that looked at the West for guidance and inspiration"[2] is incorrect. This can be said only of the Levantine groups of the capital. The difficulties into which the first organized group of Turkish Encyclopaedists ran, the relatively low-powered level at which even these investigations of Western culture took place, and the delayed effect of this group shows the "influence" of the French Revolution in real perspective. In fact, Western influences were at work at the court in a small circle which was interested—as a number of people had been in the "Era of Tulips"—in military organization and in administrative methods and also in the social life that was characteristic of court circles in Europe.

Revolution was the first great movement of ideas in Western Christendom that had any effect on the world of Islam" (Lewis, *op.cit.*, p. 105). According to him, the "success" of Western ideas in the Ottoman Empire in the nineteenth century should not be attributed to the "advance of the material might of the West" (*ibid.*, p. 106). In his opinion, "the initial attraction of these ideas . . . is rather to be found in their secularism. . . . Secularism as such had no great attraction for Muslims, but in a Western movement that was non-Christian . . . the Muslim world might hope to find the elusive secret of Western power without compromising its own religious beliefs and traditions" (*Ibid.*). This line of reasoning only serves to confuse the issue if it is not qualified and set into context. What Professor Lewis fails to mention is that the "secularism" of which he speaks was limited to palace circles, that it was stunted by the deposition of Selim III, and that it never affected the staunchly conservative masses.

[2] *Ibid.*, p. 118. This is probably based on the information given by Asım in his *Tarih*, I, 375. Cevdet Paşa, speaking of the same events, states: "And while it was necessary to bring over from Europe teachers and engineers, in connection with the introduction of new regulations, and while the training of soldiers in accordance with European practice was of great urgency, the inclinations of Sultan Selim for things strange, and new, and unusual, caused a considerable number of European style customs to appear in Istanbul and many European endeavors to be engaged in which were the prerequisites of civilization. And while changes in customs and usages are things intrinsically difficult for people to accept, viziers and officials overstepped the *Şeriat* and plunged head over heels into European ways. They geared themselves to European life in all respects whether necessary or not, and the people were shocked by those excesses" (Cevdet, *Tarih*, VIII, 147-148, citing events of the year 1217/1802-1803).

A clue, on the other hand, as to the way in which the French Revolution did affect the Ottoman Empire is found in a proclamation of the Porte to the inhabitants of Syria, which the French had invaded in 1799. Here, among the beliefs attributed to the French, figured the idea that "all men are equal in humanity and equal in being men, none has superiority or merit over the other, and everyone disposes of his life and own livelihood in this life."[3] This document makes it clear that one of the ways of gauging the extent of the penetration of Western ideas into the Ottoman Empire is to follow the changes in the attitude toward the belief in the natural equality of men and the conception that "everyone disposes of his . . . livelihood in this life." We shall see that precisely such an "activism" underlies both the reform of the Tanzimat and the Young Ottoman movement.

The gradualness with which the Turkish world view changed may be seen in that by the end of the reign of Mahmud the net increment of his rule, in this respect, had been purely and simply the establishment of the *respectability of change*. It was during his reign that the idea that "something had to be done" was given theoretical expression as well as official recognition. This idea was expressed at its earliest in the firman abolishing the Janissary corps.[4]

Two years later, in an apology that he had prepared for propaganda purposes, Keçecizâde İzzet Molla was defending the same "activist" thesis in the context of Islamic ideas. In one passage he stated, "And insofar as those who state that worldly matters may not be set into order at the time of the approach of the *Mehdi* [a figure sent by God to save the Islamic community following a 'time of troubles'] are concerned, we answer them thus: if the *Mehdi* is to appear tomorrow, let us work for justice and equity today so that He seeing

[3] Lewis, "The Impact," p. 122. Original text in Enver Ziya Karal, *Fransa-Mısır ve Osmanlı İmparatorlugu 1797-1802* (Istanbul, Millî Mecmua Basımevi, 1938), pp. 108-111.

[4] For the text of the firman, see Reed, "The Destruction of the Janissaries," pp. 242-249.

us engaged in the strengthening of justice may give us praise."[5]

Interestingly enough, though won over to change, Mahmud himself, despite his congenital ability as a political planner, used rational criteria only to a limited extent and was far behind İzzet in terms of intellectual modernization. His comparative naïveté, in this respect, appeared during a clash that developed between himself and İzzet in 1828. Mahmud's opinion, shared by those men who were known among Europeans as the "war party," was that, although the reorganized Turkish troops were not quite ready for battle, one had to rely to some extent on divine support in war. İzzet Molla, on the other hand, had dared to lay down the alternatives quite unequivocally. He began to answer the rhetorical question, "Is this the state of the Şeriat or the state of reason?" by a conciliatory statement but then proceeded to uncompromising objections to a declaration of war against Russia on grounds of reason.[6] His argument was that, military reforms having been undertaken on rational grounds, reason also had to be used in weighing the possibilities of success in warfare. He stated that merely relying on God's help in this respect was making a travesty of religion.

It was this stand which almost led to İzzet's execution, a sentence which, as related in the preceding chapter, was commuted to that of exile.

The extent to which İzzet Molla's approach differed from the earlier (or more conservative) attitude toward the same problem may be seen in the commentary made by the historian

[5] The word used for *Mehdi* in the text is *sahib-i zuhur*, a less well-known synonym. For the text see *Lâyiha* of Keçecizâde, Manuscript No. K 337, Istanbul Municipal Library; quoted by Hıfzı Veldet [Velidedeoğlu], "Kanunlaştırma Hareketi ve Tanzimat," in *Tanzimat*, pp. 169, 170. Keçecizâde's project is dated 1243 (1827-1828) and not 1253, as stated in Velidedeoğlu's article. For this date see İnal, *Son Asır Türk Şairleri*, p. 739. For the *Mehdi* see D. B. Macdonald, "al-Mahdī," *Encyclopedia of Islam*, III, 111-115.

[6] For this controversy see *Lâyiha* of İzzet Molla in İhsan Sungu, "Mahmud II'nin İzzet Molla ve Asâkir-i Mansure Hakkında bir Hattı," *Tarih Vesikaları* (October 1941), I, 170.

Vasıf Efendi[7] to a French offer extended in 1783-1784 to train Ottomans in modern methods of warfare: "These men [the Europeans] hold the erroneous belief, fostered by certain philosophers that the exalted creator has (God forbid) no influence on singular occurrences ["*umur-u Cüz'iyye*"] and since the fortunes of war are included among the latter, they advance that whichever side has superior means of waging war will overcome the other."[8]

Exactly the opposite argument that singular occurrences (i.e., in Ottoman-Islamic terminology that area of man's actions in which he was free to make a decision as to which course of action to adopt) included military planning as well as governmental measures was to gain increasing importance in the writings of the Turkish ideologues of the nineteenth century. The firman abolishing the Janissary order was the first state document whose wording amounted to a proclamation of this "activist" principle. This was so, in turn, because the document paid only lip service in its preamble to the theory that the Ottoman Empire had weakened due to a laxity in religious observance. Following the preamble, the firman went on immediately to suggest remedies that had nothing to do with religious practices. Exactly the same type of *non sequitur* may be found in the *Hatt-ı Hümâyun* of Gülhane. In this document the major purpose of the new policy, immediately following the same type of religious preamble, was stated to be the creation of new institutions to provide for the Ottoman Empire "the benefits of good administration." Lest the objection be raised that such declarations of pious principles had also in earlier times been associated with practical administrative reform, a final characteristic common to the firman and the *hatt* has to be mentioned.

One of the contributions of the Gülhane Rescript was an appeal to "all subjects" of the Ottoman Empire to band together. European and American students of the *hatt* have interpreted this aspect of the charter as a taking over of

---

[7] See above, Chapter v.　　[8] Cevdet, *Tarih*, III, 87.

European liberal ideals. It is most interesting, however, that
a similar appeal to all Ottomans appears in the firman abolishing the Janissary order.[9] Although it is difficult to go as far
as one author and see in this earlier text connotations of "the
liberty–equality–fraternity slogan,"[10] the piece does stand out
as the first official document in the Ottoman Empire which, in
effect, consists in an appeal to the "people" to band together.
The new term *"millet,"* as we shall see later, begins to appear
in the last years of Mahmud's reign to express this idea. It
replaces earlier references to the "congregation of the Muslim
people" found in the Janissary firman, but it is used for the
same purposes that appears to have molded the wording of
the firman, namely, to mobilize public opinion. Incidentally,
the modernism of Pertev Paşa, the drafter of the Janissary
firman, appears once more in this connection.

The foregoing analysis does not as yet give us precise insights into the "operative ideals" of the Tanzimat. If we turn
to Reşid himself we do not make any substantial progress.
There is very little from his pen that would enable us to
determine his aims. One of the rare documents of this nature
is a project of reforms that Reşid submitted in 1841 to the
Austrian internuncio to the Porte, Baron Sturmer. This was
to be transmitted to Prince Metternich. The contents of this
project too have been studied.[11] Yet only a fraction of the
political theory of Reşid Paşa may be gathered from it.

[9] "Hence, let all the congregation of the Muslim people, and the small
and the great officials of Islam and the Ulema, and the members of other
military formations and all the common folk be one body. Let them look
upon each other as brethren in faith. Let there be no differences between
you. Let the great ones among you look with a merciful and compassionate
eye upon the little ones, and let the minor ones, moreover, in every instance
be obedient and submissive to their superiors. And may you all strive together toward the ultimate goal to exalt the blessed word of Allah, the
preservation and the exposition of the religion and holy law of the Prophets.
And Allah grant that your union, established and preserving for this noble
aim, of beneficent reform may continue and endure for ages to come."
Reed, "The Destruction," p. 247.

[10] *Ibid.* Reed too falls into the common error of calling Pertev a "reactionary."

[11] Milev, "Réchid Pacha," p. 383 f.

Some of his fundamental political beliefs may be gathered from Palmerston's memorandum of his conversation with Reşid.[12] Here the sequel that Reşid Paşa thought would necessarily follow upon the introduction of reforms points to the influence of Enlightenment thinkers: "Meanwhile, as the new institutions would be administered with wisdom and discernment, everyone would feel the real advantages of an immutably established system, as tyranny would diminish, affection for the government would increase, the peoples [*populations*] would rally with all the strength of their heart to useful and beneficial innovations."[13]

At a later date Reşid Paşa was to clarify what he meant by "innovations" by stating that the "way of civilization" which was being adopted in the empire consisted of "education" and "the observance of laws."[14] By the latter Reşid Paşa meant organic statute law and not the law of the Koran, which it was his aim to bypass. But neither do these fragmentary considerations amount to a statement of the political philosophy of the Tanzimat.

Fortunately there exists one source which makes it possible to extrapolate some of the clues that are to be found in Reşid Paşa's "Austrian" report into a comparatively complete political theory of Turkish reforms. This source consists of the *Selected Works* of Mehmed Sadık Rifat Paşa.[15]

Mehmed Sadık Rifat Paşa was born in 1807, a year before Mahmud II's accession to the throne.[16] After having completed his primary education, which, at the time, was still in the hands of the doctors of Islamic law, the ulema, he had

---

[12] See above, Chapter IV.   [13] Bailey, *British Policy*, p. 271.
[14] Kaynar, *Mustafa Reşit Paşa*, p. 69.
[15] [Mehmed Sadık Rifat Paşa], *Müntahabat-ı Âsar* (ed. by Rauf, Istanbul, Tatyos Divitçiyan, 1290/1870).
[16] Biographical information on Sadık Rifat Paşa is based on the following sources: the introduction by Rifat Paşa's son Rauf Bey to Rifat Paşa's *Selected Works*: see *Âsar*, pp. 2-6; also Ali Fuad, "Rical-i Tanzimattan Sadık Rifat Paşa," *TTEM* (September-October, 1929), I (NS), 1-15; Abdurrahman Şeref, "Sadık Rifat Paşa," in *Tarih Musahabeleri*, pp. 115-124.

gone on to receive special training at the Palace School ("*Enderun*") and, having terminated his studies here, was appointed clerk-trainee in the Bureau of the Imperial Treasury ("*Hazine Odası*"),[17] on the strength of his father's earlier services as Head of the Military Accounting Bureau ("*Masarifat Nazırı*").[18] Upon the demand of his widowed mother, he was transferred from this employment in the imperial household to a bureau of the Porte and was apprenticed to the Bureau of the Grand Vizier ("*Mektubi-i Sadaret Odası*"). There he soon attracted the attention of his superiors and was used as confidential clerk and *rapporteur* in a succession of crises such as the Greek Uprising, the Russian War of 1829, and the Egyptian Question. In this capacity he was able again to catch the eye of Pertev Paşa, who became his protector. In 1834 he was appointed Assistant to the Undersecretary of State for Foreign Affairs ("*Âmedî Vekili*"). Thereafter his career was assured. When, however, within three years of Rifat's appointment, his patron Pertev Paşa fell out of favor and Akif Paşa was appointed in his stead to the new post of Minister of the Interior (created during his predecessor's tenure),[19] Akif discovered that many of the denunciations against himself on file at the Porte were due to the pen of Sadık Rifat.[20] He also noticed that many of the practices in the office of the Undersecretary had been altered by Rifat. Rifat was therefore dismissed from his office.

The influence that had molded Rifat into such a budding reformist was again that of Reşid's mentor and ally, Pertev Paşa.

Needless to say, the return of Akif Paşa meant the sweeping away of Rifat's innovations. Rifat escaped further persecution due to the timely appointment of Reşid Paşa as Secretary for Foreign Affairs, and he was sent to Vienna as ambassador.

---

[17] See Gibb and Bowen, *Islamic Society and the West*, Part I, Vol. I, pp. 332, 333.

[18] Heidborn, *Manuel de Droit Public et Administratif*, II, 37.

[19] İnal, *Son Asır*, p. 1315.

[20] Ali Fuad, "Sadık Rifat Paşa," p. 2.

This was in 1837, approximately a year and a half before the proclamation of the Gülhane Rescript. From Vienna, Sadık Rifat Paşa began to forward to Reşid Paşa—who filled simultaneously the offices of Ambassador to the Court of St. James and Foreign Minister—a series of dispatches which also included extensive proposals for governmental reform in the Ottoman Empire. A definite parallel exists between the ideas that are developed in these dispatches, the principles that were soon to be enunciated in the Gülhane Rescript, Reşid Paşa's own "Austrian" project of reforms dated 1841, and the actual reforms carried out in the empire in the first years of the Tanzimat.

The similarity between the ideas of Rifat Paşa and the reforms carried out in the following ten years in the empire is not surprising. In his various capacities as Undersecretary for Foreign Affairs, Secretary for Foreign Affairs, Chairman of the Council of Judicial Ordinances, Minister of Finances, and finally Assistant Chairman to the Council of the Tanzimat (*"Meclis-i Âli-i Tanzimat"*), Sadık Rifat was provided in the crucial years of Turkish reform with ample opportunities to carry out the ideas that he had presented to Reşid Paşa while he had been in Vienna.

As to the resemblance between Reşid Paşa's views, as expressed in the Rescript, and those of Rifat, this is most probably due to the close collaboration of these two men and the cross-fertilization of their ideas. In the era which followed the proclamation of the Rescript, the personal relations of the two men may not have been entirely devoid of friction, but their stand toward the reorganization of the empire was at all times quite close.[21] An indication of the similarity in their attitudes toward the fundamentals of reform may be gathered from the mistaken attribution to Reşid Paşa, by a recent biographer of his, of archival materials which are in fact from the

---

[21] Rifat has usually been labeled a "reactionary" by European publicists. In reality Rifat was only more cautious than Reşid in his stand toward reform but was in the main tradition of Turkish reform as embodied in the policies of Pertev and Galib.

pen of Rifat and which had already been published some eighty years before among Rifat Paşa's *Selected Works*.[22]

Sadık Rifat Paşa's comments on the subject of reform in the Ottoman Empire thus provide us with extremely interesting materials with which to interpret the meaning of the Rescript of 1839 and enable us to assess the nature of the reforms which followed its proclamation.

All drafts of reform prepared by Sadık Rifat Paşa and included among his *Selected Works* seem to have taken their fundamental inspiration from a report which he drafted in Vienna not long after his arrival. In this report he pointed to the basic administrative practices and governmental principles which, he believed, the Ottoman Empire should adopt for its own good.

Both extrinsic and intrinsic evidence indicate that Prince Metternich, then chancellor of the Austrian Empire, played an important role in helping Rifat Paşa to crystallize his conceptions of beneficial versus unadvisable or dangerous reform policies. This evidence, added to the already existing materials which show the close connection between Reşid and Metternich, provides us with a most important clue in understanding Rifat's and Reşid's ideas and ultimately, therefore, the *Hatt-ı Hümâyun* of Gülhane itself.

The extrinsic evidence of Austrian influences on Rifat's political ideas consists of a number of messages exchanged between Metternich and his representative at the Porte, Baron Sturmer.[23] In one of these communications dated December 1839, i.e., immediately following the proclamation, Metternich, in response to a request for advice with regard to reforms which, he stated, originated at the Porte, enunciated certain principles for the salvaging of the empire which he requested be transmitted to Reşid. These principles were closely apparented to the approach adopted by Rifat in his own "Vienna"

[22] See the project of reforms in Sadık Rifat Paşa's *Âsar*, VIII, 63-73, and cf. Reşat Kaynar, *Mustafa Reşit Paşa*, p. 202.
[23] For these messages see Milev, "Réchid Pacha," pp. 382-398.

drafts of reform. Neither should this be surprising, for in the same message Metternich also explained that he had taken advantage of the audiences requested by the Turkish ambassador, Rifat, to subject him to a barrage of his considered opinions with regard to reform. He added that he believed Rifat Paşa now well understood the points he had tried to get across.[24]

The intrinsic evidence of Metternichian influences in Rifat's writings consists of the fundamentally conservative approach of Rifat to the reforming of the Ottoman Empire and his stressing of the measures aimed at securing "efficiency" rather than abstract "liberty," as well as his fear of "excessive" freedom.

By now, after the publication of Srbik's epoch-making work on Metternich, it is no more a matter for astonishment that the Austrian chancellor should have been interested in reforms at all.[25]

An analysis of the political ideas of Rifat Paşa follows, which, by substantiating the impact on the elaboration of Turkish theories of reform, of ideas which by no means could be called "typically liberal," shows that these Turkish theories were indeed closer to the methods of governmental rejuvenation espoused at an earlier date by the great bureaucrats who created the modern European state than to the ideas propounded by the European constitutionalists of the 1830's. It is also quite clear that in his writings Sadık Rifat Paşa was carrying on a campaign in favor of the Ottoman "men of the pen" which fitted in rather snugly with the characteristic approach of reformist bureaucrats to the process of government.

The main point of Sadık Rifat Paşa's most important draft of reforms, and the statement with which he often later prefaced a discussion of reforms necessary for the well-being of the Ottoman Empire, was that a new system had been

---

[24] Metternich, *Mémoires*, VI, 386.
[25] See Heinrich Ritter von Srbik, *Metternich der Staatsman und der Mensch* (München, F. Bruckmann, 1925), 2 vols.

enforced in Europe by the European Great Powers ever since the end of the Napoleonic Wars.[26] This system, which, as the Paşa stated, was also called "civilization," was based on the determination to maintain peaceful and friendly relations between the states. It aimed at repairing the ravages caused by wars and strove to augment the well-being of all subjects. This new conception, he continued, started from the premise that a state flourished whenever its subjects were provided with the opportunity to reap to the fullest extent the fruit of their daily labor. This, in turn, was only possible where the individual benefited from the extirpation of arbitrary rule. Wherever the people were given the assurance that no unforeseen circumstances would interfere in their life, and agriculture and commerce were protected, then, explained Rifat, the state would flourish too. The extent of the territory over which the sovereignty of a state extended, he added, was no longer considered to be an accurate measure of its strength.

To make these ideas more acceptable to his audience, Rifat Paşa clothed them in the garb of the classical Islamic-Ottoman "circle of justice," linking the well-being of the state with the prosperity and the contentment of its subjects.[27] Although this conception was thereby made acceptable to a Turkish interlocutor, it would be an exaggeration to say that the idea of the prosperity of the subjects had heretofore constituted the core of Ottoman political theory. Sadık Rifat Paşa's formulation might not have been entirely new, but his emphasis on the dual concept of peace = prosperity definitely constituted an innovation.

Sadık Rifat Paşa went on to point out that wherever arbitrary rule prevailed the state would decline, for the insecurity felt by subjects in such a state would prevent them from freely

[26] [Mehmed Sadık Rifat Paşa], *Muntahabat-ı Âsar*, II, 3-4; VII, 67; VIII, 35.
[27] For this idea see Kınalızâde, *Ahlâk-i Alaî*, Bulak, Egypt, 1248/1833. Part XI and conclusion; also, *Ottoman Statecraft*, p. 17. See also above, Chapter III, for Kınalızâde's relation with Young Ottoman ideas. For Rifat Paşa's statement, *Âsar*, XI, 42.

engaging in the productive activities which he considered the
lifeline of European states. In such circumstances, he said, the
subjects would shun the accumulation of wealth, which also
was a prerequisite of production.[28]

While neither trade nor commerce nor agriculture could
progress in states where governmental caprice was rampant,
government service too would deteriorate in such circumstances. Because of the insecurity of their tenure, officials would
try to cheat the state, look after their own interests, accept
bribes, and in general wreak havoc with the administration
of the country.[29]

This, according to Rifat, was exactly what had happened in
the Ottoman Empire. The insecurity prevailing in that country had, on one hand, hindered the subjects in the development of the arts and crafts that had advanced at such a rapid
pace in Europe and, on the other hand, had driven the servants
of the state, similarly deprived of any guarantees, into accepting bribes, pressuring the subjects of the empire, and plundering state coffers.

Of these two fundamental evils which, in Rifat's opinion,
beset the empire, the first one—the insecurity of the subjects—
was so obvious to any perspicacious observer of the Ottoman
Empire that it is difficult to attribute to any statesman, whether
Turkish or European, the distinction of having been the first
man to diagnose it. Palmerston, with whom Reşid was in touch,
diagnosed it;[30] Reşid Paşa himself was aware of it;[31] Metter-

[28] *Ibid.*, VIII, 45; II, 5.
[29] *Ibid.*, VIII, 44, 59; II, 5.
[30] Palmerston gave his diagnosis in the following words: "Is it hopeless to
get them to put their finances into better condition? If, instead of granting
out monopolies which ruin commerce, they would allow the people to trade
freely and levy moderate duties on commerce, they would find their revenues
greatly improved. *If, instead of sending pashas to eat up the provinces they
govern, and then be squeezed in turn by the Sultan, they would pay their
Gov't* [sic] *officers and not allow them to* plunder, the security which such a
system would afford the population would be a wonderful stimulus to industry and production."
Instructions of Palmerston to Ponsonby, December 6, 1833, quoted by
Sir Charles Webster, *The Foreign Policy of Palmerston: Britain, the Liberal*

nich no doubt could see it.[32] Rifat Paşa's comments therefore have no great originality. Yet the conviction that all that was needed to achieve the happiness of the subjects was to provide them exclusively with practical guarantees designed to increase their usefulness—the utilitarian taint, in other words, of these reform proposals—well indicated the conservative influences under which they had been elaborated. The quiet economic pursuits of peaceful, nonrevolutionary citizens were a channel for the diversion of energies that might otherwise have been used in more violent activities. Metternich approved of such "real" improvements, which he contrasted with factitious ones, such as the drafting of new constitutions. The link between Rifat's ideas and those of Metternich are acknowledged, in this case, by Rifat himself.[33]

As to the particular emphasis placed by Rifat Paşa on the security of government officials, this latter element, which appears in various guises in his writings, consists of the blowing up of a special (and specialized) problem into one of cosmic importance. This was Rifat Paşa's grinding of his bureaucratic ax.

Both pendants to Rifat's *résumé* of Ottoman weaknesses are important. One points to a state of affairs which it took long years to remedy in the Ottoman Empire and which even today is a timely issue under the Turkish Republic; while the other provides us with some interesting insights into what is best described as the "sociological dynamic" of the Tanzimat.

Rifat Paşa believed that only one solution would solve both problems at the same time. He advised, in very general terms, that in the future greater importance should be accorded to "rules and regulations" in the Ottoman Empire than to "per-

---

Movement and the Eastern Question (London, G. Bell and Sons, 1951), p. 540, note 1. (Italics in quotation are mine.)

[31] Kaynar, *Mustafa Reşit Paşa*, p. 115 f.

[32] See above, p. 158, n. 88. Baron Sturmer's dispatch to Metternich relating conditions in the last years of Mahmud's reign.

[33] *Âsar*, XI, 45, 56.

sonal factors."[34] In fact, he advised the establishment of a new system of laws, the essence of which would be that they would "determine the limits of the permissible in a way that would proclude the exercise of personal whims."[35]

This was a bolder step for Rifat to take than meets the eye. Up to the proclamation of the *hatt*, two normative systems had existed side by side which determined the "limits of the permissible" of which he was speaking. One of them was the law of the Koran, the Şeriat, with all its appendages for elucidation, interpretation, and exegesis—theoretically the supreme and ultimate statement of the law. The second body of law operative in the Ottoman Empire was derived from the power of the sovereign to make law by edict—the ancient *'Urfi* prerogative of the sultan. Much of the first reforms of Mahmud seem to have been passed on the strength of this imperial prerogative or, at least, rationalized on such grounds. What Sadık Rifat Paşa was now proposing was to make the sultan the source of law, respect fundamental statutes of a lay character establishing principles which the sultan might or might not have approved of.

In Europe, pointed out Rifat Paşa, the current usage was for all kings to respect such fundamental laws.[36] Neither monarchs nor their ministers ever thought of themselves as above the law in those countries, nor did they exile or dismiss officers of the state in violation of existing laws.

The more selfish considerations which were submerged under these counsels appear more clearly when read in conjunction with an obituary which Rifat Paşa wrote on the occasion of Mahmud II's death. The comments made by Rifat in this piece echo almost to a word the complaints of Reşid Paşa with regard to the sultan. Rifat's assessment of the character of the sultan included such interesting items as that Mahmud had relied too much on his household staff to settle matters of state, that during his reign officials had been in the throes of a constant apprehension lest they unwittingly

[34] *Ibid.*   [35] *Ibid.*, p. 45.   [36] *Ibid.*, II, 5.

displease him, that no officer of the state was protected from his wrath, that he was inconstant, capricious, and self-contradictory in his reforming activities, and that the latter had often been only skin deep.[37]

In some of his later projects of reform, drafted after the passing of the Tanzimat Rescript, Rifat Paşa went even farther in trying to establish this new understanding of the "rule of law" on solid foundations. Encouraged by the proclamation, he now spoke of the necessity for the sultan to accept advice and cooperate with officials. "For," he stated, "the continuity of a state is not only the product of the good administration of a given sovereign. The attainment of felicity is dependent on the drafting, in a consultative manner, of such laws as shall cause the people to pray for the continuity of the state after the demise of their king."[38]

Rifat Paşa also advised that the Council of Judicial Ordinances[39] be granted more extensive powers and he went so far as to suggest that this body should reject all legislative proposals which did not conform to the principles outlined in the *hatt*.[40]

In another instance he mentioned specifically that all "complicated" matters should be settled in committee by the sultan and his Council of Ministers.[41]

In a somewhat vaguer proposal, dated after the charter, Rifat Paşa also suggested that no orders be drafted contradicting "existing regulations," by which was probably meant the Rescript of Gülhane, and that orders received contradicting these regulations should not be carried out.[42]

Government officials were to be accorded the protection of new guarantees. They were no longer to be subject to "tyrannical action" without "good reason,"[43] and they would not be liable to lose their positions for having expressed their opinions in matters of state policy. Even if there existed perfectly

[37] *Ibid.*, VIII, 54, 55.
[38] *Ibid.*, XI, 45; VIII, 60.
[39] See above, Chapter v.
[40] *Âsar*, VII, 66.
[41] *Ibid.*, p. 63.
[42] *Ibid.*, VIII, 60.
[43] *Ibid.*, VII, 64; VIII, 44.

reasonable grounds for their dismissal, such dismissals were not to be used any more as pretexts to subject their person to indignities or to confiscate their fortunes.[44]

Rifat Paşa pointed out that a state which could rely on officials who had private means of support to begin with was at an advantage over a state who recruited statesmen among upstarts, because men coming from wealthy families would not be tempted to pillage state funds as would functionaries of more modest origins. Thus he advised that a statesman should not be automatically condemned whenever he had been able to accumulate some wealth.[45]

Nowhere, however, did Rifat Paşa's espousal of the cause of the "men of the pen" come out more plainly than in a petition drafted by him which was an explicit demand that the bureaucrats of the Porte be given the privileges and the honors which had hitherto been awarded in the normal course of their careers to the "men of the sword" and the doctors of Islamic law. Rifat Paşa requested in this petition that civil employees of the state, who, he stated, toiled no less than the members of the other two "orders" of the empire, be assigned to a definite rank in the hierarchy of state employment. Just as in the case of the two other orders, the "men of the pen" too were to retain the rank that corresponded to the office they filled, even *after* they had been been dismissed. Rifat Paşa also requested that these employees be appointed only to posts to which their rank entitled them and to no office of state which was filled by men of lower rank than theirs, that they be granted the right to receive decorations and be given a fixed place in the protocol of the state.[46] In short, the sum total of this part of Rifat Paşa's proposals amounted to the whittling down of the sultan's powers concurrently with the granting of new rights to the bureaucracy of the empire.

Turning to the second facet of Rifat Paşa's political theory—his concern with the well-being of the population and the development of agriculture and commerce—the Ottoman

[44] *Ibid.*, VII, 58, 59; VIII, 44.   [45] *Ibid.*, II, 6.   [46] *Ibid.*, IX, 11-14.

ambassador believed that the first steps in eliciting this recovery would be to provide the Ottoman Empire with the protection afforded by the "European system of the Law of Nations." Under the terms of this system, the Paşa pointed out, European states had worked out a scheme of international guarantees which allowed them to concentrate on the improvement of their countries and the development of arts, crafts, and sciences. The core of this system was the peaceful settlement of disputes, which the Paşa repeatedly advised Turkey to adopt.[47]

Simultaneously with these measures taken to regulate their external affairs, continued Rifat, the European Great Powers had taken steps in their countries to prevent undue interference with the activities of their citizens,[48] had eliminated unnecessary and galling ordinances, and had encouraged commerce, industry, and agriculture.[49] Thus the prosperity of citizens was something that the state should view with favor and not with suspicion.

Again in this case the influence of Metternich can be gathered from the words of Rifat who, in describing an audience he had with the chancellor upon being recalled to Istanbul following the death of Mahmud, enumerated the counsels of Metternich as follows: "The establishment of necessary regulations and the carrying out of the latter, and, again, *since in all nations' force and vitality originate in the comfort and ease of the subjects*, never causing any action that would cause [international] order to be disrupted.[50]

Undoubtedly Rifat Paşa's fear of popular revolutions had the same Austrian origin. At one point in one of his most detailed projects of reform, Sadık Rifat Paşa went so far as to state that "governments are created for the people and not people for the governments."[51] Yet the reason for which Rifat thought this to be true comes as somewhat of an anticlimax after what we should be inclined to consider a liberal idea.

[47] *Ibid.*, VII, 67; VIII, 38, 44, 58. [48] *Ibid.*, II, 4; VII, 67; VIII, 44, 58.
[49] *Ibid.*, pp. 44, 61. [50] *Ibid.*, p. 38. (Italics in quotation are mine.)
[51] *Ibid.*, XI, 43.

In Rifat Paşa's own words, "public opinion and the inclinations of the people are like an overflowing river, and there are two situations which are impossible to overcome, one of them being religious belief and the other public opinion. Since to oppose them is dangerous and difficult, in the case of uprisings and stirrings of public opinion, the state should act accordingly to the currents of nature."[52]

Indeed, a large portion of Rifat's major essay on government is sprinkled with statements to the effect that "tyrannical rule sows the seeds of enmity and reaps the harvest of revolution and anarchy,"[53] and that "a state can guard itself against the evil wrought by agitators only through just conduct,"[54] that a government "which enforces its rule by tyranny must heed its own subjects more than its enemies."[55] That this was a general consideration that lay in the minds of the Tanzimat reformers may be gathered from Reşid Paşa's similarly inspired search, following the proclamation of the Rescript, for "*une force legale de nature à contenir* le peuple *et en même temps empêcher tout acte d'injustice.*"[56]

Again, while Rifat did point out the advantages of a system of education so organized as to be accessible to a wider strata of citizens than had been available in the Ottoman Empire, he was wary of the political consequences of increased learning. He admired the Austrian schools in which the fundamentals of geography, physics, mineralogy, and zoology were being taught, but in the same breath he warned against a system of education aiming to impart to "the common people" ... certain detailed knowledge which is of no use to them and would result in license and lack of obedience."[57]

If an over-all characterization of Sadık Rifat Paşa's ideas is in order, no description fits these better than Herman Finer's remarks on cameralism: "Jean Baptiste Colbert, comptroller of finances under Louis XIV, has given us the word *Colbertism*, the French equivalent of mercantilism in England

[52] *Ibid.*, p. 47.　　[53] *Ibid.*　　[54] *Ibid.*　　[55] *Ibid.*, p. 43.
[56] Milev, *Réchid Pacha*, p. 390. (Italics in quotation are mine.)
[57] *Âsar*, VIII, 45.

and cameralism in Germany. *In each case is meant the planning by the state of economic welfare and national strength, from the government's point of view, imposed on the people by law.*"[58] Times had changed since Colbert's formulation, but the character of his policy still showed through Rifat Paşa's theories.

The philosophical dimensions of the reform policy of Rifat Paşa appeared in his use, once again, of the term "*umur-u cüz'iyye.*" Quite boldly Rifat Paşa enlarged considerably the area already staked by İzzet Molla by stating that all measures aiming at the increase of the well-being of individuals were parts of the area of free choice. In addition, Rifat Paşa stated that in taking steps to make his proposals materialize great importance had to be accorded to the "requisites of reason" ("*mukteza-yı akl*").[59]

This survey does not exhaust all aspects of Rifat Paşa's political theory. While the Turkish envoy aimed to widen the privileges of the bureaucratic class to which he belonged, while he acted as a channel for the funneling into the Ottoman Empire of theories aimed at its rejuvenation—which, however, stopped short of introducing the "serpent" of constitutionalism into Turkey—there were also strongly idealistic aspects to his projects of reform. These aspects transcended the more selfish or utilitarian undercurrents of his proposals. An underlying theme of all his papers was his desire to establish a regime based on right and justice. Thus he stated that the source of "the power and life" of all states was justice,[60] that the sovereign had to "capture the hearts" of his subjects in his dealings with them.[61] He was indignant in his denunciation of oppression and spoke of the necessity to respect "human rights."[62]

Such an idealistic attitude does not so much rule out any connection between bureaucratic self-interest and the political

---

[58] Herman Finer, *The Governments of European Powers* (New York, Henry Holt, 1956), pp. 283, 284.

[59] *Âsar*, II, 5.   [60] *Ibid.*, XI, 43.   [61] *Ibid.*, II, 5.   [62] *Ibid.*

ideas of Rifat Paşa as it confirms it. An espousal of the "rights of the subjects" seems to have been the ideological medium through which "the men of the pen" chose to work and the idealistic cocoon which they spun around their political theory. Nor is this entirely surprising, for parallels exist in European history of the interests of a rising class having been more or less unconsciously equated with the idea of the good and the just.

It is interesting that this defense of right and justice may again be traced to Pertev Paşa. It was on the occasion of Pertev's outcry to the effect that the sultan's subjects were not his playthings that he is reported to have been exiled for the first time.[63] In Sadık Rifat Paşa's writings we come across the wide use of the expression "*halk*" to convey the European use of "the people"; Rifat also spoke of "the right to liberty" ("*hukuk-u lazime-i hürriyet*")[64] and of "all subjects."[65] The same emphasis may be found in the Gülhane Rescript; the latter was the first document in the Ottoman Empire in which was used the word "*serbestiyyet*," a Turkish neologism invented on the occasion to convey the French "*liberté*."[66] In this charter there appeared too for the first time the word "*teb'a*" in its use to mean "all subjects without distinction of religion."[67]

Sadık Rifat Paşa also was one of the first Ottomans to use the word "*millet*" which to that date had had the connotation of "religious group," as the equivalent of the French "*nation*." He made such new constructions as "the interests of the *millet*,"[68] the "servants of the *millet*,"[69] and "service to the *millet*."[70] Thus concomitantly with the rise to power of a new class in the Ottoman Empire may be seen the coming into use of a certain ideological vocabulary and the vague outlines

---

[63] İnal, *Son Asır*, p. 1314.   [64] *Âsar*, II, 4.   [65] *Ibid.*, VIII, 38.
[66] Belin, "*Charte des Turcs*," p. 22, note 1. Cf., however, T. X. Bianchi, *Vocabulaire Français-Turc* (Paris, Everat, 1831), p. 422.
[67] Belin, "*Charte des Turcs*," p. 12, note 1.
[68] *Âsar*, XI, 42, 61.   [69] *Ibid.*, p. 61.   [70] *Ibid.*, p. 46.

of an espousal of the good of "the nation" and a defense of the "rights" of a nation.

In some instances reformers such as Rifat Paşa were also led to engage in activities which later opened the way for constitutionalism in Turkey. Thus, in 1845, to determine what reforms were most urgently needed, an assembly of notables was summoned in Istanbul and it was Sadık Rifat Paşa who composed the address read to them by Reşid Paşa. True, in this address the notables were told exactly where they stood; all that was demanded was their advice. But a precedent was thus created for the idea of representation.[71]

By the end of the 1860's and the demise of Âli Paşa, the last pupil of Reşid, the residue of the Tanzimat amounted more or less to the carrying out of the type of proposal that we have investigated above. The powers of the sultan had been whittled away and transferred in great part into the hands of a new bureaucracy; a certain regularization of governmental and administrative practice had been achieved; the worst features of arbitrary rule had been curbed at all levels in the empire. The protection of private enterprise had benefited mostly the Christian subjects of the Porte and the Moslem inhabitants of the Ottoman Empire had been somewhat slow in fulfilling Rifat Paşa's hopes of the advancement of arts and crafts.

The characteristic of the type of transmission of ideas that occurred in the case of Sadık Rifat Paşa was that the process occurred at the highest governmental level, i.e., in this case from a chancellor of state to an ambassador to a vizier. One similar stream exists which resulted in the concomitant suffusion of Turkish governmental circles by European ideas. This process occurred at the level immediately below the one of which we have spoken. It consisted in the introduction into the capital of Western ideas that were brought over from Egypt. These developments occurred in the 1850's when

[71] *Ibid.*, VIII, 2.

Turkish statesmen who at one time had been in the service of Egypt began to return to Turkey because the proclamation of the Tanzimat Rescript indicated that the Ottoman Empire was being regenerated.

The earlier emigration of Ottoman statesmen to Egypt is explained by the fact that in that country the movement of reform inaugurated by Selim III had found a more fertile soil in which to grow roots. During the aftermath of the Napoleonic invasion of Egypt, Mehmed Ali, the Turkish governor of the province of the empire, who had started his career as an officer of the Imperial Army, achieved semi-independent status. Taking advantage of the personnel of Napoleon's expeditionary corps which had remained behind, he had modernized his army before Mahmud II had put his reforms into execution and had gone farther than Mahmud ever was to go with respect to Westernization.

It would seem that for many progressive-minded young men for whom reform also meant opportunities for employment, Mehmed Ali, an Ottoman who had carried out reforms in Egypt with the aid of a Turkish as well as a French staff, represented a haven and a congenial refuge. In one case— that of Yusuf Kâmil Paşa[72] (not as yet a Paşa) who smuggled himself out of Turkey to serve Mehmed Ali when he still was very young—the motivating force, a kind of "Go Southeast, Young Man," is quite clear.[73] Yusuf Kâmil Paşa spent a number of years in the service of Mehmed Ali before returning to be one of the bright intellectual lights of the Tanzimat and a protector of the mentor of the Young Ottomans, Şinasi.

Other outstanding cultural figures of the Tanzimat, most of whom later became connected, directly or indirectly, with the Young Ottoman movement had an Egyptian "internship"

[72] The translator into Turkish of Fénelon's *Télémaque*; see below, Chapter VII, 241-242.

[73] İnal, *Osmanlı Devrinde Son Sadrıazamlar*, II, 197.

on their record. This was true of Sami Paşa, Subhi Paşa, and Münif Paşa.[74] The latter also studied in Egypt.

The fact that the first work advocating representative government in the Ottoman Empire[75] was published by the grandson of Mehmed Ali, the patron of the Young Ottomans, Mustafa Fazıl, cannot therefore be considered a coincidence.[76] The earlier and more extensive Westernization of Mehmed Ali's Egypt as compared with the rest of the empire, was acknowledged by the Young Ottomans.[77]

Outstanding among the *émigré* carriers of ideas was Sami Paşa, the protector of the Young Ottomans. At one time a governmental colleague of Sadık Rifat, Sami came up in the 1850's with his own very similar brand of defense of economic activity and free enterprise and condemnation of sloth.[78] Sami

[74] Ali Fuad, "Münif Paşa," *Türk Tarih Encümeni Mecmuası* (May 1930), I (NS), 2; detailed treatment of this question will be found in İnal, *Son Sadrıazamlar*, I, 196-258, and Ergin, *Türkiye Maarif*, II, 425-448. For Kıbrıslı Kâmil Paşa's Egyptian training see Ergin, *op.cit.*, p. 438. The latter politician, one of Abdülhamid II's grand viziers, should not be confused with Yusuf Kâmil Paşa.

[75] (Mustafa Fazıl Paşa), *Lettre Addressée au Feu Sultan Abdul Aziz par le feu Prince Moustafa Fazyl Pacha: 1866* (Le Caire: A. Costagliola, 1897). Original text in the daily *Liberté* (Paris, March 24, 1867).

[76] Mustafa Fazıl Paşa was also the founder of the first social club in the Ottoman Empire. Ahmed Lûtfi, "Tanzimattan sonra Türkiyede Maarif Teşkilâtı," *TTEM* (September 1927), XVI, 316. The date given is 1287/- 1870-1871.

[77] Namık Kemal, for example, stated: "It is well known that forty to forty-five years ago the political institutions of the Empire, which were, at any rate, in a sad state, became completely ruined and European governmental systems scored a complete victory. While such was the situation, the *Vilayet* of Egypt, by dint of its imitative policy, began to get the better end of things in its rivalry [with the metropolis] with regard to power and influence in the Empire." Namık Kemal, "Tanzimat," *İbret*, 4 Ramazan 1289/November 5, 1872, quoted by Reşat Kaynar, *Mustafa Reşit Paşa*, p. 195. Also *Hürriyet*, editorial, August 10, 1868, p. 3, where Kemal speaks of the "Arabs." A contemporary of the Young Ottomans described this difference between *Vilayet* and the capital as: "Le contraste frappant qui éxiste entre la manière dont sont élevés les princes de la famille d'Osman et le système scolaire qui est suivi dans l'éducation des princes de la famille vice-royale d'Égypte." Millingen, *La Turquie*, p. 291.

[78] See below, Chapter VII, for Sami Paşa. For his economic ideas see Sami Paşa, "Ehemmiyet-i Hıfz-ı Mal," *Mecmua-i Ebüzziya*, 15 Cemaziyülahir 1298, pp. 595-605; 1 Receb 1299, pp. 620-624; 15 Receb 1299, pp. 604-608.

Paşa's conception that the Turks did indeed possess the requisites for becoming a wealthy nation if only they tried hard enough was soon to reappear among the Young Ottomans. In view of the importance that Sami Paşa's *salon* acquired for the Young Ottomans and in view of the part that his grandson, Ayetullah Bey, was to play in the founding of the Young Ottoman movement, a connection between Young Ottoman economic ideas and the earlier conceptions of the Tanzimat thus does not appear improbable. This, plus the interest shown by Europeans in the economic development of Turkey in the 1860's, sets the framework for a study of Young Ottoman economic ideas. It was that part of reformist ideology that transcended all these more down-to-earth goals, however— i.e., the idea that the subjects had rights which could not be tampered with—that was to be the main source of inspiration for the Young Ottomans.

A third source for the permeation of the architects of the Tanzimat by Western ideas was the influence of their European collaborators. An example may be provided in the case of Alexandre Blacque. It was in İzmir in 1828 that the defense of the rights of the Ottoman Empire was first undertaken in a modern medium of mass communication. Here lived a Frenchman, a Monsieur Blacque, who, on a local press owned by the French Government, published a weekly paper, the *Spectateur Oriental*. This sheet had appeared since 1825, when Blacque had taken it over from its founder. Blacque had already attracted the displeasure of the French consul once in 1827 when he had criticized the British for sending a mission to Mehmed Ali. In general his attitude was pro-Turkish and anti-French, -British, and -Russian. Following the Battle of Navarino, he began to heap "the most violent abuse" on the policies of these three states.[79] Arrested by the consul and placed on board a French ship, he was released on promise to cease publishing. His influence, however, could still be noticed in the columns of the *Courrier de Smyrne*, which started publi-

[79] MacFarlane, *Constantinople in 1828*, I, 260.

cation shortly thereafter. When the establishment of an Ottoman *Official Gazette* was being considered, Blacque was asked to edit the section published in French (*The Moniteur Ottoman*).[80]

Blacque was one of the first foreigners who were directly influential in Turkey by their control of cultural media. This influence increased with time. Following the proclamation of the *Hatt-ı Hümâyun* of Gülhane, there was a sudden influx into Turkey of French *hommes de lettres*, whose invasion a contemporary observer caustically recorded: "Why should not the French press praise to excess what it calls the Turkish Charter, when Constantinople is in the process of becoming a suburb of Paris? . . . The last steamer has just brought to the capital of the Osmanlis a small literary colony which is going to exploit liberal ideas in Turkey and proposes not to return before it has witnessed a parliamentary debate inside a Mussulman Chamber."[81]

At the time the *Hatt-ı Hümâyun* was proclaimed, it was rumored that Reşid had been influenced by Blacque in drafting the charter.[82] Other Europeans from whose counsel Reşid was alleged to have profited included his secretary Cor and a certain Barrachin. The latter caused considerable trouble to Reşid Paşa at a later date in Paris by trying to extort money from him on the grounds that the Turks still owed him huge sums for his services.[83]

With the increased number of foreign experts employed by the Porte in the 1840's and 1850's, Western popular as

[80] The most reliable account of these developments is that of Louis de Lagarde in his "Note sur les Journaux français de Smyrne a l'époque du Mahmoud II," *Journal Asiatique* (1950), Vol. 238, pp. 103-144. Cf. with Gerçek, *Türk Gazeteciliği*, p. 22 *et seq.*; [De Kay], *Sketches of Turkey* (New York, Harper, 1833), pp. 402 ff., who states he saw the first issue of the *Moniteur* coming off the press; also Babinger, *Geschichtschreiber*, p. 354.

[81] Edouard Thouvenel, "Constantinople sous Abdul Medjid," *Revue des Deux Mondes* (1840), Series IV, xxi, 68, 69.

[82] Kaynar, *Mustafa Reşit Paşa*, p. 187.

[83] Cor is the author of a competent article on the finances of Turkey. See Cor, "Le Budget de la Turquie," *Revue des Deux Mondes* (September 1, 1850), VII, 938-948. Not much more is known about him.

well as serious literature became more widely available in the Ottoman Empire. In 1845 MacFarlane found the "young men who had been educated *alla franca*" delighting in the *feuilletons* of the *Journal de Constantinople*. The Governor of Izmit, Osman Bey, showed him "a socialist proclamation recently published in Paris."[84]

The Young Ottomans were directly influenced by this type of transmission of ideas. They frequented the bookshop of a certain Roth whose partner, a Hungarian refugee of 1848 by the name of Daniel Szilagi, provided young Turks with the latest political pamphlets and treatises to appear in Europe.

[84] MacFarlane, *Turkey*, II, 430.

The Immediate Institutional and Intellectual Antecedents of the Young Ottomans

IN THE preceding chapter we attempted to describe the fashion in which the outlook of Ottomans in positions of responsibility changed during the Tanzimat era. This chapter aims to show how both the ideological changes that came during the Tanzimat and the institutional changes that had been remolding the structure of the empire ever since the time of Sultan Mahmud (and stepped up in Reşid Paşa's time) affected the Young Ottomans.

A note of caution is in order here as to the classification of the occurrences and influences which make up the strands of the Young Ottomans' background. Any categorization of these antecedents introduces a note of artificiality into the appraisal of "things as they really happened." Thus the loosest categorization in this case is probably the best, and our survey here is divided into three parts. The first one of these headings is that of "traditionalist survivals," which deals with the extent to which the Young Ottomans were affected by remnants of the traditional Ottoman world view. The second section deals with innovations; it is a study of the way in which the reformist policies of their predecessors affected the Young Ottomans. Part three surveys the attempts made by some of the older men surrounding the Young Ottomans to find a middle ground between East and West.

I. Traditionalist Survivals

As has already been pointed out, one of the most interesting features of the *Hatt-ı Hümâyun* of Gülhane, the semiconstitutional charter proclaimed by Reşid Paşa, was its internal inconsistency. As one author has stated, it was indeed a curious document that could begin by "imputing the decline of the

Ottoman Empire principally to the transgressions of old laws," proceed "to adopt new regulations in the state," and end by "praising the restoration of old manners and customs."[1]

In this dichotomy of the charter, however, lies the answer to an understanding of the Tanzimat era, for it reminds us that the noisy and colorful personal clashes between the supporters of the old order and the defenders of the new, during the Tanzimat, were accompanied by a much more subtle and subterranean antagonism between the ideas that advocated a return to an Ottoman-Islamic golden age and the theories which sought to build anew better foundations for the tottering empire.

At least three forms of traditionalist orientation that were influential in the Ottoman cultural world up to the time of the rise of the Young Ottomans may be pinpointed: one of these was the survival of the Ottoman-Islamic ideals of the "good" state; the other, the survival of popular attitudes toward authority—what may be called the "Janissary spirit"; the third, the revival of traditional Ottoman-Islamic culture.

A. THE SURVIVAL OF ISLAMIC-OTTOMAN POLITICAL IDEALS

The idealized picture of an Islamic polity had been one of the main contributions of the ulema to the culture of Islam. The outstanding feature of this theoretical construction was its defense of the principles of Islamic right and justice as against the imperial prerogative of the *'Urf.*[2] Among Turkish publicists the emphasis on just rule and equity in the dealings of the ruler with his subjects went back, as we have seen, to the eleventh century A.D. There are indications that in the eighteenth century the disintegration of the empire caused a revival of the belief that those vested with power should conform to the restrictive injunctions laid down by the doctors of Islamic law with regard to the exercise of political power. Thus it has been observed that the latest Turkish "mirror" of

[1] Sir James Porter, *Turkey: Its History and Progress* (Vol. II by Sir George Larpent, London, Hurst and Blackett, 1854), II, 24.

[2] See above, Chapter III.

any importance to have been written (it was composed at the beginning of the eighteenth century) devotes even more attention than is usual in such works to the ethical conduct of the ruler and to that of statesmen in positions of responsibility.[3]

A statement by Toderini, the author of one of the first Western histories of Turkish literature, shows that this was not an isolated example and that the concept of an ideal polity carried weight, even with the sultan, despite the realism which permeated palace politics. According to Toderini, Mustafa III had ordered the translation of Machiavelli's *Prince*, but, shocked by the amorality of this work, had also given instructions that Frederick II's *Anti-Machiavelli* be translated and appended at the end of the *Prince*. The abbé claimed that he, personally, had the opportunity to check the veracity of this incident, since the translator was an intimate friend of his.[4]

A similar preoccupation with Islamic values may be detected from the rise to popularity, during the nineteenth century, of the *Ahlâk-ı Alaî*. This work was, as we have seen, partly based on the *Ahlâk-ı Celalî* of Celaleddin-i Devvanî, who in the sixteenth century had attempted to combine the Platonic conception of the philosopher-king with the office of the caliphate.[5] The *Ahlâk-ı Alaî* was first printed in 1833[6] but continued to be reprinted, popularized, and simplified for wider and wider circulation even after the relations with the West had been established once and for all in Turkey.[7]

Sultan Mahmud's rather meager efforts to reimpose an Islamic political theory were continued on a private basis by some of the ultraconservatives during Abdülmecid's reign. Thus the Şeyhülislâm Arif Efendi (not to be confused with Arif Hikmet Bey) translated into Turkish the *Mirror* of

[3] See *Ottoman Statecraft*, p. 18.

[4] Abbé Toderini, *De la Littérature des Turcs* (trans. by Cournand, Paris, Poinçot, 1789), I, 66.

[5] See above, Chapter III, for detailed treatment of the *Ahlâk-ı Alaî*.

[6] In Egypt on the presses established at Bulak by Mehmed Ali, see Babinger, "Kınālīzāde," *Encyclopaedia of Islam*, II, 101 f.

[7] Hilmi Ziya Ülken, "Tanzimattan Sonra Fikir Hareketleri," *Tanzimat: I*, 774.

Minkarizâde Dede Efendi in which the leitmotiv was obedience to authority.[8] Arif Efendi was, as one would expect, a confirmed enemy of Şinasi and was instrumental in his dismissal.[9]

During the nineteenth century a new significance was added to this survival of Islamic-Ottoman political ideals, since, by insisting on the "right" of the Ottomans not to bow to the will of reformist sultans and statesmen, the reactionary ulema could now pose as the advocates of Islamic "natural rights" and as the idealistic foes of autocracy.

An illustration of this selfish exploiting of Islamic ideals by the obscurantist ulema may be found in the anonymous manuscript entitled *Tanzîr-i Telemak*.[10] The manuscript[11] took its title (*The Rebuttal to Télémaque*) from Yusuf Kâmil Paşa's translation of the Abbé Fénelon's *Télémaque*.[12] The latter translation, the first work to carry Western political undertones, had created a considerable stir among the Ottoman literati of the capital.

[8] For Sultan Mahmud's political theory see above, Chapter v; for Arif Efendi's translation from the original Arabic, see Minkarizâde Dede Efendi, *Siyasetnâme* (trans. by Mehmed Arif, Istanbul, 1275/1858).

[9] Ahmed Rasim, *Matbuat Tarihimize Methal: Ilk Büyük Muharrirlerden Şinasi*, (Istanbul, Yeni Matbaa, 1928), p. 27. See below, Chapter VIII, for more details on Şinasi's dismissal.

[10] Although this work was written in the 1860's, it is an accurate reflection of the grievances which the ulema had nourished against the *Tanzimat* and reforming statesmen such as Reşid Paşa ever since, beginning with the late 1830's, their sinecures had been shorn and their status downgraded.
The manuscript shows signs of having been written by someone who admired Namık Kemal, the main Young Ottoman theoretician, enough to have appropriated passages from the latter's articles; but the emphasis of the *Tanzir* is anti-Western and obscurantist, two elements which are not characteristic of Namık Kemal's writings. It may probably safely be attributed to someone who was familiar with the ideas of the Young Ottomans, but who, as a member of the ulema had his own ax to grind. Identification of the authorship of the manuscript is based on the work done by Prof. Mehmet Kaplan; see Mehmet Kaplan, "Tanzîr-i Telemak," [İstanbul Üniversitesi] *Edebiyat Fakültesi Türk Dili ve Edebiyatı Dergisi* (November 1948), III: 1-20.

[11] The following exposé is based on the extensive quotations from the original manuscript in Kaplan's article cited above in footnote 10.

[12] Yusuf Kâmil Paşa, *Tercüme-i Telemak* [Istanbul], Tabhane-i Âmire, 1279 [August 1862].

The *Tanzîr* began with a description of the wickedness of man along classical Islamic lines but highlighted the struggle of man with his environment and his own kind. This strife was made to be the leitmotiv of the human condition. It was religion which, according to the author, lifted man out of this brutish involvement with nature. Civilization too was stated to be the product of religion, and the examples of the rise of the Islamic states and the Ottoman Empire were used as proof of this condition. In time, however, religious beliefs were corrupted and ritual took the place of faith. Whenever such a natural progression was actively fostered by belittling religious belief, the result was the disappearance of a nation from the face of the earth. This was exactly what the reformers of the Tanzimat had done to the Ottoman Empire. These leaders had themselves been transformed into beasts because they had rejected the guidance of Islam. By trampling the precepts of the Şeriat they had lifted the barriers that stood in the way of personal excesses, such as the plundering of state funds. By ignoring the dicta of religious law with regard to freedom of one's person from indignities, they had jeopardized personal safety and the enjoyment of life and property. The Ottomans had thus been reduced to a miserable state.

The question as to how far the author could carry a political protest arises at this point, for it helps us to assess the extent to which the "right to rebel" was accepted by the incensed ulema.[13]

Even though Professor Kaplan, who first discovered this manuscript, is of the opinion[14] that certain passages constitute an open invitation to revolt, this stand cannot be defended on the mere strength of the passages which he offers as proof for his statements. The threat that revolts had occurred earlier under similar circumstances is there, but it does not imply more than an angry appeal to divine wrath.

After having enumerated the reasons usually set forth as

[13] See above, Chapter III.
[14] Kaplan, "Tanzîr-i Telemak," pp. 18, 19.

justifying the Tanzimat reforms, the author goes on to state that, since the Tanzimat Rescript had been proclaimed, none of the evils existing in the Ottoman Empire had been cured. On the contrary, new difficulties have been created. Morals have declined, pious foundations have been neglected, and— what is of greater importance for an insight into the motives behind these complaints—the most powerful bodies throughout the land are now the provincial councils made up of the non-ulema.[15] These new administrators come in for bitter criticism; they are accused of ignorance and—gravest of all sins— of not according sufficient importance to the ulema. Yet, continues the *Tanzîr*, official positions and the power thereby derived are divine trusts. Those who profit from the privileges accruing from these positions are not more than the temporary recipients of such privileges. In an ideal society, where the Şeriat would prevail, however, the necessity for "consultation" of a public nature would oblige such officials to act with greater regard for the public. Thus the wide gulf, which it is claimed separates the common people from the bureaucrats of the Tanzimat, is to disappear. The only difference that remains in such a situation is that the functionaries have a greater number of "holes and patches" in their clothing and that the dishes served in their houses are more modest than the cuisines of the ordinary citizen.

While traditional values could thus be transformed into the defense of vested interests by unscrupulous or ignorant members of the *İlmiye*, the emphasis on Islamic right and justice and the idea that the Şeriat, besides obedience, meant just and equitable rule may also be found in the writings of many of the "Westernists" of the Tanzimat. In the writings of Sadık Rifat Paşa, the "political theorist" of the Tanzimat,[16] for

---

[15] For the provincial councils see Engelhardt, *La Turquie et le Tanzimat*, I, 15, 105-109, 195-96; Temperley, *England in the Near East*, pp. 237-240; James Baker, *Turkey* (New York, Henry Holt, 1877), p. 143. For the extensive powers of the governor-general see Larpent, *Turkey, Its History and Progress*, p. 38; on secularization, p. 32; on the resentment of the ulema, pp. 131 ff.

[16] See above, Chapter VI.

instance, it is possible to locate statements which reproduce word for word a theory of political obligation that appears in the *Ahlâk-ı Alaî*.[17]

Perhaps the most amusing confirmation of this lingering of Islamic values may be found in the conduct of Şirvanizâde Rüşdü Paşa, himself of ulema origins who, though he was a member of the Patriotic Alliance and still plotted against Sultan Abdülaziz in the 1870's, was also engaged in translating into Turkish a chapter[18] of a treatise on the ethical qualifications to be sought in a grand vizier, written by the Islamic jurist al-Māwardī.[19]

In the light of this survival of Islamic ideas of the state it comes as no surprise to see that in the 1860's the Young Ottomans too set their sights on the ideal Islamic polity of the doctors of law,[20] considered the imperial *'Urfī* prerogative to be an usurpation of individual rights of "Mongolian" origin,[21] and admired the ulema as repositories of the Islamic theory of "individual rights."[22]

B. CULTURAL IN-GROWING

Beginning with the eighteenth century it became obvious to the Ottomans that, at least in military matters, they needed to adopt Western methods. A considerable number of trans-

[17] See Mehmed Sadık Rifat Paşa, "Idare-i Hükûmetin Bazı Kavaid-i Esasiyesini Mutazammın Rifat Paşa Merhumun Kaleme Aldığı Risale," in *Müntehabat-ı Âsar*, XI, 42-43. Sadık Rifat Paşa himself was the author of a text on Islamic ethics which was used in Ottoman elementary schools; see Mehmed Sadık Rifat Paşa, *Ahlâk Risalesi* (Istanbul, Matbaa-i Âmire, 1286/1869, reprinted many times).

[18] İnal, *Osmanlı Devrinde son Sadrıazamlar*, p. 452. One of the generals who actually deposed Aziz, Süleyman Paşa, was also the author of a "catechism" [*İlm-i Hâl*]. See Bursalı Mehmed Tahir, *Osmanlı Müellifleri*, II, 203.

[19] İnal, *op.cit.*, p. 478. The manuscript translated by Rüşdü Paşa was probably the *Kitāb Kawanin al-Wizarā*. See C. Brockelmann, "Al-Māwardī," *Encyclopaedia of Islam* (1936), III, 416.

[20] Namık Kemal, "Wa-shāwirhum fī 'l-'amr," *Hürriyet*, July 20, 1868, p. 1.

[21] Namık Kemal, "*İ'zar-ı mevhume*," *Hürriyet*, February 22, 1869, p. 8.

[22] Namık Kemal, " 'Adlu sā'atin Khayr min 'ibādati alfi sana," *Hürriyet*, June 21, 1869.

lations from Western texts of military science were thus under-taken.[23] But parallel with these undertakings may be detected an attempt to go back to translate and print the most popular "classics" of Ottoman and earlier Islamic culture. During the nineteenth century the movement culminated in a real flower-ing of translations from the Arabic and the Persian.

In the field of literature and philosophy the Tanzimat, as a whole, was an era during which translations into Turkish of Islamic literature reached unprecedented proportions.[24] Any survey of the modernization of the Ottoman Empire which does not take into account this reaction falls short of an accu-rate description. Conversely, no translations from European thinkers, philosophers, or *littérateurs* were undertaken in Turkey in the first half of the nineteenth century.

An interesting example of the way this process worked may be witnessed in the fashion in which Sultan Mahmud tackled the problem of establishing minimum standards in grammar at the elementary level. The sultan did not, as we would expect, order the writing of a new textbook suited to his edu-cational goals, but gave instructions that the commentary on the treatise on syntax of the fifteenth-century Transoxanian savant Ali Kuşçu be printed. In this he encountered considera-ble opposition because the text was unfamiliar even to the ulema.[25] It is characteristic of the difference between the reforms of Mahmud and those carried out in the reign of Abdülmecid that in the 1850's a modern grammar was finally written anew by Fuad Paşa and Cevdet Paşa[26] on order from the Ottoman Academy of Sciences.

The generation of poets preceding the Young Ottomans

---

[23] See Selim Nüzhet [Gerçek], *Türk Matbaacılığı*, pp. 70, 80, 82, 83, 85.

[24] Sadrettin Celal Antel, "Tanzimat Maarifi," *Tanzimat* I, p. 460. A preliminary, though as yet incomplete, survey based on the bibliographical materials listed below shows this statement of Antel's to be true, even though the author himself offered no conclusive proof of his assertion.

[25] Lûtfi, *Tarih*, IV, 84; for the text *Unkūd al-Zawāhir*, see Abdülhak Adnan Adıvar, "Ali Kuşçu," *Islâm Ansiklopedisi* (1941), I, 321-323. The text was eventually printed in the 1860's; see M. Belin, "Bibliographie Ottomane," *Journal Asiatique* (1869), S6, XIV, 80.

[26] See below, p. 239, n. 182.

was steeped more than ever in the rigid Persianized form of Turkish poetry.[27] It has been said of these "Council" poets[28] that never before had the distance separating "popular" Turkish from the language of the literati been so great.[29]

The Young Ottomans were directly influenced by these last figures of Ottoman classicism. Ziya Paşa was a disciple of Fatin Efendi, an outstanding figure among those fighting this rearguard action.[30] Namık Kemal had as mentor during his early years Leskofçalı Galib, a classicist imbued with Islamic ideals,[31] and shows signs of having been influenced by the Sufî revival of the early nineteenth century.[32]

Both Ziya and Namık Kemal were members of a circle of poets headed by Hersekli Arif Hikmet Bey (not to be confused with the Şeyhülislâm Arif Hikmet) which has been called the "last Pleiade" of traditional poetry to have existed in Turkey.[33]

Another variant of the attitude induced by a mixture of Islamic with Western ideas was that of Tahsin Efendi, the doctor of Islamic law who established a close friendship with Kemal in Paris and who, though he was a modernist and a popularizer of European scientific advances, also brought back from Europe the idea of the propagation of the Islamic faith by the word instead of the sword. On his return he established in Istanbul a "Society for the Study of the Geography of Islamic Lands" whose purposely innocuous name was meant to ward off the curiosity of European diplomats accredited

[27] Gibb, *Ottoman Poetry*, IV, 353.
[28] *Encümen-i Şuara Şairleri* in Turkish.
[29] Tanpınar, *XIXncu Asır*, p. 229.
[30] Ismail Hikmet [Ertaylan], *Ziya Paşa: Hayatı ve Eserleri* (Istanbul, Kanaat Kütüphanesi, 1932), p. 15. For the classicism of Ziya Paşa see also Gibb, *Ottoman Poetry*, V, 78.
[31] For the relation of Kemal with Leskofcalı Galib, see Kaplan, *Namık Kemal*, p. 34.
[32] For the Sufi revival in the nineteenth century, Tanpınar, *XIXncu Asır*, Gölpınarlı, "Namık Kemal-in Şiirleri," in *Namık Kemal Hakkında* (ed. by Dil ve Tarih-Coğrafya Fakültesi Türk Dili ve Edebiyatı Enstitüsü, Istanbul, Vakit Matbaası, 1942), p. 19.
[33] Tanpınar, *XIXncu Asır*, p. 237.

to the Porte. His real goal Tahsin stated to be a duplication of the efforts of Christian missionaries. Whether the twin purpose of unifying the Islamic people and galvanizing them to lift themselves by their own bootstraps was also included in the goals of the society is not known, but very probably this was also considered.[34]

C. THE JANISSARY SPIRIT

The annihilation of the Janissaries by Mahmud had not done away with the spirit that had animated this institution. The latter had kept alive in the Ottoman Empire a populist *esprit frondeur* which had a number of times resulted in a rebellion against constituted authority. There was something quite close to the heart of the Ottoman people in this *esprit*. Part of the latter was the legitimation of revolt directed against an administration which did not forward the aims of Islamic-Ottoman greatness. This spirit rose to the surface on at least four occasions between the date of the destruction of the Janissaries and the arrival of the Young Ottomans on the scene. In the first instance, in 1837 it took the form of a conspiracy to revive the Janissary order. The plot was discovered and silenced.[35] In 1840 a similar plot misfired. In 1853 the population of Istanbul almost took up arms against the Porte for what it thought was the cowardly attitude of the Porte toward Russia. In 1859 a fourth conspiracy organized by an *âlim* but relying on the assistance of a soldier, Hüseyin Daim Paşa, took place. This was the so-called Kuleli Incident, which has already been mentioned among the events that made the backdrop of the Young Ottoman movement.[36] What made this conspiracy crystallize again was a series of military and diplomatic reverses.[37] The aim of the conspiracy was to replace

[34] İnal, *Son Asır*, p. 1879, quoting an article by Şemseddin Sami in the periodical *Hafta* without date or page reference.

[35] *London Times*, June 26, 1837, p. 3.

[36] See above, Chapters II, III.

[37] What had happened was that in the spring of 1858 Montenegro had prepared to invade the neighboring parts of Hertzegovina on which it had claims. France, England, and Russia acted in concert to prevent Ottoman

the ministers, dethrone the sultan, and put an end to Ottoman "meekness." It is significant that Daim Paşa, who had been condemned to death but who then had benefited from a pardon, was summarily arrested upon the discovery of Mehmed Bey's plot in 1867. Hüseyin Daim Paşa was exonerated, but the authorities were quite correct in sensing that the same spirit had animated the conspirators of 1859 and those of 1867.[38]

Namık Kemal too had correctly assessed the situation when he stated that the comparative docility of the population in the years following the destruction of the Janissaries had been due to the "sight of thousands of Janissary corpses rotting in the Golden Horn."[39]

Namık Kemal himself was opposed to the violent overthrow of constituted authority. Suavi, on the contrary, was in the main stream of an old Ottoman tradition in this respect, and there was no real contradiction between his advocacy of Islamic principles and his armed coup to depose Abdülhamid.

This, then, is some indication of the extent to which traditional influences had been at work in the Ottoman society of the first half of the nineteenth century.

II. Innovations

Two cases will serve to illustrate the connection between the Young Ottomans and the new institutions established during the Tanzimat—that of bureaucratic training and that of military education.

A. BUREAUCRATIC TRAINING

The increased contacts between the Ottoman Empire and the West had resulted in the early nineteenth century in a crying need for more and better interpreters. This acute need gave rise to a crisis when, at this very same time, the suspicion

---

troops from occupying the district of Grahovo, the disputed region. Under the auspices of these powers a protocol delimiting Montenegro was signed in November of 1858. See Engelhardt, *La Turquie*, I, 154, 155.

[38] *Augsburger Allgemeine Zeitung*, June 30, 1867, p. 2951.

[39] Namık Kemal, "Hubb ul-Watan," *Hürriyet*, June 29, 1868, p. 1.

began to dawn at the Porte that the Greeks used as interpreters were disloyal to the Ottoman Government.[40] It was at this time that the study of European languages was fostered in a systematic fashion among Moslem Turks.[41] In 1822 a special section called the Translation Bureau was established at the Porte.[42] By the 1840's this bureau of the Porte had already become one of the most important centers preparing young men for governmental careers. The Translation Bureau thus slowly took over a function filled in earlier days by the Imperial Secretariat ("*Âmedî Odası*")[43] and the Secretariat of the Exchequer ("*Defterdar Mektubi Kalemi*"). An interesting example of how this process worked is illustrated by the history of the *Takvim-i Vekayi*.

When this *Official Gazette* of the empire was started in 1831, a French as well as a Turkish section had been published.[44] After some time the French section of the *Gazette* disappeared, because of the lack of a competent staff. The editor, Esad Efendi, an historian and a product of the old educational system, was thereupon dismissed and replaced by Savfet Efendi (later Savfet Paşa),[45] a young employee of the Translation Bureau who eventually became Secretary for Foreign Affairs.[46]

The mere establishment of the Translation Bureau proved insufficient even while Sultan Mahmud was still on the throne, and shortly before his death a school was opened at the Porte

[40] Şanizâde, *Tarih*, IV, 22; also, Aurel Decei, "Fenerliler," *Islâm Ansiklopedisi* (1947), IV, 549, 550.

[41] Şanizâde, IV, 33; Cevdet, *Tarih*, XI, 166.

[42] İsmail Hakkı Uzunçarşılı, *Osmanlı Devletinin Merkez ve Bahriye Teşkilâtı* (Ankara, Türk Tarih Kurumu Basımevi, 1948), pp. 71-74. This was called the *Tercüme Odası* or *Tercüme Kalemi*. A program to train young men as translators began to be implemented in 1833. Tanpınar, *XIXncu Asır*, p. 112, gives the date as 1832.

[43] Lûtfi, *Tarih*, VI, 67.

[44] For information regarding this publication see Franz Babinger, *Die Geschichtsschreiber der Osmanen und ihre Werke* (Leipzig, O. Harrassowitz, 1927), p. 353, note 1; Lûtfi, *Tarih*, III, 156 ff., 37 ff.

[45] One of the students educated by the Beşiktaş Scientific Society; see below, p. 231.

[46] Lûtfi, *Tarih*, VI, 58, 59.

called the School of Instruction.[47] The ordinance which set up
this school indicates quite clearly that the students were to be
encouraged to read the newest texts that had appeared in
France on geometry, geography, history, and politics.[48]

In earlier times, when the center of political education had
been the palace, future statesmen were being groomed at the
Palace School (*Enderun Mektebi*). An indication of the new
status acquired by the new bureaucracy in the last years of
Mahmud's reign was the closing of this school in 1833.[49]

The new School of Instruction which took over part of the
functions of the Palace School did not last more than three
years, but at least one man whose name is connected with the
Young Ottoman movement, Ziya Paşa, graduated from it;
while another, Midhat, attended it for a short time.[50]

As to the Translation Bureau, almost all the Young Ottomans started their careers as clerks in this office. This is how
Namık Kemal, and Şinasi (who was in the Translation Bureau
of the Imperial Artillery), Nuri Bey, Mehmed Bey, and
Reşad Bey of Young Ottoman fame established their first
contacts with the Western world. Münif Paşa, the author of
the first translation into Turkish from the *philosophes*, was
also employed in the same office.[51] Similarly the generation of

[47] *Mekteb-i Maarif-i Adliye* in Turkish. The use of the term *"adliye"*
here has no implication of training in jurisprudence. It is used in connection
with Mahmud's by-name of *"Adlî*, the just." See İhsan Sungu, "Mekteb-i
Maarif-i Adliyenin Tesisi," *Tarih Vesikaları* (October 1941), I, 212-225.

[48] *Ibid.*, pp. 220, 221. Efforts were also made to raise the educational
prerequisites for admission to civil service positions. At first it was decided
that candidates to the bureaus of the Porte had to pass an admission examination (in 1252/1836-1837), Lûtfi, *Tarih*, v, 102. Later, attempts to raise
the educational level of the lower employees were made. Kıbrıslı Mehmed
Paşa, a grand vizier, in the 1860's tried to carry out a policy whereby all
employees of government would be literate and equipped, in addition, with
a basic knowledge of the fundamental laws of the land, see Hayreddin,
Vesaik-i Tarihiye ve sisyasiye (Istanbul, Ahmed İhsan, 1326/1911-1912),
p. 38 *et seq.*

[49] İsmail Hakkı Baykal, *Enderun Mektebi Tarihi* (Istanbul, Halk Basımevi, 1955), p. 114.

[50] For Ziya see Ergin, *Türkiye Maarif Tarihi*, pp. 326-329; for Midhat
see İnal, *Son Sadrıazamlar*, p. 315.

[51] Ali Fuad, "Münif Paşa," *Türk Tarih Encümeni Mecmuası* (May

statesmen that succeeded Reşid Paşa got its training in Translation Bureaus either of the Porte or of the Ministry of War ("*Bab-ı Seraskerî*"). This is true of Âli Paşa and Mütercim Rüşdü Paşa, whose very name—Rüşdü Paşa, the translator—provides a clue to his earliest occupations. Ahmed Vefik Paşa, the translator of Molière's plays into Turkish and also an outstanding statesman of the Tanzimat, was originally a clerk-translator.[52]

Many of the Turkish diplomats of the Tanzimat era supplemented the training given to the young employees attached to them by encouraging them, as well as the members of their own families, to increase their knowledge of Western languages. It is under such circumstances that Âli Paşa was able to master French and that Münif Paşa learned German.[53] When, toward the turn of the nineteenth century, the American educator George Washburn displayed surprise at Vefik Paşa's knowledge of Western thought, Vefik Paşa answered that while in France, he had had the occasion to become a neighbor of Ernest Renan and that they had often discussed questions relating to religion.[54] The following remarks by a secretary of the British embassy in Istanbul in the thirties gives an inkling of the level at which conversation could be carried on with the more brilliant products of this drive to learn languages of up-and-coming young bureaucrats: "We read together the best English classics—amongst them the works of Gibbon, Robertson and Hume—and studied political economy in those of Adam Smith and Ricardo. My friend Longworth had strong Protectionist views. I was an

---

1930), 1 (NS), 2; "Münif Paşa," *Türk Meşhurları Ansiklopedisi*, p. 267; İnal, *Son Asır*, pp. 997 ff.

[52] For Âli Paşa see İnal, *Son Sadrıazamlar*, p. 5; for Rüşdü Paşa, *ibid.*, p. 102; for Ahmed Vefik Paşa, *ibid.*, p. 651.

[53] For Âli Paşa see *ibid.*, p. 5, note 3. For Münif Paşa [A. D. Mordtmann], *Stambul*, p. 173.

[54] George Washburn, *Fifty Years in Constantinople and Recollections of Robert College* (Boston and New York, Houghton Mifflin, 1909), p. 56; see also İnal, *Son Sadrıazamlar*, p. 651. Vefik Paşa did not get this knowledge "while ambassador," as Washburn states, but while on the staff of Reşid Paşa, who was ambassador to France.

ardent free-trader. We spent many an hour in fierce argument in which the effendi [Ahmed Vefik] joined in great vigour and spirit. . . . He was a perfect store of information on all manner of subjects . . . and . . . a smattering of scientific knowledge, which he afterwards considerably extended."[55]

B. HALIS EFENDI AND DIDON ARIF

A more specific example of the extent to which the employees of the bureaus of the Porte mastered the ideological tools which were being used by their European opposites may be seen in the case of Halis Efendi, an employee of the Translation Bureau and a minor poet. On the occasion of the British ambassador's pressing for a claim against the Porte in 1837, Halis Efendi used the term *"droit des gens"* to defend the Turkish position.[56] While Halis was told by the dragoman of the British embassy that he should leave the use of such concepts to his European betters, it would appear that this did not deter the poet from imbibing other ideas, such as that of nationalism. It is in one of the poems published by Halis Efendi during the Crimean War that one encounters the first poetic-elegiac use of the word "fatherland" in a vein which is reminiscent of Namık Kemal.[57] Halis Efendi was also one of the first Turkish authors of a French-Turkish grammar, although his own claim that no other work of the kind had been written before by a Turk needs to be verified.[58]

The earliest indications that the young bureaucrats of Halis' type would try to turn to direct action if dissatisfied may be gathered from the role played in the Kuleli conspiracy of 1859 by an employee of the Bureau of the Imperial Artillery. This man, Arif Bey, was Europeanized to the extent of always

[55] Henry Layard, *Autobiography and Letters* (London, John Muray, 1913), II, 48 ff.

[56] Alric, *Un diplomate*, p. 13.

[57] İnal, *Son Asır*, p. 526. The word is *"vatan."* But see also the earlier influence of the *Ceride-i Havadis*, below, Chapter VIII.

[58] See Yusuf Halis, *Miftah-ı Lisan* (Istanbul, 1266/1849-1850), listed in Fehmi Ethem Karatay, *İstanbul Üniversitesi Türkçe Basmalar Kataloğu 1729-1928* (Istanbul, Osman Yalçın, 1956) I, 266; for Halis' claim see Hayreddin, *Vesaik*, II, 85.

addressing his colleagues with the interpolation "*dis donc*" ("say there") in French; this had earned him the nickname of Didon Arif. He was one of the ringleaders in the Kuleli conspiracy, of which he most certainly thought very differently than the guiding spirit of the affair, Şeyh Ahmed. Too little is known about Arif's person to do more than indicate this link between bureaucratic contacts with the West and the earliest form of a political protest to have been recorded under the Tanzimat.

We know of one instance in which the Translation Bureau acted as a funnel for the conveying to the Young Ottomans of some of the ideas of the Enlightenment that had permeated the Balkans at an earlier date. The process had worked as follows: One of the employees of the Translation Bureau who had acted as Kemal's tutor in French was a certain Mehmed Mansur Efendi, later known as Kemal hocası Mehmed Efendi ("Kemal's teacher Mehmed Efendi"). Mehmed Efendi was a Macedonian Christian converted to Islam. He was an amateur historian, and his hobby was the study of the Greek revolutionary society known as Ethniki Etairia, of which he was a relentless enemy. He was also one of the first men to engage in a defense of the cultural achievements of Islam. It is quite possible that it was Mehmed Efendi who first taught Kemal the virtues of national cohesion. Mehmed Efendi was, at any rate, the first Turk to publish a newspaper entitled *Vatan* (1867) which was eventually closed at the same time as the *Muhbir*, in the spring of 1867.[59]

C. THE ARMY

Military training had been one of the first channels used for the introduction of Western ideas into Turkey. Up to the 1830's, however, it does not seem to have been able to create a Western frame of mind among the military reformers themselves. The architect of military reform in Turkey under

[59] Ebüzziya Tevfik, "Yeni Osmanlılar Tarihi," *Yeni Tasvir-i Efkâr*, August 28, 1909, p. 4.

Mahmud, Husrev Paşa, held the opinion that reform should stop at the refounding of the army.[60]

Husrev Paşa, paradoxically, was a pioneer in the matter of sending young boys to study military science outside Turkey. In 1830 he dispatched four young members of his household, sons of his servants or slaves, to Paris under the protecting wing of the Orientalist, Amedée Jaubert.[61] It was exactly this generation of military men who were to bring a new outlook back into Turkey. Of the four boys, one of them later became Grand Vizier, another an artillery general, and a third a colonel of the General Staff.[62] Edhem, the future Grand Vizier, graduated with highest honors in 1839.

The same year that Husrev Paşa was packing off his wards to Europe and supporting them with his private funds, a project was prepared at the Porte to send 150 students to study military sciences in Europe. The historian Lûtfi states that the project met with considerable opposition both in the palace and outside and therefore had to be abandoned.[63] This is probably the reason for which in the following year (1831) projects were being prepared at the Porte to establish an Ottoman Military Academy.[64] This school was finally inaugurated in 1834.[65] Students were sent to Europe for military education the same year. Other groups went to London, Paris, and Vienna in 1835, 1836, and 1838.[66] Officer trainees were sent in 1846, 1850, 1854, and in 1855.

One of the first results of the program of European training was that as the graduates returned to their homeland and were given teaching posts in the Military Academy, foreign instructors were brought in and lectures began to be given in the language of the instructor, while translators stood by repeating their lectures in Turkish (1846).[67]

[60] Halil İnalcık, "Husrev Paşa," *Islâm Ansiklopedisi* (1950), v, 613, 615; also, Engelhardt, *La Turquie*, I, 86.
[61] İnal, *Son Sadrıazamlar*, pp. 601, 602.
[62] *Ibid.*   [63] Lûtfi, *Tarih*, II, 171, 172.
[64] Ergin, *Türkiye Maarif Tarihi*, p. 298.
[65] *Ibid.*, p. 299.   [66] *Ibid.*, p. 306.
[67] *Ibid.*, p. 310.

Conversely, the army had been one of the earliest institutions where an extensive program of foreign-language teaching had been carried out. In 1845 MacFarlane was horrified to see the "materialistic" spirit inculcated by French teachers in students of the College of Military Surgeons. In the Military Academy he found the master of French to be "a smart young Turk, who had passed ten years of his life in Paris."[68] The textbook used here was Fénelon's *Fables*, an indication of the fashion in which Turks came into contact with the later immensely popular *Télémaque*.[69]

MacFarlane also saw two students helping each other to understand Voltaire's *Life of Charles XII*. Again, at the military hospital of Tophane, he met a Turk who had translated "the most spicy passages of Voltaire's *Dictionnaire Philosophique*."[70]

In 1855 an Ottoman school was established in Paris because the establishment of eight-year schools ("*Rüşdiye*") had proved disappointing as preparatory schools for such institutions as the Military Academy. The new school was to prepare Turkish military students for the examination of the Grandes Écoles, such as the École des Mines, the Polytechnique, and St. Cyr.[71] At least one of the Young Ottomans, Mehmed Bey, got his education in this fashion. Soon non-

[68] MacFarlane, *Turkey and Its Destiny*, II, 275.

[69] See below, pp. 241 ff.

[70] MacFarlane, *Turkey and Its Destiny*, II, p. 295. At a later date the *Life* was included among the works translated by the Ottoman Academy of Sciences (see below, p. 239, note 182) but remained at the draft stage. See Tanpınar, *XIXncu Asır*, p. 114. The reason for which the Tophane ("Imperial Artillery") was a nucleus of Europeanization was that its director Fethi Ahmed Paşa had been a strong partisan of modernization. Thus the fact that Şinasi received his scholarship to Europe while in this bureau was no coincidence. See Tanpınar, *XIXncu Asır*, p. 111.

[71] Mehmed Esad, *Mir'at-i Mekteb-i Harbiye*, pp. 65-74; Edmond Chertier, *Les Réformes en Turquie* (Paris, Dentu, 1858), p. 62. A similar attempt had been made in 1844 by Mehmed Ali; see J. Heyworth Dunne, *An Introduction to the History of Education in Modern Egypt* (London, Luzac, 1938), pp. 243-245. Halil Şerif Paşa (see above, Chapter II) had been sent to France before the establishment of this school but continued his studies in this so-called Paris Egyptian Military School after 1844.

military students arrived too, among them the later-famous poet Abdülhak Hâmid.

The early contacts of the army with the European world of ideas had already created a self-sustaining cultural effervescence by the 1870's. It was at that time that an officer who had never been to Europe composed the first systematic textbook on literary genres in Turkish. This was used in the course on Turkish literature established and taught by the compiler of the book. The compendium contained selections from Fénelon, Napoleon, Racine, and Volney.[72] Its editor was Süleyman Paşa, who at that time filled the office of Inspector of Military Schools and later was one of the four statesmen instrumental in the deposition of Abdülaziz.[73]

In Süleyman Paşa's writings we encounter an attempt to set down a theoretical expression of the activist attitude that is characteristic of the ideology of the Young Ottomans. He translated the work on free will of the Şeyh Halid of Baghdad (d. 1827) in which the Maturidite controversy with regard to free will was being revived.[74]

The Europeanization of the army was not without its direct effect on the Young Ottoman movement itself. Thus it was Edhem Paşa who encouraged the Young Ottoman Ziya Paşa to take up the study of French. The Young Ottoman Ali Suavi was patronized by Eğinli Said Paşa—known as Said Paşa the Englishman—a general who as a military trainee had studied mathematics for seven years in Edinburgh.[75]

In 1869, the year during which Young Ottoman activities were at their peak, a book expressing the same general ideas

---

[72] See Süleyman Paşa, *Mebani ül-İnşa'* (Istanbul, I, 1291/1874; II, 1289 [sic]/1873-1874).

[73] See above, Chapter IV, p. 109, n. 6. For a biography of Süleyman Paşa see [Süleyman Paşazâde Sami], *Süleyman Paşa Muhakemesi*, pp. 3-10.

[74] For this work, see Von Hammer-Purgstall, "Liste des Ouvrages imprimés à Constantinople dans le cours des années 1843 et 1844," *Journal Asiatique* (August-September 1846), Series IV, Vol. VIII, p. 256; Bursalı Mehmed Tahir, *Osmanlı Müellifleri*, I, 66, 67; for the teachings of the Maturidites, D. B. Macdonald, "Māturīdī," *Encyclopaedia of Islam*, III, 414, 415.

[75] Gövsa, *Türk Meşhurları*, p. 340.

with regard to representation that are to be found in Young
Ottoman publications stated that if a *"représentation centrale
nationale"* were to be created, "the military *representing the
intelligentsia in Turkey must also be eligible."*[76]

A most striking evidence of the role which early contacts
with the West led the Ottoman army to play may be evidenced in the career of Hüseyin Vasfi Paşa. The latter fled to
Europe when, in the fall of 1868, his plan to ram the imperial
caïque was discovered. He then joined forces with the most
radical of the Young Ottomans, Mehmed Bey, to publish the
most radical of the Young Ottoman publications, the newspaper *İnkılâb* ("Revolution") in Geneva. This was a publication which by Kemal's own admission[77]—and because of its
advocacy of violent revolution—was far to the left of the
Hürriyet. Kemal stated, in the same sentence in which he
expressed his dislike of the position assumed by the *İnkılâb,*
that, despite all, the army was still the most trustworthy
element working for reforms in the empire.

This feeling of Kemal's was confirmed in 1872 at a time
when he had been exiled by Abdülaziz. The Young Ottomans
having been scattered, Namık Kemal believed that the movement of political reform had been cut at the root in Turkey.
He was agreeably surprised, therefore, to find in his mail a
magazine entitled *Çanta* ("The Knapsack"), which was being
published by a young staff officer by the name of Menemenli
Rifat and which included patriotic-literary articles as its main
staple. The *Çanta,* a sort of "Officer's Literary Magazine,"[78]
more or less overtly tried to create a stereotype of the officer
as a bulwark of the empire.

To the publisher Kemal wrote: "Long live the Young

[76] Moustafa Djelaleddine, *Les Turcs Anciens et Modernes* (Constantinople, Imprimerie du Courrier d'Orient, 1869), p. 211.

[77] Kuntay, *Namık Kemal,* I, 435, note 31. For Ziya Paşa's dissociation
with Hüseyin Vasfi, see below, Chapter XI. It is probably more than a coincidence that Vasfi Paşa was the son-in-law of another former military man,
Rüşdü Paşa, who eventually was to unseat Abdülaziz. See above, Chapter IV.

[78] *Çanta* (Istanbul, Cemiyet-i Tedrisiye-i Islamiye, 1290). The editor,
Menemenlizâde Rifat, later married Kemal's daughter.

Ottomans.... If ten years ago, at a time when the state, having decided to publish a military journal could not find among the officers more than two or three ex-clerks [competent enough to do the job], an angel had descended from Heaven and announced that within ten years, officers of the age of twenty and twenty-two, and even our own pupils, were to become the leaders of the nation and maybe the inventors of its literature, who could have believed it? ... Who are those who are so rash as to deny all hope for this nation . . . and who proclaim that the education of its people is an impossible task . . . ?"[79]

Finally it was the military who had the most important role to play in the deposition of Sultan Abdülaziz in 1876. The general who provided the armed forces that supported the coup relates in his memoirs that it was the despair he felt at the Ottoman Empire's ever catching up with the West that made him rebel.[80]

If the "men of the pen" and the "men of the sword" had been molded in a comparatively short span of time into a new and Westernized elite, the influence of the West was not entirely without its effect on the third order of the Ottoman Empire, the doctors of Islamic law who made up the institution of the *Ilmiyye*.

D. THE ULEMA

The obvious decay of the institution of the *Ilmiyye* had led students of this order to make hasty generalizations about the ulema which are incorrect and misleading. The contention is thus advanced that the ulema "naturally" thwarted all attempts at reform. It would seem, however, that the role played by this estate of the Ottoman realm was much more subtle than one gathers from such sweeping generalizations. While examples may be given of ulema who were adamant in their

[79] Kuntay, *Namık Kemal*, II, 231.
[80] Süleyman Paşa, *Hiss-i İnkılâb*, pp. 4 ff.

antireformist attitude,[81] a number of them appear to have worked in collaboration with the reformist sultans.

Even in the time of Sultan Selim, the *Şeyhülislâm* Ahmed Esad Efendi had incurred the wrath of the reactionary ulema because he approved of the innovations of the sultan, and the *Şeyhülislâm* Hamidizâde Mustafa Efendi was dismissed due to the uproar caused by his attempts to reform the ulema.

Şanizâde, the brilliant member of the Beşiktaş Society, was also an *âlim*. The classical statement of the case for the establishment of the *Nizam-ı Cedid*, the new troops organized on a European model by Selim, is from the pen of an *âlim*, Mehmed Münib Efendi.[82] One of the projects of reform presented to Selim was that of Tatarcık Abdullah Molla,[83] a member of the religious estate.

The educational background of Kethüdazâde Arif Efendi, the lecturer in philosophy of the Beşiktaş Society,[84] gives an indication of the range covered in training the more sophisticated ulema. Geometry, mathematics, astronomy, and philosophy, all more or less suspect in Islam, made up more than one half of the subjects which Kethüdazâde had studied.[85] This is borne out by other surprising examples of ulema interest in physical sciences and association with attempts to introduce new Western cultural implements. Thus when the permission was first granted to establish a Turkish-run printing plant, the committee which was to supervise the printing of "dictionaries, and works on history, philosophical sciences, astronomy and geography" was made up of ulema. When the School of Engineering was established in 1734, algebra and geometry were taught by ulema. It was another *âlim*, the translator of İbn Haldun, Pirizâde, who ordered experimental apparatus from France for this school.[86]

[81] Such as, for instance, the *Şeyhülislâm* Topal Ataullah Efendi who was the ringleader in the movement to depose Selim.
[82] See Babinger, *Geschichtsschreiber*, pp. 344, 345.
[83] Cevdet, *Tarih*, VI, 43-52.
[84] See below, p. 229.
[85] İnal, *Son Asır*, pp. 34, 35.
[86] Esad, *Mir'at-ı Mühendishane*, p. 7; see also p. 34 for another mathe-

During the reign of Mahmud, Keçecizâde[87] and the *Şey-hülislâm* Arif Hikmet Bey helped to carry out reforms.[88] The latter was sent to Rumelia in 1840 to see whether the principles enunciated in the charter of Gülhane were being carried out. Another liberally inclined *âlim* was Çelebizâde Hafidi Mehmed Zeynülabidin Efendi. He had to be dismissed because of minor uprisings among the students of theology caused by his efforts at reforming the ulema.[89]

Kemal Efendi (later Kemal Paşa), who carried out the decision taken in the *Meclis-i Vâlâ* in 1838 to secularize primary education by establishing the modernized eight-year schools called *Rüşdiyes*, was a member of the ulema. When Kemal Paşa reached the point where he began interfering with religious educational institutions, his life was threatened and he had to be spirited out of the capital and given a diplomatic post in Germany.[90]

Sami Paşa, the Abdülmecid's first Minister of Education, one of the statesmen instrumental in the secularization of education and a protector of the Young Ottomans, although a layman himself, came from a long line of ulema.[91]

The preceding argument as to the open-mindedness of the ulema does serve to dispel some of the fog cast on nineteenth-century Turkish social history. Yet the argument is really of no use in explaining the association of ulema with Young Ottomans, for by the 1860's the sophisticated and open-minded ulema were almost extinct. With the one exception of the historian Cevdet Paşa, who in part owed his open-mindedness to the mentorship of Reşid Paşa, the concentration of the educational resources of the empire to train better civil servants

---

matician, Hoca İshak, the author of the first (four-volume) modern textbook of mathematics in Turkish.

[87] Cevdet, *Tarih*, VI, 29.

[88] Fevziye Abdullah [Tansel], "Arif Hikmet Bey," *Islâm Ansiklopedisi* (1940), I, 564-568; İnal, *Son Asır*, p. 621; Ubicini, *La Turquie Actuelle*, p. 172; Lûtfi, *Tarih*, VI, 101.

[89] Cevdet, *Tarih*, X, 236 f.

[90] Ergin, *Türkiye Maarif Tarihi*, pp. 369-372.

[91] İnal, *Son Asır*, p. 1649.

had resulted in a decrease of the well-educated, broad-minded ulema. Cevdet Paşa himself considered the date of the death of the *Şeyhülislâm* Arif Hikmet Bey (1859) to be a landmark in this process. With his demise, the really learned *âlim* had disappeared, according to Cevdet.[92]

In reality, as has been pointed out before,[93] the causes for the closeness between the Young Ottomans and the doctors of Islamic law were a common loss of status and a common dislike for the "official" ulema, the *Ulema-i Rusum*, or ulema who were granted diplomas as the result of their connections. An illustration of the way their alliance worked may be found in the establishment of the *Cemiyet-i Tedrisiye-i İslamiye*, an association which began as an adult education society and eventually laid the foundation for a *lycée* where Islamic ideals prevailed, although instruction was carried on along modern lines. Even today this *lycée*, the *Darüşşafaka*, has remained as a center of conservatism. The following were the influences which led to the creation of this institution.

The ulema had not reacted constructively for a long time to the efforts of the Tanzimat leaders to spread education among a wider strata of the population. The challenge of providing the means to establish modern educational institutions was not taken up by an Islamic group until 1864-1865. That year instruction began to be provided which had as a goal the elementary education as well as the religious training of indigent Moslems—shopkeepers and poor government employees who had not had the benefits of formal schooling.

At first the school was named *Cemiyet-i Tedrisiye* ("Instruction Society"), but this name was later changed to that of *Cemiyet-i Tedrisiye-i İslamiye* ("Islamic Educational Society"), to show that the primary purpose of the organization was Islamic. What is striking in this case is that the impetus to

[92] Cevdet Paşa, "Ma'ruzat," *TTEM* (July 1925), XV, 271; (May 1926), XVI, 167, 168.

[93] See above, Chapter IV.

[94] *Cemiyet-i Tedrisiye-i İslamiye Salnamesi* (Istanbul, 1332/1913-1914), p. 8; Belin, "De l'Instruction," p. 230.

establish this new educational institution came not from the ulema but from a group of government employees.[95]

A breakdown of charter members of the organization reveals that a number of ulema were also among the sponsors; none of the sponsors, however, were of top rank, i.e., undersecretary or higher. This already establishes an affinity between the social origins of the sponsors and those of the Young Ottomans. A complete survey of the sponsors reveals again an alliance between the lower- and middle-level bureaucrats, the less important ulema, and the military, the proportion of each of these elements among the founders reflecting the proportion in which they are also found among the Young Ottomans.[96]

In the case of the Cemiyet the collaboration with the military can be traced fairly accurately. The society, for instance, for a few years published a periodical entitled *Mebahis-i İlmiye* (*"Scientific Questions"*), which is reported to have been in great demand among the students of the Imperial Military Academy.[97] Again, it is interesting that the proceeds of the first "officers' literary magazine" in the empire, the *Çanta*, were to go to the Educational Society.

The Educational Society was also an institution which greatly interested the intellectuals who gathered in the editorial offices of the *Tasvir-i Efkâr* and, in particular, the

[95] The three initiators of the new Islamic school were Yusuf Bey, later Minister of Finances; Muhtar Bey, an officer (later known as Gazi Ahmed Muhtar Paşa); and another military man, Tevfik Bey (later known as Müş'ir Vidinli Tevfik Paşa). Later, on the advice of Sakızlı Esad Paşa, a former director of the Ottoman school in Paris, the institution was enlarged and made a military preparatory school on the model of the French "Prytanée Militaire de la Flèche." *Salname*, p. 13. For Tevfik Paşa see Gövsa, *Türk Meşhurları*, p. 380; Tahir, *Osmanlı Müellifleri*, III, 258. Tevfik Paşa's works, interestingly enough, were almost all on mathematics.

[96] The following were these sponsors: two employees of the ministry of education (ulema), five employees of the ministry of finances, five employees of the bureaus of the ministry of war (employed mostly in financial capacities), two employees of the ministry of foreign affairs, three employees of the bureau of the Undersecretary of State for Foreign Affairs, two field officers, one police department head, one librarian, one *âlim* sitting on commercial courts.

[97] *Salname*, p. 11.

Young Ottomans.[98] Namık Kemal while still in the capital was a volunteer instructor in spelling at the school.[99]

Quite apart from this specialized case of cooperation between the ulema and the Young Ottomans, what seems to have happened in a more general context is that, with the arrival on the scene of men who were bent on saving traditional Ottoman values, the thousands of ulema in training, the students of Islamic law with only a mediocre future to look forward to, were provided with an instrument of protest. The manifestations of students of religion (*Softas*) which were decisive in 1876 in forcing the appointment of Rüşdü Paşa to the grand vizierate become intelligible in this perspective. It is due to these factors that the Young Ottomans were able, for the first time, to gather the students of theology of Istanbul under the banner of such an essentially Western course as political representation. These were the same students who earlier had been used by obscurantist ulema to protest against reforms. Furthermore, the Young Ottomans, more religiously inclined than the generation of statesmen who had succeeded Reşid Paşa, could also become a rallying point for the liberally inclined ulema, to the very limited extent to which the latter still existed.

It might be useful to remember in this connection that the ulema, despite theoretical strictures against disobedience to authority, were quite turbulent. In 1859 the Kuleli conspiracy to unseat Abdülmecid was led by a certain Şeyh Ahmed of Süleymaniye, i.e., a member of the ulema. Among the liberal-minded members of the *İlmiyye* who were associated with the Young Ottomans were such figures as Veliyeddin Efendi, whose imprisonment in 1867, at a time when the Young Ottomans were obliged to flee Turkey, caused the religious students studying under him to band together and manifest noisy displeasure in front of the palace gates.[100] On the same occa-

---

[98] For a few paragraphs of praise see *Tasvir-i Efkâr* (15 Safer 1283/-June 30, 1866), p. 2.

[99] *Salname*, p. 9.

[100] Kuntay, *Namık Kemal*, II, 471, and above Chapter II.

sion, the Young Ottoman Aksaraylı Şeyh Hasan Efendi was exiled to Cyprus.[101] When five years later Namık Kemal himself was exiled to Cyprus, there were five people in all who were believed to be so dangerous that they had to be banished to far-flung corners of the empire. One of them, Bereketzâde Ismail Hakkı Efendi, was an *âlim.*[102]

The most colorful of the Young Ottoman leaders, Ali Suavi, was himself a member of the ulema. The eventful career of Suavi had made him stand out in Turkish political and intellectual history; thus lesser figures of *Ilmiyye* origins whose contributions are also important have been relegated to the background. The attitudes of these men, however, are an essential ingredient in the temper of the times. Two enlightened *âlims* in particular deserve notice—Hoca Tahsin Efendi and Sarıyerli Hoca Sadık Efendi.

Hoca Tahsin Efendi had been sent to France by Reşid Paşa to study natural sciences in an attempt to create a Westernized ulema elite.[103] He remained there for twelve years, where he acted at the same time as the "chaplain" of the Ottoman embassy. Hoca Tahsin was also given the responsibility of keeping track of the faith and morals of the students at the Turkish school in Paris. Two wards who were personally entrusted to Tahsin Efendi were Abdülhak Hâmid, of later poetic fame, and Hâmid's brother Nasuhi.[104] During his stay he got to know the *émigré* Young Ottomans and established a close friendship with them. He returned to Istanbul in 1869 with the body of Fuad Paşa, who had died at Nice.

He was then made the dean of the Ottoman University which had been inaugurated a year before. An experiment in physics in which he engaged soon made him the target of the attacks of the ulema. To illustrate the notion of vacuum, he had placed a pigeon underneath a glass bell. When he began

[101] *Ibid.*

[102] *Ibid.,* p. 167.

[103] Necib Âsım, "Hoca Tahsin," *TTEM* (June 1, 1928) XVII-XVIII, 57-63; *Sicill-i Osmanî,* II, 51; Gövsa, *Türk Meşhurları,* p. 176.

[104] İnal, *Son Asır,* p. 544.

to empty the receptacle and the bird suffocated, Tahsin Efendi
thought he had proven his point. All he had done, in reality,
was to expose himself to accusations of performing magic. He
was thus charged with being a heretic, had to discontinue his
lectures, and was eventually dismissed.[105] The university too
was closed because the advanced opinions of Tahsin Efendi
were being reinforced by those of Cemaleddin el-Afganî. The
latter had caused a scandal when his remarks on the subject of
the "Advancement of Arts, Crafts, and Industry" were erroneously interpreted by an ignorant—though influential—*âlim*
as placing arts and crafts and divine inspiration on a footing
of equality.[106]

Tahsin Efendi's modernism may be witnessed in his publication of the first Turkish treatise on psychology.[107] He also
wrote the first exposé of modern astronomical theories at a
popular level.[108] To him is also attributed a translation of
Volney's *Loi Naturelle*,[109] which Namık Kemal also translated.[110] Tahsin's charge, Nasuhi, apparently followed in the
steps of his tutor, for like Tahsin he engaged in a translation
of Volney's *Ruins of Palmyra*. Hâmid himself has been

[105] Lewis Farley lists four of the lecturers in physical sciences, all of whom
were ulema, and one of whom, Selim Sabit Efendi, had been sent to Paris
with Tahsin. Selim Sabit Efendi is also known for having attempted to open
one of the first elementary schools where modern principles of education
were applied. See Lewis Farley, *Modern Turkey* (2nd ed., London, Hurst
and Blackett, 1872), p. 154; Ergin, *Türkiye Maarif Tarihi*, p. 384.

[106] Ergin, *Türkiye Maarif Tarihi*, II, 465-468. The university was
closed in December 1870. For further details see Mehmed Zeki Pakalın, *Son
Sadrıazamlar ve Başvekiller* (Istanbul, Ahmed Sait Matbaası, 1944), IV,
140-156; İnal, *Son Asır*, p. 1873. For the text of this speech in English see
E. G. Browne, *The Persian Revolution of 1905-1909* (Cambridge, Cambridge University Press, 1910), p. 7.

[107] Hoca Tahsin, *Psikoloji veya İlm-i Ruh* (2nd ed., Istanbul, Şirket-i
Mürettibiye Matbaası, 1310/1892-1893).

[108] Hoca Tahsin, *Esas-ı İlm-i Hey'et* (Istanbul, Matbaa-i Safa ve Enver,
1311/1893-1894); disregarding the earlier treatise by the Imperial Astrologer (*Müneccimbaşı*) Osman Saib, see *Ta'lim ül-Küre* (Istanbul, n.p., 1848,
1850).

[109] Âsım, "Hoca Tahsin," p. 60; İnal, *Son Asır*, p. 1875. See Constantin
François Chasseboeuf Comte de Volney, *La Loi Naturelle ou Catéchisme du
Citoyen Français* (ed. by Gaston-Martin, Paris, Armand Colin, 1934).

[110] See below, Chapter X.

quoted as having said that it was through reading his brother's translations of Volney over and over that he became interested in Western literature.[111]

By the end of his life Hoca Tahsin, living in a room cluttered with scientific instruments, was trying to establish Islam on naturalistic foundations, taking as his point of departure the indivisibility of the atom. With this came strong humanitarian convictions which—not unlike those of Mazzini and d'Azeglio, who had set the mood of the times only a decade earlier—were combined with a desire to unite and enlighten his "own people." These Hoca Tahsin understood to be first the Ottomans and then, in the narrower sense, the Albanians, to whom he felt attached by ties of local patriotism, for he had been born in Yanya (Yannina).[112]

Tahsin Efendi's incursions into modernism were mostly cultural; Sarıyerli Hoca Sadık Efendi, on the other hand, incurred the disfavor of the Porte because he mentioned the evils of oppression in his sermons. Because of these sermons Sadık Efendi was accused of favoring the Young Ottomans and was exiled to Syria.[113]

A contemporary French periodical made the following comment on this banishment: "It is not only among the Christian populations that reigns at this moment a lively and deep seated agitation. This is much more prevalent among the Moslem populations. . . . The discontent of the Moslems is mostly evidenced by the daring shown in religious publications against the governments of Âli and Fuad Paşa. . . . Ulemas who were delivering sermons on the Ramazan . . . in the presence of the Sultan have dared state to his face that he

<hr />

[111] İnal, *Son Asır*, p. 1106; for Volney, Constantin François Chasseboeuf, Comte de Volney, *Les Ruines ou Méditations sur les Révolutions des Empires* (2nd ed., Paris, Desenne, 1792). For Kemal's translation see [Namık Kemal], *Fransız Müelliflerinden Volney nam zatın "Les Ruines de Palmyre" unvaniyle yazmış olduğu makalattan bazı fıkraların tercümesi* . . . ([Istanbul], 1288/1871).

[112] Lemi Elbir, "Hoca Tahsin," *Aylık Ansiklopedi* (Istanbul, 1945-1949), p. 1486.

[113] "Sadık Efendi," III, 196; Gövsa, *Türk Meşhurları*, p. 335.

would lose his empire and his people."[114] After having described the saintliness of Sadık Efendi, the author of the article added: "Such is the man that the government of Âli Paşa has just arrested and interned in the fortress of St. John of Acre. For he preached in Istanbul [the merits of] democracy, liberty, equality, brotherhood between all men be they Christian or Moslem, Greek or Ottoman."[115]

Sadık Efendi is credited with the writing of a manuscript taking up the ideas of the Abbé Fénelon's *Télémaque*.[116] The significance of the overwhelming preoccupation of the intellectuals of the time with this work will be discussed later.

This, then, was the extent to which the ulema had kept up with the times. Reşid Paşa and his colleagues had been only partially successful in influencing the ulema into European ways; they had achieved much more in the Westernization of the bureaucracy and the army on the lines that had already been laid down by Mahmud. What advances were made in spreading general knowledge, however, must be laid at the door of Reşid Paşa's reforms.

E. THE REFORM IN LANGUAGE AND THE ATTEMPTS TO GENERALIZE EDUCATION

Even in the 1830's Sultan Mahmud had established eight-year schools called *Rüşdiye* ("maturity schools") which aimed at providing a wider program of studies at the elementary level than the local Koranic schools (*"mahalle mektebi"*). In 1845 a commission was created at the Porte to reorganize the entire educational system. In 1847 a Ministry of Education was created.[117] This was an attempt to wrest education from the exclusive grip of the ulema, who had controlled it at the primary and secondary level to that date. By 1866 one author

---

[114] Gustave Flourens, "Sadyk Efendi," *l'Illustration* (February 27, 1869), LIII, 134; for a letter of Namık Kemal referring to this incident see Kuntay, *Namık Kemal*, I, 419, *Hürriyet*, February 15, 1869, p. 6.

[115] *Ibid.*

[116] Gövsa, *Türk Meşhurları*, p. 335.

[117] Ergin, *Türkiye Maarif Tarihi*, pp. 368, 369.

could make the categorical statement that, with the establishment of the Commission on Education, the secularization of education had become an accomplished fact.[118] One of the decisions of the commission was to found an Ottoman university. This proved more difficult than had been anticipated. Thus efforts were concentrated on the founding of institutions which would help break the ground for the university.[119] One of these was the Imperial Academy of Arts and Sciences (*Encümen-i Daniş*), inaugurated in 1850.[120] Many of the members of the academy were later to become famous statesmen (Âli, Fuad, Cevdet), while some, like Reşid Paşa and the *Şeyhülislâm* Arif Hikmet Bey had already reached the highest points of their career.[121] One of the immediate tasks of the academy was to be the preparation of texts to be used in the Ottoman university.[122] The writing of an Ottoman grammar was assigned to Fuad Efendi and Cevdet Efendi.[123] This book is one of the three texts that ever reached print; the others remained in the draft stage.[124]

That more was meant by the creation of the Ottoman Academy of Arts and Sciences than the mere preparation of texts, and that there was envisaged an Encyclopedist movement having as its goal the simplification of the Ottoman language and the spreading of knowledge, is clear from the introduction to the statutes of the academy. These statutes declared, in most refined Ottoman, that in the past ". . . most writers limited their ambition to making a show of eloquence and vying with each other for the palms of success; they lived only to overembellish their style with ornamentation and did not go beyond various types of poetry and rhetoric. Conse-

[118] Belin, "De l'instruction publique," p. 222; cf. Engelhardt, *La Turquie*, I, 77.
[119] Ergin, *Türkiye Maarif Tarihi*, p. 368.
[120] E. d'Eschavannes, "Académie des Sciences de Constantinople," *Revue de l'Orient de l'Algérie et des Colonies* (1852), XII, 361-372.
[121] *Ibid.*, pp. 370 ff., for a list of members.
[122] *Ibid.*, p. 362.
[123] Tanpınar, *XIXncu Asır*, p. 115.
[124] *Ibid.* For the names of the other books and the manuscripts which were not printed, see p. 239, n. 182.

quently the pearls which had been previously retrieved from the ocean of science remained hidden in the shells of an abstract terminology and ideas were enveloped in the veil of subtleties. Similar to the virginal betrothed they could not make their face seen to the gaze of all. Such writings, as may well be imagined, were accessible only to the intelligence of the cultivated minds, the lower classes eliciting no profit from them. Yet it is well known that the salutary goal of general civilization can only be reached by the prior diffusion of diverse kinds of knowledge. Consequently, while encouraging the production of purely literary works aiming to entertain men of discrimination, insistence is [hereby] placed on the drafting of scientific and technological books written in a single style and fitted to the needs of popular intelligence so as to provide the means of widening and completing its instruction.

"Thus praises be to God that from the day on which he ascended the imperial throne our most exalted and most powerful master has directed his attention to intellectual culture in all provinces of the empire . . . and has in particular undertaken to propagate civilization among the popular classes."[125]

This certainly was not an attitude which could have been said to be favored by Ottoman classicists. The contempt felt by Selim III's envoy to France, Atıf Efendi, for political ideas expressed "in easily intelligible words and phrases"[126] is characteristic of the earlier disdain with which linguistic simplicity was regarded. The new approach to language indicated that the general reader and the man in the street were beginning to be given an importance which they had not been able to acquire in the eyes of the intellectuals of a bygone social order.

It is hard to determine under what circumstances the feeling originated that the Ottoman language ought to be simplified. In the mind of Reşid Paşa it was undoubtedly formulated as

[125] d'Eschavannes, "*Académie*," pp. 363, 364.
[126] Lewis, "The Impact," p. 121.

a means of facilitating communication at all levels, and especially the official level.[127] The *Ottoman Gazette*, one of the fruits of the personal efforts of Reşid at a time when his star had not as yet risen,[128] was visualized as a medium of information for the people.[129] Developments along the same line occurred independently of the will of Reşid Paşa, however— a fact which showed that the general increase in communications exerted a driving force in the direction of language reform. Thus the first time the practice of teaching Turkish by using Arabic grammars was abandoned was in 1846. In that year a professor at the Imperial Military College had to compose a Turkish grammar because military science did not lend itself to the use of the intricate and overloaded Ottoman of the time.[130]

Even Akif Paşa, a contemporary Turkish poet and statesman who cannot be described as anything but a "pure" reactionary, was led, without realizing it, to fall in with linguistic simplification. As E. J. W. Gibb points out, "This faithful disciple of the old classic teachers who neither knew nor cared to know a word of any Western language . . . was yet moved . . . to cast aside the old, cumbersome phraseology which swathed and shackled Ottoman prose, and to create for himself a style at once simpler, freer, and more natural, which he handed down as a priceless legacy to his successors."[131]

The next stage in this process was the consolidation of these linguistic gains by the Young Ottomans. Before the Young

[127] Agâh Sırrı Levend, *Türk Dilinde Gelişme ve Sadeleşme Safhaları* (Ankara, Türk Tarih Kurumu Basımevi, 1949), p. 97.
[128] For this aspect of Reşid Paşa's activities, see Ergin, *Türkiye Maarif Tarihi*, p. 446.
[129] "Mukaddeme-i Takvim-i Vekayi," in Lûtfi, *Tarih*, III, 158. "*Kâffe-i teb'a-yı devlet-i Aliyye*" is the expression used.
[130] Ergin, *Türkiye Maarif Tarihi*, p. 446.
[131] Gibb, *Ottoman Poetry*, IV, 328. Although Ahmed Hamdi Tanpınar disagrees with Gibb's interpretation (see A. Hamdi Tanpınar, "Akif Paşa," *Islâm Ansiklopedisi* [1941], I, 245-246), it is significant that both Namık Kemal and Ziya made the same judgment about Akif as Gibb. The process of simplification may be traced even earlier to the style of the historian Âsım; see F. Köprülü, "Âsım," *Islâm Ansiklopedisi* (1942), I, 665-673.

Ottoman movement had reached a noticeable momentum, Münif Paşa in the 1850's was elaborating a style accessible to as wide an audience as possible.[132] Later we come across Şinasi's use of clear, concise, and simple Turkish, Suavi's protests against classical double talk,[133] and the task undertaken by Ziya Paşa, despite his strong classical bent, to go back to the original, "unspoilt" Turkish of the pre-Islamic era.[134]

Thus the setting was prepared for another development, which also reminds us of the activities of the Encyclopedists. It took place in the 1860's and was the proliferation of *salons*.

F. THE SALONS AND THE FIRST TRANSLATIONS

Private discussion groups of a literary nature were not unknown in traditional Ottoman culture. One of the first serious contacts between the Ottoman intellectual world and the Western intellectual realm at a nongovernmental level was established in such a *salon*—the so-called Beşiktaş Scientific Society (*Beşiktaş Cemiyet-i İlmiyesi*). The society devoted its sessions to the study of mathematics, astronomy, literature, and philosophy.[135] Its members met in the *yalı* ("seaside mansion") of Ismail Ferruh Efendi between Beşiktaş and Ortaköy. Ferruh Efendi himself was a man of considerable learning in Islamic subjects. The curiosity that the members of this circle felt with regard to "Frankish" customs, and the lengths to which they would go to satisfy that curiosity, is vividly depicted by one of them, Kethüdazâde Arif Efendi (1777-1849), a member of the ulema and a state official of high rank who was the society's lecturer on philosophy: "In the time of the Janissaries, I would go to Beyoğlu [the European section of Istanbul also known as Pera] to the church which had an organ, and would step up

---

[132] Tanpınar, *XIXncu Asır*, p. 153.

[133] Ali Suavi, reply to a reader's letter, *Muhbir*, 27 Zilhicce 1283, p. 1.

[134] Ertaylan, *Ziya Paşa*, p. 150; for Ziya Paşa's own theory of simplification see Ziya Paşa, "Şiir ve İnşa'," *Hürriyet*, September 7, 1868, pp. 4-7.

[135] See Ismail Hakkı Uzunçarşılı, "Nizam-ı Cedid Ricalinden Valide Sultan Kethüdası Meşhur Yusuf Ağa ve Kethüdazâde Arif Efendi," *Belleten* (July 1956), XX, 485-525; also, Lûtfi, *Tarih*, I, 168, 169; Cevdet, XII, 184.

to the gallery and sit quietly without taking off my *kavuk*
[long conical hat around which the turban was wound]. They
would offer me snuff, take me into their rooms and feel
pleased. And at one time I used to go to the British embassy
ball. There would be as many as four or five hundred *Franks*
with black hats and no Moslem other than myself. I would
sit with a white turban over my *kavuk*. One Moslem among
all these Franks was a funny sight. But after the *Nizam* arose
[after the abolition of the Janissary corps and the establishment of the new army of Mahmud II] and the Janissary
order was abolished I did not go."[136]

The reason Arif Efendi "did not go" any more was that he
was accused, eventually, of favoring the Bektaşi, a religious
order dissolved because of its connection with the Janissaries,
and he did not want the Porte to use this excuse to banish
him. The latter pretext was eventually used to get rid of the
leader of the Beşiktaş Society, the historian Şanizâde.

Şanizâde was the closest approximation to an Encyclopaedist
who ever lived in the Ottoman Empire. He has been described
as "an unusual Ottoman learned man"[137] in that he spoke and
wrote French fluently and had a wide knowledge of military
affairs and organization, mathematics, physics, medicine and
astronomy, poetry, music, painting, and even matchmaking.[138]

According to the historian Lûtfi, the Beşiktaş group was
soon suspected of "disrespectful attitudes," by which is probably meant that Sultan Mahmud, who was quick to take um-
brage at any activity which he did not control, began to fear
they were a nucleus of political conspiracy. This, added to the
palace intrigues of the court physician Mustafa Behçet Efendi,
who was jealous of Şanizâde's learning in the field of medicine,

[136] Uzunçarşılı, "Nizam-ı Cedid," p. 504, quoting Arif Efendi's *Menakib*,
p. 138.
[137] Howard A. Reed, "The Destruction of the Janissaries," p. 96.
[138] Babinger, *Die Geschichtsschreiber*, p. 346. Şanizâde was also one of the
first Ottomans to give a description, in his works, of European representative
institutions. See Şanizâde, *Tarih*, IV, 3. Also, İnal, *Son Asır*, pp. 110, 116,
118.

caused Şanizâde to be exiled on the official grounds that he had connections among the spiritual mentors of the Janissaries, the Bektaşi.[139] Lûtfi also indicates that an important job of proselytizing was being carried on by the members of the society, who provided free instruction to anyone who showed an interest in the learning its members could offer.

Among the students trained at this center were many who later rose to important positions. Such were Ahmed Tevhid Efendi,[140] later Minister of Pious Foundations and the author of a text on surveying; Emin Efendi, later teacher of Persian at the Imperial School of Music, from which at least two Young Ottomans were to graduate; Kabuli Mehmed Paşa (died 1877), later Minister of Foreign Affairs; Savfet Paşa, who was to serve six times as Minister of Foreign Affairs in the Tanzimat era; Yusuf Kâmil Pasa, the first man to translate a mildly political work from Western sources.[141] Midhat Paşa, of reformist and constitutionalist fame, as a boy took lessons from Kethüdazâde. More important still, the Beşiktaş Society trained Melek Paşazâde Abdülkadir Bey, whom we see next as chairman of the committee of the Porte which in 1845 reorganized the Ottoman educational system.[142]

Hammer, the historian, referred to Melek Paşazâde Abdülkadir as *"l'un des oulemas les plus érudits de l'empire Turc."*[143] By citing his correspondence with Abdülkadir, Hammer also

[139] Although these accusations are usually dismissed as false, the fact that Şanizâde's great-grandfather Şani Ahmed Dede was a Bektaşi leader is thought-provoking. It may be that the family had retained contacts with the Bektaşi even in the early nineteenth century. *Ibid.*, p. 110, note 1.
In the case of Kethüdazâde the accusation of Bektaşism, which was made equivalent to that of "freethinker," barely missed its mark. Kethüdazâde was saved by the intercession of a friend. *Ibid.*, p. 35.
[140] The following information about the men who were trained in the society is based on the information given by Uzunçarşılı in "Nizam-ı Cedid," pp. 513, 514.
[141] The translator into Turkish of Fénelon's *Télémaque*; see below pp. 241ff.
[142] Ergin, *Türkiye Maarif Tarihi*, p. 368. For the importance of this committee see below, pp. 241-242. Ahmed Cevdet Paşa's instructor of Persian was Ferruh Efendi, another member of the Beşiktaş Society. See İnal, *Son Asır*, pp. 236-380.
[143] Hammer, *Histoire*, XVII, *post face*, p. xxii *et seq.*

gives indications that the communications of foreign savants were being read in the Beşiktaş group.

Apart from *salons* there had also existed in the Ottoman Empire a tradition of grooming the children of a household for government service and of making the children of slaves and domestics participate in this educational process. This was called the *gulâm* system.[144] Husrev Paşa was engaged throughout his life in educating the members of his household in this fashion and found time to train scores of young men who later became government officials of the highest rank.[145]

But during the reign of Sultan Abdülaziz mansions became centers of discussion, as well as educational institutions, and the foci of intensive cultural activities. When the Young Ottoman movement was in its inception these *salons* were at the peak of their activity. Every owner of a large mansion tried to get at least one learned man "in residence."[146] The task of this guest of distinction was to serve as teacher for the instruction of guests or members of the household.

All the members of the Young Ottoman movement were active in these circles, and at least one of them, Ayetullah Bey, was brought up in such surroundings. Ayetullah Bey's father, Subhi Paşa,[147] whom we have already encountered as one of the Turks in the service of Mehmed Ali, was an historian in his own right[148] and had gained fame as a Maecenas who harbored well-known European as well as Eastern scholars in his house. In this, Subhi Paşa was continuing a tradition inaugurated in his family by his father, Abdurrahman Sami Paşa,

[144] Halil İnalcık, "Husrev Paşa," p. 612; also, Helmuth von Moltke, *Briefe über Zustande und Begebenheiten in der Türkei* (4th ed., Berlin, Mitler, 1882), p. 99.
[145] Moltke, *loc.cit.*, and above, p. 212.
[146] İnal, *Son Sadrıazamlar*, II, 235; Ergin, *Türkiye Maarif Tarihi*, II, 316. See also Fatma Aliyye, *Ahmed Cevdet Paşa ve Zamanı* (Istanbul, Kanaat, 1332/1916), p. 25, for another *salon* organized by one of the servants of a member of the Beşiktaş Society who seems to have made good in a surprisingly short time.
[147] *Sicill-i Osmanî*, III, 220 ff; *Türk Meşhurları*, p. 344.
[148] Babinger, *Geschichtsschreiber*, p. 368 ff.

the first Minister of Education under Abdülmecid.[149] Both Paşa's children were tutored in history, philosophy, and law by the orientalist Mordtmann.[150]

Sami Paşa was a protector of Ali Suavi and gave him shelter for some time before this Young Ottoman had to flee Turkey in 1867. One of Sami Paşa's innumerable sons, Baki Bey, was a true *libertin*, a confirmed enemy of the reactionary ulema, and caused a minor scandal by the publication of an article of his on education expressing his secular convictions.[151] Baki Bey greatly admired Ali Suavi.[152]

Salons were also to be found in the houses of Eğinli Said Paşa, known as "Said Paşa the Englishman" because he had studied mathematics at Edinburgh. Said Paşa also accorded his protection to Ali Suavi. The same holds true for the mansion of Yusuf Kâmil Paşa, a man whom we shall study in detail later. Kemal was often seen at this house.[153] The discussions undertaken in these mansions were accompanied by a simultaneous attempt to introduce into Turkey the ideas that were part of the cultural patrimony of the West.

The most active in fostering this movement was Münif Paşa,[154] who was born in 1828.[155] His father was an âlim who, at the time of İbrahim Paşa's invasion of Syria, had been

---

[149] See above, Chapters II, VI.

[150] For Sami Paşa see *Sicill-i Osmanî*, III, 7, 8; *Türk Meşhurları*, p. 344; İnal, *Son Sadrıazamlar*, I, 200. Also, İnal, *Son Asır*, pp. 1649-1661.

Andreas David Mordtmann was a German orientalist, the founder of Sassanid numismatics. Sent as a consular representative of the Hanseatic towns to Istanbul in 1846, he was appointed judge in the newly formed Turkish commercial courts in 1860. He remained in this position until 1871 when he was dismissed by the grand vizier, Mahmud Nedim Paşa. For a full biography, see A. D. Mordtmann, *Anatolien* (ed. by Franz Babinger, Hanover, Heinz Lafaire, 1925), pp. VII-XIII.

[151] Kuntay, *Sarıklı İhtilalci Ali Suavi*, p. 16.

[152] *Ibid.*

[153] İnal, *Son Sadrıazamlar*, p. 237.

[154] Ali Fuad, "Münif Paşa," *TTEM* (May, 1930), 1 (NS), 1-16. For biographical data, see İnal, *Son Asır*, pp. 997 *et seq.*; for a treatment from the literary viewpoint, see Tanpınar, *XIXncu Asır*, pp. 151-154; İnal, *loc.cit.*

[155] See above, p. 209.

taken on the staff of the latter as an instructor of Persian and Arabic for his children. Münif Paşa therefore completed his studies in Egypt. He later returned to Turkey and entered the Translation Bureau in 1852. In 1855 he was appointed Second Secretary of the Ottoman embassy in Berlin. In 1859 he returned to the Porte and reentered the Translation Bureau. In this year he provided the Ottomans with the first translation into Turkish of what may be termed the ideas of the Enlightenment.

As early as 1850 an attempt at familiarizing Ottoman audiences with the foundations of Western culture had been made when an Armenian translated from the French into Turkish a history of Greek philosophy.[156] This was a bolder move than meets the eye since philosophical speculation divorced from theology was considered heretical in Turkey.[157]

The literary product of Münif Paşa's Westernization still was a novelty, however, because what was now being presented to an Ottoman audience was a small booklet made up of selected dialogues from Voltaire, Fontenelle, and Fénelon.[158] The translation contained the following dialogues:

1. Dialogue between the Greek Philosopher Democritus and Heraclitus.[159]

[156] Cricor Chumarian, *Abrégé de la Vie des Plus Illustres Philosophes de l'Antiquité* (Smyrne [*sic*], Imprimerie Daveroni et Sougioli, 1854). Turkish text facing French.

[157] In the reign of Sultan Mehmed II a prize had been offered by the sultan for the best refutation of the liberal stand toward "natural philosophy" represented by the Islamic philosopher İbn Rüşd and confirmation that the opposite stand taken by the philosopher Gazalî was correct. A member of the ulema by the name of Hocazâde had won this prize and his work was used thereafter as a standard reference to settle any similar argument. See Abdülhak Adnan Adıvar, *Osmanlı Türklerinde İlim* (Istanbul, Maarif Matbaası, 1943), pp. 39, 40.

[158] *Muhaverat-i Hikemiyye: Fransa Hükema-yı Benamından Voltaire ve Fénelon ve Fontenelle l'elifatından* (Mütercimi Münif Efendi, ez Hulefa-yı Oda-yı Tercüme-i Bâb-ı Âli, Dersaadet [Istanbul], Ceridehane Matbaası, 1276/1859-1860).

[159] Fénelon, "Démocrite et Héraclite," *Oeuvres* (Lebel Edition, Paris, 1820-1830), XIX, 181-183.

2. Dialogue between a Philosopher and a Gardener Regarding the City of Cashmere.[160]

3. Dialogue between the King of Athens, Demetrius, and Erostratus.[161]

4. Dialogue between Bayard and the High Constable on the Bearing of Arms Against One's Country.[162]

5. Dialogue between two philosophers by the name of Posidonus and Lucretius on the Proof of Predestination.[163]

6. Dialogue between the Wife [sic] of Louis XV, Madame de Maintenon, and Mlle. de l'Enclos, her Old Friend.[164]

7. Dialogue between a Philosopher and a Minister of Finance Regarding Public Administration.[165]

8. Dialogue between a French Savage and a French Educator on the Subject of Man.[166]

Five of Münif Paşa's *Dialogues* had been selected from Voltaire's *Dialogues et Entretiens Philosophiques*, one of them was from Fontenelle's *Dialogue des Morts*, and two of them were from the *Dialogues* of the Abbé Fénelon.

It is difficult to determine, in the Voltairian dialogues translated by Münif Paşa, whether there was a deliberate choice. The translations follow the order in which the dialogues are placed in the complete edition of Voltaire's works, with the omission of one dialogue concerned with a Jesuit, which would not have meant much to an Ottoman audience. It is

[160] Voltaire, Dialogues et Entretiens Philosophiques, "Les Embellissements de la Ville de Cachemire," Oeuvres (Renouard Edition, Paris, 1819-1825), XXXII, 1-8.

[161] Fontenelle, "Erostrate et Démetrius de Phalere," Nouveaux Dialogues des Morts (Nouvelle Edition, Amsterdam, Pierre Mortier, 1701), pp. 133-139.

[162] Fénelon, "Le Connétable de Bourbon et Bayard," Oeuvres, XIX, 375-378.

[163] Voltaire, "Lucrèce et Posidonus," loc.cit., pp. 39-56.

[164] Ibid., "Madame de Maintenon et Mademoiselle de l'Enclos," pp. 14-19.

[165] Ibid., "Un Philosophe et un Contrôleur Général de Finances," pp. 19-27.

[166] Ibid., "Un Sauvage et un Bachelier," pp. 57-66.

interesting to note, however, that of the points made in these dialogues, the strongest set forth an "activism" which we have already encountered as a leitmotiv of Turkish progressive thought in the early nineteenth century. Thus the first dialogue of Voltaire begins by painting a picture of Cashmere which reminds one of the stagnation of the Ottoman Empire:

"Le Royaume de Cachemire avait subsisté plus de treize cent ans, sans avoir eu ni de vrais philosophes, ni de vrais poètes, ni d'architectes passables, ni de peintres, ni de sculpteurs. Ils manquèrent longtemps de manufactures et de commerce, au point que, pendant plus de mille ans, quand un marquis Cachemirien voulait avoir du linge et un beau pourpoint, il etait obligé d'avoir recours à un juif ou un Banian."[167]

The thesis advanced by Voltaire's *philosophe* is that nothing lies in the way of exploiting natural and human resources for a country like Cashmere. As he states, *"Pour éxécuter les plus grandes entreprises il ne faut qu'une tête et des mains."*[168]

Again, in the advice given by the philosopher to the controller of finances, the general idea is the same: *"La richesse d'un état consiste dans le nombre de ses habitants et dans le travail."*[169] *"La vraie richesse d'un royaume . . . est . . . dans l'industrie et le travail."*[170] This, as we saw, was the very argument advanced at an earlier date by Sadık Rifat Paşa in his economic analyses, and an approach which may also be found among the partisans of Mahmud's reforms.[171] Eventually this standpoint and attitude was to culminate in its purest form in

[167] Voltaire, "Les Embellissements de la Ville de Cachemire," *Oeuvres,* XXXI, 1.

[168] *Ibid.,* pp. 5, 6.

[169] Voltaire, "Un Philosophe et un Contrôleur Général des Finances," *op. cit.,* p. 21.

[170] *Ibid.,* pp. 21, 22.

[171] The first work to appear in Turkey on modern European economic theories was a translation of J. B. Say's *Catéchisme d'Économie Politique.* This work of the popularizer of Adam Smith's doctrine appeared in 1852. The translation was by Abro Sahak Efendi, a member of the Imperial Academy of Sciences. See *İlm-i Tedbir-i Menzil* (Istanbul, 1268); Karatay, *Türkçe Basmalar,* p. 724; Schlechta-Wssehrd, "Verzeichnis," *ZDMG* (1853), VII, 250.

an exposition, by the Young Ottomans, of the benefits of hard work as such. Thus both Namık Kemal and Ali Suavi were to write articles on this very subject.[172] But the contrast with the fatalism prevalent at the end of the eighteenth century was striking even in these pioneer endeavors of Münif Paşa.[173]

Of the other dialogues by Voltaire selected by Münif Paşa for translation and included in the *Muhaverat*, the one between Mme de Maintenon and her friend probably was a hint of the benefits that could be derived from the education of women.

A more difficult problem into which to venture was Voltaire's discussions of the Prime Mover, settled by his assertion that nature could not be understood without the idea of a "supreme intelligence."[174]

Political implications come out in the final dialogue, in which the Spirit of Laws was, somewhat cynically, made to consist of the right of the propertyless to work for property owners. In the same dialogue, however, the best laws were also stated to be those that were made by consulting the interest of the greatest number.[175]

In the case of Fontenelle dialogue, Münif Paşa's purpose is obscure in selecting a piece which amounts to the defense of the thesis that "passions do and undo all in this world."[176]

Another theme encountered in these translations is that of patriotism. This is the subject of the second of Fénelon's dialogues included in the *Muhaverat*. This again was the first instance of a theme treated at great length by the Young Ottomans.[177]

[172] Namık Kemal, "Sây," in *Makalât-ı Siyasiye ve Edebiye* (ed. by Ali Ekrem [Bulayır], Istanbul, Selanik Matbaası, 1327 [Malî]/1912), pp. 27-33; Ali Suavi, "Mukaddeme," *Muhbir*, 25 Şaban 1283/January 3, 1867.

[173] See also Ahmed Midhat, *Sevda-yı Sâyü Amel* (Istanbul, 1879). A good exposé of the fatalistic attitude is contained in Gibb and Bowen, *Islamic Society*, Part I, Vol. II, p. 206.

[174] Voltaire, "Lucrèce et Posidonus," *Oeuvres*, XXXII, 43.

[175] *Ibid.*, "Un Sauvage et un Bachelier," pp. 64, 65.

[176] Unless it be meant as an additional proof of human control over events. Fontenelle, *Nouveaux Dialogues*, p. 39.

[177] Namık Kemal, "Vatan," *İbret*, March 10, 1872, in Özön, *Namık Kemal ve İbret*, pp. 263-271.

The intellectual stand taken in all of these dialogues was quite mild by comparison with a nineteenth-century European thought that had just begun to consider man in terms of biological evolution. But it should not be forgotten that even by the publication of these innocuous pieces Münif Paşa was exposing himself to censure. He was, in fact, to be highly criticized for his work by the ulema, who thought of him as an atheist.[178] A good reminder of the extent to which the *Dialogues* constituted an innovation may be gathered from the rebuke that another Western-minded *littérateur*, Ahmed Midhat, suffered two decades later for having used the term "Islamic philosophy." The protest came from ulema, who pointed out that the term "Islamic philosophy" was a contradiction of terms.[179]

Hardly had three years gone by after the publication of the *Dialogues* when Münif Paşa founded, in 1861, the Ottoman Scientific Society.[180] The society published a periodical, the *Journal of Sciences*,[181] which appeared for three years. A glance at the titles of some of the articles that appeared in the *Journal* is all that one needs to establish a parallel between the activities of this organization and the earlier work of scientific popularization undertaken by the encyclopedists in France. The first government-subsidized program envisaged

[178] [Mordtmann], *Stambul*, p. 174.
[179] Mustafa Nihat [Özön], *Muasır Türk Edebiyatı Tarihi* (Istanbul, Devlet Matbaası, 1934), p. 668, 669, states that the protest came from the censors; in fact the piece appears to have been written by ulema, who might or might not have had an official connection. See "Mektup," *Dağarcık* (1288/1871-1872), No. 6, p. 173. This periodical did not bear publication dates other than the year.
[180] *Cemiyet-i İlmiye-yi Osmaniye.* The Ottoman Scientific Society was established by an imperial decree of the 24th of Zilkade 1277 (June 2, 1861); it had forty members and was presided over by Sami Paşa (see above, pp. 192, 232). It offered a reading room open every day except Tuesdays from 3 to 11, European newspapers, and a library of 600 volumes. The society provided free instruction in French, English, and Western jurisprudence. Belin, "De l'Instruction Publique," *Le Contemporain* (1866), XI, 230.
[181] *Mecmua-i Fünûn.* Referred to hereafter as *MF* (1279-1281/1862-1863, 1866-1867).

by the Ottoman academy in 1850 had not been successful.[182] But now a number of essays appeared which gave Ottoman audiences their first contacts with the scientific ideas of the West. The following are the titles of some of the articles that ran in the *Mecmua-i Fünûn* during its three-year publication: "Comparison between learning and ignorance";[183] "The Science of the Wealth of Nations";[184] "Introduction to the Science of Geology";[185] "University Lectures";[186] "History

[182] See Schlechta-Wssehrd, "Mittheilungen aus Dem Orient: Ueber den Neugestifteten Turkischen Gelehrten-Verein," *ZDMG* (1863), XVII, 682-684.

Three books had resulted from the first activities of the Ottoman Academy of Sciences. One was J. B. Say's *Catéchisme d'Economie Politique*; (see above, p. 236, note 171; the second, an Ottoman grammar by Cevdet and Fuad of which thirteen editions appeared between 1851 and 1893-1894. This book was entitled *Kavaid-i Osmaniye*. (See Karatay, *Türkçe Basmalar*, I, 130). The third work was a manual containing biographies of famous European statesmen. It was aimed at familiarizing the employees of the Porte with diplomatic history and practice. Its author was Abro Sahak Efendi, a member of the Academy who later became Fuad Paşa's secretary. See [Abro Sahak] *Avrupada Meşhur Ministroların Tercüme-i Hallerine Dair Risale* (Istanbul, Takvimhane-i Âmire, Şaban 1271/April-May 1855). Another product of these activities was Cevdet Paşa's *History* which was ordered by the Academy, but appeared much later. Associated with these activities too was the Turkish translation of Buffon's *Histoire Naturelle*, not directly sponsored by the Academy and which also appeared much later as a serial in the *Tasvir-i Efkâr*. See below, p. 262, note 35. Much of the work done for the Academy remained at the draft stage. Such is Abro Sahak's translation of Voltaire's *History of Charles XII*. There also exists a *General History* of Abro Sahak's in draft form; similar were Ahmed Ağribozi's *History of Ancient Greece*, Todoraki Efendi's translation of a *History of Europe*, and Aleko Efendi's book on the last campaigns of Napoleon. See Tanpınar, *XIXncu Asr*, p. 114. In July 1865 a Translation Committee was established anew and attached to the Ministry of Education. This committee, presided over by Münif, was given the task of translating into Turkish texts which the committee had decided were of "scientific and commercial interest." See Lûtfi, "Tanzimattan Sonra Türkiyede Maarif Teşkilâtı," *TTEM* (September 1927), XVI, 308; Belin, "De l'instruction," *Le Contemporain* (1866), XI, 229. The two products of this later activity were a translation of what has been described as "Chamber's History" in an article by a European correspondent (probably *Historical Questions*, London, 1865), and the antiquated text on Geography of the French geographer Cortanbert. For both these works see *Augsburger Allgemeine Zeitung*, February 2, 1867, p. 531; Karatay, *Türkçe Basmalar*, pp. 133, 138.

[183] *MF* (Muharrem 1279/July 1862 approx.), I, 20.

[184] *Ibid.* (Safer 1279/August 1862), II, 86.

[185] *Ibid.* (Safer 1279/August 1862), II, 65.

[186] *Ibid.* (Receb 1279/January 1863), III, 301.

of the Telegraph";[187] "History of the Sages of Greece."[188]
The economic themes of work, sobriety, and action, which
appeared about the same time in Sami Paşa's essay on "The
Importance of Thrift," were also taken up in the *Mecmua.*
Thus there were articles in this periodical on "The Necessity
to Work,"[189] "The Unity of Theory and Practice,"[190] "The
Praise of Work and Criticism of Inactivity."[191] Simultaneously,
the first outlines of an interest in Moslems who lived outside the Ottoman Empire was evidenced[192]—an interest which
was to acquire considerable importance among the Young
Ottomans.

When it first came out, the *Mecmua* was considered a great
step in the Westernizing of Ottoman culture. It certainly
exerted a lasting influence on the generation that saw its first
appearance. Later, in the 1870's, the Young Ottoman Ali
Suavi published a periodical, the *Ulûm,* which undoubtedly
was the intellectual heir of the *Mecmua-i Fünûn.*[193] The

[187] *Ibid.* (Zilkade 1279/May 1863), XI, 448.
[188] *Ibid.* (Serial from XV, 94, Rebiülevvel 1280 to XIII, 400, Zilkade
1281/August 1863 to September 1865.) Agâh Sırrı Levend, in his *Türk
Dilinde Gelişme ve Sadeleşme Safhaları,* pp. 167, 168, gives the text of a
lecture by Münif Paşa at the Ottoman Scientific Society in which Münif
proposed the simplication of the Arabic alphabet as a measure to increase
literacy. The text of this lecture apparently appeared in the *Mecmua-i Fünûn*
in 1280 (No. 14, pp. 74-77). This material was unfortunately overlooked
in my survey of the *Mecmua.*
[189] Mehmed Şerif, "Lüzum-u Sây-ü amel," *MF,* Şaban 1279/Jan-Feb
1863, pp. 333-337.
[190] Mehmed Said Efendi, "Nazarî ile amelî arasında olan cihet-i vahdet,"
ibid., Ramazan 1279/Feb-Mch 1863, pp. 368-376.
[191] Ethem Pertev, "Meth-i sây ve zemm-i betalet hakkında meşahir-i
Ulema-yı İslamiyeden Kemalpaşazâdenin Arabî risalesi tercümesidir," *ibid.,*
no date [1281/1864-1865], pp. 281-289. For further information on Pertev
Paşa see Tanpınar, *XIXncu Asır,* I, 239; İnal, *Son Asır,* p. 1329.
[192] Münif [Paşa], "Çinde bulunan ehl-i İslam," *MF,* Şaban 1279/Jan-Feb
1863, pp. 317-320.
[193] Suavi Efendi, *Ouloum Gazatasy* [*sic*], Journal Encyclopédique Turc
Bi-mensuel, 44 Avenue de la Grande Armée, Paris, I, No 1, 8 Cemaziyülevvel 1286 (August 8, 1869). "Recueil périodique ayant pour but de
répandre le goût des sciences, des lettres et des arts. La première partie de ce
recueil est encyclopédique. Le seconde partie contient des romans scientifiques
et divers articles ayant pour but de mettre les sciences et les arts à la portée
des gens du monde."

Ulûm was distinguished mostly by its mediocrity, due to Suavi's determination to be a single-man editorial board, contributor, and publisher. But even at the time of Münif Paşa's pioneer endeavors, a process was at work which quickly made his work of popularization, and later that of Suavi, appear dated. For lack of better expression this process might be termed the "politicization" of intellectual productions. What had happened was that the center of gravity shifted within ten years from works aiming to enlighten to works intending to convince. This is why in the 1870's the cultural pretensions of Suavi had a hollow ring even for his companions, the Young Ottomans.[194]

The first imperceptible step in this change of emphasis had already occurred with the appearance of Yusuf Kâmil Paşa's translation of the Abbé Fénelon's *Télémaque*.[195] *Télémaque* had been translated in 1859. It circulated for some time in manuscript form in Ottoman *salons*. It was printed in August 1862 for the first time.[196]

The book was a mythical account of the upbringing of a prince of a royal household and his grooming for future kingship, in the best philosophical, Platonic tradition. The translation was an immediate success. The reason for this popularity is perhaps best indicated in a book review which the poet and journalist Şinasi Efendi wrote when the work was first printed: "While on the surface, the work of the famous French author, Fénelon, entitled the Adventures of *Télémaque*, conveys the impression of being a romance, its true meaning is in the nature of a philosophical law which includes all the arts of government that have as purpose the fulfillment of justice and happiness for the individual.

[194] Even though Ebüzziya, one of the Young Ottomans, was to state later that the *Philosophical Dialogues* had been influential in shaping the ideas of his generation. See Tanpınar, *XIXncu Asır*, p. 153, citing an article by Ebüzziya in *Yeni Tasvir-i Efkâr* (1910), Nos. 251-253, without page reference.

[195] Özön, *Türkçede Roman*, p. 144.

[196] Yusuf Kâmil, *Tercüme-i Telemak* (1st ed., Istanbul, Tabhane-i Âmire, 1279-1862; 2nd ed., Istanbul, Tasvir-i Efkâr Gazetehanesi, 1279/1863 [*sic*].)

"A superior work concerning such an exalted craft was in need of being translated into Turkish by an author possessing poetic talent and lofty style."[197]

What this "philosophical law" was, for an Ottoman audience, is not hard to establish. Fénelon was the tutor of the Duke of Burgundy, the son of Louis XV. His *Télémaque* was a means of indicating the path that he felt should be followed by a just ruler. The work was therefore comparable to the Ottoman "mirrors."[198] It also included a strain of Platonism that could be found in Islamic political treatises.[199]

But if treatises taking up the discussion of the ends of government were known to Turkish audiences, this new "mirror" differed from those they knew in two respects. First it was couched in the form of a novel. Although traditional literature such as the Ottoman version of the fables of Bidpay did include stories with a political moral, *Télémaque* had more to do with every day life. It possessed the attraction which came from combining the ideal with the practical. At an earlier time Sadık Rifat Paşa had presented his projects of reform either in the shape of state reports or in that of forbiddingly didactic pamphlets. Now, similar ideas were made pleasant, easy to read; at least for the *literati*. Namık Kemal, who was one step ahead of Kâmil Paşa, was later to criticize him because Kâmil did not have a popular enough style.[200]

[197] Şinasi, "Payitaht," *Tasvir-i Efkâr*, 2 Ramazan 1279/February 21, 1863, p. 1. Yusuf Kâmil Paşa himself was quite worried that the deeper implications of his translations would not be understood. Özön, *Türkçede Roman*, p. 145.

[198] See above, Chapter III.

[199] According to one author, for example, the philosophy expressed in *Télémaque* was an attempt to revive the Platonic idea of the state, see Kingsley Martin, *French Liberal Thought in the XVIIIth Century* (ed. by Kingsley Martin, London, Turnstile Press, 1954), pp. 55, 56. See also Roland Mousnier, "Les Idées Politiques de Fénelon," *XVIIe Siècle: Revue des Etudes du XVIIe Siècle* (1949), I, 190-206.

Another student of Fénelon has remarked, "In his emphasis on the danger of luxury, the evils of the idle class, and the necessity for education as the basis of national well-being, there is, clearly enough, something revolutionary. . . ." Harold Laski, "The Rise of Liberalism," *Encyclopedia of Social Sciences* (1932), I, 117.

[200] Kuntay, *Namık Kemal*, I, 343, note 36.

Secondly, just as the shape of the message conveyed by *Télémaque* was devised to obtain a cohesive effect, so too its content was directed toward what has been described somewhat pedantically as "social mobilization."[201] Here we come across the familiar injunction, already found in Sadık Rifat Paşa, that the ruler should love his "*reaya*," i.e., lowliest subjects, like his own children.[202] We encounter such remarks as that the satisfying of animal pleasures should be subordinated to the acquisition of knowledge,[203] that commercial education should be encouraged,[204] that rulers should look after the interests of their subjects rather than indulge in costly wars so as to satisfy their ego,[205] that those citizens who contributed to arts, sciences and commerce should be honored for these vital contributions,[206] that affairs of the state should be entrusted to "councils."[207] The word *kanaat* (frugality), which often recurs, brings to mind what has been said about the capitalist "ethos" and its ramifications.[208] It is stated that artists should devote their attention to the glorification of those great men who had been of use to the fatherland[209]— *vatan*—an incidental insight into the extent to which the aim of mobilizing national energies had already crystallized at the time of Fénelon. The use of political intimidation is decried[210] and luxurious living is condemned as a social evil of great magnitude.[211]

In addition, Fénelon was protesting against the very same types of abuses that had accompanied reforms in Turkey during the Tanzimat, such as corruption, graft, and "enlightened" despotism.

---

[201] A thesis developed in Karl W. Deutsch, *Nationalism and Social Communications* (New York, 1953).

[202] [Fénelon], *Cümel-i Hikemiye-yi Telemak* (translated by Yusuf Kâmil Paşa, Istanbul, Matbaa-i Ebüzziya, 1310/1892-1893), p. 7. I am using this shortened edition of *Télémaque* because it was edited by one of the Young Ottomans, Ebüzziya Tevfik. The selection of Ebüzziya consists precisely of those sections of the book that are the most obviously directed to social mobilization.

[203] *Ibid.*, p. 2.   [204] *Ibid.*, p. 10.   [205] *Ibid.*, p. 11.

[206] *Ibid.*, pp. 12-13.   [207] *Ibid.*, p. 17.   [208] *Ibid.*, pp. 23, 26.

[209] *Ibid.*, p. 37.   [210] *Ibid.*, p. 53.   [211] *Ibid.*, p. 55.

Fénelon's ideas were revolutionary in that the good Abbé did yearn for the reestablishment of a perfect bygone order of the state which lived mostly in his imagination. One of his complaints was that the "párlements" were an essential ingredient of monarchic government in France and that by not convoking them the king erred grievously.[212] The Young Ottomans too were to state at a later date that their demands for representation was only the revival of the Ottoman governmental mechanism of the *Meşveret*.[213]

Another point of interest with regard to Fénelon was that this writer took issue with the bureaucracy created by Louis XIV. This complaint is echoed by the Jeune Turquie with regard to the bureaucracy of the Tanzimat.

A final indication of what *Télémaque* was meant to convey to Turkish audiences may be gathered from Sami Paşa's introduction to the second edition. In this Sami Paşa pointed out that even though foreign works might be impossible to understand in the language in which they were originally written, *meaning* was universal. It was this aspect of the book which he asked his readers to keep in mind. This idea of the universality of knowledge was one which went back to Enlightenment thinkers.[214]

A somewhat different manifestation of the trend of politicization in the 1860's may be seen in the sudden proliferation of newspapers and the creation of a new journalistic intelligentsia combative and political rather than didactic and encyclopedic in its approach. The people who staffed these journals were the somewhat different generation of "angry young poets," such as Âli and Müşfik, to whom reference was made in Chapter IV. The first clash between the encyclopedists and the journalists materialized as a row between Münif and Refik Bey, a close friend of Kemal. Refik, also an employee of

---

[212] Mousnier, "Les Idées Politiques," pp. 198 ff.; Martin, *op.cit.*, p. 58.
[213] Namık Kemal, "Usul-u Meşveret Hakkında . . . ," *Hürriyet*, September 14, 1868, p. 6, and the series following in the *Hürriyet*.
[214] Özön, *Türkçede Roman*, p. 145 f.

one of the bureaus of the Porte, had established in 1863 the short-lived periodical *Mir'at*.[215]

Refik apparently thought that Münif Paşa's account of the purposes of the *Mir'at* in the *Mecmua-i Fünûn* was a misrepresentation of the lofty goals he had set himself. Without mincing words he answered Münif Paşa in the *Mir'at*. This, in turn, infuriated Âli Paşa, who could easily upbraid Refik since the latter was a government employee. Âli ordered Refik to apologize; Refik refused and was dismissed from his job.

Namık Kemal became a part to a controversy similar to that in which Refik had taken part when in the summer of 1866 he objected and wrote a rebuttal to an article of Münif's in which the latter defended the thesis that with the spread of science and education recourse to force in relations between states would eventually be abandoned. Namık Kemal stated that there was no indication that this was about to happen and that it was those nations that had known how to distinguish themselves in war that were spoken of as "great."[216] Namık Kemal was also affected by the trend from Encyclopaedism toward political consciousness and became one of its spokesmen. Typical of this new disdain for people who were not politically *engagé* was Namık Kemal's criticism of Subhi Paşa, Sami Paşa's son. This criticism was made on the grounds that Subhi Paşa's achievements in the field of numismatics could be considered only a meager contribution to the modernization of the Ottoman Empire.[217]

A general indication of the restlessness of the Turkish men

[215] The first issue appeared on the 1st of Ramazan 1279/February 19, 1863, and the publication was ceased after the third issue. İnal, *Son Asır*, p. 1405, note 1. See also Bianchi, "Bibliographie Ottomane," *Journal Asiatique* (August-September 1863), Series VI, II, 269.

[216] Namık Kemal, "Redd-i İtiraz," *Tasvir-i Efkâr*, 16 Rebiülahir 1283/August 28, 1866 in *Müntahabat-ı Tasvir-i Efkâr* (ed. by Ebüzziya Tevfik, Parts 1 and 2, 2nd ed., Istanbul, Matbaa-i Ebüzziya, 1311/1893-1894), p. 36. This article was identified as Namık Kemal's only after Ebüzziya's collection of Kemal's articles was obtained. The article is therefore quoted from this collection.

[217] Kuntay, *Namık Kemal*, II, 2, p. 215.

of letters in the early 1860's may be seen in that the organ
of the Society of Writers (*Cemiyet-i Kitabet*), the *Ibar-ı
Intibah* was suspended almost immediately after the first number appeared (6 Receb 1279/February 1863).[218]

III. The Assessment of Western Influences and the Study of "Intermediate Types"

A. THE "SALONS" AS CONSERVATIVE CENTERS

Even though cultural Europeanization was one of the
results of *salon* activities, it would be an oversimplification to
dwell only on this aspect of their influence. The main targets
of the *salons* were the "over-Westernized" generation of
Tanzimat statesmen (such as Fuad and Âli Paşa), willing as
they were to jettison more of the Ottoman-Islamic elements
in modernizing the state than had been their predecessor,
Reşid Paşa.

Again, the *Şeyhülislâm* Arif Hikmet Bey, although an outstanding cultural leader, an advocate of reform, and a member
of the Imperial Academy of Sciences, protested in his verses
against the corruption of these statesmen and condemned
their lavish style of life and the harshness with which they
had sometimes enforced their decisions.[219]

Subhi Paşa, the most important *salon* leader, charged the
same statesman with being shallow and inept. A typical complaint of his was that by setting a uniform ten per cent tax on
agricultural produce, the reformers had instituted a harsh
and blind system of taxation in place of the old custom of
assessing taxes in accordance with the fertility of the land. A
petition embodying this criticism was presented to the sultan
by Subhi Paşa in 1867, the very year the Young Ottomans had

[218] Belin, "*De l'Instruction publique*," p. 231. Also, Rasim, *Şinasi*, p. 6, unnumbered note.
[219] Fevziye Abdullah, "Arif Hikmet Bey," *Islâm Ansiklopedisi*, I, 565, (citing Arif Hikmet, *Divan*, pp. 133, 164).

to flee Turkey.[220] Similar theses may also be found in the articles of Ziya Paşa published in the *Hürriyet*.[221]

Such an onslaught on reform as originated in some of the *salons* and as taken over by the Young Ottomans was not so alien to Western ideas as one would expect. Men like Subhi Paşa and later the Young Ottomans could find in the West ideas and theories justifying a stand against what was considered excessive change. One of these European sources of an antireformist stand was "exoticism," as illustrated by the viewpoint from which David Urquhart surveyed the Turkish reform movement.

B. DAVID URQUHART'S SENTIMENTAL EXOTICISM

To consider the people of the East "half children" and the "white man's burden" was only one of the attitudes adopted by British officials toward their "backward" charges throughout the world. Others, under the influence of the romantic ideas of the "noble savage," considered that Eastern societies had their own justification and looked at the attempts to Europeanize these societies as the rash works of ignorant men. This was the attitude which motivated the stand toward reforms taken by David Urquhart, the influential secretary of the British embassy in Istanbul, in the 1830's.

Urquhart considered that it was not through the grafting on of alien institutions that Turkey would prosper, but by a judicious development of those features of the Ottoman Empire that would enable it to keep pace with Western progress.[222] In a work published in 1839 he did not disguise his

[220] For the text of this petition see *Türkiye Ziraat Tarihine bir Bakış* (ed. by Birinci Köy ve Kalkınma Kongresi, Istanbul, Devlet Basımevi, 1938), p. 255 ff.

[221] Ziya Paşa, "Yeni Osmanlılardan bir Zat Tarafından Matbaamıza Gönderilip Derc Olunan Hatıraların Maba'didir," *Hürriyet*, April 5, 1869, p. 6.

[222] Bailey, in his *British Policy and the Turkish Reform Movement*, p. 230, states: "Palmerston never favored extensive constitutional developments in the Ottoman Empire. In this he was supported by his ambassador at Constantinople, Lord Ponsonby, and David Urquhart." The successor of

admiration for the foundations on which, according to him, Ottoman society rested. These Ottoman characteristics, stated Urquhart, would astound any unprejudiced Englishman who studied them with impartiality. Such an Englishman, he commented, ". . . will perceive an abundance of the necessaries and the comforts of life within the reach of the whole mass of the population. He will be struck by the absence of pauperism, of litigation, of crime, and, above all, will have to remark an absence of party spirit and political animosity."[223]

Urquhart was aware that by the destruction of the Janissaries a great and natural safety valve in the Ottoman system had been wrecked without thought of the consequences. To an old Turk who had witnessed the reforms of Mahmud II he attributed the following reflections: "Above all the Ulema of Constantinople were to blame. They should have secured a permanent divan [Council], before sanctioning and effecting the destruction of the Janissaries. How has the Sultan maintained himself, hitherto? What is his Nizzam [new formations on the European model]? What are their numbers or instruction? They will, no doubt, become powerful but what have they been hitherto but boys of ten and twelve years of age who know not what religion or duty means and who already presume to despise their betters and will grow up to divide the Musulmans into two factions?"[224]

By pointing out the essential excellence of Ottoman institutions, Urquhart was paving the way for the Young Ottoman's protonationalism and the parochialism that was associated with it. That Ali Suavi, who had set out to prove the superior aptitudes of the Turks for sciences,[225] should have nourished

Ponsonby, Stratford de Redcliffe followed a somewhat different policy, but Bailey points out again that his influence has been exaggerated. *Ibid.*, p. 231.

[223] D. Urquhart, *The Spirit of the East* (London, Henry Colburn, 1838), II, 49.

[224] *Ibid.*, I, 172.

[225] In an article in the periodical *Ulûm* on the scientific contributions of the Turks, *Ulûm* (Paris, 1870), I, 1. See also Mordtmann, *Stambul*, p. 66, who speaks too harshly, in my opinion, of the aims of the Young Ottomans as *"vor allen Dingen die Herstellung alt-türkischer und mittelalterlicher Zustände."*

a great admiration[226] for Urquhart is, therefore, not surprising.

In Ahmed Vefik Paşa we may find a representative of a similar attitude. Vefik Paşa was adamant in salvaging the best of Ottoman culture, but not because he had never been in contact with the West. As one of his intimates described him: "To the opponents of Reshid Pasha may be added a small body of able, enlightened, thoughtful and honest men of which Ahmet Vefyk [sic] Efendi became the type, who whilst anxious that the corrupt and incapable administration of public affairs should be reformed and purified, were of the opinion that the necessary reforms could only be safely and effectually accomplished upon Turkish and Mussulman lines, and great prudence and caution were required in putting them into execution. . . . They maintained at the same time, that the ancient Turkish political system and institutions and the Mussulman religion contained the elements of progress, civilization and good and just government, if they were only honestly and justly developed."[227]

From this stand to the contention that European representative institutions had existed for all times in Islam was only a step, and this step was taken by the Young Ottomans.

[226] Kuntay, *Sarıklı İhtilalci Ali Suavi*, pp. 28, 120; Mordtmann, *Stambul*, p. 226.
In the *Diplomatic Review* which he directed, Urquhart spoke of Ali Suavi's *A Propos de l'Hertzegovine* (Paris, 1875) as "an enthusiastic partisan treatise by an eminent Osmanli whose uprightness of character and opposition to corrupt government in Turkey have forced him to live in banishment, but who is, nevertheless, as devoted as a patriot [sic] to the welfare of the Turkish monarchy." Reverse of title page, *Diplomatic Review* (July 1876), XXIV.

[227] Sir Henry Layard, *Autobiography and Letters*, II, 89. Safvet Paşa, a statesman who was grand vizier, and Minister of Education and Foreign Affairs during the Tanzimat, and whose understanding of Western culture cannot be questioned, also had a different approach to the problems of reform than Âli and Fuad Paşa. Even though his remarks on the subject, as reported by the Turkish historian, Abdurrahman Şeref, are based on hearsay, the attitude described reflects accurately the stand toward reform taken by some of his contemporaries; what Safvet Paşa had to say about legal reforms was the following: "Sir, we have neither judges nor courts; under such circumstances legal reforms are condemned to be a dead letter. First we must train judges, then build court-houses and then only attempt to reform and enlarge the legal system in our country." Şeref, *Tarih Musahabeleri*, p. 296.

The latter were in touch with Urquhart in London. Urquhart's influence was bolstered by another romantic trend to
whose soothing music Suavi was quite sensitive. This was the
new interest in linguistic and anthropological studies which
so greatly contributed to building the foundations of nineteenth-century European nationalism. The instrumentality
through which these ideas affected Suavi was a book on
Turkish grammar by Arthur Lumley Davids, published in
London in 1832 and in a second French edition in 1836.[228]
The author's preface to this work with its recounting of
the past glories of the Turks and its sympathetic approach to
their civilization apparently deeply influenced Suavi, who read
the French edition.[229] Davids also had reference in his preface
to the ideas earlier expounded by J. S. Bailly, the mayor of
Paris, to the effect that "the plains of Tatary" had given arts,
sciences, and civilization to the world, and that its ancient
inhabitants were the "enlightened preceptors of mankind."[230]
Suavi was stirred by this acknowledgment of the Turkish
contribution to civilization, and, attributing it to the "Englishman Bailey," used it to bolster his statements about the outstanding qualities of his people.[231]

Thus, in Suavi, eighteenth-century Encyclopaedism was
crowded in with nineteenth-century historical romanticism.
Such a mixture, added to an Islamic substratum, was what,

[228] Arthur Lumley Davids, *Kitab 'ilm un-nafi fi tahsil-i sarf ve nahv-i
Turki*, (A Grammar of the Turkish Language) (London, Allen, Parbury, and
Taylor, 1832).

[229] Ali Suavi, "Türk," *Ulûm*, 8 Cemaziyelevvel 1286/August 8, 1869,
p. 1.

[230] Davids, *op.cit.*, Introduction, p. v, paraphrasing Jean Sylvain Bailly,
Lettres sur l'Atlantide de Platon et sur l'Ancienne Histoire de l'Asie (London,
Elmesly; Paris, Delure, 1779).

[231] Moustafa Djelaleddine's *Les Turcs Anciens et Modernes* (see above,
p. 215) is worthy of study in this respect. The author, a Polish convert to
Islam, devoted the above-mentioned work to the thesis that the Turks were
an Aryan "lost tribe" and therefore more European than the Europeans. The
influence of other European refugees from the repressions of 1848 in the
Austrian Empire and in Poland who established themselves in Turkey has
not, as yet, been studied; see, however, Ahmed Refik, *Türkiyede Mülteciler
Meselesi* (Istanbul, Matbaa-i Âmire, 1926).

in general, made up the fundamental beliefs of that "inter-mediate" type of Westernist who went by the name of Young Ottoman. Not the least extraordinary facet of the movement which these young men founded was the synthesis which they created out of such diverse elements—a synthesis which, though condemned to be short-lived, mightily sustained their own spirit and left an indelible mark on Turkish thought.

CHAPTER VIII

Şinasi: the Birth of Public Opinion

ALTHOUGH the Young Ottoman movement was the product of many influences, it devolved upon one person to establish its intellectual foundations. This was the poet Şinasi Efendi, whose publications familiarized Turkish intellectuals with literary, social, and political conceptions current in Europe in the middle of the nineteenth century. Namık Kemal himself placed full credit for the intellectual mentorship of the Young Ottomans on the shoulders of Şinasi.[1]

Ibrahim Şinasi Efendi was born in 1826.[2] He came from a moderately well-to-do family, his father having been an officer in the Turkish army. Şinasi began his career at a very early age as a clerk in the bureau of the Imperial Ottoman Artillery (*Tophane Kalemi*). While in this post he learned French from a French artillery officer, a convert to Islam who had abandoned his original family name of Chateauneuf for the more romantic one of Reşad Bey. Şinasi soon acquired considerable proficiency in French. Encouraged by a patron of modernization, Fethi Ahmed Paşa, and by Reşid Paşa, he petitioned the commanding general of the Imperial Artillery to be sent to Europe for study (1849). This request was granted and Şinasi remained in Paris until 1853 studying public finance and literature. During his stay in Europe he

---

[1] Kuntay, *Namık Kemal*, I, 377.

[2] The following biographical information is based on: Hikmet Dizdaroğlu, *Şinasi: Hayatı, Sanatı, Eserleri* (Istanbul, Varlık Yayınları, 1954). Upon close examination this work will be seen to have been based to a great extent on Ahmed Rasim, *Matbuat Tarihimize Methal: İlk Büyük Muharrirlerden Şinasi* (Istanbul, Yeni Matbaa, 1928). However, the more recent work was used as basic source since some of the information contained in the earlier biography of Şinasi has proved to be inexact and has been corrected by Dizdaroğlu. A very good but short article by Kenan Akyüz, "Şinasi'nin Fransadaki Öğrenimi ile İlgili Bazı Belgeler," *Türk Dili Dergisi* (April 1954), III, 397-405, enables one to correct some of the erroneous information contained in the above sources.

established a close friendship with Samuel de Sacy, the son of the orientalist Sylvestre de Sacy. He also knew well the French liberal poet Alphonse de Lamartine. He seems to have been in touch with a variety of liberal circles in the French capital.

Şinasi had obtained his scholarship thanks to the patronage of Reşid Paşa. When he returned to Turkey in 1853, he was appointed to his old post and then in 1855 to the Educational Committee (*Meclis-i Maarif*),[3] which was gradually taking education out of the hands of the ulema. However, the same year, at a time when Reşid Paşa was temporarily out of power, Şinasi was dismissed by Âli Paşa, who had replaced Reşid. Âli, an earlier protégé of Reşid had by then become a statesman of considerable stature and was already competing with Reşid. It is not entirely out of the question that Şinasi, in turn, should have frightened Âli as a potential rival.

Şinasi was reinstated in 1856. Soon thereafter (in 1858) Reşid Paşa died. Although Şinasi was still able to reply on the protection of such statesmen as Yusuf Kâmil Paşa, the brilliant administrative career to which many thought Şinasi destined never materialized.

During his second appointment Şinasi had begun to devote most of his energies to publishing. In 1859 appeared his first work, an anthology of poems entitled *Divan-ı Şinasi*,[4] in keeping with classical usage. Here appeared the panegyrics of Mustafa Reşid Paşa which constitute one of the more important sources for a study of Şinasi. It was this work of Şinasi, bought at a second-hand book dealer's stall, which made Kemal aware of Şinasi's stature. He admits having been spellbound as soon as he began reading the first page. The same year Şinasi published a diminutive pamphlet entitled *Translation of Poems*, an anthology of translations from the French classics, in particular Racine and LaFontaine, with a few short

[3] See above, Chapter VII. My source for these dates is Mustafa Nihat Özön, "Şinasi," *Aylık Ansiklopedi*, (1944-1945), I, 159.

[4] The edition used here was the second edition. The copy used had no title page and bore only the date Şaban 1287/1870.

excerpts from Fénelon's *Télémaque*.[5] In 1860, in collaboration with his friend Agâh Efendi, Şinasi began the publication of the first privately owned Turkish newspaper. This was the *Tercüman-ı Ahval* which appeared in the fall of 1860.[6] Within six months Şinasi had, for some unknown reason, broken with Agâh Efendi and left the *Tercüman*. In 1862 he started his own newspaper, entitled *Tasvir-i Efkâr*, which appeared twice a week.[7]

The *Tasvir-i Efkâr* soon became a forum for the expression of new literary as well as political ideas. It was used by Şinasi to disseminate a knowledge of European intellectual advances and break the classical molds of Ottoman literature. In the meantime on July 2, 1863, Şinasi had once again been dismissed from his job. Documents recently uncovered[8] show that this last dismissal was due to the sultan's objections to Şinasi's timid libertarianism. "Mentioning too often matters of state" in the *Tasvir* was the official reason given for his dismissal. The fact that an article by Şinasi explaining the principle of "no taxation without representation" appeared in the *Tasvir* the day before the imperial order for Şinasi's expulsion was drafted may be the solution to a problem which heretofore has puzzled his biographers. Then too, the first budget of the Ottoman Empire had been published in 1862-1863, and this probably was a complicating factor. Meanwhile, Şinasi's relations with the Porte were improving. This was at least true of his relations with Fuad Paşa. In 1864 Fuad, who was temporarily made the Minister of Defense, asked Şinasi's help in publishing the *Ceride-i Askeriye* (*"Military Gazette"*), which was the second official journal to have appeared in the Ottoman Empire. At least one authority has stated that Şinasi regained official favor to the extent of being considered for a

---

[5] Chinassi [*sic*], *Extraits de Poésies et de Prose Traduits en Vers du Français en Turc* (Constantinople, Imprimerie de la Presse d'Orient, 1859).

[6] On October 22, 1860/6 Rebiülahir 1277.

[7] The first issue appeared on June 28, 1862/30 Zilhicce 1278.

[8] See Akyüz, "Şinasi'nin Fransadaki Öğrenimi ile İlgili Bazı Belgeler," p. 405.

position on the *Meclis-i Vâlâ*, the sequel to the earlier consultative assembly established by Reşid Paşa.[9] Soon thereafter,
however, Şinasi left for Paris. The usual explanation given
for this precipitous flight is that Şinasi had participated in a
plot against Âli Paşa engineered by a certain Said Sermedi
about whom little more is known than that he did exist.[10]
Şinasi's escape on a French ship was arranged by the publisher
of the *Courrier d'Orient*, who later also helped Kemal to get
to Paris. Şinasi had left the editorship of the *Tasvir-i Efkâr*
to Namık Kemal, who still divided his time between the
Tasvir and his governmental work.

When, four years later, Kemal was also obliged to flee and
came to visit Şinasi in Paris, he found to his surprise that his
former employer had given himself entirely to the study of
literature and linguistics. In addition, the Young Ottomans
were given a rather chill welcome by Şinasi. Only Reşad was
able to establish contact with him.[11] About the same time
Şinasi's wife took advantage of the voyage of Sultan Abdülaziz to Europe to ask Fuad Paşa to intercede with the sultan
for Şinasi's return. Şinasi was pardoned, but this action was
far from pleasing to him. Incensed at his wife's part in it, he
returned to Istanbul for only five days—the time needed to
divorce her—and then went back to Paris.

According to Ebüzziya, back in Paris Şinasi devoted himself entirely to the writing of an Ottoman dictionary and spent
most of his time at the Bibliothèque Nationale. The War of
1870 forced Şinasi to return to Istanbul, where he lived in
great destitution, accepting only essential help from Mustafa
Fazıl Paşa. As in Paris, he was a recluse there too. Şinasi's
strange conduct and increasing misanthropy were probably

[9] Ahmed Rasim, *Şinasi*, p. 27.
[10] Namık Kemal speaks in one of his letters of this conspiracy as having
been hushed up; Kuntay, *Namık Kemal*, I, 1, 95. Şinasi fled in the spring of
1865; see Ebüzziya, "Yeni Osmanlılar," *Yeni Tasvir-i Efkâr*, October 31,
1909.
[11] Ebüzziya Tevfik, "Yeni Osmanlılar Tarihi," *Yeni Tasvir-i Efkâr*,
February 7, 8, 1910.

caused by the brain tumor from which he eventually died on September 13, 1871 (27 Cemaziyülahir 1288).

I. Şinasi's Thought

Şinasi is unanimously considered by historians of Turkish intellectual history the first outstanding advocate of Europeanization in the Ottoman Empire.[12] However, none of these historians explicitly takes up one of the characteristic features of this contribution, namely, that Şinasi was the first *private* exponent of such views. Up until Şinasi's time, schemes of modernization that had been thought of had been the result of an official concern with reform. The reformers were statesmen and sovereigns. The crucial importance of Şinasi consists in that during his lifetime and owing to his influence the modernists were split into two camps. Within the ranks of the reformers now appeared a new breed, the reformist intellectual. Later the same intellectuals were to spearhead the Young Ottoman movement. Even these new intellectuals had originated in the bureaus of the Porte. Despite the fact that it had been nurtured in the service of the Ottoman state, however, the new group differed from the reformers of the Porte in that it had an ideology to offer. These young men debated the problem of reform and set their own theoretical framework without being content with the prospect of rising to high offices of state and subsequently implementing whatever policy they chose. In that sense the group led by Şinasi was the first one to have the earmarks of a true intelligentsia.

The development of this intelligentsia, in turn, seems to have been closely associated with the history of Turkish journalism. Turkish journalistic growth had been rather slow at first. The *Official Gazette (Takvim-i Vekayi)*, which appeared in 1831, was the only newspaper in Turkish available until

[12] See Ahmed Rasim, *op.cit.*, whose book deals with this idea throughout, and also the following works: Levend, *Türk Dilinde Gelişme*, p. 101; M. N. Özön, *Son Asır Türk Edebiyatı Tarihi* (Istanbul, Maarif Matbaası, 1941), p. 417; Ismail Habib, *Edebi Yeniliğimiz. Birinci Kısım* (Istanbul, Devlet Matbaası, 1931), p. 71; Tanpınar, *XIXncu Asır*, I, 170.

1840. The *Takvim* contained the latest administrative and governmental decisions. In 1831 the foreword to the first issue explained that it was meant to inform the subjects of the day-to-day business of the state. The *Takvim* was the beginning of a flow of information with regard to the state, which was later to be swelled by annuals, budgetary reports, and diplomatic "color" books. Its audience was limited to Ottoman civil servants, embassies, and businessmen. For a long time the *Takvim* appeared at irregular intervals and difficulties were encountered in keeping it in operation.[13] The first privately owned Turkish newspaper, on the other hand, was owned and published by the infamous Mr. Churchill whose indemnization had cost Akif Paşa his post. Part of this indemnization had consisted of a concession to establish a newspaper in Istanbul. In 1840 Churchill took advantage of this concession and founded the *Ceride-i Havadis.* In the beginning the *Ceride* attracted little attention and was distributed free to serve as an advertising handbill.[14]

During the Crimean War Churchill's personal dispatches from the Crimea caused sales to increase considerably and the newspaper acquired a steady clientele.

The social background of the men who were running the *Ceride* for Churchill and their dissatisfaction with things as they were has already been taken up above, but the cultural ripples created by the protojournalists who congregated in its editorial rooms has not been mentioned. These were not negligible.

It was on the *Ceride-i Havadis* that the ex-diplomat Mustafa Sami began to use the "journalistic" Turkish that was perfected by Şinasi.[15] In 1840, the same year the *Ceride* first appeared, Mustafa Sami, in a work entitled *Avrupa Risalesi* (*"Pamphlet on Europe"*), spoke of the fact that he had engaged in a reporting of European life because he considered

[13] Selim Nüzhet [Gerçek], *Türk Gazeteciliği* (Istanbul, Devlet Matbaası, 1931), pp. 30 ff.
[14] *Ibid.*, p. 37.   [15] Kaplan, *Namık Kemal*, p. 135.

it a duty to his *vatan* (fatherland).[16] From the very beginning
of its appearance the *Ceride-i Havadis*, under the rubric "Foreign News," gave a wealth of encyclopedic information to its
readers about the New World, India, modern methods of
locomotion, paleontology, and insurance. It also had articles
on human reason[17] and, most significantly, was a precursor of
the *Tasvir-i Efkâr* in articles describing European parliamentary government[18] and news items in which it was pointed
out that in France government expenditures had to be approved by parliament.[19] It was also the *Ceride* that started
the use of serials.

The Young Ottomans always remembered with gratitude
such erstwhile contributors to the *Ceride-i Havadis* as Hafız
Müşfik and Ali Âli as precursors of themselves in creating the
new, simplified journalistic language and style. The chief
characteristic of this style was that it aimed at conveying ideas
rather than at titillating the brain. This in itself had little to
do with Westernization but it was, nevertheless, an important
step in the modernization of Ottoman society.

The influence of the staff of the *Ceride* was sometimes
manifested in indirect ways which it is not easy to trace but
which had an undeniable importance. Thus Hâlet Efendi, one
of the early members of the editorial staff of the *Ceride*, later
took up an administrative career and made his own important
contribution to the modernization of the empire by inaugu-
rating the practice of preparing an official yearbook for each
province. He began this practice in Aleppo and it was then
adopted by the central administration.[20] Hâlet was also one of
the first Ottomans to experiment with the theater as a literary
genre. While in Aleppo he also started a local paper in
Arabic.[21] Hâlet was a close friend of Kemal and while he was

[16] Mustafa Sami, *Avrupa Risalesi* (Istanbul, 1256/1840), p. 4.
[17] *Ceride-i Havadis*, Gurre-i Şevval 1256/November 26, 1840, p. 3.
[18] *Ibid.*; 18 Muharrem 1257/March 12, 1841, p. 3; 14 Cemaziyülahir 1257/August 3, 1841, p. 2.
[19] *Ceride-i Havadis*, 2 Rebiülahır 1257/June 5, 1841, p. 3.
[20] See Ahmed Rasim, *Şinasi*, p. 7; İnal, *Son Asır*, pp. 441, 1410.
[21] Rasim, *loc.cit.*

ŞINASI

on the staff of the *Ceride*, he worked in the Customs Bureau with Kemal.

Said Paşa, Abdülhamid's grand vizier, was also on the staff of the *Ceride* in his youth and so was Mehmed Süreyya, the author of the Ottoman *Who's Who*.[22]

In 1860 a rival to the *Ceride-i Havadis* appeared—the *Tercüman-ı Ahval*, which was started by Agâh Efendi with the cooperation of Şinasi. Agâh Efendi was later to become a charter member of the Paris Young Ottoman Society; yet this association with them was not wholehearted, for Agâh Efendi was essentially a nonpolitical person. Neither was he an ideologue. What interested Agâh above all were the more pedestrian benefits of European civilization. Thus as director of the Ottoman Postal Service he had introduced into the Ottoman Empire the use of the postage stamp.[23] It is in the same spirit—that of introducing into the empire the benefits of useful European institutions—that he established the *Tercüman-ı Ahval*. In this sense he was doing for Ottoman journalism what Münif Paşa had already done for encyclopaedism. It is not certain whether the politicization of its contents was due to the influence of Şinasi or that of Agâh. Şinasi's introductory article in its first issue pointed in this direction. But then he was also a very careful man. Yet this newspaper, published by two of the coolest heads of the Ottoman Empire, was the first to be suspended because it had displeased the Ottoman government. It was likewise a hothouse for Turkish ideologues. The most famous of its products was the editor of the short-lived *Mir'at*, Refik Bey, who died at the age of twenty-three during the cholera epidemic of 1865 without having been able to fulfill the expectations of his friends.[24] Refik Bey was considered by the Young Ottomans to have been an important precursor of the Young Ottoman movement. Süleyman Nazif, in his work on Kemal, speaks of him

[22] Gerçek, *Türk Gazeteciliği*, p. 38.
[23] Server Iskit, "Agâh Efendi," *Aylık Ansiklopedi* (1944-1945), I, 163.
[24] For Refik see İnal, *Son Asır*, pp. 1404-1412. Also, above, Chapter VII.

as having "opened Kemal's eyes" to the liberal ideas of the West.[25] Again, it is in Refik's *Mir'at* that Namık Kemal's translation of Montesquieu's *Considerations on the Grandeur and Decadence of the Romans* is reported to have appeared.[26]

The *Mir'at*, from contemporary reports describing it, seems to have been an exponent of the idea—one encountered often among the Young Ottomans—that work and industriousness were basic to Western civilization.[27] Refik, as we have seen, was also quite outspoken in his convictions that political affairs were the concern of all citizens, and he was dismissed from the government because of his sneers at Münif's mildness. After Refik's death, Kemal himself worked for a while on the *Tercüman-ı Ahval* and speaks of Refik with the greatest admiration.[28]

The competition of the *Tercüman-i Ahval* forced Churchill's son, to whom the rights of publication had passed in 1864, to ask Münif Paşa to recast the *Ceride* and publish the latter as the *Supplement to the Ceride*. Yet the *Ceride* was doomed because of the new popularity of the *Tasvir-i Efkâr*. Münif Paşa had been summoned to help the *Ceride* because serials of the type that he had published in the *Mecmua-i Fünûn* were becoming increasingly popular, but the *Tasvir* offered both serials more sophisticated than those of the *Ceride* and analyses of political affairs, which were a complete innovation. In using his newspaper to make cautious and indirect, but yet continuous reference to political and social matters, Şinasi had stolen a march on the *Ceride*. Şinasi had the additional advantage of being able to rely on the contributions of such Encyclopaedists as Yusuf Kâmil Paşa. In general,

[25] Süleyman Nazif, *Namık Kemal* (Istanbul, İkdam Matbaası, 1922), p. 5.
[26] Kaplan, *Namık Kemal*, p. 31. For the text see Ahmet Hamdi Tanpınar, *Namık Kemal Antolojisi* (Istanbul, 1946), pp. 33, 34.
[27] Bianchi, "Bibliographie Ottomane," *Journal Asiatique* (August-September 1863), Series VI, II, 269.
[28] Ahmed Rasim, *Şinasi*, p. 9, 10, basing his information on Ebüzziya Tevfik, *Salname-i Hadika*, p. 1-11, without date or publishing reference for this annual of the newspaper *Hadika* published by Ebüzziya.

the *Tasvir-i Efkâr* was also far ahead of other Turkish newspapers and periodicals of the time in the quality of its educational articles, i.e., those devoted to the illustration of the
methods used in the new branches of knowledge that had
come into their own in Europe in the nineteenth century.

To emphasize the European content of natural-law theories,
for example, Şinasi chose to publish as the first serial to appear
in the *Tasvir-i Efkâr* a translation of Vattel's *Droit des Gens*.[29]
Vattel's conviction that natural law was the ultimate basis of
all legal institutions[30] was thus brought to a Turkish audience.
To counteract the classical Islamic conception of history as a
process guided by the hand of God, Şinasi published serials on
ancient history by Sami and Subhi Paşa, where historical
events were taken up as part of a causal chain.[31] It is in the
columns of the same newspaper in the serials on historical
methodology written by Ahmed Vefik Paşa that for the first
time in Turkey history was called a "science."[32] A number of
these historical serials were also devoted to discovering the
causes of the decline of the Ottoman Empire,[33] and at least
one of them was an attempt to recapture the glorious doings
of the Turks in their original homeland of Central Asia.[34]
Şinasi also tried to include the best of Europe's scientific thinking in his journal; Mustafa Behçet Efendi's translation of

[29] "Hukuk-u Milel," *Tasvir-i Efkâr*, 4 Safer 1279-17 Muharrem 1282/
August 1, 1862-June 12, 1865. Almost none of these serials appeared in
consecutive issues, as can be seen from the long-drawn-out publication of the
above serial, spread over three years. The method used here has been to
mention the first and the last serial dates.
[30] Rolf Knubben, "Vattel," *Encyclopedia of Social Sciences* (1935),
XV, 232.
[31] Abdurrahman Sami Bey, "Rumuz ül-Hikem fi Ahlâk ül-Âlem," 14
Safer 1279-12 Rebiülahır 1282/August 17, 1862-September 4, 1865.
Abdüllatif Subhi Bey, "Uyun ul-Ahbar fi nukud ül-Âsar," Selh-i Zilhicce
1278-18 Rebiülevvel 1279/June 28, 1862-September 13, 1862.
[32] Ahmed Vefik Efendi, "Hikmet-i Tarih," 8 Ramazan 1279-20 Şevval
1279/February 27, 1863-April 11, 1863. For the traditional Ottoman view
see Hammer, *Histoire*, XVII, *post face*, p. XLVI.
[33] Mehmed Şefik Efendi, "Şefiknâme," 21 Rebiülahır 1282-1 Ramazan
1282/August 14, 1865-January 18, 1866.
[34] Ebu'l Gazi Bahadır Han, "Evsal-ı Şecere-i Turkî," 14 Rebiülahır 1280-
16 Ramazan 1280/September 28, 1863-February 24, 1864.

Buffon's *Histoire Naturelle*[35] was such an attempt. One of the rare editorials written by Şinasi was a complaint that scientific education was being neglected in the new normal schools.[36]

In a single series entitled "The Financial System of France" Şinasi, who attributed these articles to a "well known French personality," attempted to get across to his readers the essentials of parliamentary government.[37]

Şinasi's ability to take advantage of the best brains of the *salon* groups is one aspect of his continuity with earlier developments in Turkish intellectual history; his espousal of linguistic reform was another. It is significant that the prestige of the *Tasvir-i Efkâr* reached a peak as a result of the fame Şinasi gained from a full-fledged battle against the partisans of classical Turkish style.[38] As E. J. W. Gibb describes the *Tasvir*: "Not merely was it the first unofficial journal in Turkey [*sic*], it was the first utterance of the modern school. . . . Here, for the first time, an Ottoman man of letters conversant with and appreciative of a great European language and literature deliberately set out to reconstruct from its very foundations the whole edifice of Turkish literary style."[39]

The real innovations brought by Şinasi, however, are apt to be overlooked if we analyze them only from the vantage point of the history of Turkish literature. The best method to appraise the full extent of the change brought about by him is to look at his contributions from the broader viewpoint of "communications."

In Chapter VII an attempt was made to isolate, among the

[35] Buffon, "Tarih-i Tabii," 24 Safer 1281-4 Rebiülevvel 1282/July 29, 1864-August 27, 1865. Trans. by Hekimbaşı Mustafa Behçet Efendi.

[36] *Tasvir-i Efkâr*, 4 Receb 1279/December 26, 1862.

[37] "Fransa Umur-u Maliyesi Hakkında," 16 Muharrem 1280-5 Rebiülevvel 1280/July 3, 1863-August 20, 1863.

[38] This debate has been published in pamphlet form as Şinasi, *Muntahabat-ı Tasvir-i Efkâr, İkinci Kısım. Mebahisat-ı Edebiyye, Mes'ele-i Mebhuset-u Anha* (Ed. by Ebüzziya Tevfik, 1st ed., Konstantiniyye, Matbaa-i Ebüzziya, 1303/1885).

[39] Gibb, *Ottoman Poetry*, v, 26.

strands of Young Ottoman thought, two elements which may be included under the general heading of "communications"; these were the simplification of the Turkish language and the first translations of Western literary productions into Turkish. Both of these moves had been steps taken toward the establishment in Ottoman society of a level of communications roughly comparable to that which existed in the West. Both moves had been sponsored at first by the state. It is only with the growth of journalism, however, that a significant acceleration occurred in the rate at which channels of communication were established. Here too, the important transition was from state support to private journalism. Three forces which had existed only potentially in state journalism were thereby unleashed: one was the feeling of intimacy, the direct contact between reader and editor that was established (despite what to many modern readers would appear as the epitome of aloofness); the second was the minimum of realism that had to infuse any literary product that explained factual occurrences; the last was the powerful instrument provided by a knowledge of such European liberal expressions as "the people" or "the nation."

All of these characteristics, and therefore also the extent to which Şinasi differed from Agâh, may be witnessed in Şinasi's first piece of journalistic writing, the foreword to the first issue of the *Tercüman-ı Ahval*. This introduction ran as follows: "Since people living in a given social community are circumscribed in their actions by multifarious legal obligations, it is quite natural that they should consider the expression of ideas aimed at the protection of the interests of the fatherland part of the totality of their vested rights. If tangible proof of this assertion is sought, it is sufficient to point at the political gazettes of those people the limits of whose understanding have been enlarged by the power of knowledge."[40] In this piece may be singled out Şinasi's characteristic contributions of antiesotericism, realism, and political rationalism.

[40] "Mukaddeme," *Tercüman-ı Ahval*, 2 Rebiülahır 1277/October 8, 1860, p. 1.

By the mere use of direct and intelligible prose addressed to the many, Şinasi was already an innovator. This was so because a most essential part of the culture of Islam was its esotericism—a conception that knowledge was dangerous when indiscriminately placed in the hands of everyone. Thus far, information couched in a language understandable to all had been suspect. Technical innovations which would facilitate learning were also accepted with misgivings by most conservatively inclined Ottoman men of learning. When, for instance, the first Turkish printing press was established and the printing of books on "philosophy, geography, and history" considered, the ulema did not protest against the printing of the scientific works per se, but grumbled that this new invention would increase the circulation of religious books to an extent where it would become dangerous.[41] It is a telling difference between the attitudes of the East and the West that in the West, on the contrary, the Bible should have been the first book printed.

Again, when at the beginning of the nineteenth century the great calligrapher Mustafa Rakım Efendi proposed a new, simplified system of calligraphy, opposition to its use was only quashed because the sultan, a calligrapher himself, had admired the new characters.[42] Later a simplified alphabet had been devised by Fuad Paşa and Cevdet Paşa, who used it to increase the speed of reading among elementary school students.[43] It is true that as early as 1840 one comes across an attempt to translate into simple, everyday Turkish a work on Islamic dogmatics,[44] but there is no doubt that for a long time the general feeling prevailed that simplicity and clarity—in short, accessibility—went against the grain of the old Otto-

[41] Server İskit, *Türkiyede Neşriyat Hareketleri* (Istanbul, Devlet Basımevi, 1939), p. 7.
[42] Ebüzziya Tevfik, "Rical-i Mensiye," *Mecmua-i Ebüzziya* (1317/1899-1900), XIX, 438.
[43] Bianchi, "Bibliographie Ottomane," *Journal Asiatique* (October-November 1860), V, 16.
[44] Kadı Birgevî's *Tarikat-ı Muhammediye*. See Hammer, "Liste," *Journal Asiatique* (March 1843), IV, I, 247.

man conceptions of knowledge. Esotericism, in the sense of an unwillingness to divulge the aims of the society, was still present in the Beşiktaş Society. Although the aim of the first simplifiers of the Ottoman language had been to conjure this secretiveness, its corollary, exclusiveness, had remained operative even in the Ottoman Scientific Society in the sense that appointments to this body were considered politically useful sinecures. Even the audiences of the *salons* which were beginning to grow were a select group.

In short, then, when Şinasi coupled clarity and intelligibility with the conception of a people's right to know what was happening, his approach was entirely new. It is useful to remember in this connection that as late as the end of the nineteenth century the historian Lûtfi, preparing notes for a history of education during the Tanzimat, jotted down his notes that the main drawback in the abortive attempt to create an Ottoman university in 1870 had been having the lectures open to the public.[45]

Şinasi's concern with reporting political and social changes, his emphasis on facts—what we may call his realism—was also a departure from the norm. E. J. W. Gibb makes this point quite succinctly when he states, "Şinasi is justly regarded as the true founder of the Modern School of Ottoman literature, since he was the first who seriously and systematically strove to raise literature from being . . . a mere plaything for the amusement of the learned into an instrument for the moral and intellectual education of the whole people."[46]

Forty years later this earlier state of affairs had been forgotten by Ottoman audiences. Ebüzziya Tevfik, one of the survivors of the heroic times of Turkish journalism, thus reminded his readers in 1900 that in his own youth not much had been available to those like himself who were eager to know what was happening in the world. To that part of the

[45] See Lûtfi, "Türkiyede Maarif Teşkilâtı 1267-1287," *TTEM* (1927), XVI, 305.
[46] Gibb, *History of Ottoman Poetry,* V, 28.

public that did not make it a specialty to study one branch of knowledge, he said, the only works available had been romances twisted into almost identical shapes by an array of conventions. Ebüzziya recalled that relating an event without emasculating its distinguishing traits by fitting it to a given mold was so rare a happening that a letter of Akif Paşa[47] describing a boat ride had been deemed worthy of printing because of the comparative freshness of his description.

Finally, Şinasi's idea of "rights" of the people as a pendant of their obligations was a product of Western political rationalism. The earlier emphasis placed on saving the empire from disintegration, already transformed in Sadık Rifat Paşa's ideas into the protection of the well-being of subjects, was now being metamorphosed into a defense of the rights of the people. This was Şinasi's outstanding contribution to the development of Turkish political thought.

Şinasi was set apart from his followers, the Young Ottomans, in that he was much more a man of the Enlightenment than they were. What Şinasi shared with Kemal, for example, was a concern for the "people," stemming in both men from a belief in the perfectibility—if not always the essential goodness—of man. What separated Şinasi from Kemal was the strongly emotional attachment of Kemal to an imaginary golden age of Ottoman culture which he took as an ideal to be approximated in the present. These points at which Kemal and Şinasi differed showed the affinity between Kemal's ideas and his own time. It pointed to the emotionalism, irrationalism, and parochialism that began to pervade the European theories which slowly replaced natural-law theories. Şinasi's espousal of earlier currents of ideas made him more of a universal man and more of a cosmopolitan sage. In general, Şinasi's writings show a definite concern with and an approval of what he called the "civilizing mission" of Reşid Paşa.

[47] Ebüzziya Tevfik, "Rical-i Mensiye," *Mecmua-i Ebüzziya* (1317/1899-1900), XIX, 439 ff.; *ibid.*, "Süleyman Nazif Beyefendiye," *Mecmua-i Ebüzziya* (1329/1911), XXX, 579.

Şinasi equated the well-being of the empire with the process of Europeanization which had set in since the Tanzimat. According to him, the highest achievement of Reşid Paşa was that he had brought to Turkey "the European climate of opinion."[48] Thus a large part of the poetry written by Şinasi was composed of panegyrics to Mustafa Reşid Paşa. Repeatedly he heaped praise on the grand vizier for having introduced "reason" in the Ottoman Empire; in one instance he went so far as to thank Reşid Paşa for having liberated "the people" from "fanaticism."[49] Again, in one of his poems, the achievements of the grand vizier were compared to those of Plato and Newton. This need not indicate the European origin of Şinasi's ideas, for Plato was held in considerable esteem in traditional Ottoman culture. The comparison made between Reşid and Newton and the selection of Newton as a standard of excellence did, however, show the extent of Şinasi's identification with Western rationalism.[50] In the same vein, according to Şinasi, the most important gift bestowed on human beings was the gift of reason. Only in the light of such a divine grant, he stated, could the meaning of the divine "gift of tongues" be appreciated.[51] This was an indirect attack on the current Islamic conception that the main use of language was to praise the Lord and spread His word. Again, in Şinasi's conception of man, "the will of the soul" was "chiefly guided by reason."[52] God had granted reason to man as a means of investigating the world around him.

[48] *Şinasi: Müntahabat-ı Eş'arım* (Ed. by Muallâ Anıl, Istanbul, A. Sait, 1945), p. 18. To appreciate the extent to which Şinasi had identified himself with the West, it is sufficient to compare this statement with a similar one of Ziya Paşa, one of the Young Ottomans, which takes the reverse view that the subservience to European ideas "in all matters" was a shocking development which had never been witnessed before in the empire. See Ziya Paşa, "Terciibend," in Ertaylan, *Ziya Paşa*, p. 146.

[49] Anıl, *Şinasi*, p. 13.

[50] There is, in fact, an element of astronomical description which, as Kaplan has shown, pervades Şinasi's poetry and shows the extent to which he was impressed by the idea of "the harmony of the spheres." Kaplan, "Şinaisi'nin Türk Şiirinde Yarattığı Yenilik," p. 29.

[51] Anıl, *Şinasi*, p. 12.

[52] *Ibid.*, pp. 5, 12.

Many of Şinasi's poems show him to have been religiously inclined and a firm believer in Islam. Yet it is a type of religiousness which is expressed in an entirely new language. One of the most interesting of his couplets is the following:

> To seek the way of God is an obligation of right reason
> If He wills [you] to distinguish the road,
> He shall appoint Her as guide.[53]

This couplet, by making religion an obligation imposed by reason, shows an approach to faith which is the reverse of the traditional Islamic approach; the latter proceeded from faith to reason. Even though the many pantheistic and mystical orders of Islam sometimes did describe God as intelligence, the conception of God as reason, which appeared in Şinasi's poems, was novel. In particular, his lines where the worship of God was stated to consist of nothing but the expression of the purest form of man's reason are indicative of a radical change as between the Islamic approach to matters of faith and Şinasi's treatment of the same question. With time, disillusionment with politics led Şinasi to anchor himself increasingly to the humanistic rationalism which was basic to his thought, but in his youth this rationalism had, as we have already noted, not only a literary but also a political expression.

While one is ascertaining the answers that Şinasi provided to the political problems which were singled out for usually quite short discussion in the *Tasvir-i Efkâr*, a most important matter which has to be kept in mind is that he was a very cautious man. This pusillanimity probably had a pathological origin, for it eventually took the form of a deep misanthropy. Şinasi also had good reasons for being cautious, since all the

[53] Şinasi, "Nef'iye Nazire," Dizdaroğlu, *Şinasi*, p. 47. For a study which considers rationalism to have been the original contribution of Şinasi to Turkish literature see Dr. Ali Nihat Tarlan, "Tanzimat Edebiyatında Hakikî Müceddid," in *Tanzimat*, p. 603 ff. I find that my approach to Şinasi's "deism" has already been explored by Professor Mehmed Kaplan in his Şinasi'nin Türk Şiirinde Yarattığı Yenilik," 27.

pains he took to approach politics indirectly did not prevent his being expelled from his job. The raw materials that we have to work with in analyzing Şinasi's political thought consist, therefore, of allusions or indirect references to reform. We never come across a full-fledged statement of principle. That Şinasi approved of the separation of church from state, for example, can only be inferred from the large space he devoted to the papal problem in the columns of the *Tasvir-i Efkâr* and the side he chose to defend—the Italian government.[54] This was the only way the question could be approached without raising various susceptibilities. His reference to Reşid Paşa as "the president" of the people is an indication that he did not entirely set aside republican considerations.[55] Yet the fabric of his political thought which has to be reconstituted from indirect references in his poetry and his articles is not so tight as to give us a precise indication as to whether he would have advocated the creation of a republic in Turkey. One thing can be ascertained and that is the fact that his rationalism resulted in his taking an entirely new approach to political matters. This can be gathered by the attitude he adopted toward three questions: first, there are indications that he believed in politics as an activity having its own inner dynamic; secondly, he had a rationalistic approach to law which was at variance with the main current of the Ottoman-Islamic tradition; finally, he introduced into the Turkish public opinion which he created the idea of a public or of "the people." One other element that he brought to Turkish thought has no relation to his rationalism and constitutes the nineteenth-century aspect of his thought. This is Şinasi's conception of "the nation."

[54] See *Tasvir-i Efkâr*, "Roma Meselesi," Selh-i Zilhicce 1278/June 28, 1862; "Avrupa," *op.cit.*, 8 Muharrem 1279-6/July 1862; "Avrupa," *op.cit.*, 26 Cemaziyülahir 1279/December 19, 1862. This fact was first noticed by N. Eruygur, in N. Eruygur, *Şinasi ve Tasvir-i Efkâr Gazetesi*, Istanbul Üniversitesi Türkoloji Enstitüsü, Tez. No. 393 (1953), (unpublished B.A. paper, Institute of Turcology of the University of Istanbul), p. 38.
[55] Anıl, *Şinasi*, p. 13.

II. Laws of Politics

Şinasi's rationalism led him to consider politics as a science which had its basis in what he called moral or philosophical laws. The following evaluation that he made of the Turkish translation of Fénelon's *Télémaque* shows this quite strikingly:

"While, on the surface, the work of the famous French author Fénelon, entitled *The Adventures of Télémaque*, conveys the impression of being a romance, its true meaning is of the nature of a philosophical law which includes all the arts of government that have as purpose the fulfillment of justice and the happiness of the individual.

"A superior work concerning such exalted a craft was in need of being translated into Turkish by an author possessing poetic talent and a lofty style."[56]

It is interesting to note that in Namık Kemal's writings remarks can be found which are entirely at variance with this attitude. Such, for example, is the statement that ethical norms are not the result of philosophical insight but that they are given by religion.[57]

III. Şinasi's Conception of Justice and Law

An insight into Şinasi's Western-mindedness can be gained by an examination of his idea of justice. It should be clear by now that one of the ways of viewing the history of the Ottoman Empire is to look at it from the perspective of the struggle between the imperial prerogative embodied in the sultan and the upholders of the divine law, the ulema. Thus the idea of justice was an important one among the influences that went into the making of any cultivated and intelligent individual in the empire. It has also been pointed out that the decay of the Ottoman Empire had placed the idea of justice in the forefront of Ottoman problems and that publica-

[56] "Payitaht," *Tasvir-i Efkâr*, 2 Ramazan 1279/February 21, 1862.
[57] Cf. below, Chapter x.

tions idealizing the "rule of law" upheld by the ulema began
to have wide circulation. Even in the writings of the Westernist Şinasi, when the problem of political freedom was
touched, it was not by the defense of an abstraction such as
"freedom" (the latter word does not appear in a political
context in his writings); but what was mentioned as an ideal
was the establishment of justice with the concrete meaning
of equality before the law. Şinasi thus indicated the extent of
his ties with traditional Ottoman-Islamic conceptions. Yet an
analysis of the context in which "justice" is used in the writings of Şinasi shows that already European pressures were
becoming influential. This is due not only to Şinasi's extreme
rationalism; even though Şinasi was a rationalist in the field
of law it would not have been sufficient proof to separate his
thought from traditional Ottoman-Islamic conceptions, for
there did exist among the doctors of law of Islam a tradition
of rationalism introduced by the *Mu'tezilite* order. This rationalism was not held to be of the highest respectability in
orthodox circles, but it was still part of the corpus of Islamic
thought. The aspects of Şinasi's conception of law which differed from the traditional Islamic conception were, first of all,
that Şinasi believed rulers to be responsible for their actions
in this world as well as in the next. This appears in the passage
which Şinasi placed at the head of his *Selected Poems* translated from the French. The passage, a selection from Racine's
Esther, follows:

> Ce Dieu, maître absolu de la terre et des cieux
> N'est point tel que l'erreur le figure à nos yeux;
> L'Éternel est son nom, le monde est son ouvrage,
> Il entend les soupirs de l'humble qu'on outrage,
> *Juge tous les mortels avec d'égales lois,*
> Et du haut de son trône interroge les rois.[58]

Secondly, Şinasi's thought differed from the traditional Islamic approach in that it included the conception of a human

[58] Chinassi, *Extraits de Poésie et de Prose*, p. 11. (The italics in the
quotation are mine.)

lawgiver. For him, for example, one of the most important contributions of the grand vizier was that the latter had established a fundamental law which set limits to the power of the sultan.[59] It is this idea of a lawgiver other than the ruler which is quite foreign to earlier Ottoman thought where law is either the law of God, set once and for all (only to be modified by dint of interpretation or by outright distortion of the meaning), or that of the ruler, the edict of the sultan.

That the idea of keeping the law as close as possible to its original source, the Koran, had not changed in the 1860's and that the step undertaken by Şinasi was a very daring one can be gathered from the difficulties encountered by the Tanzimat historian and jurist Cevdet Paşa in regard to the mere codification of the Islamic law of obligations, that part of the law which fulfilled the function of a civil code in Islam. Cevdet Paşa was entrusted by the Porte with the codification of this section of Islamic law, but he ran into considerable resistance in the preparation of such a man-made code and to overcome the criticism of the ulema he had to have reference to a work of Celaleddin-i Devvanî.[60]

Şinasi, on the other hand, considered that the man-made law of Reşid Paşa (i.e., the Tanzimat Rescript) would provide the basis for the development and the rise of the Ottoman Empire "eternally." It thus seems, Şinasi thought that Reşid Paşa had built a new polity for the Ottoman Empire and had grounded it in a new law—again, a highly heretical conception if one takes into consideration that according to the Ottoman-Islamic scheme the laws of the polity were the existing laws of God. In Şinasi's scheme what was being praised was neither divine law nor the less orthodox *Kanunnâme*, the product of the sultan's will. It was the vizier's law which was praised. Thus both from the Islamic and the Ottoman point of view Şinasi's ideas were new. Şinasi's emphasis on man-made

[59] Anıl, *Şinasi*, p. 11.
[60] Mardin, *Medenî Hukuk Cephesinden Ahmet Cevdet Paşa*, p. 61. For Devvanî, see above, pp. 100-101.

law is also one which comes close to Reşid Paşa's own statements regarding his goals.[61]

IV. Şinasi's Conception of Public Opinion

For Şinasi, the right of the people to express "ideas of benefit to the fatherland" was one which was engendered by the obligation which the people assumed toward society.[62] The crux of the matter was the vagueness of Şinasi's conception of "the people." The prevailing conception among liberal circles in Europe at the time was that of wide or universal suffrage. But Şinasi seems to have been more conservative in his approach, and while he stated in the foreword of the *Tasvir-i Efkâr* that he considered it to be his duty to determine what the people believed to be in their own interest, a new approach to politics in Turkey, he did not mention how large a group he meant by his use of the word "people."[63] The mention he made in the preface of the *Tercüman-ı Ahval* of using language directed to "the people in general"[64] indicated that he had in mind a wider strata than the Ottoman elite, but there are indications that Şinasi believed only in having reference to the opinion of those individuals "who had acquired experience."[65]

Just as in the case of Münif Paşa, it is probable that Şinasi addressed himself to an imaginary anthropocentric man, a type of *homo politicus* similar to the *homo oeconomicus*, a product of the mathematical imagination of the Enlightenment. Şinasi, however, was also the first Ottoman thinker to

---

[61] It is not so easy to establish a connection between Şinasi's conception of law and that of Montesquieu, as attempted by Kaplan. But there does seem to exist some influence, such as when Şinasi calls Reşid Paşa "the president of the virtuous people." Montesquieu did state that virtue was the principle basic to a republican democracy; cf. Kaplan, "Şinasi'nin Türk Şiirinde Yarattığı Yenilik," pp. 35 and 39.

[62] Şinasi, "Mukaddeme," *Tercüman-ı Ahval*, 2 Rebiülahır 1277/October 8, 1860.

[63] Şinasi, "Mukaddeme," *Tasvir-i Efkâr*, 28 Zilhicce 1278/June 26, 1861.

[64] *Ibid.*, *Tercüman-ı Ahval*, 2 Rebiülahır 1277/October 8, 1860.

[65] *Ibid.*, "Maraz-ı Umumi-i Osmanî," *Tasvir-i Efkâr*, 8 Şevval 1279/March 29, 1862.

add a new dimension to the generally felt concern for the salvation of the Ottoman Empire by his wide use of the word *"millet,"* with the connotation of the French word *"nation."* This term appears quite often in his poetry and articles. Such phrases as "your presence in the heart of the nation is a divine miracle"[66] and his reference to Reşid Paşa as the saviour of the "nation"[67] or the "Great Ottoman Nation"[68] are illustrations of this new context in which the word was used. Şinasi, however, did not, as did Namık Kemal, hold a nationalism which was based on an appeal to feeling and emotion.

V. *Şinasi on Representative Government*

In Şinasi's writings there is an instance of Reşid Paşa being called the "representative appointed for the obtainment of the people's well-being." This too is new terminology and one which has telling political implications. True, the term "representative" or "deputy" is used here to mean that Reşid Paşa was the God-appointed vicar whose task it was to establish the well-being of the people, and therefore the style is not at loggerheads with the Ottoman-Islamic ideals prevailing at the time. But this is certainly the first instance of the vicarage of God being mentioned in a vocabulary more suited to the repertory of a European statesman than to that of a doctor of Mohammedan law. Actually, the use of slightly modified classical Islamic imagery to convey new ideas to his readers— a stratagem adopted by the pusillanimous Şinasi to make his remarks less obviously European—led later to considerable misunderstanding. It is in this light that we can understand why the more religious-minded Namık Kemal was, in his own words, "dazzled" when he first came across a volume of

[66] Anıl, *Şinasi*, p. 11.

[67] See also Şinasi, "Mukaddeme," *Tasvir-i Efkâr*, 28 Zilhicce 1278/ June 26, 1862. Cf. however, with Şinasi, "Millet-i Museviye," *Tasvir-i Efkâr*, 4 Receb 1279/December 26, 1862, where *"millet"* is used throughout in the same sense of "religious minority."

[68] Anıl, *Şinasi*, p. 11.

Şinasi's works.[69] To a certain extent Şinasi's disguised approach to reform was one of its causes of success, but because these same ideas were not enunciated clearly enough, it undoubtedly created a basic ambiguity which weakened the foundations on which the Young Ottomans attempted to build their intellectual constructions.

In one respect Şinasi was quite in agreement with the Young Ottomans. It was his conviction that the real nub of Western strength lay in the European encouragement of arts, crafts, and manufactures. In fact, there does not seem to have been a single nineteenth-century Turkish thinker who was not convinced of this.

Şinasi's influence on the generation immediately following cannot be overemphasized. The impression given by his works, however, is that although he looked to the West for inspiration, he chose to think of European intellectual advances and political conceptions as superior ones which he did not try to conciliate with Islam. In his mind the separation between the state and religion as affected by the reforms of the early Tanzimat posed no problems. By adopting this attitude Şinasi placed himself in an awkward position with regard to those who realized that this separation was not so simple.

In another way Şinasi was in advance of his time. His rationalism and humanistic approach was to be equaled only by one other Turkish thinker, the poet Tevfik Fikret, and that fifty years later. His fluent pen and control of all media of literature enabled him to appeal to many who approached his works for their literary as well as their cultural and political value. Often, however, this resulted in his followers' not appreciating the extent to which he had traveled on the road to Westernization.

[69] Tanpınar, *XIXncu Asır*, p. 165, note 2.

Mustafa Fazıl Paşa: Mid-Nineteenth-Century Liberalism

ONE of the more important contributions to the propagation of the idea of constitutionalism in Turkey had been the translation by the Young Ottomans, in the year 1867, of Mustafa Fazıl Paşa's *Letter* to Sultan Abdülaziz. The resulting pamphlet circulated in Turkey by the Young Ottomans caused a considerable stir throughout the empire. Ali Suavi relates that the low state of his morale was suddenly uplifted by the news that a former dignitary of the Ottoman Empire had gathered enough courage to suggest a plan for the salvation of the empire.[1] Ebüzziya considers it to have been the foundation stone of political writing in Turkey. He points out that it was felt at the time that the *Letter*, by submitting to clinical analysis the causes of the decadence of the Ottoman Empire, introduced a new approach to matters of state, viz., that the decline of the Ottoman Empire was not an inevitable process, but a state of affairs for which there existed a remedy. In the *Letter* Mustafa Fazıl Paşa took up an idea which had already been enunciated in the Gülhane Rescript—the idea that by structural changes one could work for the arrest of the process of decay in the empire. This time, however, the earlier attempt to create a more efficient administrative procedure had given way to the idea that this machinery should be controlled.

Just as the Gülhane Rescript had proclaimed eighteen years before, the *Letter* started by pointing out the lowering in ethical standards that had taken place in Turkey in the preceding century.[2]

---

[1] Ali Suavi, *Ulûm* (undated [1870]), p. 918.

[2] For the various printings of the *Letter*, see above, p. 38, n. 61. Quotations here are taken from *Lettre Adresse* [sic] *au feu sultan Abdülaziz par le feu Prince Mustafa Fazil Pacha (1866)*, (Le Caire, A. Costagliola, 1879). Turkish text: *Paristen bir Mektup. Sultan Abdülaziz Han'a Pariste*

"We Ottomans," stated Mustafa Fazıl Paşa, "are letting ourselves be invaded by a moral degeneration which every day becomes more visible, deeper and more universal."[3] Yet this time, and in contrast to the overt purposes of the Rescript of 1839, as outlined in the Rescript's preamble, the *Letter* did not interpret this "degeneration" to be a result of the slackening of religious observance. The factor, often alluded to before, that the earliest glory of the Ottoman Empire was due to the purity of the religious ideals of the Ottomans was now relegated to the status of a contributing rather than a principal factor. In the foreground appeared a notion, unknown to Islam—that of a lay ethic. This shifting of the main emphasis from one factor to another was done with considerable ingenuity. Mustafa Fazıl started by pleading: "Sire, when our ancestors, more than four centuries ago gave an end to the Eastern Empire and gloriously established themselves in the city of which Constantine had made the capital of the world, they did not only owe this great conquest which is one of the most memorable dates of history to their religious 'élan' and to their military courage. Rather, this 'élan' and this military courage were only the reflection of their moral values."[4] In a later part of the letter Mustafa Fazıl Paşa was to go far beyond this new secular approach to politics to affirm with reference to religion: "It is not it [religion] which regulates the rights of peoples."[5] The reason for this somewhat unexpected change is easy to determine. Ali Suavi provides us with the wisdom of hindsight that places the *Letter* in perspective and allows us to pinpoint the origin of

Cemiyeti Ahrar Reisi Mısırlı Mustafa Fazıl Paşa Merhum Tarafından Gonderilen Mektubun Tercümesidir (Dersaadet, Artin Asadoryan Matbaası, 1326/1908).

Because of the difficulty in locating these texts, references to the following widely available recent edition of the letter follow the first reference to the Cairo edition: Marcel Colombe, "Une lettre d'un prince egyptien du xixe Siècle au Sultan Ottoman Abd al-Aziz," *Orient*, (1958), II, 23-58.

[3] *Lettre*, p. 3; *Colombe*, p. 30.
[4] *Lettre*, p. 5; *Colombe*, p. 30.
[5] *Lettre*, p. 12; *Colombe*, p. 37.

such innovations. According to Suavi, the draft of the letter had, in fact, been composed by a Rumanian by the name of Ganesco and had then been rewritten by Mustafa Fazıl.[6] Yet the *Letter* is still important to study in detail. For it is undeniable that the missive had wide repercussions in the Ottoman Empire, that it was accepted by the Ottoman intelligentsia at the time of its circulation in the capital as an adequate statement of goals, and that it was one of the sources of inspiration of the Young Turks, who in the 1890's were to repeat the feats of the Young Ottomans. Up to this point, however, the *Letter* did not offend the feelings of anyone. What then, according to Fazıl Paşa, was the core of this "moral value" which he held to be of greater worth than religious guidance? It consisted in the fact that the Turks "were giving allegiance to their chieftains but they were so in virtue of a principle freely accepted by them, they had all the proudness of the heart and the mind and some kind of feeling of freedom native to them . . . which knew how to discipline itself."[7] There could hardly have been drafted a sentence more evocative of Rousseau, and at the same time of the regulating "invisible hand" of nature held in such high esteem by eighteenth-century thinkers. Thus virtue, in Mustafa Fazıl Paşa's new conception, was not only knocked off its religious pedestal, but at the same time appeared equated with the peculiar love for liberty and proudness which, for some time, had been believed to be the hallmark of man in the state of nature. Moral decay, i.e., a departure from the independent character which was native to the earliest Turks,

[6] Ali Suavi, "Faziliye," *Ulûm*, 15 Safer 1287/May 17, 1870, p. 1119. Ganesco was a contributor to the *Liberté* in which Mustafa Fazıl Paşa's *Letter* first appeared. On June 23, 1866 he had written an article warning against the results of a Hohenzollern Prince being made the ruler of Roumania. There thus exists the possibility that this revelation of Suavi is accurate. Ebüzziya Tevfik states that a Greek by the name of Revelaki who was employed by a number of Embassies as a go-between in their transactions with the Porte was instrumental in having the French text printed. See Ebüzziya Tevfik, "Yeni Osmanlılar," *Yeni Tasvir-i Efkâr*, June 1, 1919, pp. 3, 4.
[7] *Lettre*, p. 6; *Colombe*, p. 31.

was the result of the injustices to which the population of the Ottoman Empire had been subjected. While on one hand these injustices made men weak and servile,[8] on the other hand it caused the decay of arts and sciences, since slave nations had no use for these activities.[9] Nothing proved this better than the backward state of commerce and industry in the Ottoman Empire. No one could, according to Fazıl Paşa, deny the fact that the supremacy of modern European states was based on the availability of a pool of "intelligent and the educated."[10] This is also an emphasis we have already encountered in the ideas of Sadık Rifat Paşa. Thus the Prussian victory at Sadowa was due to the superior instruction of the Prussians as compared to the Austrians—an idea which is later to recur in Namık Kemal.[11] Yet Mustafa Fazıl Paşa could not accuse the administration of the empire of having neglected the dissemination of knowledge. A great effort in that direction had been undertaken by the early statesmen of the Tanzimat, and Âli Paşa was then at the beginning of the negotiations which were to result in the creation of the *lycée* of Galatasaray. The contention put forth by Fazıl Paşa, a new and arresting one, was that education alone was not sufficient to cure the ills of the empire. Neither were the attempts to reform and modernize the administrative system of Turkey and the efforts to establish a centralized state. According to Fazıl Paşa, efficiency in the state machinery could not be obtained by a mere increase in control, as was attempted in the centralizing moves of Mahmud II but, on the contrary,

[8] *Ibid.*

[9] *Lettre*, p. 8; *Colombe*, p. 32. *Cf.* with the statement by Herder, whose writings are examples of the liberal nationalism having prevailed in early nineteenth-century Europe. "Under the yoke of despotism even the noblest people in a short time will lose its nobility: its highest talent will be abused for falsehood and fraud, for crawling, for servility, and luxury." Hans Kohn, *The Idea of Nationalism* (New York: Macmillan, 1944), p. 447. Ganesco, to whom Suavi attributes the first draft of the letter, was influenced by Herder; see Gregory Ganesco, *Diplomatie et Nationalité* (Paris, Librairie Nouvelle, 1856), pp. 64, 144.

[10] Mustafa Fazıl Paşa, *Lettre*, p. 8.

[11] See above, p. 62; *Colombe*, p. 32.

by decreasing the grip of the state over the citizen. This was the only way to eliminate the oppressions which neither the ruler nor the officials desired but which resulted "from the very nature of government."[12] Fazıl Paşa contended that the truth of the matter was that the first mentor of the people was liberty itself. Liberty was the "original schoolmaster which gave rise to all others."[13] Only when their rights were guaranteed could people make use of their knowledge.

The "tyranny" existing in Turkey was attributed by Mustafa Fazıl Paşa to the irresponsibility of "subordinate functionaries" who, Mustafa Fazıl Paşa stated, were only nominally dependent on the authority of the sultan, since the sultan had no way of knowing if they were conforming to his "paternal orders." In short, since "there is no public opinion in Turkey and the innumerable agents of your government, not responsible to public opinion, become consequently not responsible to your Majesty, . . . there is nothing that is not permitted to these subaltern tyrants."[14] By the term *"tyrans subalternes"* Fazıl Paşa meant to characterize the governmental elite, and his appeal to the sultan was ostensibly meant to enlist the sovereign's support against these men. In reality, Mustafa Fazıl Paşa was appealing to a section of the Turkish intelligentsia which already had shown its distaste for the high-handed rule of these ministers.

In the opinion of Mustafa Fazıl Paşa the excesses of these statesmen would be checked by the establishment of a responsible government. But an examination of what he believed to be the function of this government shows that the constitution which he proposed for Turkey would not have established in Turkey responsible government in the sense meant, for example, by Locke. Mustafa Fazıl Paşa's constitution, in the words of its sponsor, would only take away one right of the sultan—that of "making mistakes." In short, Mustafa Fazıl

[12] *Lettre*, p. 5; *Colombe*, p. 30.
[13] *Ibid.*, p. 8; *ibid.*, p. 32.
[14] *Ibid.*, p. 6; *ibid.*, p. 31.

Paşa meant the "responsible government" to be a purely consultative organ.[15]

The origin of Mustafa Fazıl Paşa's ideas can be pinpointed in the light of his respect toward the sovereign and his desire to see the sovereign leading the constitutional state. It was the sovereign who was to guide the Turkish nation on the road to progress, and there was no question in his scheme of a government responsible to the people. The idea of guidance by the sovereign on the constitutional road was one which had become fashionable in Europe toward the middle of the nineteenth century. It was expounded at length in the works of the Italians, such as Mazzini and d'Azeglio, and Mustafa Fazıl Paşa's emphasis on the ethical aspects of government are also reminiscent of the moralistic tinge of Gioberti's work, the *Prolegomeni del Primato Morale e Civile degli Italiani.*[16] In fact, Mustafa Fazıl Paşa spoke of a "revolution" which was to be undertaken by the ruler himself. The example that Mustafa Fazıl Paşa gave of the king of Italy as the leader of the movement of liberalization in his own country confirms this point.

Although Mustafa Fazıl Paşa knew quite well that a close relationship existed between matters of faith and matters of state in Islam, he did not hesitate to give a new interpretation of this relation in his *Letter*. The least that can be said about this interpretation is that there was no precedent for it. According to him, religion commands the soul "and opens for us the perspectives of future life, but it does not regulate the rights of the people and it loses itself by losing all the rest when it does not remain in the sublime domain of eternal verities." "Sire," he went on, "there are no Christian politics or Moslem politics, for there is only one justice and politics is justice incarnate."[17] This, of course, was a conception which came to complete another one advanced in an earlier part of the

[15] *Ibid.*, p. 12; *ibid.*, p. 34.
[16] [Vicenzo Gioberti], *Prolegomeni del Primato Morale e Civile degli Italiani* (Brussels, Caus & Co., 1846).
[17] *Lettre*, p. 9; *Colombe*, p. 37.

Letter—the conception of an ethic ultimately based on liberty.

Mustafa Fazıl Paşa stated that it was his "patriotism" which had spurred him on to make his proposals.[18] Again there was talk, in the *Letter*, of the "lofty sentiments inherent" in "the Turkish race." Something had indeed been added to Sadık Rifat Paşa's conception of the fatherland in the intervening years: Rıfat Paşa had not mentioned the word "race," for in Islam no such conception existed. Similarly, the talk of "sentiments" inherent in a people was the hallmark of romantic European thought and the far echo of the idea of the soul of a nation which through the German historian Herder had come to be associated with liberal nationalism. In general, it can be said that Mustafa Fazıl Paşa's letter shows the same influence of liberal nationalism as was to appear in Kemal but with an absence of Islamic references, which leads us to suspect that the journalists who congregated around him in Paris had a hand in drafting it.

In a letter which he wrote two months later Mustafa Fazıl Paşa summed up his program as "seeking to base the Ottoman Empire upon constitutional liberty which would establish equality and harmony between Musulman and Christian and which, in waiting for better things, would give to Turkey the moral superiority over such and such one of its neighbors."[19]

Just as with the Young Ottomans, Mustafa Fazıl Paşa was stimulated to make proposals for a constitution for the empire by the disintegrating pressures coming from its component nationalities. But in Mustafa Fazıl's ideas may be perceived a strand of genuine, if somewhat naïve, universalism—a quality the survival of which later became known as "*kozmopolit cereyanlar*" ("cosmopolite movements.") The absence again in Mustafa Fazıl's opus of the idea, fundamental in Kemal's pieces, that the Şeriat be made into the capstone of the political system showed the extent of the ideological rift that separated the "Egyptian" prince from the Turkish patriot.

---

[18] *Lettre*, p. 4; *Colombe*, p. 29.
[19] *Levant Herald Daily Bulletin*, April 16, 1867, p. 1.

CHAPTER X

Namık Kemal: the Synthesis

OF ALL the men who participated in the Young Ottoman movement, one above the rest, Namık Kemal, has retained in modern Turkey the fame which he achieved in the middle of the nineteenth century.

That Kemal's fame should have endured is hardly astonishing, for the directness and the incisiveness of his prose compares favorably with that of modern Turkish writers. The nature of this achievement can be appreciated only by comparing his writings with those of his contemporaries. The latter are still riddled with the Arabic and Persian vocabulary of the Classical Era of Turkish literature, a written language which was the privilege of only a minority to enjoy. Namık Kemal, on the other hand, went further in the use of the vernacular than his predecessors such as Şinasi and Münif Paşa and thereby reached an even wider audience than these precursors of the simplification of the Turkish language. Besides the simplicity of his Turkish, the power of his style was remarkable. Among the political writings of the era, his articles stand out as closely argued, precise pieces of work devoid of the circumlocutions of the written Turkish of the nineteenth century and a far cry from the ornate style used in official correspondence and documents.

Today his works are still the most readable of those published in his time. His patriotic poetry, filled with exhortations to save the fatherland, is still a standard part of Turkish anthologies and, like the prose of Renan, which in earlier times used to familiarize the French schoolboy with the notion of *patrie*, constitutes the Turkish citizen's earliest introductions to such concepts as "the fatherland."

Whenever protests have arisen against the curtailments of what are considered to be the basic rights of the citizen under the Turkish Republic, these too have been voiced in his name and expressed in his words. But it is seldom realized that this second contribution of his, i.e., the popularization of the notion of *"Hürriyet,"* was the most original, in terms of the contrast with earlier Ottoman values,[1] and that in the long run it proved of greater worth in the modernization of the Empire.

Namık Kemal was born in the town of Tekirdağ in December of 1840.[2] For a few months, in his youth, he studied at the *Rüşdiye's* of Beyazit and Valide. These were the new types of westernized, eight year schools that had been established during the Tanzimat. Most of his time between the ages of ten to sixteen was spent in extensive travel throughout the empire. He accompanied his grandfather Abdüllatif Paşa to the border town of Kars, and followed him later to Sofia.

Kemal's father was the Court Astronomer Mustafa Asım Bey. The latter's functions had little to do with astronomy proper. Mustafa Asım Bey was actually the court astrologer at the time when even in the Ottoman Empire kings were beginning to take astrology with a grain of salt. His functions were to determine the propitious time for any of the Sultan's actions. In 1861, on the occasion of Abdülaziz's accession to the throne, it was Mustafa Asım Bey who was charged with the determination of the propitious time for the ceremony to be performed. Yet on this occasion the ceremony was held ahead of time because other bureaucratic considerations had to be put in the forefront.[3] This event is symbolic of the influences that surrounded Namık Kemal during his boyhood. On one hand, the family of Kemal was associated with ancient tradi-

---

[1] According to a standard French-Turkish dictionary of the time, the word *hürriyet* was used to characterize the state of a person who was not a slave, i.e., it was a noun used in connection with freedmen. The same source indicates that the contemporary Turkish equivalent for *civil liberty* was *ruhsat-ı şeriyye*, textually "permission of religious law," i.e., what could be done without overstepping the law. T. X. Bianchi, *Dictionnaire Français-Turc* (Paris, Dondey-Dupré, 1850), II, 293. As early as 1831, however, *hürriyet* was used as a *fifth* meaning of *liberté*. See T. X. Bianchi, *Vocabulaire Francais-Turc* (Paris, Everat, 1831), p. 422.

[2] Kaplan, *Namık Kemal*, p. 11.

[3] Kuntay, *Namık Kemal*, I, 7, note 8.

tions and distinguished itself by service to the state. His grandfather on the paternal side, Şemseddin Bey, had been the first chamberlain to Selim III, and his family traced its lineage to Topal Osman Paşa, the victor over Nadir Şah of Persia (circa 1743-1746).[4] On the other hand, the family was slowly losing its importance with the arrival on the scene of a new class of Ottoman functionaries. His father had to rely on others for the support of the family,[5] and his paternal grandfather's house was seized by creditors.[6]

In 1857-1858, when Namık Kemal was seventeen, he came to Istanbul and entered the Translation Bureau of the Customs and then that of the Porte. At the time of his arrival in the capital, eighteen years had passed since the proclamation of the Rescript of 1839, and the Europeanizing drive of the Tanzimat had begun to affect markedly the cultural life of the empire. Münif Paşa was publishing his translations from the French *philosophes* and at literary gatherings questions relating to the Westernization of Turkey were being discussed. Yet the influences to which Kemal was subjected were not only Western. Through his maternal grandfather, Abdüllatif Paşa, Namık Kemal came under the influence of the classicist poet, Leskofçalı Galib. The latter, apart from having had considerable experience as a government official, was the upholder of those Islamic standards of justice which constituted the core of the teachings of the ulema. Namık Kemal's oft-quoted poem "On Liberty" appears to have been directly inspired by a similar poem written by Galib. At the same time Kemal was meeting Şinasi, and became a member of the poetic circle known as the Council, of which both Şinasi and Galib were members.[7]

[4] Theodor Menzel, "Kemal," *Encyclopaedia of Islam*, II, 847-851.
[5] Kuntay, *Namık Kemal*, I, 6.   [6] *Ibid.*, p. 8.
[7] Kaplan, *Namık Kemal*, p. 43; Abdülbaki Gölpınarlı, "Namık Kemal'in Şiirleri" in *Namık Kemal Hakkında*, p. 19, also, pp. 68, 69 for Alid inclinations, i.e., emphasis on the person of the caliph Ali which was one of the forms that "folk" Islam had taken in Turkey, and Fevziye Abdullah Tansel "Süleyman Hüsnü Paşa ile Namık Kemal'in Münasebet ve Muhaberatı," *Türkiyat Mecmuası* (1954), XI, 140, for the Sûfi use of "freedom."

Namık Kemal's activities from 1865 onward, his numerous exiles, and his death while still comparatively young have been recounted above.[8] No indication has been provided as yet of the voluminous literary-historical productions which he managed to complete while being driven from pillar to post. During his lifetime in addition to large numbers of articles he wrote six plays, a series of short biographies, three novels, the first volume of a projected twelve-volume Ottoman history, two extensive essays (one on the Ottoman past and the other on his dream of the ideal Ottoman society), two long critical-literary essays in verse, and completed several translations.[9] His political conceptions run throughout his works and should therefore be studied in the context of all his productions. The core of his political theory, however, is found in the articles he wrote for the *Hürriyet* and the *İbret*. It is to these articles that we have to turn to recapture his political thought.

More philosophically inclined than his colleagues, Namık Kemal concentrated on the discussion of fundamental theoretical issues and thus produced a body of political philosophy which is the only one worthy of that name among the writings of his time. The privileged position which his political theory occupied only came to an end at the beginning of the twentieth century, when Ziya Gökalp, the second important modern Turkish political theorist produced the second, more or less systematic body of political thought. This does not mean that Kemal's ideas have not left a characteristic imprint on Turkish political thought as well as in literature. Exactly the contrary is true. The extraordinary extent to which his editorials set the tone for Turkish journalistic style may be followed even today. The echo of his patriotic exhortations may be found in any occasional speech delivered by a contemporary Turkish political leader. Kemal's political philosophy, then, may be studied from two viewpoints: first, in relation to his attempted

[8] See above, Chapter II.
[9] For a complete bibliography of Namık Kemal's works see Şerif Hulusî, "Namık Kemal'in Eserleri," in *Namık Kemal Hakkında*, pp. 305-421.

synthesis between Islamic and Western political conceptions and therefore in terms of purpose, origin, and internal consistency; and secondly, in terms of having introduced into Turkey certain key political concepts which affected subsequent generations of Turkish thinkers.

I. The Political System of Namık Kemal

In 1940 there appeared in Turkey a volume entitled *Tanzimat I: 100 ncü Yıldönümü Münasebetile*, aiming to summarize the achievements of the Tanzimat on the one hundredth anniversary of the proclamation of the Rescript of Gülhane. Among the contributions to the commemorative volume was an article on the Young Ottomans by İhsan Sungu, an official of the Ministry of Education and an expert on the intellectual history of the Tanzimat.[10] This article raised considerable interest among Turkish scholars because it purported to refute a myth, that of the Young Ottomans as advocates of thorough Westernization. Sungu showed, by lengthy excerpts from the *Hürriyet*, that in fact this mouthpiece of the Young Ottomans had consistently taken an Islamic approach to the problem of government, and that religion was given an undeniably major role in its schemes of reform. This reminder had certainly become necessary at a time when the nationalism of Kemal, used by subsequent generations of less religiously inclined reformers, had become identified with the lay nationalism that was part of the ideology of the founders of the Turkish Republic. Yet it is probable that this discovery did not surprise many of those who had made the study of the Tanzimat their specialty, for throughout the writings of Kemal there reappear the themes of divine justice, of religious law, and of observance of the principles of Islam. Namık Kemal's background does, to a certain extent, explain this emphasis. His strong classical cul-

[10] İhsan Sungu, "Tanzimat ve Yeni Osmanlılar," *Tanzimat I: 100 ncü Yıldönümü Münasebetile* (ed. by Türk Tarih Kurumu, Istanbul, Maarif Matbaası, 1940), pp. 777-857.

ture and the contacts which he established with the Council poets, as well as the mentorship of the classicist Leskofçalı Galib, are other factors which must have confirmed his Islamic faith quite early. It is probable that, among the poets known to Kemal, there were mystics who gave him an insight into what many Turks have considered to be the more sophisticated aspects of religion, into that universalism and semipantheism which has been associated with the *tasavvuf* or Islamic mysticism. At any rate, such inclinations did exist in his family, which has been called "a Bektaşi family."[11] The Bektaşi order of dervishes, on the other hand, is well known for its contributions to the intellectual life of the Ottoman Empire and for its espousal of the griefs of the "common man."[12] Thus Namık Kemal's interest in "the people," which has often been erroneously interpreted as a belief in the value of universal suffrage, originally had religious and probably mystical bases. When, later on, Namık Kemal became acquainted with European liberalism, the idea of the participation of the people in the political process, which was gaining strength all the time in Europe, found a ready reception in his mind.

There are indications that, even during the first years of his stay in Istanbul, Namık Kemal was already comparing the ideas of the Enlightenment regarding government with the traditional political thought of Islam. The following letter written to his spiritual mentor, Leskofçalı Galib, shows the evaluation of the ideas of Voltaire he made at the time: "This man has devoted himself to the destruction of existing precepts of religion, yet in so doing he follows the same road as that blasted by Ahmed Vefik Paşa in Bursa, and which resulted in the opening of many straight paths, but which has also been

[11] Kaplan, *Namık Kemal*, p. 18. On the influence of the religious leader of the Kadirî religious order Osman Şems on Kemal, see Gölpınarlı, "Namık Kemal'in Şiirleri," *Namık Kemal Hakkında*, p. 19.

[12] It has been pointed out that in Turkey, in particular, mysticism has been made the vehicle for the expression of the discontentment of the unprivileged. See John Kingsley Birge, *The Bektashi Order of Dervishes* (London, Luzac, 1937), p. 69.

the cause of much tyranny and disorder. In particular his [Voltaire's] information on the subject of Islam having been gathered from work on homiletics, and consisting of hearsay, is as mistaken as the sources which he uses. Yet this is more the result of his ignorance than of his evil intentions. While in most parts of the book the reasoning used is so strong as to appear superhuman, there are some parts in it that can be refuted as easily as the words of Senih Efendi. I consider [the case of Voltaire] to provide quite strong proof of the impotence of reasoning in the face of the deed of God."[13]

On the bases of his Islamic culture, Namık Kemal evolved a system which has the distinction of fitting rather closely the prerequisites of the type of liberalism that was current in Europe in the middle of the nineteenth century. This was done, however, by emphasizing certain factors in Islamic political thought and conveniently relegating others to the background. At certain times the contradiction between the system of Namık Kemal and that of Islam became quite obvious.

II. The Origin of Government

For Namık Kemal good government is government which fulfills the political desiderata of the religious law, i.e., the Şeriat. Yet there are many instances where it is not entirely clear whether according to him government in the abstract and the principle of political authority are divinely ordained categories or due to a purely mundane development, such as the "natural sociability" of man. The first of these theories is the one encountered in the works of the Islamic jurists; the second is one which is found both in Islamic and Western philosophers.

In one of the most important articles he wrote on the subject,[14] Namık Kemal would seem to have adopted this second

[13] Kuntay, *Namık Kemal,* p. 24. Senih Efendi (1822-1900) was a bureaucrat disliked by Kemal for his reactionary tendencies.

[14] Namık Kemal, "Wa-shāwirhum fi'l-'amr," *Hürriyet,* July 20, 1868, pp. 1-4.

The structure of Namık Kemal's political system and its points of contact

stand. In this piece he started from the idea that men are naturally inclined to harm one another and that the power to protect man from the attacks of his kin can be provided only by an association of men.[15] Thus the freedom of man can be protected only in society. In his own words, "the service rendered by society in the world is the invention of . . . an absolute normative force for the protection of freedom. The life of humanity is dependent on the continuation of this force."[16]

Government, the organ which uses "this force," exists because all members of the community cannot busy themselves with governmental matters. Thus government arises as the result of an agreement among citizens to appoint a "specialist" in government, and may be considered the natural product of a division of labor brought about by the greater complexity that arises with an increase in population.[17] As Kemal states: "Since it is impossible that the community perform the tasks

---

with Islamic theory as well as its similarities with the ideas that were current in Europe in his time have not been well studied as yet. The only attempt to trace European influences is an article of Behice Boran entitled "The social ideas of Namık Kemal," ("Namık Kemal'in Sosyal fikirleri," in *Namık Kemal Hakkında*, pp. 249-278). This article, however, does not try to place in perspective the Islamic elements in Namık Kemal's political theory.

[15] Namık Kemal, "Wa-shāwirhum," p. 1. The idea of the essentially predatory inclinations of man is not, as advanced by Boran, a reflexion of Hobbesian influences, but an Islamic conception. "And God said 'Get ye down . . . enemies one to the other.' " *Koran*, Sura XX, verse 121, Bell, I, 301. According to one authority this has led to the conception of law as "a permanent struggle against the wicked instincts of man." David de Santillana, "Law and Society," *The Legacy of Islam* (ed. by T. W. Arnold and Alfred Guillaume, London, Oxford University Press, 1931), p. 295. Namık Kemal stated in another article that even though human nature could be bettered by education it would take "a few thousand years" to achieve it. See Namık Kemal, "Bazı Mülâhazat-ı Devlet ve Millet," *İbret*, October 9, 1872, in Mustafa Nihat Özön, *Namık Kemal ve İbret Gazetesi* (Istanbul, Remzi Kitabevi, 1938), p. 131.

[16] Namık Kemal, "Wa-shāwirhum," p. 1. Cf. John Locke, *The Second Treatise of Civil Government and a Letter Concerning Toleration* (ed. by Gough, Oxford, 1948), par. 134. For the dissimilar views of Rousseau, see Robert Derathé, *Rousseau et la Science Politique de son Temps* (Paris, Presses Universitaires, 1950), pp. 174-177.

[17] Namık Kemal, "Bazı Mülâhazat-ı Devlet ve Millet," in Özön, *Namık Kemal ve İbret. . .*, pp. 131, 132, cf. Locke, *Second Treatise*, par. 156.

which befall it . . . the appointment of an *Imam* [leader of the Islamic community] and the formation of government is a necessity. This, on the other hand, is nothing other than the delegation of certain individuals by society for the perform-ance of the above-mentioned duties."[18]

Namık Kemal, then, seems to imply that there are two stages in the establishment of government. First society is created. Society is a form of association which is distinguished by its being regulated by certain principles generally agreed upon (the "absolute normative force") which keep men from hurting one another. Thereafter, and as the result of a division of labor, government is created and some members are as-signed the task of enforcing this "force."

Now the mere secular explanation of the origins of society encapsulated in such a scheme need not indicate that Namık Kemal was going outside the bounds of Islamic political theory. The Falāsifa had also relied on a secular explanation of the origins of society.[19] Unencumbered by Rousseauan in-fluences, however, they left the issue conveniently vague. Where Namık Kemal entangled himself in contradictions was in his idea that the force which had regulated the workings of the first stages of association was the same as that which had obtained during the second stage, i.e. after government had come into being. In the second stage this force was the Şeriat. But Namık Kemal implied that the first force was identical with the second. This he had to do because if he had not he would have agreed that a natural law of secular nature had

---

[18] Namık Kemal, "Wa-shāwirhum," p. 1. Compare with the classical Islamic accounts of the origins of society: the beginnings of society "are traced by Muslims much in the same way as in Christian theory. A moment existed at the dawn of history when mankind was a single flock. Ignorant of evil they lived in a peaceful anarchy, according to the precepts of natural law. The end of the golden age came with the crime of Cain. The passions of men gained the upper hand and brought about social disaster, the loss of true faith, and the introduction of particular law." Santillana, "Law and Society," *The Legacy of Islam,* p. 304.

The mere assumption of a "state of nature" then need not indicate the influence of the Enlightenment on Kemal's ideas.

[19] Rosenthal, *Political Thought,* p. 125.

preceded the Şeriat. As we have tried to show in Chapter III this could not be so because Islamic natural law did not consist of a continuum but of the Şeriat itself and of the very special duties, political, economic, and social, which it prescribed.

A similar problem which Namık Kemal encounters at this early stage is that of the problem of good and evil. As he stated: "With us good and evil are determined by the Şeriat. Again whether the relations between compatriots conform with the abstract good is known by the application of the guage of [religious] justice to these relations."[20]

There is nothing preceding the Şeriat, then, which may be called good or evil because only the Şeriat enables one to determine these qualities.[21]

There are other passages of Kemal where we can see that in fact he did not involve himself in such patent absurdities but came dangerously close to it. Thus the Rousseauan context in which he explains the origins of the Şeriat[22] is unconvincing: "When societies became larger, states and governments were formed and it became necessary to enact a binding thread which would elicit common opinion in matters of general administration for the individuals who made up every

[20] Namık Kemal, "Hukuk," in *İbret*, 19 June 1872, Özön, *Namık Kemal ve İbret*, p. 51.

[21] "Is law a primal principle for the presence of which we search the universe or is it the product of the will of humanity? The second alternative can in no case be admitted, for the will of humanity is either completely free, or is limited by a norm. If it is free then no man would want to bow to the orders of others on the sole basis of caprice, neither could they be forced to obey these orders. If [on the other hand] there exists such a limitation of will, what does this limitation consist in? . . . According to our belief, [this limitation] consists in the good and evil with which the Ruling Power has endowed nature. Consequently, the name of law is given to 'the necessary relations which arise from human nature in accordance with the idea of good.' . . ." Namık Kemal, "Hukuk," in Özön, *Namık Kemal ve İbret*, p. 49.

[22] I have considered the article from which the following quotation is taken to have been written by Kemal as attributed in Kaplan's list of the *Hürriyet* articles written by Namık Kemal. See Kaplan, *Namık Kemal*, pp. 173-177. The emphasis on a state of nature, a favorite point of Ziya Paşa's, does not rule out entirely its having been due to Ziya's pen. But even were the article to be Ziya's there are other similar statements by Kemal.

civilized society. This binding thread is the Şeriat which is the political law serving to protect and govern the members of society jointly and severally. Its interpretation is determined by the assent of the community but its basis is natural law. For us that natural law is the same divine justice as has been set by the Koran."[23]

The origin of this juxtaposition of secular and religious elements in Kemal's political theory went back to the dual origin—half European and half Islamic—of his thought. The reason for which he chose the secular explanation of the origin of government was that such an argument naturally led him to the conclusion that "the right of sovereignty belongs to all."[24] Such a conclusion would have been hard to elicit from Islamic political theology. In fact, what he was attempting to achieve was what Robert Dérathé has stated was the overriding aim of Rousseau, namely, the transformation of the idea of a *pactum subjectionis* into one compatible with the idea of freedom.[25] For in reality the first pact in Islamic theory was not one between men but one between God and men and a true *pactum subjectionis* in this respect.[26]

Having taken care of the question of the origin of political power, Namık Kemal then goes on to ascertain the specific form in which men are bound by this power. This brings Kemal to a discussion of what is essentially the second pact, the pact of government. The specific form in which the allegiance to the ruler is legalized is, according to Kemal, the institution of the *Biat* ("*Baia*" in Arabic). It has already been indicated that this process of confirming the authority of the caliph played an important role in the theory of the jurists.[27]

[23] "Devlet-i Aliyyeyi Bunlunduğu Hal-i Hatarnaktan Halâsın Esbabı," *Hürriyet*, August 24, 1868, p. 2.

[24] Namık Kemal, "Wa-shāwirhum," p. 1.

[25] Dérathé, *Jean Jacques Rousseau*, p. 182.

[26] See above, Chapter III.

[27] "Given these requisites, [the qualities necessary to a good monarch] it is evident that the choice of a chief for the Islamic community cannot be left to chance or violence, but must be founded on the ripe reflection of those best qualified to appreciate whether the candidate is a fit subject for choice.

According to Khadduri, this institution was also considered to constitute the second contractual step in the Islamic theory of contract.[28] At this stage the contract becomes one between the Muslim community on one hand and the Caliph on the other. The bonds which bind the subjects to the ruler are not as strong here as in the first contract.

Since, in the theory developed by the jurists, the social compact was binding only on condition that the caliph enforce divine law, Namık Kemal was justified in stating that he based himself on Islamic fundamentals when he enunciated the theory that the community had the right to break the contract if the ruler did not carry out his obligations.

"If the people of a country," he stated, "gather and pledge allegiance to a man for the Sultanate or the Caliphate, this man becomes Sultan or Caliph, the Sultan or Caliph preceding him is invalidated, for the imamate is a right of the community."[29] But if Namık Kemal was justified in pointing out that the Islamic contract was revocable, he failed to draw attention to the fundamental ambiguousness of the theory of the Islamic jurists, the fact that they had never mentioned

---

The elective body cannot therefore be the whole of the Muslim people, but only those who by their culture, their social rank, their experience of worldly affairs, and their morality, are suited to be judges. The electorate will be entrusted to the 'men of the pen and the sword,' in other words to the civil and military notables; to them is given power 'both to bind and to loose,' that is to say, to stipulate in the name of the whole community the bond on which rests the power of the prince and the obedience due from his subjects. Election is in the law the act by which the people, or the notables on their behalf, confer the supreme power on the object of their choice; it is an offer of contract (*'iqād*), which, if accepted, by the person chosen, becomes a binding contract (*'aqd*). . . . By accepting the investiture, the caliph binds himself to exercise his power within the limits laid down by the divine law."

The caliph, in turn, "undertakes to provide for the temporal interests of Islam, such as the protection of the frontiers, the conduct of war against the unbelievers, internal security, management of public property, and the administration of justice." Santillana, "Law and Society," *The Legacy of Islam*, pp. 297-8.

[28] Khadduri, *War and Peace*, p. 11.
[29] Namık Kemal, "Wa-shāwirhum," p. 1.

the specific steps by which the mandate of the caliph could be revoked in case such a fundamental disagreement arose between the caliph and his flock.[30]

In fact, Namık Kemal never evolved a theory of justified revolt (a conception which in Europe was the crude and embryonic predecessor of the idea of the responsibility of government).[31] His own position in this matter was similar to that of the Islamic jurists and he strictly opposed any such conception as a right of rebellion. There was no question in his mind that the sultan-caliph could not be deposed by an armed revolt or conspiracy, nor could he by any stretch of the imagination be said to have thought that "the tree of liberty" should be "watered by the blood of tyrants."[32]

Namık Kemal even went further than denying the right of revolution; he made it extremely difficult for the mandate of the ruler to be revoked. For, according to Namık Kemal, the right to break the contract is not a right of the individual; neither is it, as in traditional Islamic theory, the theoretical privilege of the notables. It is, according to him, a right of the community as a whole, assembled for this purpose, to

[30] The most widely accepted Islamic attitude appeared in the following saying traced to the Prophet: "When you meet God (on the day of the judgment) say, 'O Lord, Thou didst send us Prophets and we obeyed them by Thy permission, and you set over us Caliphs and we obeyed them by Thy permission, and our rulers gave us orders and we obeyed them for Thy sake'; And God will answer, 'Ye speak the truth; theirs is the responsibility and you are quit of it.'" Sir Thomas Arnold, *The Caliphate* (Oxford, Clarendon Press, 1924), p. 49. Cf. with Locke, who describes legislative power as "only a fiduciary power to act for certain ends" so that "there remains still in the *people* a supreme power to remove or alter the legislative when they find the legislative act contrary to the trust reposed in them." *Second Treatise*, VII, para. 149.

[31] "The right of resistance was, however, merely the Medieval method, clumsy in idea and technique for the realization of a more general principle, for which a technically more suitable procedure of enforcement was afterwards found. This principle was the responsibility of government, which in the middle ages meant the responsibility of the king and his Council." Fritz Kern, *Kingship and Law in the Middle Ages* (trans. by S. B. Chrimes, Oxford, Basil Blackwell, 1939), p. 195 ff.

[32] Namık Kemal, "Yeni Osmanlıların ilân-ı resmîsi," *Hürriyet*, October 12, 1868, p. 3. "Hubb ul-watan," *Hürriyet*, June 29, 1868, p. 2.

break the contract. Just as the selection and the rejection of a person to the office of *imam* is the right of the congregation which gathers for this election.[33]

Namık Kemal's emphasis on the *biat* is quite consistent with his use of such concepts as "the people," "the interests of the people," and "public opinion"; but these are definitely new terms to be used in connection with the *biat*. They replace the much more narrow terms of "the men of the pen and the men of the sword" or "the binders and looseners" which are found in Islamic theory.

Another point which Namık Kemal relegated to the background was that concomitantly with the theory of *biat* had been developed the Islamic theory of trusteeship or *wilāya*, the net effect of which was to countermand the theory of the *biat*. The Islamic theory of trusteeship was a basically authoritarian theory. In contrast with the liberal theory of trusteeship as evidenced in Locke, for example,[34] in Islam the trustor was not identical with the beneficiary; there was no trust which the people set for their own benefit. In Islam, the trustor was God and the trustee was the ruler. It was a trust meant in the reverse of its libertarian meaning.

What emerges at this stage as a fundamental characteristic of Namık Kemal's theory is his attempt to devise some means by which ultimate reference in matters of government would be the will of the community while still remaining true to Islamic principles.

Namık Kemal's argument, when summed up, was that such a basis did exist in Islamic theory. According to Kemal, one of the results of the existence of such an Islamic principle of reference to the will of the community is that the particular form that an Islamic government takes is not important. The monarchical system, for example, is not necessarily the only possible Islamic political regime. He goes on from there to

[33] Namık Kemal, "Usul-u Meşveret," (1) *Hürriyet*, September 14, 1868, p. 6; "Wa-shāwirhum," p. 1.

[34] J. W. Gough, *John Locke's Political Philosophy* (Oxford, Clarendon Press, 1950), p. 143.

make the statement that, in fact, the Islamic state was "a kind of Republic" at its inception.[35] In his own words: "What does it mean to state that once the right of the people's sovereignty has been affirmed, it should also be admitted that the people can create a republic? Who can deny this right? That a republic would cause our [Turkey's] downfall is a different matter which nobody will deny, and this idea would not occur to anybody in our country, but the right to create [such a system] has not lapsed, because of the mere fact that it has not been used."[36] Or, as he stated it on another occasion: "There is no quality of the *Padişah* which gives him the right to govern men other than that which, under the name of *Biat*, is granted to him and with which the ministers are vested by way of appointment. This is the connotation of the saying of the Prophet to the effect that 'the masters of the tribe are your servants.' "[37]

The contradictions which appeared in Namık Kemal's account of the origin of government also carried over to some of the other key concepts of his political theory. A good example of that is the conception of "liberty," which was so important to him. There is no doubt that Kemal's most deeply felt attitude with regard to liberty was conveyed by such a passage of his as the one in which he stated: "Man is free. He always requires freedom. To deprive humanity of it is as if one were to deprive it of food."[38]

This, however, was an attitude which differed considerably from the one which conceived of liberty as having been a divine grant (i.e., God had given Moslems the religious law which provided them with this liberty).[39] It also differed from the theory that man "created free by God is . . . obliged to profit from this divine gift,"[40] or the one whereby "the right

---

[35] Namık Kemal, "Usul-u Meşveret," *Hürriyet*, September 14, 1868, p. 5; also, "Sadaret," *ibid.*, March 1, 1869, p. 1.

[36] Namık Kemal, "Wa-shāwirhum," p. 1.   [37] *Ibid.*

[38] Namık Kemal, "Hürriyet," *Hürriyet*, August 31, 1868, p. 4.

[39] *Ibid.*, August 2, 1869, p. 2.

[40] Namık Kemal, "Wa-shāwirhum," p. 1.

and purpose of man is not only to live but to live with liberty";[41] and from the conception according to which "man's freedom results from the fact that he is free in his actions and his freedom derives from the fact that he has been endowed with reason."[42]

Again, the fact that Namık Kemal was unaware of essential differences between his position and that of European advocates of responsible government appears clearly in the confusion that existed in his mind as to the place of the individual in government. Namık Kemal advocated a political system in which the individual would be held in as high esteem as he was held in Western constitutional states. This he tried to achieve by stressing the Islamic theory of the inviolability of the person, by referring to the saying in the Koran which made man "sovereign over things."[43] Yet he did not realize that the basis of the individualistic concept of European government was one in which he as the upholder of Islamic principles could not acquiesce, i.e., that in Europe the individual owed his emancipation to a postulate inherent in the liberal world view according to which "the state is regarded not as a natural necessity arising out of man's needs and social nature with a purpose transcending the subjective will of the individuals, but as an artificial instrumentality based on the claims of individuals."[44]

This Namık Kemal could not accept, for in the first place the Şeriat was not based on the satisfaction of such individual claims. Namık Kemal's attempt to look at government as an

[41] Namık Kemal, "Medeniyet," in Özön, *Namık Kemal ve İbret*, p. 215. Cf. editorial, *Hürriyet*, August 10, 1868, p. 2.

[42] Namık Kemal, "Hürriyet-i Efkâr," *Hadika*, November 24, 1873, *Külliyat-ı Kemal, Makalât-ı Siyasiye ve Edebiye*, Birinci Tertip (ed. by Ali Ekrem [Bulayır], Istanbul, Selanik Matbaası, 1328/1910), p. 40. Hereinafter cited as *M.S.E.* This is a collection of articles written by Namık Kemal in various newspapers.

[43] Namık Kemal, "İfade-i Meram," *İbret*, September 1872, in Özön, *Namık Kemal ve İbret*, p. 125.

[44] John H. Hallowell, *Main Currents in Modern Political Thought* (New York, Henry Holt, 1950), p. 114.

"invention" was an effort made to introduce this individualistic element. But the spirit and the letter of the Şeriat, based on the idea of a divinely ordained purpose, i.e., the providing of justice and harmony, engulfed this attempt and what remained was only an internal contradiction in Kemal's theory. In the second place, in the West the validity of such individual claims ultimately rested on other basic postulates such as the essential goodness of men and their ability to guide themselves by the sole light of reason, which Namık Kemal could not accept.

If the community is made the source of sovereignty in Namık Kemal's scheme and if the "binding force" is the same as the pressures of the majority in the community it does not follow that the *majority is entitled* to transgress the boundaries of the moral law set by the Şeriat. The majority is not justified in "touching a hair of the most insignificant Ethiopian child."[45] Just as the majority cannot transgress the boundaries of the moral law, neither can the community as a whole delegate to anybody a task which does not conform to the dicta of the Şeriat: "Every community can delegate command to a greater or lesser degree, according to its needs and character. However, it is a precept of reason [*Kavaid-i hikem-iye*] that 'regardless of the time, the place, or the method used, the government should choose the road which will least limit the freedom of the individual.' No community can agree on, or confirm in the office, an individual as an absolute ruler, nor can it bestow legislative powers on a single individual. And even if it so desires, it cannot rightfully do so. For it neither has the right to tyrannize an individual nor to violate the rights of all."[46]

This brings us to one of the most striking characteristics of

[45] Namık Kemal, "Bazı Mülâhazat-ı Devlet ve Millet," *İbret*, October 9, 1872, in Özön, *Namık Kemal ve İbret*, p. 132; editorial, *Hürriyet*, November 30, 1868, p. 1.

[46] "Furthermore, since the influence of one era over the succeeding era is a law which is based on the necessity of nature, no society has a right to choose a way of acting which shall affect its successors." Namık Kemal, "Wa-shāwirhum," p. 1.

Kemal's system: his stand against the conception of a general will. Namık Kemal does not assign the *state* any attributes which distinguish it from the *government*, and he uses the terms "government" and "state" interchangeably. As he expresses it: "The 'government' or the 'state' is the name given to the way in which this delegation [the delegation of the powers of the community] is exercised. On the other hand, the name 'community' is used for the whole of a civilized society when one sets aside this delegation."[47]

In other words, Namık Kemal does not have any use for an organic theory of the state or for a state which would embody the general will and would therefore justify individual sacrifices on its behalf. Reference has already been made to the fact that Namık Kemal did not consider any majority, however strong, warranted in committing an injustice. But Namık Kemal went farther to point out that the state *qua* state was not entitled to special privileges, but only consisted in the sum of the individuals which made it up. This thesis was advanced by Namık Kemal's two articles in the *İbret* in which he criticized the attitude assumed by two newspapers, the *Basiret* appearing in Istanbul and the *Gülşensaray* appearing in Bosnia, in a controversy that was raging between the two.[48] To the arguments of the *Gülşensaray*, which were based on the conception of the moral personality of the state, Kemal objected, "Is it possible that a quality which is not present in any of the parts be found only in the sum of these parts?"[49]

According to Namık Kemal, it was this very conception of the state as embodying the general will which in Europe made it an offense punishable by death to say "Long live the monarch!" one day, and attached the same penalty to the utter-

---

[47] Namık Kemal, "Bazı Mülâhazat," Özön, *Namık Kemal ve İbret*, p. 132.

[48] Namık Kemal, "Dostane bir Vesatet," *İbret*, 20 Rebiülahir 1289/June 27, 1872; "Herkesin maksadı bir ammâ rivayet muhtelif," *İbret*, 25 Rebiülahir 1289/July 2, 1872.

[49] Namık Kemal, "Hukuk-u Umumiye," *İbret*, July 8, 1872, in Özön, *Namık Kemal ve İbret*, p. 97.

ance of "Long live the empire!" four months later, and resulted in similar sanctions against those who shouted "Long live the republic!" four years after the first manifestation of enthusiasm.[50] It is for the same reason, says Kemal, "that a member of the police—I saw it with my own eyes—could beat and insult a gentleman in public."[51]

"In reality, sovereignty is not an abstract right which is attributed to the totality of the people, it is the right of sovereignty which is congenitally present in every man. . . .

"The sovereignty of the people, which consists in that the source of the power of the government is the people, and which is called *biat* in the religious law, is not a power that derives from the abstract meaning attached to conceptions such as the 'majority' or the 'people.' It is a right which derives from the congenital independence with which every individual is endowed at his creation, and follows from personal independence. 'Every one is the ruler of his own world.' "[52]

It is from this vantage point that Namık Kemal approached the problem of majority rule. Even if there were no question as to *what* the will of the majority was, and assuming that all government action were geared to the *interest* of the majority, Namık Kemal felt that government could still be tyrannical. Under these circumstances, for example, the state would be justified in condemning to death all those suffering from incurable infectious diseases as a permanent danger to society.[53]

According to Kemal, these clearly inhuman consequences showed the limitations of the idea of the interest of the majority. For Namık Kemal, the real source of sovereignty, as well as the ultimate standard against which the action of the government had to be measured, was the inviolability of the private person of the citizen. "This particular sovereignty can never separate itself from the nature of the individual. It

[50] *Ibid.,* p. 100.   [51] *Ibid.,* p. 101.   [52] *Ibid.,* p. 97.
[53] Namık Kemal, "Hukuk," *İbret,* June 19, 1872, in Özön, *Namık Kemal ve İbret,* p. 50.

cannot be abandoned to anyone. It is impossible to rightfully execute laws in the name of a person or a corporation or a committee without obtaining at first a special permission by use of one of the available means such as the *biat*, election, or delegation or without taking a secondary authorization from one who holds this privilege."[54]

While this constitutes the negative side of Namık Kemal's ideas regarding the limitation of government, a positive side to these ideas also existed. Namık Kemal was also convinced that the state should not play the role of a mentor vis-à-vis the citizen. This is how Namık Kemal expressed this characteristically European conception: "There is no doubt that government is neither the father, nor the guardian, nor the mentor, nor the governess of the people. If it renders services for the betterment of the individual, for the upbuilding of the country, for the maturing of humanity and for the advancement of civilization, it then will have extended a help which is of benefit to itself, to its people and to the entire world . . . but can we criticize it if it limits itself to the execution of justice? Do we have the right to ask it to act as our governess?"[55]

All considered, Namık Kemal's political system is based on a peculiar ideal of the state as a rather amorphous entity, but some of the peculiarity of this approach vanishes when its origins are investigated. The Islamic roots of this attitude can be stated as follows: Nothing in the Koran indicates that a state is to be formed which has been granted the right to protect itself or foster its own growth *qua* state, i.e., without reference to the individuals who make it up. One of the things that never permeated Islam was a real theory of the state. This is the meaning of Namık Kemal's use of the term "community" when European writers would have used the

[54] Namık Kemal, "Hukuk-u Umumiye," *İbret*, July 8, 1872, in *ibid.*, p. 97.
[55] Namık Kemal, "İbret", *İbret*, June 5, 1872, *ibid.*, p. 43, "El hak," *Hürriyet*, June 29, 1868, p. 2.

term "state." This point has been well expressed by one recent student of Arab nationalism:

". . . In the *hadith* and the teachings of the 'ulama' . . . the theories about al-Umma al-Islamiyya [the Islamic community], although they appear to be similar to western organic theories of government, in fact insist on the benefits which the individual reaps in such a solidary community and on the material services rendered by one individual to another, they do not know a collective being higher than the individuals who make up society."[56]

Most of the sayings of the Islamic theorists show that the idea of the Leviathan state was one with which they were not familiar, even though they had comments to offer regarding the misuse of the principle of authority and the abuses of the ruler. Even though the subservience to *authority* became a subservience to the *state* in the Ottoman Empire, Namık Kemal's theory is conspicuous in the first place because it is a theory which sets itself against the state. In the face of such developments as the controlling drive of the Tanzimat, Namık Kemal revived the teachings of the ulema in regard to the evil of unjust rule. But Namık Kemal was obliged to face a new problem unknown to the ulema, and his arguments against the state *qua* state could not be taken from the availa-

[56] Sylvia G. Haim, "Islam and the Theory of Arab Nationalism," *Die Welt des Islams* (1955), NS IV, 128, 129. On the absence of an Islamic conception of the Leviathan state, one author states: "Nous avons vu l'enseignement théologique qui fut longtemps le plus officiel, celui de l'école Ash'arite affirmer un occasionalisme atomistique, ou les atomes discontinus et juxtaposés, trame dernière de tout être contingent, sont crées et recrées par Dieu seconde par seconde. Cette vision du monde peut nous servir d'image symbolique et comme representative de l'Umma. Les individus, atomes discontinus d'un même tout qui les englobe, les absorbe et fait leur grandeur, maintiennent cependant et affirment leur discontinuité individuante. Forme 'd'individualisme' si l'on veut, mais qui risque beaucoup moins de compromettre de simple valeurs humaines que ce reniement d'un au delà de la terre où s'enracine l'individualisme de l'Occident moderne. . . . Le role de la communauté ne sera pas de créer, préparer l'épanouissement de la personne, il est vrai, mais non plus de travailler a créer l'être collectif." Louis Gardet, *La Cité Musulmane, Vie Sociale et Politique* (Paris, Librairie Philosophique J. Vrin, 1954), p. 207.

ble ideological arsenal of the ulema. We are therefore led to suspect that while Kemal's *attitude* toward this issue was determined by his Islamic background, his *argument* had European roots. What these roots were will be investigated below.

One final fact that has to be taken into consideration here is that Namık Kemal did not take a consistent attitude in regard to the nature of the state. This is the case, for example, in the following passage taken from one of the first articles in the *Hürriyet*: "The state is a moral personality. The making of laws is its will, their execution its actions."[57]

It is therefore probable that the anti-Rousseauan trend in his thought was also the expression of his more mature political thought, which he developed after his stay in England. At that time he was able to compare the system of France, which he had criticized even in the earlier stages of his stay in Europe,[58] with that of England, which he admired.[59] Yet again we find that this explanation is also unsatisfactory, for in the last work which he wrote, his *Ottoman History*, we find again: "There can be no age of maturity for the moral person called civilized society."[60] It would seem that the difference here lies between Namık Kemal's conception of the state and his conception of society. Societies, which Namık Kemal identified with a particular type of culture (such is the use by Namık Kemal of the term "Ottoman Society"), did, according to him, possess qualities which made them live and progress in the stream of history. They were personalities, but the state had no reason to claim a personality for itself since it was only a means to provide the well-being of the community. Here again, the idea of cultural uniqueness and

---

[57] Namık Kemal, "Wa-shāwirhum," *Hürriyet*, July 20, 1868, p. 1.

[58] Namık Kemal, "Usul-u Meşveret," *Hürriyet*, September 14, 1868, p. 6.

[59] Namık Kemal, "Terakki," *İbret*, No. 46, November 1872, in Özön, *Namık Kemal ve İbret*, p. 176.

[60] Namık Kemal, *Osmanlı Tarihi* (Istanbul, Mahmud Bey Matbaası, 1326/1910-1911), pp. 4, 5.

personality are new conceptions which can be traced to the influence of the romantic theory of history in the intellectual circles of the Turkish capital.[61]

Namık Kemal was able to take exception to a conception of the "general will" because political authority had firm bases in Islam. Notwithstanding his stress on popular sovereignty he unconsciously relied on these traditional Islamic bases of authority. He therefore did not feel impelled to undertake a search for the rational bases of political obligation. This stand, however, involved Kemal in certain difficulties in terms of internal consistency of which he was not entirely aware. The problem may be stated as follows: Namık Kemal proposed certain definite reforms to eliminate the ills that were besetting the empire. These remedies and Namık Kemal's synthesis might have been rejected by a sizable portion of the Ottoman citizens. Indeed, during his lifetime Kemal witnessed the fact that this could happen.[62] How, then, did Kemal expect his suggested remedies to be enforced? The answer to this lies in Kemal's belief in harmony—an attitude in which it is rather difficult to separate the Islamic from the Enlightenment strands.

What this theory amounted to was, in essence, a belief that, once the people had been given the opportunity to take a share in the ideal (viz., representative) government, they would be led in their individual paths to do the same things. The Enlightenment origin of this conception is clear. For one, Namık Kemal had great faith in the ability of the "common man" (in this case, the provincial delegates to Parliament) to reach politically sound decisions.[63] He had an unbounded

---

[61] See Cevdet Paşa's statement about the influence on his own thought of the French romantic historian Michelet in Ebül'ülâ Mardin, *Medenî Hukuk Cephesinden Ahmet Cevdet Paşa*, pp. 30, 31, note 56. Michelet himself has been described as a "zealot." See Boyd C. Shafer, *Nationalism: Myth and Reality* (London, Gollancz, 1955), p. 179.

[62] See above, Chapter II.

[63] Namık Kemal, "Usul-u Meşveret," *Hürriyet*, September 29, 1868, III, 6.

admiration also for the mechanics of discussion and the exchange of ideas which, according to him, led to truth.[64]

Of a similar origin was Namık Kemal's reference to the harmony of the universe: "It is well known that strength increases in proportion to mutual aid and not only in the human world but in the world of matter too a binding order is [provided by] the harmony and unity which are inherent in things. If the smallest wheel of a factory were to get out of order, all of its parts would suffer; if the smallest satellite of Jupiter were to move from its accustomed path, the conditions regulated by our sun would probably be completely upset."[65]

But in this very article Namık Kemal, after such a preamble, went on to investigate the reasons for which the Islamic "nation" had disintegrated. It is in this transition that one encounters the second Islamic source of Kemal's emphasis on harmony, for Kemal showed that what he was longing for was the ideal harmony of an ideal Islamic state which had existed in the golden age of Islam. This attitude went back to the idealized picture of the harmonious state as expounded both by the jurists and the Falāsifa.[66] To it may be traced other ideas of Kemal, such as the thought that ideal government in addition to providing justice establishes social harmony and cohesion.[67] This stand also expresses itself in Kemal's objection to politics as a clash of opposites.

"Since to thus consider government and the people two opposites running counter to each other, just as the currents of the Bosphorus flow in opposite directions, is a conception which has such a bad effect on the political situation and on public opinion as to make it completely undesirable."[68]

[64] Namık Kemal, "Ikhtilāfu Ummatī Raḥma," *Hürriyet*, July 6, 1868, p. 4.

[65] Namık Kemal, "İttihad-ı Islâm," in Özön, *Namık Kemal ve İbret*, p. 75.

[66] Particularly the conception of the "pure city" in Farabî which reappears in the *Ahlak-ı Alaî*. See Chapter III.

[67] Namık Kemal, " 'Inna'llāha ya'mur bi'l 'Adl wa'l iḥsān," *Hürriyet*, January 18, 1869, p. 1.

[68] Namık Kemal, "Bazı Mülâhazat-ı Devlet," in Özön, *Namık Kemal ve*

Namık Kemal's idea of harmony is also interesting in that it constitutes a locus where meet (*a*) the Irano-Mongolian theory of classes, (*b*) the ideas of the Enlightenment, and (*c*) the ideas of the Islamic jurists. In Montesquieu's *Considerations on the Grandeur and the Decadence of the Romans* a passage may be found in which the author states:

"Dans l'accord du despotisme Asiatique, c'est à dire de tout gouvernement qui n'est pas modéré, il y a toujours une division réelle; le laboureur, l'homme de guerre, le négociant, le magistrat, le noble ne sont joints que par ce que les uns oppriment les autres sans résistance: et si l'on y voit de l'union, ce ne sont pas des citoyens qui sont unis mais des corps morts ensevelis les uns apres les autres."[69]

Montesquieu goes on to say that the ideal state should, on the contrary, be "une union d'harmonie qui fait que toutes les parties, quelqu'opposées qu'elles nous paraissent, concourent au bien général de la societé, comme des dissonances, dans la musique, concourent à l'accord total."[70]

Namık Kemal who stood, with the orthodox Islamic jurists, in opposition to the Irano-Mongolian despotic arrangement of powers to which Montesquieu referred, found in the latter a Western thinker whose theories with regard to the checks to be imposed on the executive were combined with a theory of harmony which Kemal had already espoused on Islamic grounds.

In general, Kemal could find in the ideas of Montesquieu more of a common ground than is apparent at first sight, for Montesquieu was still bound by invisible threads to ancient philosophical conceptions which had found an echo in Islamic

---

İbret, p. 130. The idea of harmony also colored the conception of law held by Kemal. One of the examples which Kemal gave to prove the superiority of the *Şeriat* was that, since it was based on religious authority, it based obedience on stronger grounds both "materially and morally." Namık Kemal, " 'Inna'llāha," *Hürriyet*, January 18, 1868, p. 5.

[69] Montesquieu, *Considérations sur les Causes de la Grandeur des Romains et de leur Décadence* (in *Oeuvres*, ed. by Masson, Paris, 1950), I, IX, 415.

[70] *Ibid.*

civilization. As Isaiah Berlin points out: "Montesquieu's concept of types is not empirical, it springs from the ancient doctrines of natural kinds; it is thoroughly metaphysical and Aristotelian. According to him each type of society possesses an inner structure, an inner dynamic principle of force which makes it function as it does—and this 'inner' force differs from type to type. Whatever strengthens the 'inner' principle causes the organism to flourish, whatever impairs it causes it to decay. His catalogue of these forces is very famous— monarchy rests on the principle of honor, aristocracy on that of moderation, the republican régime on that of virtue."[71]

Namık Kemal who criticized both Locke and Rousseau for their failure to base their system on empirical evidence,[72] found thus in Montesquieu a thinker who organized a wealth of facts into an ancient framework with which he as an Ottoman was not entirely unfamiliar.

III. Representative Institutions

While in its more fundamental and abstract aspects Namık Kemal's theory was not quite convincing, those sections of his writings that took up the impassioned defense of representative government were much more consistent and coherent. In all fairness to Kemal it should also be pointed out that a defense of liberal ideals carried out on such practical grounds made up the bulk of his contributions to political literature. Most of Kemal's articles were so built that they naturally led to a common conclusion—the necessity to establish in the Ottoman Empire the "system of *meşveret*," the word coined by Kemal for "representative government." Thus, starting from the premise that freedom was a divine grant, he would go on to state that a community ("*ümmet*") could be free only when it had been assured of its personal rights ("*hukuk-u*

---

[71] Isaiah Berlin, *Montesquieu*, Reprint *Proceedings of the British Academy* (London, Oxford University Press, 1956), Vol. 41, p. 277.
[72] Namık Kemal, *Osmanlı Tarihi*, I, Part 1, p. 8.

şahsiye") and of its political rights (*"hukuk-u siyasiye"*).[73]
Securing personal rights was dependent upon the institution
of impartial and competent courts, while political right depended upon the separation of powers (*"kuvvetlerin taksimi"*)
and the establishment of representative government.

Some characteristics of Namık Kemal's use of the term
"usul-u meşveret" are worth analyzing. In Kemal's writings
this term has only rarely the connotation of "constitutionalism"; more often it is used as the equivalent of "representative
government." The reason for which constitutionalism was not
accorded a place as a primary political goal was that according
to Kemal the Şeriat already provided a set of fundamental
political principles to guide statesmen.

Thus Kemal did not choose to stress the drafting of a constitution or the wresting of a charter from the government
with as much vehemence as had been the case among the
advocates of constitutionalism in nineteenth-century Europe.
What Kemal *did* insist on, however, was that the laws of the
land other than the Şeriat be made accessible to all. Kemal
had two purposes in mind. First, he desired that laws and
regulations be written in "a language understandable to all."[74]
Namık Kemal was referring here to his suspicion that the
official style of the Porte (*"kitabet-i resmiye"*), devised centuries before, was meant to prevent the people from understanding governmental affairs.[75]

---

[73] See Namık Kemal, "El ḥaḳḳ yaʿlū" *Hürriyet*, June 29, 1868, p. 3. This
idea went back to Montesquieu. See *Esprit*, I, 3.

[74] Namık Kemal, "Wa-shāwirhum," p. 1.

[75] A point elaborated by him in the preface to his translation of the
Bahar-ı Daniş. See Ismail Habib Sevük, *Tanzimattanberi: II Edebiyat Antolojisi* (İstanbul, Remzi Kitabevi, 1943), pp. 208-209. For a similar article of
Ziya Paşa, see "Şiir ve İnşa," *Hürriyet*, September 7, 1868, p. 4. The necessity for accessibility was an idea that had been quite common among
Enlightenment thinkers. In particular, in Volney, whom Kemal knew well
(see below, pp. 315 f.), we find the following statement: ". . . et l'administration étant secrète et mysterieuse, il n'éxista aucun moyen de réforme ni
d'amélioration." C. F. Volney, *Les Ruines ou Méditations sur les Révolutions
des Empires Suivies de la Loi Naturelle* (Paris Décembre-Alonniers, 1869),
p. 46.

In addition, Namık Kemal pointed to the unwieldiness of the masses of Imperial Rescripts in force and the inconvenience of having to depend on various laws and charters proclaimed at different dates (such as the Gülhane Rescript and the Rescript of 1856) which were all part of the fundamental law of the empire; he suggested a codification of these laws.

The document which was to underpin the system of representation proposed by Kemal was to consist of a consolidation and a revision of the Rescripts of Gülhane and of 1856. These revising activities were to be inspired by "existing foreign constitutions."[76]

Every one of the clauses to be included in the new constitution of the Ottoman Empire was to be in harmony with a precept of Islamic law. Furthermore, the establishment of a constitutional regime in Turkey would not, according to Kemal, be an innovation. According to him, to institute a mechanism of governmental control would only mean the refining of a mode of government which had been in use in the Ottoman Empire before the centralizing moves of Mahmud and the rise of a new bureaucracy had put an end to it.[77]

According to Kemal, in reality the Ottoman system of government, despite the external trappings of an autocracy, had always been a "legitimate government" in which the ulema held the legislative power, the sultan and his viziers the executive power, while the people in arms represented by the Janissaries controlled the action of the executive.[78]

This, however, he admitted was a fairly primitive arrangement which resulted in continuous friction between the government and the Janissaries and in the needless shedding of blood during palace revolutions. Thus, concluded Kemal, historical evidence "unfortunately" pointed to the necessity of confining government to the hands of "a well-qualified group" of limited size which would take care of the matters of state. There was

[76] Namık Kemal, "Usul-u Meşveret," *Hürriyet*, September 14, 1868, I, 6.
[77] *Ibid.*, p. 6.
[78] Namık Kemal, "Hasta Adam," *Hürriyet*, December 7, 1868, p. 1.

no other way to invest this group with legitimate authority and to control their actions than by having "recourse to delegation."[79]

Most of the space that Namık Kemal devoted to constitutionalism treated of the various modes in which the group of limited size or government was to be controlled.

According to Namık Kemal, the constitution which was to serve as model to the Turks was the constitution of the Second Empire of France. This result was arrived at by a method of elimination rather than by choice. Namık Kemal ruled out the constitution of the United States because it was a republic; he ruled out the constitution of Prussia and England because both were partly based on the representation of an aristocracy which, he said, did not exist in the Ottoman Empire.[80] To Namık Kemal, the French constitution appeared to include the most suitable combination of checks and balances for Turkey, for it had been able to create "an era of happiness" in France, a country generally given to violent revolution.[81] Using the French model, Namık Kemal advised the creation of a system of government composed of three organs—a council of state,[82] a senate,[83] and a lower chamber,[84] with the whole arrangement supervised by the sultan. In this scheme, the council of state was given the task of preparing laws and ironing out difficulties that might arise in administrative practice.[85] The *corps législatif* (composed of elected members in contrast to the members of the council of state who were to be nominated by the sovereign) and the senate were to approve or reject the projects of law prepared by the council of state, and the lower chamber was to control the budget.[86]

[79] Namık Kemal, "Usul-u Meşveret," *Hürriyet*, September 14, 1868, I, 6.
[80] *Ibid.*, p. 7.
[81] *Ibid.* In his "Memur," *İbret*, October 7, 1872, *M.S.E.*, pp. 135-148, Kemal speaks of the Belgian constitution as the best available. The influence of this document also shows in the Ottoman constitution of 1876.
[82] *Meclis-i Şura-yı Devlet* in Turkish.
[83] *Senato* in Turkish.   [84] *Meclis-i Şura-yı Ümmet* in Turkish.
[85] Namık Kemal, "Usul-u Meşveret," *Hürriyet*, September 21, 1868, II, 6.
[86] *Ibid.*

Namık Kemal stated that the two primary goals of the government thus created should be the enforcing of law and the "securing of progress."[87] For Namık Kemal, as earlier for Şinasi, this meant that reforms had to be pushed by the state and could not be left entirely to the efforts of individuals. This would seem to contradict the earlier statements of Namık Kemal to the effect that the state was not the governess of individuals; but in the former case what he alluded to was the necessity for Turks to work and thus create wealth without state support, while in this case what he meant was the cultural development of the empire. Other statements of Namık Kemal in the context of the question of state support confirm this distinction which he made in regard to the state's intervention in cultural as opposed to economic matters. He mentioned, for example, that if Yusuf Kâmil Paşa, instead of spending his time translating the Abbé Fénelon's *Télémaque*, had opened a few high schools while he was Minister of Instruction, he would have done more for his country.[88]

What was to be the position of the sultan in this scheme? The answer provided by Namık Kemal to this question was that the Ottoman Empire could not imitate the French system, which lifted some of the responsibility from the shoulders of the government and placed it on the emperor, made solely responsible to the people. Neither could the Ottoman Empire choose to divest the ruler of all responsibility, as in England, and make the government solely responsible; for the Padişah, according to Kemal, is "designated by religious law for the carrying out of justice."[89] Namık Kemal proposed the ambiguous compromise of making the sultan "responsible for his own actions," i.e., for those actions that could be traced to his own will.[90] What Namık Kemal really meant was that the sultan

[87] *Ibid., Hürriyet*, September 29, 1868, III, 5.

[88] Namık Kemal, "Bazı Mulâhazat-ı Devlet ve Millet," in Özön, *Namık Kemal ve İbret*, pp. 133, 134.

[89] Namık Kemal, "Usul-u Meşveret," *Hürriyet*, September 14, 1868, I, p. 7.

[90] *Ibid.*, p. 8.

would also be limited by the laws of the realm.[91] After having spelled out this feature quite uncompromisingly, Kemal went on to bury the harshness of this new conception under a series of compliments to the sultan and the House of Osman. He also pointed out that as matters stood the sultan was little more than a prisoner of his ministers.

IV. Namık Kemal's Idea of Law

Most of the criticism of the Young Ottomans and particularly that of Namık Kemal can be summarized as a cry for justice. To a large extent what this meant in practice was a demand for the implementation of the religious law, the Şeriat. There are statements of Namık Kemal which show that he believed the ulema needed to be shorn of what he considered obscurantist elements, but, as for the "spirit" of that law itself, Namık Kemal believed that the Şeriat provided the surest guide. Namık Kemal's position was quite similar to that which, at an earlier date, had made Sir Edward Coke oppose James I. Just as in Coke's case, Namık Kemal too believed that it was the Ottoman equivalent of the common law "which assigned to the King his powers, to each of the courts of the realm its proper jurisdiction and to every Englishman [or, in this case, to every Ottoman] the rights and privileges of his station."[92] He also believed that the Şeriat included all that then could be counted as constitution, both the fundamental structure of the government and the fundamental rights of the subjects. This belief of Namık Kemal's was strictly orthodox and emphasized the teachings of the ulema.[93]

It is because Namık Kemal believed in the "common law" that he attacked the continental European conception of a public law which, in the form it took during the nineteenth century, started from the basic tenet of the superiority of the

[91] For these ideas see Namık Kemal, "El haḳḳ ya'lū," *Hürriyet*, June 29, 1868, p. 3.

[92] Sabine, *History of Political Theory*, p. 425.

[93] See H. A. R. Gibb, *La Structure de la Pensée Religieuse de l'Islam* (Paris, Editions Larose, 1950), p. 35.

moral personality of the state.[94] From there, Namık Kemal went to attack the conception of the general will.

The comparison which was made between Coke and Kemal may be carried farther to the points on which Namık Kemal and Sir Edward differed. This difference is of fundamental importance. In his stand against James I, Coke had spoken about the particular reason of law which the king, who was not a lawyer, could not therefore fathom. But then, this "particular reason" was not an essentially religious element. It was something which derived from the nature of legal reasoning. On the other hand, the Şeriat being the law of God could have no secular inner logic. This is why, for example, Namık Kemal would state that he did not believe law could be based on ethics. For, according to him, "the science of what is just and what is unjust" was based on religion; it was the Şeriat.

On the other hand, ethics he considered to be "mere philosophical speculation."[95] Morality without religion, argued Kemal, could not by itself constitute a check on man's actions. This, he said, was what was meant by Voltaire when the latter stated that "if there were no God, it would be necessary to invent one."[96] Consequently, a positivistic interpretation of law was anathema to Kemal. He did, however, accept Montesquieu's statement that law was the sum of relations which stemmed from the very nature of things, since this statement was vague enough to be set into religious context.[97] According to Kemal, not only did the religious foundation of law solve the problem of a fixed standard of good and bad, but, in addition, it had great practical advantages. Since God had ordered the study of the Koran, every citizen was held to know the general principles embodied in it. If laws were passed in accordance with these general principles, it meant that every true believer would automatically have a sufficient knowledge

[94] Namık Kemal, "Hukuk-u Umumiye," *İbret*, July 8, 1872, in Özön, *Namık Kemal ve İbret*, p. 93 ff.

[95] Kuntay, *Namık Kemal*, II, 484.

[96] *Ibid.*, p. 435.

[97] *Ibid.*, p. 488. For Namık Kemal's difficulties in this respect see below, p. 318.

of the laws of the realm. In a country like France, where law was not drafted in accordance with such basic standards, it was of course impossible for the citizen to know the law.[98]

With regard to the Ottoman Empire, Namık Kemal was in keeping with the tradition of Ottoman thought which related the downfall of the empire to a slackening in the observance of religious law.[99] He was violently opposed to the movement for the secularization of law which had started with the Tanzimat.[100] He stated: "Up to the present courts with wide jurisdiction [the new secular courts of the Tanzimat] have been founded and all kinds of laws made. Of what use have these been, other than weakening the Mohammedan Şeriat? Are these courts more impartial than religious courts and are these laws more perfect than the precepts of the Şeriat? Since it [the Şeriat] is under the protection of the Unique One, even the greatest of tyrants cannot alter it. All he can do is suppress it. We would seek our salvation in conforming to these standards. . . ."[101]

Yet it would seem that he had enough respect for a Western, secular, natural-law interpretation of the decline of the Ottoman Empire to have taken the pains to translate it.[102] This was the French historian Volney's *Ruins of Palmyra*, and the case of Kemal's attraction to his ideas is important enough to merit somewhat extended treatment. Volney was the Toynbee of his era, and his book on the *Ruins of Palmyra* was a consideration of the general causes of the decadence of empires. While the main bulk of this work was devoted to the analysis of the causes for the decline of ancient empires, Volney also included

[98] *Ibid.*, p. 493.
[99] Namık Kemal, "Devlet-i Aliyye-yi Bulunduğu Hal-i Hatarnaktan Halâsın Esbabı," *Hürriyet*, August 24, 1868, pp. 1, 2.
[100] *Ibid.*, pp. 2, 3; editorial, November 30, 1868.
[101] *Ibid.*, p. 3.
[102] [Namık Kemal], *Fransız Müelliflerinden Volney nam Zatın "Les Ruines de Palmyre" unvaniyle Yazmış Olduğu Makalâttan Bazı Fıkraların Tercümesidir* [n.p.], 1288/1871. For the attribution of this translation to Namık Kemal see Kaplan, *Namık Kemal*, p. 102, note 2. For a corroboration by Ebüzziya see [Namık Kemal], "Volney Tercümesi," *Mecmua-i Ebüzziya*, 15 Muharrem 1298, pp. 280, 281.

the Ottoman Empire in this study and gave it considerable attention. The method he used in undertaking this analysis was an application to the philosophy of history of an essentially Rousseauistic approach. Volney explained the origins of society in a Rousseauan fashion, but his originality consisted in the analysis of the rise and fall of empires by the same method. According to Volney, empires declined because they did not heed the principles of natural law inherent in human beings. Thus, for example, in trying to find the mysterious signs by which it could be determined whether an empire was on the wane, men were fooling themselves. The only remedy against such decline was to follow the law of nature.[103]

In addition, Volney conveniently made the specific point that the Ottoman Empire had declined because its rulers had neglected this law and become tyrannical and unjust.[104]

In view of his concern for the decline of the Ottoman Empire, the idea that the decline of the latter could be explained by a deterioration of its government was a very helpful one for Namık Kemal. Namık Kemal had probably undertaken the translation of Volney's work for the same reason that had prompted him to translate Montesquieu's *Grandeur and Decadence of the Romans*.[105] His purpose in both cases was to show what happened when what he had called in one instance "natural law,"[106] i.e., the Şeriat, stopped being observed.

[103] ". . . l'homme reporte en vain ses malheurs à des agents obscurs et imaginaires, il recherche en vain à ses maux de causes mystérieuses . . . l'homme est régi par des lois naturelles, régulieres dans leur cours, conséquentes dans leurs effets, immuables dans leur essence." C. F. Volney, *Les Ruines* (Paris, Décembre-Alonniers, 1869), p. 24.

[104] "Voilà par quels principes sont jugés les peuples. . . . Interrogez vos ancêtres. Demandez leur par quel moyen ils élevèrent leur fortune alors qu'idolâtres, peu nombreux et pauvres, ils vinrent des deserts Tartares camper dans ces riches contrées. . . . Alors le Sultan lui-même rendait justice et veillait à la discipline, alors était puni le juge prévaricateur, le gouverneur concussionnaire, et la multitude vivait dans l'aisance, le cultivateur était garanti des rapines des Janissaires et les campagnes prosperaient, les routes publiques étaient assurées et le commerce repandait l'abondance." *Ibid.*, pp. 58, 59.

[105] For this translation of Kemal's see Kaplan, *Namık Kemal*, pp. 49, 50.

[106] Namık Kemal, "Devlet-i Aliyyeyi," *Hürriyet*, August 24, 1868, p. 2.

He forgot that the natural law which Volney spoke of was not the Şeriat and that, while on the surface the type of conduct advocated by Volney and that required by the Şeriat had similarities, there were fundamental differences between the Islamic and the Western conception of natural law. He forgot that in the West there had begun since the seventeenth century "a gradual process of releasing political philosophy from the association with theology."[107]

Basic to Volney's approach to natural law were the following conceptions:

a) That human societies were regulated by natural laws and that flaws in human institutions were due to a departure from a fixed norm of nature and reason;

b) That these laws could be grasped by men's intelligence because they were inherent in human beings;

c) That these laws were immutable in their essence.

All of these conceptions were foreign to orthodox Islam, if not outright heretical. True, there had been Western thinkers in whose conception natural law and, even more important, revelation had played an important part. Thus, for example, Locke's inspiration on the subject of natural law had been the Bible.[108] But the answer given by Locke to the questions "Can the law of nature be known by the light of reason?" and "Can reason attain the knowledge of natural law through sense experience?" was an unqualified "Yes."[109] To the same questions an Islamic thinker would have replied, "No." Furthermore, "Locke's notion that the law of matter is immutable" implied "that the binding force of it does not lapse even at

---

Also, for Kemal's conviction that statute law was based on natural law with citations from Martens and Puffendorf see Namık Kemal, "Redd-i itiraz," Müntahabat-ı Tasvir-i Efkâr, I-II, 41, 42.

[107] Sabine, A History of Political Theory, p. 415.

[108] J. W. Gough, John Locke's Political Philosophy, p. 22.

[109] John Locke, Essays on the Law of Nature. The Latin text with a translation, introduction, and notes, together with transcripts of Locke's shorthand in his journal for 1676. (ed. by W. von Leyden, Oxford, Clarendon Press, 1954), pp. 123, 147.

God's own command."[110] This would have been crass heresy by Islamic standards.

In fact, Volney was much farther on the road of the secularization of natural law than was Locke. For Locke, as for Kemal, the law of nature had been "a moral standard to which all men, including governors themselves, should conform.[111] For Volney, it was a semideterministic norm of growth and decay which presented men with the simple alternative of conforming to the laws of history or perishing. There were even similarities between the attitude of Volney and that of the most extreme representative of the secularization of natural law, the materialist d'Holbach.[112] Finally, Volney's conception of natural law was based on the idea of the essential goodness of man, while Namık Kemal's idea was postulated on the essentially predatory nature of men.

Namık Kemal's espousal of the ideas set forth by Volney is, again, one point at which there can be found internal contradictions in his thought. But Namık Kemal was not aware of these contradictions and thought that these ideas would blend in with his Islamic theories. In reality, it was this Islamic texture which was preponderant in his thought.

In one instance, again, Namık Kemal tried to conciliate Montesquieu's definition of law as "the relations stemming from the nature of things" with the Islamic conception of law, and he came to the conclusion that these two conceptions were not antithetical since it was God who was the Author of the "nature of things."[113] Yet, as has been stressed in an earlier chapter, this deistic conception of the role played by the

[110] *Ibid.*, p. 57.

[111] Gough, *John Locke*, p. 22.

[112] See Volney, "L'Espece Humaine s'Améliorera-t-elle," *Les Ruines*, pp. 65-73. The cure Volney was advocating for humanity's ills showed an amazing similarity with those proposed by d'Holbach which Sabine has described as follows: "Enlighten them [men], remove the obstacles set up by superstition and tyranny, leave them free to follow the light of reason, convince rulers that their interests are identical with those of their subjects and a happy state of society will follow almost automatically." Sabine, *op.cit.*, p. 570.

[113] Namık Kemal, "Hukuk," in Özön, *Namık Kemal ve İbret*, pp. 49, 50; cf. *Esprit*, I, 1, for a similar conception.

divinity had no orthodox Islamic equivalent. Kaplan's thesis[114] that by the standards of Islamic mysticism such a conciliation was possible, and that this was what Namık Kemal had in mind, does shed light on the mental processes of Kemal. It also corroborates the link established earlier in this chapter with regard to Kemal's idea of freedom. This explanation, however, does not dispel the great philosophical difficulties in which Kemal had involved himself by attempting to conciliate Montesquieu with the Şeriat. These difficulties and the divergence between these two approaches to law stand out quite clearly in view of the specific injunctions, legal, political, and other, contained in the Koran. Montesquieu's main contribution to the theory of law, on the other hand, was thoroughgoing relativism, something with which Namık Kemal could not agree in view of his allegiance to the principles enunciated in the Koran.

The all-embracing aspect of Islamic law and the importance it had for Kemal have to be grasped to place in their true context other concepts he used, such as *equality*. For Kemal, equality meant before everything else equality before the law, and equality which derives from the dignity of the human person and the divine origin of the creation of man.[115] In practice, this meant for Kemal that high government officials would not be treated more leniently than ordinary citizens in the courts.[116] This was the equality that had existed between the Prophet and his followers and was identified with an idealized Islamic golden age.[117]

V. Namık Kemal's Idea of Progress

Of all Namık Kemal's ideas that can be traced back to the influence of Europe, the most obvious is his conception of progress. One finds this conception in the articles that he wrote

[114] Kaplan, *Namık Kemal*, p. 115.
[115] Namık Kemal, "Müsavat," *M.S.E.*, p. 377.
[116] *Ibid.*, p. 378.
[117] *Ibid.*, p. 379.

after his sojourn in Europe and particularly in those he composed under the influence of his stay in England.

A great many of the articles published by Kemal in the years following his European exile were devoted to demonstrating the practical benefits reaped by Europeans from their attitude toward the family and their fellow citizens, or to show the material advantages provided by the West. It is in these articles that we can see an aim of Namık Kemal which always accompanied his political liberalism but which he expressed most vehemently at the time he stopped being an expatriate. This aim was to overtake the West in the race for progress. It is to the materialization of this progress that Namık Kemal attributed the superiority of the British in a variety of fields. Thus British courts were, according to him, so just as to inspire in the people who were brought before them more confidence than they had in their own fathers.[118] Every aspect of life in England aroused the enthusiasm of Kemal who, in one and the same breath, praised the Crystal Palace, the British system of education, British printing presses, and the uses to which steam and electricity were put in Britain.[119] Even the fact that in England policemen did no more than regulate traffic and pacify a few drunken brawlers was due to progress.[120]

According to Kemal, this flow of progress was part of the dynamic move of every society and reflected the natural ability of individuals to progress.[121] Furthermore, Namık Kemal believed that progress was irreversible; like the hands of a clock, it could not be turned back. Kemal considered Western progress to have been due to the sum of events which had occurred in Europe in the two centuries preceding the middle of the nineteenth century.[122] This progress was advancing at

[118] Namık Kemal, "Terakki," İbret, November 1872, in Özön, Namık Kemal ve İbret, p. 178.
[119] Ibid., p. 183.
[120] Ibid., p. 186.
[121] Ibid., p. 212.
[122] Namık Kemal, "İbret," in Özön, Namık Kemal ve İbret, p. 39.

an increasingly fast pace[123] and its most important characteristic was that it had brought "lasting order" in society.[124]

Kemal argued that Europe had achieved these results by separating existing laws from "abstractions" and "superstitions" and had thus established science on "experiment and deduction."[125] One of the consequences of this "dawning of truth" had been the French Declaration of the Rights of Man. This progress, continued Kemal, had not been followed in the Ottoman Empire. True, the Tanzimat had introduced reforms and new institutions, but the only way in which the population of the Ottoman Empire had been made to participate in the Tanzimat was through the language reform of Şinasi. Specially in regard to its commercial backwardness, in regard to the fact that the people had not contributed their share toward the creation of a prosperous country, Turkey could not be said to have progressed.[126] If the Ottomans desired to make use of their natural abilities, they should take notice of what had happened in Europe. The Islamic injunction to look for science and learning even so far as China pointed to the way for changes.[127]

Part of Namık Kemal's attitude toward progress was his advocacy of a regeneration of Turkish agriculture through tax reforms, the arresting of the decrease in the Turkish element of the empire by extending conscription to the non-Moslem population, the elimination of the tariff policy which had led to the ruin of local manufactures, and the establishment of favorable credit for the growth of local industry.[128] All of this was part of a general activist attitude of Kemal which made him scoff at the idea of resignation to one's fate as utterly non-Islamic.[129]

[123] Namık Kemal, "Medeniyet," in Özön, *Namık Kemal ve İbret*, p. 212.
[124] *Ibid.*, p. 216.
[125] Namık Kemal, "İbret," in Özön, *Namık Kemal ve İbret*, p. 39.
[126] *Ibid.*
[127] Namık Kemal, "Terakki," in Özön, *Namık Kemal ve İbret*, p. 188.
[128] Namık Kemal, editorial, *Hürriyet*, August 10, 1868, p. 1.
[129] Namık Kemal, "Memalik-i Osmaniyenin Yeni Mukasemesi," *Hürriyet*, November 9, 1868, p. 4.

Namık Kemal saw clearly that one of the elements that made for progress in Europe was the internal safety provided by good government. Yet this did not stop him from clinging tenaciously to a number of Islamic cultural institutions in matters of dress, social intercourse, and manners. In addition, for him, European civilization included many institutions that had been invented in Islam to begin with and which had been perfected by Europeans. By considering nineteenth-century Europe to have brought back to life ideas and institutions which "in fact" were Islamic, Namık Kemal showed the zealot strain in his approach to reform. Yet, in the case of progress too, Kemal fostered a new approach.

It should be clear from the Islamic conception of the immanence of God that progress as a self-perpetuating process activated by human reason is an idea which is far from being Islamic. The Islamic vantage point chosen by Kemal was expressed in two sayings—one, that one should look for science as far as China and the second, a saying attributed to the Prophet to the effect that temporal changes justified a change in mores.[130] But it is far from these bases to the "innate ability of man to progress" of which Kemal spoke. There is no better indication of Kemal's innovation in this respect than his advice to take advantage of the office of prayer leader to prod the members of the congregation to diligence and cleanliness as a means of encouraging progress. In Kemal's words: "If the preachers, instead of theologizing in the Mosques would apply themselves to teach subjects which would be of use in both this world and the next, and [thus] contribute to guarantee the life of the nation, lots of misconceptions on this subject, which are present in public opinion, would be eliminated."[131]

This essentially European social activism recurs in Namık Kemal's article entitled "Work."[132] Here he dwells at length

---

[130] Namık Kemal, "Karınca Kanatlandı," *Hürriyet*, February 22, 1869, p. 2.

[131] Namık Kemal, "Nufus," *İbret*, June 25, 1872, in Özön, *Namık Kemal ve İbret*, p. 70.

[132] Namık Kemal, "Sây," *M.S.E.*, p. 27 ff.

on the evils of sloth and makes the statement that man, although mortal, should look at life as if he were to live forever. In fact, this strain in Namık Kemal's thought is a continuation of one to be found in Şinasi and Sadık Rifat Paşa. With these authors, Namık Kemal was convinced that the future development of the empire depended on intense effort accompanied by education.[133]

A final aspect of Namık Kemal's views on progress which must not be overlooked is that it was part of the general "social mobilization" to which we have already pointed out in connection with the significance of *Fénelon*. Namık Kemal believed, for example, that literature should be used as a means of inspiring the Ottomans to lift themselves by their own bootstraps.[134] Similarly his injunctions to establish a streamlined civil service, and to look for talent in the provinces rather than only in the capital, were part of an effort to harness all available resources to what today would be called the "development" of the Ottoman Empire.[135] His criticism of the ulema's assuming a double function as "professors" in traditional Ottoman institutions of higher learning and judges in Ottoman courts, amounted to a desire to see both of these functions performed with the efficiency that was required by a modern society.[136] His articles on economics[137] repeat economic themes first encountered in the writings of Sadık Rifat Paşa.

---

[133] Namık Kemal, "Vatan," *M.S.E.*, p. 330.

[134] Namık Kemal, "Bend-i Mahsus," *Tasvir-i Efkâr*, 16 Rebiülahir 1283-28 August 1866. In *Müntahabat-ı Tasvir-i Efkâr: Edebiyat: Namık Kemal* Cüz 1-2. (2nd. ed., Istanbul, Matbaa-i Ebüzziya, 1311/1893-1894), p. 8. In the same piece the transition from purposiveness to puritanism can be quite clearly seen. At the end of the article Namık Kemal argues that the Ottomans have no more time to devote to the "titillating" classical Ottoman literature which is branded as immoral because it leads to a waste of national energy.

[135] See Namık Kemal, "Memur," *M.S.E.*, pp. 135-148. Similar was his theme that women should be educated. See Namık Kemal, "Terbiye-i nisvan hakkında bir Lâyiha. . . ," *Tasvir-i Efkâr* 4 Şevval 1283/February 9th, 1867.

[136] *Ibid.*, p. 139.

[137] Namık Kemal, "Nüfus," *İbret*, 25 June 1872, in Özön, *Namık Kemal ve İbret*, p. 60; "Terakkî," *İbret* (No. 45) October 1872, *Ibid.*, pp. 176-189.

VI. Namık Kemal and European Philosophy

With all the emphasis he placed on Western progress Kemal was not as yet ready to use the new philosophical world view associated with the advances that he admired so much. This attitude which seems to have crystallized in the last years of his life was essentially an extension of an earlier one which had led him to reject any bases for the state other than the Şeriat. It is true that in this later phase he attacked the materialism of Renan, who had gone quite far beyond the deism of the eighteenth century. It may be that while Kemal still felt some affinity with the Enlightenment he could not swallow the philosophical desiccation of Renan.

Kemal's specific target was this French thinker's allegation that there existed no philosophy in the true sense of the word in Islam. Renan had relied on an argument similar to the one that has been advanced in this study, namely, that Islam had not been able to achieve so great a distinction in the field of science as Europe because it did not have a major tradition of secular thought independent of theology.[138] Namık Kemal's defense, even though passionate, was quite weak, for he obviously was unable to understand his adversary's position.[139] While on one hand he defended the thesis that nothing in Islamic doctrine forbade the study of the exact sciences and mathematics,[140] he showed his own inclination in the matter by stating that science was not merely "an instrument to gain control over nature and create wealth."[141] "It can never be known," he stated, "of those who use science for practical goals if they have been able to attain a higher status [i.e., if they have evolved morally] or reached maturity."[142] The antiutilitarian and strongly moralistic-religious aspect of this statement is striking. Again, Kemal protested that Renan should have

[138] For the text of this lecture of Renan's see Ernest Renan, *Oeuvres Complètes* (Psichari ed., Paris, Calman-Levy) (1947), I, 945-959.

[139] Namık Kemal, *Renan Müdafaanamesi* (ed. by Ali Ekrem Bulayır, *Külliyat-ı Kemal*, Birinci Tertip Istanbul, Selanik Matbaası, 1326/1910-1911).

[140] *Ibid.*, p. 14.　　[141] *Ibid.*, p. 16.　　[142] *Ibid.*, p. 17.

equated science with mathematics and natural sciences. If this method were to be adopted, he stated, he would agree that Islamic culture had thwarted the growth of science.[143] To Renan's contention that there was no such thing as an Arab philosophy, he opposed the fact that the science of *hikmet*, an Islamized version of the physics and metaphysics of Aristotle, was being taught in the religious schools of the capital.[144] But he did not take into account the fact that this Islamic scholastic approach to philosophy was quite barren and that the spirit of hair-splitting which permeated these teachings was no more part and parcel of European philosophy. The argument that was used by Kemal to counter Renan was that one could not make statements about philosophical freedom in the Western world in the face of such events as the death of Socrates, the attitude of the Inquisition toward Galileo, and the burning of the copies of Rousseau's *Emile*. He did not mention the fact that a qualitative change had taken place in Europe in the attitude taken toward philosophy after the end of the Middle Ages and that the Europeans themselves attributed a great part of the progress that had been accomplished in Europe to the gradually widening limits of freedom of thought, and, in particular, that the rise of political liberalism had been associated with two parallel movements—the emancipation of philosophy from religion and the conceptualization of a mechanistic system of nature. Although Kemal protested the notion advanced by Renan that astronomy had never made any progress in Islam because of the different world view that such a study would entail, on another occasion he stated quite unequivocally his disbelief in a conception of society deriving its strength from astronomy, by which words he tried to convey to his readers his opposition to a mechanistic conception of society as was current in nineteenth-century Europe.

The de-emphasizing of the mechanistic aspect of Enlightenment thought was accompanied, in Namık Kemal, by an

[143] *Ibid.*, p. 21.   [144] *Ibid.*, p. 34.

emphasis on sentiment and feeling. It is only fair to remember here that in the elaboration of the political system of Kemal a considerable amount of rationalism had crept in, but it is characteristic of Kemal that in the discussion of cultural issues he preferred to emphasize emotions rather than reason. There is a striking difference, in this respect, between Namık Kemal's utterances and the much more staid writing and the constant emphasis on reason of the poet Şinasi Efendi. The characteristic emphasis on feeling of Namık Kemal is best seen in his patriotism.

VII. Namık Kemal, the Patriot

As much as the word *"hürriyet"* is an invention of Kemal, it is to him too that is credited the first extensive use of the word *"vatan"* in the sense of "fatherland" in Turkish literature. The word *"vatan,"* the Turkish equivalent of the French *"patrie,"* had been coined before, in the early nineteenth century, but its widespread use and its popularization are due to Namık Kemal.

Namık Kemal's brand of patriotism was one of the most fiery and romantic and was linked with his advocacy of feeling. It is significant, for example, that it is in his article entitled "The Fatherland" that Namık Kemal gave one of his most complete and clear statements about his belief in the insufficiency of reason. As he expressed it, in the preamble of this article: "With all the benefits to which it has given rise, the experimental method, which has contributed more than anything else to the maturing and the progress of the world, has not been able to clear itself of the onus of having overstepped all boundaries and having placed whatever beliefs there were in the mind and whatever feelings there were in the soul under the light of reality and investigation. Among those who have made it a habit to use the experimental method in their search for truth there are certain super-critics who limit their quest for answers to material occurrences and who would like to consider everything that cannot be touched or seen as either unreliable apparitions or as inferior to the manifestations of nature."[145]

For Namık Kemal, sentiment had its own logic differing from the logic of reason: "If the Lord had created the mind of man [on the model of] the multiplication table, his conscience like a geometric measure, it would have been impossible for such concepts as 'the nation,' 'the fatherland,' or 'family' to exist."[146] The defense of the concept of "the fatherland" on this basis by Kemal reminds one strikingly of the speech of Ernest Renan entitled "Qu'est-ce qu'une nation?" Like Renan, Namık Kemal spoke of the fatherland as being not only a geographical unit, but also an emotional bond in which the memories of ancestors, the recollections of one's own youth and earliest experiences all had a place.[147] Kemal stated, "One should love one's fatherland because the most precious gift God has bestowed on us, life, began with the breathing of the air of the fatherland.[148] He added: "The fatherland is not composed of the vague lines traced by the sword of a conqueror or the pen of a scribe. It is a sacred idea resulting from the conglomeration of various noble feelings such as the people, liberty, brotherhood, interest, sovereignty, respect for one's ancestors, love of the family, and childhood memories.[149]

Key words in Namık Kemal's patriotic statements, in addition to the word *"vatan,"* are the expressions *"Osmanlı"* ("Ottoman"), *"Ümmet"* ("community"), *"millet"* (used both for "nation" or in its traditional meaning of "religious group in the Ottoman Empire"), *"Türk"* ("Turk"), *"kavm"* ("tribe"), and *"mezheb"* ("denomination"). Every one of these words was used by Namık Kemal at one time or another to denote the focus of national allegiance. This, by itself, is indicative of the fact that Namık Kemal, enthusiastic as he was in eliciting an

---

[145] Namık Kemal, "Vatan," *İbret*, March 12, 1873, in Özön, *Namık Kemal ve İbret*, p. 263.

[146] *Ibid.*, p. 264.

[147] *Ibid.*, p. 265. "Qu'est-ce qu'une nation?" in Ernest Renan's *Oeuvres* (1947), I, 887-906.

[148] Namık Kemal, "Vatan," p. 264.

[149] *Ibid.*, p. 265.

undivided allegiance to "the fatherland," was not entirely clear as to what the fatherland consisted of.

The difficulty lay in that the Ottoman Empire was composed of people who spoke different languages, had various ethnic origins, believed in a number of religions, and also belonged to many denominations. The number of possible combinations and permutations within these four basic categories is quite large and almost all of them were present in the empire as groups with separate personalities.

By and large Namık Kemal wrote his articles on "the fatherland" with a view to activating the individual's allegiance to the *vatan*, i.e., to the territory contained within the borders of the Ottoman Empire. Within this territory the great unifying force was to be the projected representative assembly itself. It would then seem to follow that all the categories of citizens within this area were Ottomans. And indeed in some writings Namık Kemal uses "Ottoman" as a name to describe all the citizens of this ideal empire.[150]

Sometimes, however, the term "Ottoman" is used with reference to the past instead of the future. In this case it applies to the Ottoman Turks. It is used usually to refer to the outstanding qualities of the Ottomans. An example is the statement, "The blood that runs in our veins too is that Ottoman blood which bears the distinction of having been shed to provide even the smallest benefits to the fatherland."[151]

In this reminiscing context "Ottoman" is sometimes replaced by "Turk": "Are not the Turks the nation [*"millet"*] in whose *medresses* Farabis, Ibn Sinas, Gazalis, Zemahşeris propagated knowledge?"[152]

But while *"millet"* is used in the sense of "nation," *"hem millet"* ("co-nationals," "compatriots") appears in a religious context. The Circassians are the *hem millets* of the Turks.[153]

---

[150] Namık Kemal, "Usul-u Meşveret," November 23, 1868, p. 6; editorial, *Hürriyet*, December 7, 1868.

[151] Namık Kemal, "Hubb ul-Watan," *Hürriyet*, June 29, 1868, p. 1.

[152] *Ibid.*

[153] Editorial, *Hürriyet*, May 10, 1868.

In the same passage in which he uses *"millet"* in the sense of "nation," Kemal states the very same Turks to have been "an *ümmet* ["community"] which has achieved the position of teacher of the world" and a few lines farther on he speaks of "the fatherland" as having been ruled by the caliph Omar and the sultan Süleyman I. Comparisons with the vocabulary Namık Kemal uses to describe other nations do not help to untangle the puzzle. The Romans are a "great community," the Jews "a small tribe" but superior to the Romans in that they were able to maintain their cultural personality longer.[154]

Kemal's attitude can be clarified only if reference is made to an element which for centuries had constituted the core of Ottoman culture. This was the spirit of *gazâ* and *fütüvvet*— the Ottoman "pioneer spirit" of conquest. The Ottoman popular classes were thoroughly permeated by this spirit and its latest manifestation (in the nineteenth century) had been seen in 1853. At that date a popular rebellion had almost taken place in the capital because the official attitude toward Russia had been considered too cowardly. Namık Kemal used both *gazâ* and *fütüvvet*, in the context of his patriotic exhortations. Thus he said,

"Such [courageous] *Padişahs* were seen that some died on the field of war ["*gazâ meydanı*"] and some perished in horrible dungeons."[155]

and

"Is it not strange that European cabinets should attempt to apportion by a stroke of the pen countries which our ancestors conquered by their sword?"[156]

If *gazâ* was the existing psychological substratum on which Namık Kemal built his patriotism, the preservation, rehabilitation, and development of the Ottoman state was his primary practical purpose. In this respect Kemal was sincerely ready to

[154] Namık Kemal, "Devlet-i Aliyyeye," *Hürriyet*, August 24, 1868, p. 2.
[155] Namık Kemal, "Hubb ul-Watan," *Hürriyet*, June 29, 1868, p. 1.
[156] Namık Kemal, "Memalik-i Osmaniyenin Yeni Mukasemesi," *Hürriyet*, November 9, 1868, p. 1.

work for the creation of a new focus of allegiance transcending that provided by the spirit of *gazâ*.

Neither the idea of the preservation of the Ottoman state nor that of an ethnically diversified empire were entirely new. The first one was a traditional Ottoman ideal, while the second was the very base on which the empire was built, as Namık Kemal himself argued. Thus we may say that Namık Kemal found the ground already prepared for his idea of the harmonious symbiosis of ethnically and religiously differing populations. His own contribution, an important one which should not be overlooked, was that the idea of a *union* of populations (all to be known as Ottomans) replaced the previous conception of people living side by side in harmony but still separated by religious barriers in the absence of a feeling of nationality. This intellectual evolution is somewhat analogous to that from the conception of "equal but separate" status to that of a fully integrated citizenry.

To bring about this intertwining Kemal relied on the conception of an equal guarantee of the political rights of the entire Ottoman population and on a system of education accessible to everyone. To him, sitting side by side on the same benches was the best way of fostering such a unity. Once these conditions were fulfilled, the future of the Ottoman Empire would be assured, he thought.

Quite early, however, alternative methods of strengthening the Ottoman state were being considered by Kemal which had a characteristically Western stamp. On one hand, Namık Kemal stated that he did not believe in an internationalism which consisted in loving humanity as a whole at a time when nations were in arms and one's fatherland was in danger.[157] On

---

[157] Namık Kemal, "Vatan," in Özön, *Namık Kemal ve İbret*, p. 266. These conceptions seem to have been formed quite early. In the summer of 1866 Kemal was already objecting to the thesis set forth by Münif Paşa, the Encyclopaedist, that with time and advances in science and education, force would become obsolete in relations between states. This was indicative of the new European trend toward *realpolitik* in Kemal's time. See Namık Kemal, "Redd-i İtiraz," *Tasvir-i Efkâr*, 16 Rebiülahir 1283/August 28, 1866, in *Müntahabat-ı Tasvir-i Efkâr* 1-2, p. 35.

NAMIK KEMAL

the other hand, even during the first period of activity of the Young Ottomans, he was already thinking of reuniting all geographically accessible Moslems by extending to them the same benefits of representative government.[158]

Namık Kemal's early ideas on the subject of "the fatherland" are thus quite complex. They consist, on one hand, of the continuous mention of the prowess of the ancient Ottomans which, according to Kemal, obligated succeeding generations to live up to it and, on the other hand, of suggestions regarding the building of a unified state and the establishment of the conception of an imperial Ottoman citizenship regardless of religion or race. These two ideas are usually set forth within one and the same article. Although the emphasis on the superiority of the Ottomans can already be encountered in the *Letter* of Mustafa Fazıl Paşa, in Namık Kemal it is a constant theme. There was an explosive element which did not escape Sultan Abdülhamid II in this praise of Ottoman valor of bygone days and the simultaneous attempt to build a state to which non-Turks would willingly give their allegiance. If the Turks were glorified, it became difficult to convince the rest of the races entering into the composition of the empire that they would be placed on an equal plane in the constitutional empire that Kemal was offering them. It is probably this contradiction which, in part, caused the government to exile Namık Kemal when his appeal to patriotic sentiment in his play *The Fatherland* got an enthusiastic response from his audience. The play[159] was a glorification of Turkish courage and patriotism. It showed that Namık Kemal was not conscious of the impossibility of convincing the minorities of the empire of the value of a theory which united the glorification of Turkish conquests and of a Moslem army with a sincere concern for the problems of the nations which made up the empire. During his last exile, by writing an Ottoman history, the idea of which had been suggested to him by a desire to investigate the military ac-

[158] Editorial, *Hürriyet*, May 10, 1869.
[159] See above, Chapter I.

331

complishments of the Turks, Namık Kemal showed himself to be more concerned with the glorious past of the Turks than the creation of a new Ottoman nation. He could hardly be blamed for this in view of the already obvious fact that the people making up the Ottoman Empire were not interested in Ottomanism. Toward the end of his active life as a theorist and pamphleteer, Namık Kemal, faced with an increasingly strong current of Pan-Slavism in the Balkans, gave up the idea of an *Ottoman nation* made up of various national and religious groups and seemed resigned to the loss of the greater part of the European holdings of the empire. His attention was turned toward the "Islamic people." What he hoped was that the *Ottoman state* could now be reinforced by the union, within its fold, of all Moslems,[160] with the help of the Ottoman "elder brothers."

VIII. The European Origins of Kemal's Ideas

Most conveniently for those interested in his ideas, Namık Kemal mentions in one of his writings those men in the stream of Western tradition of political thought to which he attributes the greatest importance. They are the following: Plato, Aristotle, Zeno, Cicero, Descartes, Bacon, Rousseau, Voltaire, Condorcet, Turgot, Robespierre, Danton, Garibaldi, Silvio Pellico.[161] In other sections of his works Namık Kemal praises Montesquieu, whom he calls "one who has reached the status of

[160] Namık Kemal, "İttihad-ı İslâm," *İbret*, June 27, 1872, in Özön, *Namık Kemal ve İbret*, pp. 74-78. On the occasion of a Yemenite demand for protection to the Ottoman Empire in 1872 Kemal was stimulated to respond as follows: "It is only from here that the multifarious achievements of our century can be heralded to Arabia. Thus the desired future prosperity of the Islamic Caliphate will be the contribution of the Turks in the first degree but also of the Arabs in the second." Namık Kemal, "Mütalaa," *İbret*, June 20, 1872, in Özön, *Namık Kemal ve İbret*, p. 53.

[161] Fevziye Abdullah Tansel, "Namık Kemalin Hukukî Fikirleri," *Türk Hukuk Tarihi Dergisi* (1949), I, 57, 58. Ebüzziya mentions among Kemal's unpublished translations Condorcet's *Sketch of a Historical Picture of the Progress of the Human Mind* and "some" of Bacon's works. Kaplan, *Namık Kemal*, p. 32.

[supreme] teacher in the science of politics"[162] and speaks of his *Esprit des Lois*. Still other political thinkers whose works, as well as names, are mentioned include Locke, whose Carolinian constitution is referred to in one instance,[163] and Rousseau whose *Contrat Social*[164] and Polish constitution are mentioned.[165] To these influences must be added that of the French historian Volney.[166]

Finally the French romantic writers as a whole influenced Kemal. Of these Western antecedents Namık Kemal derived the theory of popular sovereignty from Rousseau. He seems to have obtained his ideas about the double contract from Locke; he definitely owed his theory of the separation of powers to Montesquieu; he was indebted to Volney for his analysis of the decadence of the Ottoman Empire and to the romantic writers for his emphasis on feeling and emotion as well as for his conception of culture.

That Namık Kemal owed his conception of popular sovereignty and of the origins of society to Rousseau may be seen in the fashion in which he described the creation of the first "normative force" to be "invented" in society. Note the similarity of his wording with Rousseau's expression: "Trouver une forme d'association . . . par laquelle chacun, s'unissant à tous, n'obéisse pourtant qu'à lui-même, et reste aussi libre qu'auparavant."[167]

Again, in the instances in which Kemal speaks of the state as a "moral person," it is the reflexion of Rousseau's "Corps moral et collectif."[168] Rousseau, however, did not accept the

[162] Namık Kemal, "Sadaret," *Hürriyet*, March 1, 1869, p. 1. Ebüzziya mentions an unpublished translation of the "Esprit des Lois." Kaplan, *Namık Kemal*, p. 32.
[163] Namık Kemal, *Osmanlı Tarihi*, p. 8.
[164] Namık Kemal, "*Usul-u Meşveret*," p. 5. According to Ebüzziya, Namık Kemal translated the *Contrat* although this translation was not published. Kaplan, *Namık Kemal*, p. 32.
[165] Namık Kemal, *Osmanlı Tarihi*, p. 8.
[166] See above, p. 316f.
[167] *Contrat Social* in Vaughan, *The Political Writings*, II, 32. Liv. I, ch. vi.
[168] *Ibid.*, p. 33.

double contract and Kemal, who was loath to get involved in the consequences that stemmed from a theory of the "general will," therefore turned to Locke for the double contract.

Kemal's opposition to the idea of a general will may be traced, in turn, to the ideas of Emile Acollas. Acollas was a French jurist who for some time gave Kemal private lessons in law in Paris. He had been fairly well known under the Second Empire in France as an advocate of the reduction of the power of the central government. Imprisoned for conspiracy on the eve of the Franco-Prussian War, his first move in 1871 upon the foundation of the French Republic, was to demand the authorization to teach courses in civil law to the workers. According to Acollas, democracy's most important component was individual independence. His life, which he lived along clearly Proudhonian-humanitarian-socialistic lines, links him in the last analysis to an aspect of continental liberalism which had been evolving in an anti-Rousseauan direction.[169]

Of all the European ideas to which he was exposed, Kemal seems to have been impressed by that of the separation of powers almost as much as that of popular sovereignty. To him it was quite clear that as long as legislation was enacted and executed by the same body, the system of government would be absolutistic.[170]

Cevdet Perin, in his work on the influence of French literature on the literature of the Tanzimat, reaches the conclusion

---

[169] For Acollas, see Georges Weill, "Acollas," *Encyclopedia of Social Sciences* (1930), I, 420. Compare Namık Kemal's ideas with Acollas' following statement: "La société n'est qu'une collectivité qui n'a ni plus de droits ni plus de devoirs que les individus dont elle est composée." Emile Acollas, *La Declaration des Droits de l'Homme de 1789 Commentée* (Paris, A. Chevalier Moresc, ed., 1885), p. 192.

I am drawing a parallel between Acollas' and Kemal's ideas fully aware that the report of the contact between the two men has been questioned as resting only on Ebüzziya's words. See Fevziye Abdullah Tansel's bibliographical criticism in *Belleten* (1943), VII, 207. Kemal's taking lessons from Acollas was first reported in *Kemal Beyin Tercüme-i Hâli* (Istanbul, 1326), a work I could not see. The similarity between Kemal's ideas and certain aspects of Acollas' theories remains striking.

[170] Namık Kemal, "Wa-shāwirhum," p. 1; "El hak," p. 4.

that Namık Kemal's literary works show him to have been in
the romantic tradition.[171] Perin goes on to state that what made
Namık Kemal a romantic was his personality and not the
influences to which he was exposed. A much more plausible
explanation, however, is suggested by the same author when
he admits that the generation that was influential in the 1860's
in Turkey, and therefore the generation that influenced Kemal,
had studied in Europe at the height of the romantic movement
and that for this generation, which was out of touch with
Europe, Europe still meant the romantic Europe of the
1830's.[172]

Also of romantic origin in Namık Kemal's writings is his
conception of the hero.[173] Kemal's biographies of the great
figures of Islamic history,[174] as well as many of his plays,[175]
show his attraction to charismatic figures who galvanize the
people into action. This glorification of the individual is different from that which had existed in Ottoman popular
épopées of the classical times, for Kemal uses it with the aim of
arousing the patriotic feelings of his audience. It was a call to
action rather than a mere recounting of prowesses.[176]

There is no doubt that Kemal's insistence on feeling as
sometimes superior to reason as well as the fieriness of his
style were of romantic origin. It is probably to this that Ziya
once alluded in dismissing Kemal's style as being copied from
"French poets."[177]

A final romantic strain reminiscent this time of Herder

[171] Cevdet Perin, *Tanzimat Edebiyatında Fransız Tesiri* (Istanbul, Pulhan Matbaası, 1946), p. 153.

[172] *Ibid.*, p. 152.

[173] This point has been extensively analyzed by Kaplan, *Namık Kemal*,
pp. 150-158. However, Kemal's highest admiration was for the French
classics. See *ibid.*, p. 149.

[174] See Namık Kemal, *Evrak-ı Perişan* (Istanbul, Matbaa-i Osmaniye,
1301/1883-1884).

[175] *Vatan Yahut Silistre* (Istanbul, 1290/1873-1874); *Akif Bey* (Istanbul,
1290/1873-1874); *Celaleddin Harzemşah* (Istanbul, 1292/1875).

[176] For Namık Kemal's own conception of the theater as a call to action,
see Kaplan, *Namık Kemal*, p. 142.

[177] Ismail Hikmet [Ertaylan], *Türk Edebiyatı Tarihi*, I, 169-170.

appears in Kemal's preface to his *Ottoman History* in such statements as:

"Human society, which is a moral presence every parcel of which is made up of a man, cannot divest itself of all content and inheritances suddenly and . . . assume new form and content.

"It is on the strength of this conclusion that the divine law posits that while statutes may be changed with time, customs are unchangeable."[178]

It is to such utterances that must be traced back the ideas of Turkish nationalism as they developed during the twentieth century.

[178] Namık Kemal, *Osmanlı Tarihi*, p. 3. For the influence of Montesquieu's historicism as a possible origin of such conceptions see below, Chapter XI.

Ziya Paşa: Philosophical Insecurity

BOTH the personality and the career of Ziya Paşa differed from those of Kemal. The outstanding characteristic of Ziya Paşa, and one which has been often mentioned, was his experience as an administrator; Namık Kemal, on the other hand, was more of a theorist. Thus, while Kemal's articles more often than not have to do with general principles of politics, Ziya Paşa's are, in the majority, concerned with bettering administrative practice in the Ottoman Empire. With regard to their respective personalities, Ziya was a much more cautious man than Kemal. He did not entirely approve of Kemal's romantic *panache* and thought of the rest of the Young Ottomans as somewhat naïve. This might be due to the fact that at the time he joined the Young Ottomans, Ziya had already had considerable political experience and a somewhat longer record of opposition to Âli Paşa than had the Young Ottomans.

Ziya's comparative lack of fervor is one of the reasons for which he has not been accorded the same position as Kemal in the Pantheon of Turkish patriots.

Ziya Paşa's father was a minor customs employee.[1] His son, born in 1825, was able to complete the local Koranic school and was then admitted to one of the two academies established by Reşid Paşa.[2] The recollections of one of Ziya's school companions shows that even at this time students were aware of the upper-class status acquired by the children of important Tanzimat statesmen. The latter were being sent to the *Mekteb-i Maarif-i Adliyye*, one of the two schools mentioned above, where they were provided with special amenities. The twin

---

[1] Ismail Hikmet [Ertaylan], *Ziya Paşa: Hayatı ve Eserleri* (İstanbul, Kanaat Kütüphanesi, 1932), p. 5.

[2] [Ziya Paşa], "Ziya Paşanın Evvan-ı Tıfliyeti Hakkında Makalesi," *Mecmua-i Ebüzziya* (15 Rebiülahir 1298-1 Cemaziyülevvel 1298), I, 404-409.

school to which Ziya Paşa went, however, was one which provided scholarships to every student but which also lacked the amenities that were to be found at the *Mekteb-i Maarif*. This "poor man's school" was called *Mekteb-i İrfan*. The competition between the two institutions seems to have been fierce, the overtones of a moralistic crusade against favoritism being present both in the attitude of the students and that of the teachers of the *Mekteb-i İrfan*.[3]

Upon graduating from this school, Ziya Paşa entered the Translation Bureau. There he came under the influence of one of the last Turkish classicists, the poet Fatin Efendi, under whose guidance he acquired a vast store of classical Ottoman-Islamic culture.[4]

Ziya Paşa, like Şinasi, was a protégé of Reşid Paşa. He did, therefore, feel the greatness of the Westernizing moves of Reşid Paşa, whom he praised in his poetry composed during the happy days when the latter was still alive. But an examination of these very verses showed that he divided his admiration between the grand vizier and that enlightened member of the ulema, the Şeyhülislâm Arif Hikmet Bey.[5]

In 1855 Ziya Paşa was appointed secretary to the Imperial Palace. Edhem Paşa, a product of the École des Mines, was, at the time, commanding general of the palace troops, and he advised Ziya to learn a foreign language. It was as a result of his influence that Ziya Paşa concentrated on French and started translations from this language. The first of these was a translation of Viardot's *History of the Moors of Spain*.[6] This was followed by Lavallée's *History of the Inquisition*.[7] The second of these works was an indirect defense of Islam in that it pointed to the inhumanity of the methods used by the Inquisition. Thus quite early the defensive cast of Ziya's thought was

---

[3] We gather this from the remarks of Ziya's schoolmate, İbrahim Halil Aşçıdede, whose unpublished memoirs are quoted in Ergin, *Türkiye Maarif Tarihi*, p. 325 ff.

[4] Ertaylan, *Ziya Paşa*, p. 15.

[5] *Ibid.*

[6] *Endülüs Tarihi* (Dersaadet, Eser Kütüphanesi, 1304/1886-1887), 4 vols.

[7] *Ibid., Engizisyon Tarihi* (Istanbul, Matbaa-i Ebüzziya, 1299/1881-1882).

visible. It is probable at that time too that he set out to translate Rousseau's *Emile*.

In 1859 Mustafa Reşid Paşa died, and shortly thereafter (in 1861) Sultan Abdülmecid died too. The preponderant influence of Reşid Paşa thus gave way to the influence of Fuad and Âli Paşa. An attempted intrigue by Ziya to discredit Âli failed and earned Ziya Âli's enmity. Ziya Paşa was progressively pulled away from the main stream of the business of the state, being appointed first Minister of Police, then Minister to Athens, and finally assistant governor in an Anatolian province.[8] In the following four years he was sent to various distant posts in Anatolia, and purposely given new assignments as often as possible. This was Âli's way of making him expiate his intrigues. During Ziya Paşa's final stay in the Province of Amasya, Âli Paşa had it so arranged that an investigation committee was sent to check on his activities. The relentless hatred of Âli Paşa and the abuses he had witnessed during his administrative career convinced Ziya Paşa that he should take a hand at the problem of political reform in Turkey. This accounts for his collaboration with the discontented element in the capital. Even though misunderstandings arose between the two main Young Ottoman leaders during their common exile in Europe,[9] he was the closest collaborator of Namık Kemal for a long time, and some of the more important articles in the *Hürriyet* came from his pen.

When Sultan Abdülaziz was finally deposed, and a constitutional commission created, he participated in its work.[10] When, shortly thereafter, the first Turkish parliament was dissolved by Abdülhamid II, not to be convened for thirty-two years, Ziya Paşa was made to resume his administrative posts. Cut off from the intellectual world of the capital, he lived a miserable life in various provinces until 1880, the date of his death (May 17, 1880).

[8] Ertaylan, *Ziya Paşa*, pp. 26-31.

[9] See above, Chapter II.

[10] Although there is no evidence, as stated in Tanpınar, *XIXncu Asır*, p. 287, that he prepared the drafts of the Ottoman constitution.

Namık Kemal had failed to achieve a true synthesis between East and West. Yet in his system East and West were more or less in equilibrium. This is true both of his writings and of his life, through which runs a strong vein of commitments to the achievement of such an ideal synthesis. Neither Ziya's life nor his writings are so consistent. There are times when modern ideas are definitely on the upsurge. This appears, for instance, in his articles in the *Hürriyet* entitled "Şiir ve Inşa'," where Ziya[11] destroys the Turkish classical style as cumbersome, complicated, and a means of keeping the people in subservience. Yet, on his return to Turkey, in his preface to his anthology entitled *Harabat*, he seems to have been of the opposite opinion.[12]

A similar ambivalence appears, as we shall see below, in Ziya's proposals for political and educational reform. The best way to pinpoint the origin of this vacillation is to follow closely some of the themes in his poetry. The overriding metaphysical anxiety which has been found to prevail there is the best indication of the deep spiritual crisis created in him by his encounter with Western thought.[13]

Ziya Paşa's ideas concerning the state are quite similar to those of Kemal, but there are three aspects of his contributions which distinguish them from the latter. First, Ziya was a man intimately acquainted with the Palace and thus obsessed with the idea of the imperial function. A special facet of this approach was Ziya's study of the decline of this function, which according to him paralleled and was the cause of the decline of the empire. Secondly, Ziya was a cultural traditionalist in more ways than Kemal. This accounts for his vehemence against the adoption of "Frankish customs" and his fear that the *geist* of Ottoman culture was about to disappear. Finally, he was not so much interested in freedom as he was in the elimination of the new bureaucrats.

[11] See Ziya Paşa, "Şiir ve Inşa," *Hürriyet*, September 7, 1868, pp. 4-7.
[12] For this work see Gibb, *Ottoman Poetry*, v, 78. For the opposite view see Ismail Hikmet, *Ziya Paşa*, pp. 95-98.
[13] See Tanpınar, *XIXncu Asır*, pp. 294, 295.

The most complete statement of his fundamental political theory may be found in a series of articles which appeared in the *Hürriyet*.[14] In this series he first turned his attention to the origin of society and built step by step an explanation of Ottoman decline.

Ziya Paşa explained the origin of the earliest political ties as follows:

"If one ever brings to mind the fashion in which society arose and which in turn gave rise to tribal origin and government, reason leads one to the following explanation: at first a few families were roaming completely naked through the mountains, remaining on an elevation in summer and living in lower parts in the winter, inside caves and feeding on wild fruit. With the establishment of contacts between families, this roaming was undertaken [by a few families] at one time. The single families who saw two or three families gathered in one place joined them, and thus a new form was evolved and the community progressively came into being. However, ambition and greed and the desire of the victorious to subjugate the defeated being congenital tendencies of human character, the result of daily intercourse between families was the rise of dispute and enmity. To settle these disputes a principle became necessary [*bir hükmün vucudu iktiza etmiştir*]. Thus the wisest and the oldest [man] among the families was chosen and these words were said to him: 'Because of your superior qualities, the members of the community have agreed that you be brought to the office of government. You shall serve them by taking care of such and such a matter. Since you consequently will not have time to gather nourishment like others, as long as you occupy this function everybody or every family shall give you thus much victuals every day. If you do not fulfill your duty satisfactorily, they shall find somebody to replace you.' In short he was brought to this office with the words:

[14] Ziya Paşa, "Hâtıra," *Hürriyet*, December 14, 1868, pp. 5-8; January 4, 1869, pp. 4-8; February 15, 1869, pp. 1-5; March 1, 1869, pp. 6-8; March 8, 1869, pp. 6-9; March 15, 1869, pp. 6-8; March 29, 1869, pp. 7, 8; April 5, 1869, pp. 5-8; April 12, 1869, pp. 7, 8; May 3, 1869, pp. 1-4.

'You shall be a paid servant of the community.' When with the passing of time the community grew and houses and villages were built and other families began to gather in various places in a similar fashion and were shaped into society, and when disputes began to arise between them and the judge who had been chosen to settle disputes was not sufficient any longer, the need was felt for a superior chief to protect the community from the attacks of the enemy and to enforce the execution of the orders of the judge. Thus, again the one person who was best known among all families, for his ability and material spirit, was again brought to the executive office of government with a salary. Thus the Emirs and the monarchs were at first paid servants of the community who were given the duty of ministering to its needs and performing services for its benefit. Later, when societies grew larger and took the form of tribes and nations, the task fulfilled by the Emir assumed greater importance and since naturally respect and prestige [for the office] increased as it became more and more important, the title of Emir was transformed into that of King or 'Padişah,' and with the passing of time and centuries, the foundations [of this institution] were forgotten, and it was believed that pomp and luxury and the executive power were beyond question. Thus a situation arose which completely contradicted the original purpose. It was now believed that the people were no more than the servants of the King, among the majority the King was believed to be the master. Matters went so far that to keep the people from being enlightened about this secret, i.e., the seizure of their natural rights, the governments of antiquity used them as they would cattle, and undertook by guile to keep science and learning a monopoly of the spiritual caste, and the simple people were always kept in blind ignorance, and the cultural patrimony of the majority of humanity began to consist of such things as stones and trees and spiders and hellfire. And this was only natural, for just as insects who live in dirt think that no other state exists than that in which they find themselves, when men are born in centuries of

oppression they go on in life believing oppression to be custom-
ary and slavery to be a requisite of nature. And after a while
they meet with disaster and decline. The number of nations
which have thus been born and lived and died has not been
ascertained. However, these precautions were effective only as
long as ignorance and blindness continued, but when civilization
began to spread and the eyes of humanity began to open with
the light of science, all nations saw the state in which they were
and began to sue for their rights.

"Those whose support was derived from being in power
decided not to change their unbounded rule, and used the very
power and force they had taken from the people against the
people. This conflict gave rise to many civil revolutions and
national wars. A few nations such as Rome and Sparta and
Athens established republican rule to escape from unbounded
tyranny, but even then, those who were appointed to political
office made it their aim to use this power without recognizing
any bounds. This too gave rise to innumerable clashes and
troubles. While these clashes were taking place in the world,
the exalted religion of Islam arose. The saintly person of the
Prophet did not establish a sultanate, and the four [first]
Caliphs were brought to power by the election of the Companions of the Prophet. The affairs of the state were decided by
the votes of selected Companions of the Prophet and carried
out in accordance with the sacred law of the Şeriat."[15]

Ziya Paşa went on from there to show that Islamic rulers
had never taken the title of "king" but were content with
being called "the leader of the faithful" and the "successor of
the prophet of God." Then he added, "Later independent
cities and government and states and Sultanates arose by way
of forceful imposition, and every Islamic government, as long
as it exercised its duty of providing justice and right by way of
conforming to the principles of the Şeriat, reached a state of
progress and happiness and the people had richness and

[15] Ziya Paşa, "Hâtıra," *Hürriyet*, 25 Şaban 1285/December 14, 1868,
pp. 7, 8.

repose."[16] This was the state of the Ottoman Empire up to the end of the sixteenth century.

It appears from this exposé that, like Kemal, Ziya Paşa believed the state of nature to have been an historical occurrence.[17] As to the particular characteristics of this state of nature, the similarity with Kemal is also apparent. Ziya Paşa did not regard the state of nature as a state of "peace, good-will and mutual assistance."[18] He considered it a "perpetual contention for Honours, richess and authority."[19] However, the comparison between Ziya's ideas and those of English political theorists would be somewhat misleading since there are no indications that Ziya ever came directly in contact with their thought. A comparison that would be justified, on the other hand, is one that would link him with Rousseau. Ziya Paşa is known to have translated the *Émile*.[20] The *Émile*, on the other hand, although basically a treatise on education, is larded with frequent references to such ideas as the state of nature, the social compact, and the general will. While there are no extensive descriptions of the state of nature in the book, another work of Rousseau, the *Discours sur l'Inégalité*, contains an analysis of the formation of societies which is strikingly reminiscent of Ziya's theory. Rousseau states:

"Les hommes érrant jusqu'ici dans les bois ayant pris une assiette plus fixe se rapprochent lentement, se réunissent en diverses troupes et forment ensuite dans chaque contrée une nation particulière, mure de moeurs et de caractère non par des

[16] *Ibid.*, January 4, 1869, p. 4.

[17] Ziya Paşa, "Hâtıraya zeyl," *Hürriyet*, January 4, 1869, p. 4. Locke's stand is the same. See Gough's "Introduction" to Locke's *Second Treatise*, p. XVIII, for Locke's position. For the most complete and authoritative argument that Rousseau believed in the state of nature as an historical event see Dérathé, *Rousseau et la Science Politique*, p. 132.

[18] Locke, *Second Treatise*, II, 17.

[19] Thomas Hobbes, *Leviathan or the Matter, Forme and Power of a Commonwealth Ecclesiastical and Civil* (ed. by Michael Oakeshott, Oxford, Basil Blackwell, 1946), p. 460.

[20] See Ziya Paşa, "Jean Jacques Rousseau ile Émile'i hakkında," *Mecmua-i Ebüzziya* (15 Cemaziyülevvel 1330/May 2, 1911), pp. 104-110.

règlements et des lois mais par l'influence commune du climat."[21]

The first point at which traces of Islamic political theory at odds with Rousseau appear in Ziya's scheme is his conception of the "community," which is much looser than that of "society" found in Rousseau. In Ziya Paşa's theory the community comes about as a result of an agreement which appears to be tacit, but which is so tacit as to be almost nonexistent. Here again, the looseness of the Islamic conception of the community as primarily a "union of proselytizers"[22] with no tight juridical definition of the nature of the union permitted Ziya to leave his thought unclear. It should be noted, in this connection, that just like Kemal and in contradistinction to Rousseau, Ziya had in mind a double contract of society.

The next step in the establishment of government, the so-called "contract of government," consists, in Ziya's theory, in giving some power to a judge so that he can arbitrate disputes arising in the community. Since the aim of the Enlightenment thinkers had been to devise a theory by which the executive could be held responsible, the investigations of these thinkers was primarily an investigation of the nature of the relations between the community and the executive. It is significant, then, that Ziya Paşa exploited another line of thought and made the judge the first person to whom authority had been delegated in the name of the community.

It is probable that this characteristic of Ziya Paşa's system reflects again an aspect of Islamic theory, namely, the precedence of law over the state. It points to the fact that Ziya Paşa, just as Kemal, was not accustomed to think of government as machinery and that for him government meant the dispensation of justice rather than the presence of a machinery of the state. The second facet of Ziya Paşa's theory, i.e., the statement that the community does not surrender its sovereignty to its magistrate but holds him continuously responsible, indicates an

[21] Vaughan, *The Political Writings*, I, 173.
[22] Khadduri, *War and Peace*, p. 17.

even more extensive conception of responsibility than that which is to be found in Locke,[23] for Ziya Paşa speaks of the judge as a "paid servant" of the community. This absence of a surrender of sovereignty may reflect the influences of Rousseau, and be traced to such statements contained in the *Emile* as that a people cannot unconditionally alienate its liberty to its chief.[24] That no surrender of sovereignty is meant in Ziya Paşa's theory can also be seen in the fact that he does not consider this step—the appointment of the judge—to be indicative of a qualitative change in the fabric of civil society. The qualitative change, or, to use Ziya Paşa's own terminology, the change-over from "community" to "society," occurs only at a later date and is simply the result of the growth of the community.

The appointment of the judge is followed by the appointment of an executive solely to help the judge in this task. Thus it appears that for Ziya Paşa the command of a sovereign is only a subsidiary factor in the growth of government. The next stage in this theory is that the ruler, once he has established a monopoly of power, uses this power to foster the idea that the sovereign is not responsible to the people and also to establish his own tyrannical rule over them.

What is striking about this interpretation of the history of government is that, as Kemal did, Ziya neglects to mention the fact that in Islam authority is a divine category and that this theory is based on the Koranic dictum to obey leaders. In Ziya Paşa's writings, the Şeriat seems to lose entirely its characteristic of a fundamental statement of political obligation and becomes no more than a perfect statement of law—the best available means for keeping the ruler from oppressing people. In general, Ziya Paşa's theory of contract, by making this contract one between the people and their magistrates, is completely at odds with the Islamic theory of a contract entered

---

[23] Sabine, *A History of Political Theory*, p. 534. Locke "retained the older view that the grant of the community divests the people of power so long as the government is faithful to its duties."

[24] *Emile*, in Vaughan, *The Political Writings*, II, 150.

into between the people and God. What Ziya Paşa was attempting to do here is fairly easy to grasp. He was trying to establish the theoretical bases—whether at odds with Islam or not—to justify such statements of his as: "The efforts of the Young Turkey Party are primarily directed to the substitution of the *will of the nation*, that is to say of the population of the Empire without distinction of race or religion, for the arbitrary power of a few individuals."[25] Ziya Paşa did not seem to think that this attempt to by-pass the religious foundations of obligation should deter him from demanding, as he repeatedly did, a wider use of religious law.[26]

A certain parallelism has emerged from the comparison between the system of Ziya Paşa and the ideas of Rousseau. But then the positions adopted by the two differ considerably in the steps that they indicated would remedy the ills of government. For Rousseau, the theoretical premise of an unalienable sovereignty was reflected in the criticism he made of parliamentary government as giving the right to the people of legislating only once, i.e., at the time they delegated their powers to the government; thereafter, Rousseau pointed out, the hands of the community were tied.[27] Rousseau therefore concluded that only in small communities could one devise practical means of providing for the continuous control of government. This view appears in the *Emile*, in Rousseau's proposals to set up a "federative association," a conglomerate of politically wieldy units of small size.[28]

But Ziya Paşa had quite different plans, for if he believed like Namık Kemal that the salvation of the empire lay in the creation of a national assembly; he was extremely timid even in proposing such a mild step toward establishing the responsi-

---

[25] Ziya Paşa, letter to the French newspaper *Liberté*; French original and English translation in the *Levant Herald* (Istanbul), October 20, 1868. (Italics in quotation are the author's.)

[26] Ziya Paşa, "Mes'ele-yi Müsavat," *Hürriyet*, October 5, 1868, pp. 1, 2; "Hâtıra," *Hürriyet*, December 14, 1868, p. 8; Ziya Paşa, "Fuad Paşanın Vasiyetnamesi," *Hürriyet*, November 1, 1869, p. 1.

[27] Sabine, *History of Political Theory*, p. 535.

[28] *Emile*, in Vaughan, *The Political Writings*, II, 157, 158.

bility of the sultan. The ideals that he held on this subject were expressed in an article that Ziya Paşa wrote about an imaginary conversation that he had with Sultan Abdülaziz in a dream. The striking element in this piece was the fact that, while in the article Ziya Paşa tried to establish a vague parliamentary mechanism for Turkey, at the same time he exerted himself to explain away the "revolt" of the Young Ottomans. The tone of this dialogue[29] and the anguish manifested by Ziya Paşa in trying to explain to the sultan why he had been driven to criticize government showed his respect for the monarchy. Ziya Paşa's actions at the time he wrote this article also substantiated such an attitude, since it is known that while he was in London in 1867 he could not resist the temptation of preparing a long petition which he expected to submit to the sultan during the latter's official visit to France and about which his colleagues were in the dark.[30]

The scheme of government proposed by Ziya Paşa in the "dream sequence" article reflected quite clearly his respect for the monarchic principle. For one thing, despite his proposal to create a national assembly, Ziya Paşa immediately qualified this proposal by the statement that the "legitimate independence" of the monarch would in no way be curtailed: "For since the National Assembly, which has been thought of by your humble servant, would not be anything that would trespass the limits set by the order of the Şeriat, just as the independence of the Sultan is bound by religious law, so with the [new] system would it be limited. For example, what is there in holding ministers responsible before a National Assembly for their actions that could be considered a limitation of your will? Can it be considered a sign of your independence if

[29] Ziya Paşa, "Sultan Abdülaziz Han-Ziya Bey-Âli Paşa," *Hürriyet*, October 1869, p. 2. Published separately as a pamphlet in Latin script, *Edibi Muhterem Ziya Paşanın Rüyası* (Istanbul, Şirket-i Mürettibiye Matbaası, 1932).

[30] Kuntay, *Namık Kemal*, I, 436. For the text of this petition see *Cennetmekân Sultan Abdülaziz Han'in Londraya Azimetinde Takdim Olunan Merhum Ziya Paşanın Arzuhali* (Dersaadet, n.p., 1328/1909).

ministers feel free to oppress the people and rob the treasury? Would you want such independence?"[31]

Ziya Paşa agreed that the subjects of the Ottoman Empire had not as yet reached the state "where they can distinguish their own interests," but he was adamant in stating that it was good government and the institution of representation itself which would achieve these results. Characteristic of this very same stand, however, were his protestations that the sultan should take a more active hand in the affairs of the state and restrain his grand vizier from doing the same. Up to the last, Ziya Paşa was faithful to the monarchic principle and when he was the only person left on the editorial staff of the *Hürriyet* which he published by lithography in Geneva, he spent his energies rebuking Mehmed Bey's *İnkılâb* and its advocacy of tyrannicide.

Thus, while Namık Kemal hid behind a screen of praises for the House of Osman his fear that a sultan as incompetent as Abdülaziz would undermine the prestige of this dynasty, Ziya Paşa earnestly believed that the decline of the Ottoman Empire was due to the degenerescence of the imperial function. Since Ziya was affected by European libertarian currents, he also included in his proposals a scheme whereby the bureaucrats whom he despised would be made responsible to a national assembly, but he was in no way frightened by the prospect of a resurgence of irresponsibility on the part of the sultan. He lived long enough, though, to witness the sight of exactly such a resurgence during the reign of Sultan Abdülhamid II (1876-1909).

The tacit assumption that no harm would come from the sovereign and that therefore he did not need to be held accountable was one which was in harmony with Islamic conceptions of government. On the other hand, one of the implicit elements on the theory of parliamentary government was that the king was responsible to the people. This responsibility had later been thrown on the shoulders of the prime minister as

[31] Ziya Paşa, "Sultan Abdülaziz Han-Ziya Bey-Âli Paşa," *Hürriyet*, October 11, 1869, p. 2.

the result of the historical development of parliamentary practice in England. But the theory of parliamentary government was elaborated under the dark aura of a royal execution and it reflected this origin. For Ziya Paşa, however, rebellion was such a bogey as to cause him to write the following letter of protest to the editor of the French newspaper *Liberté* while he was in exile:

"A letter of the 29th September, published in the North Eastern Correspondence and reproduced by other organs, states that a conspiracy had been discovered at Constantinople and that twenty-six persons have been arrested. Among the number are mentioned M. Condouri, a rich merchant of Odessa and a Russian subject, M. Altinji. . . . The other individuals arrested are alleged to be Ottomans belonging to the Young Turkey Committee, I protest against the assertion relative to that party. M. Condouri and Altinji are totally unknown to us and the idea of associating the Young Turkish Party with Greek or Russian subjects is as burlesque as the project of assassination attributed to these men is criminal."[32]

Ziya Paşa's use of the state of nature as a starting point for his political analyses, his use of the conception of an unalienable sovereignty and his secular theory of contract are all factors which point to the Western origins of his theory. As in Namık Kemal's ideas, the influence of the Enlightenment may also be seen in his attempt to use the concept of the state of nature and the law of nature in historical interpretations. But in introducing these principles in his political theory he had to do violence to some of his Islamic precepts.

The first thing that comes to mind in this respect is his ambivalent attitude with regard to the "natural goodness" of man. It would seem that, since he translated the *Émile*, a treatise of education based on the assumption of the naturally good instincts of man, he was confident that the "natural inclinations" of man were toward goodness. Yet we have seen

[32] Ziya Paşa, letter to *Liberté*; French original and English translation in the *Levant Herald* (Istanbul), October 20, 1868. This was a reference to Huseyin Vasfi Paşa's conspiracy. See above, Chapter VII.

that this is not true. To a basically Islamic pessimism about the "nature of man" Ziya added his own peculiar sense of foreboding.[33] Two explanations come to mind at this point in elucidating his stand: first, it has been shown that Rousseau's ideas about the "natural goodness" of man are much more complex than one usually allows for and we might expect the contradictions in Ziya's thought to reflect this complexity. In the light of Ziya's other writings, however, a simpler explanation suggests itself. Ziya admired the quality of simplicity, unclutteredness, common sense that showed in the educational system of Rousseau. Already he had protested against the complication of the traditional methods of instruction in the empire. Now he tried to show what could be substituted for it. The deeper philosophical implications of his educational stand did not trouble him. Yet, if he was not obliged to clarify his stand in the matter of an educational philosophy at odds with some of his fundamental beliefs, in political theory he involved himself in contradictions which showed the divergent sources of his inspiration more clearly.

Another way in which to place Ziya Paşa's educational ideas in perspective is to view them as part of the activism which is so characteristic of the thought of Ottomans who were influenced by Western ideas. Ziya Paşa's article on his own youth which was part of the preface he had prepared for his translation of the *Émile* shows this quite clearly.[34] The entire piece is a recounting of the waste of talent that resulted from entrusting children to male governesses ["*Lala*"], usually older domestics who were too feeble to do household chores.

According to Ziya, man is not very different from animals in his "natural condition," and while he stands out from among animals by his ability to manufacture tools, he shows even greater ability in decimating his kind.[35] It is only the Prophet's divine message in the form of the Şeriat which brings an end

[33] Tanpınar, *XIXncu Asır*, p. 297.

[34] [Ziya Paşa], "Ziya Paşanın Evvan-ı tıfliyeti hakkında makalesi," *Mecmua-i Ebüzziya* (15 Rebiülevvel 1298), I, 404-409.

[35] Ziya Paşa, "Hâtıra," *Hürriyet*, December 14, 1868, p. 6.

to this social chaos. But there are instances in which Ziya Paşa speaks of "civilization" and "the opening up of men's minds" as being significant forces in history which made for progress without the benefit of the Şeriat. Even more striking are the instances where he specifically attributes political evolution and betterment to the impersonal forces of history. "Since the present century is the time of humanity's youth, the idea of liberty is spreading through the world like a river which has overflown its banks so that such ways of self-defense adopted by tyrants as imprisonment and exile and even murder cannot make up a dam that will stop its flow."[36]

Another variant on the same theme is the idea that tyranny has a degenerative effect on people and that civilization is dependent on good government. Which idea, then, did Ziya accept as true? That man's appetites could be controlled by a scheme devised by himself—i.e., good government, or did men have to wait for the divine message of the Şeriat?

Ziya Paşa's ultimate rationale for "freedom" was that God had congenitally endowed man with freedom. The vagueness of such a conception allowed it to be elaborated in various ways. What Ziya Paşa used it for was to expand the idea that freedom without law could not be conceived: "Elaborate laws were made according to the particular composition of every nation and according to its characteristics and mores. There has never existed at any time a tribe which lived in society without being tied to a more or less regular system of laws. Even among the savages, there have been found traditions special to them which had the force of law. Thus liberty is found with attachment to laws."[37]

Ziya stated further that these laws were part of a system which was germane to a given people and that whenever changes were brought to the system, these people began to decline. In reality, what he wanted to express was the idea that the Şeriat could not be abandoned without the danger of

---

[36] Ziya Paşa, "Yeni Osmanlıların Ecille-i Azâsından . . . Ziya Beyefendi," *Hürriyet*, July 6, 1868, p. 2.
[37] *Ibid.*

degeneration and loss of cultural identity for the Ottomans. Here the consequence of Ziya's stand was not so much doing violence to Islamic fundamentals as getting involved in somewhat absurd conclusions. This happened when he attributed all European emigration to the American continent to such an abandonment of their old ways: "Every nation [*"millet"*] has its distinctive customs and ways of administration and civilization. It is one of the laws of nature that every individual earns his living in accordance with these laws. Thus every time these foundations are shaken a nation's means of livelihood is destroyed, and whenever this happens every type of mischief and upheavals and revolutions occur. An example of this may be seen in the situation of the people of France, England and Germany, many millions of whose artisans were living from the product of their handicraft. Then, with the advancement of education, inventions too increased and many of the products which used to be produced by hand began to be manufactured by machine."[38] Ergo, these populations migrated to America. It is difficult to trace the origin of this emphasis of Ziya's on the "spirit" of a society. Romantic origins do not stand out so clearly as in Kemal. Montesquieu's writings, however, yield some interesting parallels which might constitute the answer to the problem. Montesquieu did, indeed, believe in a "general spirit" animating a given state, a belief which has earned him a place among the fathers of historicism. Thus it is quite probable that Ziya's ideas originated in such theories of Montesquieu as that "there is in every nation a general spirit upon which power itself is founded. When it shocks this spirit, power settles its own foundation and thus necessarily checks itself."[39]

[38] Ziya Paşa, "Hâtıra," *Hürriyet*, May 3, 1869, p. 7.

[39] The passage runs: "C'est une erreur de croire qu'il y ait dans le monde une autorité humaine à tous les égards despotique; il n'y en a jamais eu, et il n'y en aura jamais; le pouvoir le plus immense est toujours borné par quelque coin. Que le grand-seigneur mette un nouvel impôt a Constantinople, un cri general lui fait d'abord trouver des limites qu'il n'avait pas connues. Un roi de Perse peut bien contraindre un fils à tuer son père ou un père de tuer son fils; mais obliger ses sujets de boire du vin, il ne le peut pas. Il y a dans

Ziya Paşa's ideas on the origin of obligation and his proposals for a national assembly were only part of what can be
called his political theory. For Ziya Paşa was also a patriot and
his greatest concern was for the weakening of the Ottoman
Empire that he alleged had come about after the Tanzimat.
The description he gave of this latter process sheds considerable light on the reasons for the crystallization of Turkish
patriotism in the middle of the nineteenth century. In his
articles he described at length the ruin of the Turkish trading
classes by European traders due to the privileges that had been
granted to the latter, the extent to which the Porte had been
cowed by Western Great Powers and the insolence of foreigners who exploited their privileged status to the utmost,
the humiliation of seeing the Christian subjects of the Porte
granted the special protection of the West, the financial ineptitude of the government, which because of the increased corruption was obliged to have recourse to larger and larger loans,
the fact that the Turkish traders seeing that they were being
pushed out of commerce went into government service and
thus placed an additional burden on the shoulders of the state,
the ignorance of the governmental elite and their inability to
muster any respect for the Ottoman state outside of Turkey—
all these were treated as factors having aggravated the developments which he had outlined in the series on the decline
of the Ottoman Empire.

Of all these factors the one that seemed to interest Ziya
Paşa most was the guarantee of equal treatment which had
been embodied in the Firman of Reforms of 1856. At the
time, one of the major accusations leveled against the Porte
had been that the Christian subjects of the Porte did not have
governmental careers open to them. The Porte had at first
countered by the argument that the Rescript of Gülhane had

---

chaque nation un esprit général, sur lequel la puissance même est fondée,
quand elle choque cet esprit, elle se choque elle-même, et elle s'arrête
nécessairement." Montesquieu, *Considérations sur les Causes de la Grandeur
des Romains et de leur Décadence* in *Oeuvres* (ed. by Masson, Paris, 1950),
I, Ch. XXII, 519.

established such equality in the law. Ziya Paşa saw the speciousness of this argument: "The equality which was proclaimed with the Hatt-ı Hümayun of Gülhane was restricted to private law, that is to everybody being afforded judicial remedy. Consequently to say that the Porte proclaimed complete [political] equality in the first place by passing the Rescript of Gülhane, is a statement of ignorance which is contrary to fact and merits being laughed at."[40] What Ziya Paşa objected to was the conception of what he called "equality in honors," viz., the provisions of the Firman of 1856 according to which employment was forcibly opened up to the minorities on a proportioned basis. And what he criticized was the basic postulate on which such provisions were founded, namely, the conception that the religious groups making up the Ottoman Empire should be granted civil and military offices in rough proportion to their numbers in the empire. He argued that to thus have one Moslem, one Jewish, one Catholic, and one Orthodox Greek general in the army would no more mean the granting of equality of status to the various minorities than would an obligation imposed on the sultan to change the color of his trousers every day of the week. Ziya Paşa concluded that what was really meant in the demands of the Great Powers was the establishment of "political rights." These, however, would not be obtained by employing Christians in the highest state functions but by providing them with an opportunity to control the government.

Despite a common attraction for historical explanations, one of the main differences between the political thought of Ziya and that of Kemal is that over and above his traditionalism Kemal may be described as deeply committed to the ideas of the Enlightenment, specially that of progress. Kemal's historical analyses are not so much devoted to find out *why* the Ottoman Empire declined as to discover *how* a juncture could be effected between Ottoman culture and the stream of Western progress. This factor is much less important in Ziya, whose

---

[40] Ziya Paşa, "Mes'eleyi Müsavat," *Hürriyet*, October 5, 1868, p. 3.

main contribution consists in a description of the causes of the disintegration of the empire.

According to Ziya, the main reasons for this decline should be sought in an event which happened approximately at the time of the death of Sultan Süleyman, namely, the practice fostered by the grand viziers of keeping princes of the imperial household in the dark about the affairs of the state.[41] Ziya Paşa illustrated this contention as follows: "None of the grand viziers of Mehmet the IInd or Selim the Ist or Süleyman the Magnificent were ever defeated in battle, but the Sultans who thereafter acceded to the Ottoman Throne became the victims of their ministers or of 'rowdies' or of those who used the latter as instruments of their policies. The Imperial power thus weakened day by day."[42]

In these historical passages appeared once again the theme of *gazâ* found in Namık Kemal's writings. According to Ziya it was the latter which had provided the cohesive force in the Ottoman Empire. In his opinion in earlier times the Ottoman army had relied for its strength on the "religious principle of rising to the beatific state of a *gazi*, while the men who made up European armies were dragged to the battlefield under the threat of the whip." With time this religious fervor waned,

---

[41] "Up to that date, princes of the Imperial family were sent to the provinces, and since it was part of imperial usage to study the 'achievements of man' and administrative practice under the guidance of the Ulema and savants who were detailed to their side, when these princes acceded to the throne, they personally took the reins of the state in their hands, and worked most diligently for the advancement and happiness of the state and the subjects." Ziya Paşa, "Hâtıra," *Hürriyet*, January 4, 1869, p. 4.

"The weekly *divans* met in the very presence of the *Padişah*, and the lowest individuals as well as the most highly placed, and Moslems and non-Moslems, all were secure in their rights as set in the *Şeriat*, and every judge was aware of the penalties to which he would be subject if he strayed from the path of the sacred law." *Ibid.*

These statements had a basis in historical fact. According to Gibb and Bowen, the decline of the sultan's power "corresponded to a growth, at least during the earlier part of the period during which it took place, in the power of the Grand Vizier. But it marked also a growth in what may be called caprice of government . . . the Ottoman government became decidedly less 'constitutional' than it had been." Gibb and Bowen, *Islamic Society*, I, I, 197.

[42] Ziya Paşa, "Hâtıra," *op.cit.*, p. 5.

thus causing a weakening of the army; on the other hand, Europeans devised better methods of induction and training. The reason which Ziya Paşa gave for the decrease in religious belief was that the Şeriat had not been enforced by the usurpers of the imperial function.[43]

Another consequence of the change of the sultan's position was that palace intrigues became the rule, and profit the most attractive aide of an official position.[44]

A vivid example of the consequences of the misrule of the viziers—and one which Ziya Paşa used to explain the reverses suffered by the Ottoman army during the eighteenth century —was the following: "Thus while Damad Ibrahim Paşa constructed waterfalls on the stream emptying into the Golden Horn, and decorated both banks with pleasure spots, and stuck candles on the back of turtles when tulips were in bloom, and let them loose in tulip gardens . . . thus aiming to erase from the mind of Sultan Ahmed the very thought of struggle, on the other hand, the Tsar of Russia, Peter, was building up St. Petersburg and the naval yards of Kronstadt, and reinforcing his army and his navy by the introduction of modern methods of training."[45]

Other illustrations followed; Ziya Paşa made the point, for example, that while every European power of importance had resident envoys in Istanbul, the Ottoman Empire for a long time had no such representative in Europe. The Ottoman Empire was thus unable to follow the changes which were taking place in Europe. Conversely, in Istanbul, European representatives rarely wandered outside of Pera, and used Greek interpreters to communicate with the Ottomans. These representatives thus got an erroneous idea of the "national customs of the Ottoman Nation." This mutual estrangement had been a

---

[43] "As the result of the Imperial power getting into the hands of the ministers and any Tom, Dick and Harry, the commands of the *Şeriat* began to be abandoned and as a consequence of the tyranny thereby created, other dispensers of justice arose, and these were the Janissaries, and every time despotic power became unbearable, the latter took action to modify its mode." *Ibid.*, p. 7.

[44] *Ibid.*   [45] *Ibid.*

factor which the Russians used to great advantage in their Middle Eastern policy. Empress Catherine the Second, for example, while on one hand engaged in waging war against Mustafa IV on the Danube, did not neglect, on the other hand, to win to her side such famous Europeans as Voltaire, Diderot, and d'Alembert, "whose very words were law in Europe" by such simple stratagems as honoring them with a few lines in her own handwriting and "clever pronouncements" and gifts, and reaped good will by distributing bribes among the European press. This policy caused a reversal of opinion with regard to the Ottoman Empire among Europeans, and prepared the ground for the doctrine which was then propagated—that the Christians in the Ottoman Empire were like "sheep being tended by wolves." Yet the Ottomans never took pains to answer these allegations. In addition, the widening of the scope of education, following the French Revolution of 1791 (*sic*), and the new emphasis placed on the study of ancient Greek and Latin, which made the graduates of such schools believe that "Athens was a land of philosophy, harboring within its walls a host of Socrates and Platos" and that the Ottomans were "habitual tyrants," gave strength to the anti-Ottoman feelings.[46]

Ziya Paşa gave the following example to illustrate the contention that even during the reign of Sultan Mahmud II the same factors that had caused the decadence of the Ottoman Empire were still silently undermining its structure: "The *silahtar* ["imperial sword bearer"] Ali Ağa and Husrev Paşa and Fevzi Ahmed Paşa and Pertev Paşa and Akif Paşa . . . were rulers all but in name and when the Russian and the Egyptian questions arose, such men caused the weakness of the state, for, as a natural result of [their rivalry with one another] . . . the pay of the military was reduced, currency debased, and internal trade thereby greatly affected."[47]

[46] *Hürriyet*, February 13, 1869, pp. 1, 2.
[47] Ziya Paşa, "Hâtıra," *Hürriyet*, February 13, 1869, p. 1.

Finally came Reşid Paşa and the proclamation of the Tanzimat Rescript, but Reşid Paşa, because he wanted to "become famous" in Europe,[48] made the Europeans believe that the privileges which had been granted to the subjects of the sultan in this charter were new in Islam. This in turn led to two evils: on the one hand, Europeans became confirmed in their conviction that Islamic law did not provide such rights; and, secondly, the successors of Reşid Paşa, Fuad and Âli Paşa, adopting the policy of their master, went on confirming this erroneous impression. Again, no importance was given to the Şeriat during these years, and yet the successful reforms carried out by Midhat Paşa, the governor of the Danubian Province, showed that it was individuals who were important in matters of state, and it was religious belief which in turn formed good men.[49]

The foregoing analysis has shown the extent to which Namık Kemal's ideas were more radical than Ziya's. Yet the libertarian content of Ziya's writings cannot be denied. True, "popular sovereignty" was not a concept as widely used by him as by Kemal. True again, Ziya vitiated his schemes of governmental responsibility by his adulation of the sultan, but an outstanding aspect of his theory was that government meant justice for the people.

Speaking of the attempts made in the Firman of 1856 to establish "equality" among Ottomans, he pointed out that "equality" was a meaningless term as long as the "upper classes" of Istanbul would be steeped in wealth while the paupers in Izmir had to drown their children because they were too poor to afford any.[50]

[48] *Ibid.*, April 5, 1869, p. 6.
[49] *Ibid.*, March 29, 1869, p. 7.
[50] *Ibid.*, "Mes'ele-yi Müsavat," *Hürriyet*, October 5, 1868, p. 3.

Ali Suavi: the Zealot

Whether the products of Ali Suavi's mind are worth analyzing in detail is a question which anyone willing to follow his adventurous life has to consider seriously. The dominant pathological traits of his personality are so striking as to require no special *expertise* to single them out, and yet there is more to him than his eccentricities. In recent times his figure has been surrounded by an aura of reverence due to the fact that he was the first modern Turk to die in the pursuit of democratic ideals.[1] But there is very little of the real Suavi in that image, the product of a belated political canonization. To his political companions Suavi was a charlatan and, to many of his contemporaries, a crank. Such a harsh judgment is not surprising coming as it did from an age not as yet steeped in the cult of the colorful and the bizarre. There is one reason, however, for which Suavi's conduct as well as his ideas should be given serious attention today: they were the product of the same kind of frustrations as have produced the ambivalent personality of the demagogic ulema of our time. Suavi was an Islamic radical quite akin in his ideals and his conduct to the leaders of the various modern Islamic politico-religious associations which have made an undeniable contribution to the instability of the contemporary Middle East. Like them too, his essential force consisted in being in touch with that large, inchoate mass of dissatisfaction which modern political manipulators usually equate with "the people."

Suavi was born in Istanbul in 1839, the son of a paper merchant of modest means. He received his primary education at a *Rüşdiye*. Sometime after his graduation he studied religious sciences and went on a pilgrimage to Mecca. He then entered the service of the state in a governmental bureau.

[1] For a booklet taking up this theme see Falih Rıfkı Atay, *Baş Veren bir İnkilapçı* (Istanbul, 1954).

Three years later Suavi got a position as a teacher in a *Rüşdiye* in Bursa by obtaining the highest score in a competitive examination organized by the Ministry of Education. It should be kept in mind that Ali Suavi was by then trained primarily in religious sciences, although he later acquired a wide store of rather muddled encyclopedic information. When the *Vilayet* of Edirne was reorganized in accordance with the new law of Vilayets he was appointed to an administrative post in Filibe (Plodiv) and then to a teaching position. Because of a conflict with the administrator of the region, the historian Atâ Bey, he was dismissed. Atâ Bey had accused Suavi of inciting the people to revolt during his weekly sermons. We know that at this time he was a reader of the *Tasvir-i Efkâr* and was promising it scholarly contributions which apparently never came forth.[2]

Suavi now returned to the capital and was taken under the protective wing of Abdurrahman Sami Paşa, the Minister of Education whose attention he had first caught during the competitive examinations he had entered some years before and whose *salon* was a gathering place for the literati of the capital. It is at this time (1867) that Suavi began writing for Filip Efendi's *Muhbir*. Suavi was, at the same time, preaching at the Şehzâde mosque. When the *Muhbir* was closed in March of 1867, Suavi was sent into exile to the Black Sea, but by the end of May he had been able to make his getaway, and in the beginning of June he was already in Paris. This escape was planned and financed by Mustafa Fazıl Paşa. On his way to Paris Suavi was joined in Italy by Kemal and Ziya. The three companions thus arrived in Paris together.

The reasons for which Suavi was placed in charge of the first Young Ottoman publication to appear in Europe immediately after these developments are not clear. The fact that the Young Ottoman weekly also was to be named *Muhbir* and that it claimed to be a reincarnation of the first *Muhbir* provides some clue to this selection. Suavi had already made him-

[2] Kuntay, *Namık Kemal*, I, 50, 51.

self a reputation as being able to appeal to a popular audience
and he probably was thought of as being the right person to
keep the effervescence of the capital at the level which it had
reached in the early spring of 1867. Suavi's real limitations as
a journalist, however, as well as the primitiveness of his style
and the lusterlessness of his defenses of liberty and constitutionalism became apparent as soon as the first few issues of the
Muhbir had come out. Not much could be done to change the
Muhbir because of Suavi's extraordinary pride and self-assurance. The difference in style between the various unsigned
articles which appeared in the *Muhbir* make it clear, however,
that some amount of editing was taking place. Such a basic
variety makes it difficult to select Suavi's own contributions to
the *Muhbir*. The most effective test is to look for the characteristic primitiveness of Suavi's style, but this is not always conclusive since there are some pieces that seem to have been
corrected by Kemal after having been written by Suavi.

Finally, in April of 1868, Kemal and Ziya requested Suavi
in writing to delete from the first page of the *Muhbir* the
notation that it was the organ of the Young Ottoman Society.[3]
Sometime later a meeting was convened in Paris, the difficulties
were discussed, and the decision was taken to publish the
Hürriyet; the *Muhbir* was also to continue publication. When
the *Muhbir* ceased to appear shortly thereafter, it was because
a Greek printer's apprentice who worked at the printing plant
had absconded with some of the key implements of the press.[4]
This, of course, brought great relief to the Young Ottomans
but infuriated Suavi. The following year seems to have been
spent by Suavi in drifting around in London. Still in the pay of
Mustafa Fazıl Paşa, he poured his bile into anonymous letters
to the wives and fiancées the Young Ottomans had left behind,
exposing imaginary engagements, flirtations, or marriages of
the latter with English girls. The factual material for such
descriptions of illicit bliss was directly available to Suavi since

---

[3] Kuntay, *Ali Suavi*, p. 57, for this letter.
[4] *Hürriyet*, December 28, 1868.

he himself had attached to his person a young and beautiful Englishwoman whom he was later to bring back to the capital. In July-August of 1869 began in Paris the publication of the *Ulûm*. This journal, subtitled "Journal Encyclopédique Turc," was one place where Suavi could parade the all-embracing knowledge of which he was so proud.

The *Ulûm* was discontinued during the Franco-Prussian War. From Lyons where he found refuge Suavi began to publish a successor to the *Ulûm* under the title *Temporarily: to the clientele of the Ulûm*.[5] In this sheet both Young Otto-man personalities and Young Ottoman goals were being lam-pooned. At the same time Ali Suavi was attempting to show his real attachment for the monarchy. This new emphasis placed by Suavi on the sultan's leadership of his community, combined with the idea of government as an activity tailored to suit the needs of the "small man" and a concomitant suspi-cion of any intermediate political forces—whether Ottoman politicians or Turkish reformist groups—was an important aspect of Ali Suavi's philosophy which hardened at this junc-ture. Suavi now placed both Young Ottomans and Ottoman statesmen under the same heading of enemies of the people. He also saw a basic similarity between the two groups. Thus his earlier praises of Midhat Paşa in the *Muhbir* were replaced by silence and later by vituperations against him. It is this feeling which quite probably kept him from returning to the capital in the first days of 1876 after the destitution of Abdü-laziz. The change-over had been publicized as a triumph of Midhat Paşa's reformist conceptions, but this did not seem to attract Suavi. Only after Abdülhamid was brought to the throne did he come back, after having heralded his own new beliefs with regard to reform, constitutionalism, and the people in articles he sent to Turkish newspapers pending his return.[6]

[5] *Muvakkaten Ulûm Müşterilerine.* I have been unable to find this periodical.

[6] According to Kuntay, *Ali Suavi*, p. 160, note 2, Suavi had requested permission to return to Turkey during Abdülaziz's reign but permission was not granted. However, the articles sent by Suavi to Turkey before his arrival

Upon his return, Ali Suavi was made the director of the lyceum of Galatasaray, a school established by Fuad Paşa in 1868 where the standard French *lycée* program of studies was being carried out by a partly French faculty. Suavi, on this occasion, scandalized many socially conservative Turks by establishing his English wife in the headmaster's suite. It was his incompetence, however, which led to his dismissal soon thereafter. On the occasion of Midhat Paşa's banishment, he showed, once again, considerable activity as a publicist. In letters sent to the newspapers of the capital he condoned Abdülhamid's action, attacked Midhat, expressed once more his belief that liberty was something of which the people should profit, not just ministers like Midhat. Soon thereafter Suavi established a "society of hearing and obedience" which, using the transcription into Turkish of the French *contre-révolution*, he described as a conservative force.[7]

With this background in mind it is not easy to explain Ali Suavi's attempted coup in May of 1878, which aimed to bring Murad V back to the throne. Murad had been confined to the palace of Çirağan. Suavi, gathering a few hundred refugees who had fled before the Russians' advances in the Balkans, attempted to seize the palace, but he failed and was killed in the process.[8]

A tentative explanation of Suavi's conduct is that he had been disappointed by Abdülhamid's failure to lead "the nation in arms" in an inch-by-inch defense of the Ottoman soil against the Russian invaders.[9] The apocalyptic figure for whom Suavi

---

make it quite clear that what attracted him back to Turkey was not the triumph of those political forces which collaborated in bringing about the downfall of Abdülaziz. See Kuntay, *Ali Suavi*, pp. 91-97.

[7] This name had reference to the Koranic line, "we heard and believed," Sura II, 285, Bell, I, 42. Kuntay, *Ali Suavi*, p. 153. Ali Suavi was also working against Midhat, see A. Clician Vasif, *Son Altesse Midhat-Pacha Grand Vizir* (Paris, Kugelmann, 1909), pp. 132-133.

[8] See Ismail Hakki Uzunçarşili, "Ali Suavi ve Çirağan Sarayi Vak'asi," *Belleten* (1944), VIII, 71-118.

[9] Public opinion in the capital was running against the sultan because of this failure. See E. de Keratry, *Mourad V-Prince, Sultan, Prisonnier d'Etat 1840-1878* (Paris, Dentu, 1878), p. 251.

yearned did not appear in this instance. Such a personage was to rise up only much later at the end of the First World War and thus fulfill a deeply seated popular need for success in battle which had been cumulating since the great Ottoman military reverses in the eighteenth century. This contribution of the *Gazi*, Mustafa Kemal Atatürk, explains the extent to which he was able to ride over popular conservatism and carry modernization much farther than anybody had dared until that time.

While Suavi's writings are devoid of the literary polish which makes the products of Kemal's pen such captivating reading, they too bear a characteristic stamp—that of an unmistakable, rather primitive, and crude style. The confused but fervent world of his ideas, often dismissed as the lucubrations of a maniac by his Young Ottoman colleagues, is thus best set in focus by capturing the "atmosphere" of a passage in which Suavi develops one of his favorite themes. In the following piece Suavi counters the accusation that the *Muhbir* (11) was more interested in inflammatory polemics than in the truth:

"Strange. If a poor man steals, or if he commits any other well-known infraction of the law, his failures are spelled out in large characters on a piece of paper, hung on his neck, and the man made to stand in a busy avenue and exhibit it to all passers-by.

"All right. But if there are no objections to exhibiting the poor in such a fashion for their infractions why should the exhibiting of governmental wrongs which wreak havoc with the entire fatherland and the nation be considered excessive? . . .

"Why, blast it, the same is true if leaving aside personal rights we consider the rights of the community. . . .

"What now is it that provides a guarantee of the rights of the community? Is it the personality and the will of the Sultan or the Şeriat which sets limits to all men and the Tanzimat which is the instrument it uses to this purpose?

"Well, by what are the Şeriat and the Tanzimat secured if not by the assemblies? It follows, then, that the assemblies are indirectly the guarantors of the rights of the community. Why then should our assemblies be made the instruments of the whims of one or two men? . . . When the rights of millions of people are given in trust to such [corrupt] assemblies how can one expect the security of the people not to be frittered away? How can one but expect part of the population to change nationality? How can one expect the Moslems, who are denied protection, not to decrease in number? How can one expect those who are trampled not to take under their feet those who trampled them regardless of the consequences that such actions would incur? . . . Do all members of the Government believe themselves to be free of responsibility for this state of affairs? If there are any of them who harbor such beliefs they are mistaken. To provide justice is the greatest, the first duty of government, for it is the very reason of its establishment and a pledge of its continuation."[10]

One of the shortest ways of making the fundamental characteristics of Ali Suavi's theories stand out, on the other hand, is to compare them with those of Kemal. Once this is done, three fundamental disagreements between the two men emerge. First, while the nub of Namık Kemal's political theory consists of a determined effort to introduce into Ottoman political thinking the concept of popular sovereignty, Suavi finds the term to be meaningless from the point of view of Islamic political theology and false from the vantage point of European political philosophy. Second, while Kemal attempts to work into his scheme the principle of the separation of powers, Suavi replaces this by the principle of the "unity of the imamate." Finally, while Namık Kemal was opposed to any act of civil disobedience that would go beyond verbal protests, Suavi was ready to go much farther.

In following Ali Suavi's discussion of popular sovereignty, one cannot but feel that Suavi is, in fact, arguing against Kemal

[10] Ali Suavi, "Şahsiyat," *Muhbir*, March 23, 1868, p. 2.

and trying to show as far-fetched Kemal's efforts to make popular sovereignty an element which had always existed in Islamic theory. His own arguments on the subject are quite clear: "There exists a term which has gained considerable notoriety nowadays, 'popular sovereignty,' as the expression goes. This term is a translation from the French. Its original reads: 'souveraineté du peuple.' Now let us inquire into the meaning of these French words. What does 'souveraineté' mean? This word is originally from the Latin 'soprenos' which means 'does what he desires.' Sole master of his self [*"hâkim-i binnefs"*], absolute authority [*"âmir-i mutlak"*], free in his actions [*"fail-i muhtar"*]. Well, what is it, in fact, that rules by itself and has absolute power over things? Something which cannot be qualified with any attribute other than that of Divinity. Thus, in this sense, there does not exist a single human being who possesses 'souveraineté.' "[11]

According to Suavi, the sovereignty that man possessed was of a relative nature, i.e., he was sovereign over his own self with regard to his fellow humans in that none of them had the right to interfere with his activities as long as he observed the dicta of divine law.

Suavi then went on to argue that even the "natural" philosophers [*"tabiiyyun,"* the philosophers of the Enlightement] were obliged to admit, ultimately, the presence of an all-pervasive ordering force. To Suavi this was a poor substitute for God.[12]

Again, with regard to the separation of powers Suavi's reaction was characteristic of what we would expect from an *âlim* when faced with the doctrine of Montesquieu. Suavi stated that first of all the *separation* of powers existed in Islam, as could be gathered from the division of labor between the *müftü* (the interpreter of the Şeriat), the *kadı* (the judge sitting on the Islamic court), and the *vali* (the governor acting as the arm of the executive). This was a point that had already

---

[11] Suavi, "al-Ḥākim Huwullāh," *Ulûm,* 22 Rebiülahir 1286/August 1, 1869, p. 18.
[12] *Ibid.,* p. 24.

been made by Kemal. But while Kemal went on to accept the concept of checks and balances, Suavi claimed that this was impossible. According to him the only three-way division that Islam allowed was one based on a separation of functions. There was no way of considering these three functional orders as powers working at cross-purposes with one another. Suavi made the point that the principle of the "unity of the imamate" required that though these forces carry out different tasks they be linked to one another in a hierarchical chain reminiscent of Kınalızâde's "circle." This he described as follows: "The *ümera* rule over the people and the ulema rule over the *emirs* and divine law rules over the ulema."[13]

It is noticeable that Suavi had in fact reversed the order of hierarchy to place the ulema over the military ruling class, but apart from that he was quite right in stating that in a nomocracy a system of checks and balances did not make any sense, for the process of checks and balances is a purely secular, mechanical arrangement taking its origin in the idea that in making laws and carrying them out man had no way of looking up to precise, absolute norms. In Islam these norms existed; consequently what the separation of *functions* (instead of powers) aimed to provide was the faithful application of the divine orders. It was unthinkable (in theory, if not in practice) that once the ulema had determined what the law was, the *ümera* would not follow suit but veto their proposal.

Suavi's argument did not take historical precedent into account, but there is no reason why it should have. Insofar as historical precedent had precisely meant the whittling of the powers of the ulema, Suavi was trying to avoid it.

This attitude of Suavi's is also relevant with regard to the final point at which his theories differed from those of Kemal, namely, the ease with which, as we shall see below, he took to a theory of justified resistance.

In the more general context of all his writings, both in the

[13] *Ibid.*, 8 Cemaziyülevvel 1286/August 8, 1869, p. 80. *Ümera*, the plural of *Emir*, are the warriors mentioned in the "circle" of justice.

Muhbir and in the *Ulûm*, it may be said that Suavi's ideas converge at three points which are: first, his desire to infuse a new energy into the veins of the Ottomans and his own readiness to take drastic measures so as to elicit the recovery of the Ottoman Empire; secondly, his self-identification with the underprivileged; and, thirdly, his willingness to resist constituted authority. This latter factor is often extremely ambiguous as it is accompanied by a search for the right type of ruler to which to surrender the administration of the affairs of the state. But this again is a preindividualistic view of the functions of authority and government and may be found even in medieval Europe.

In its most general sense Ali Suavi's activism consisted in a conviction that the Ottomans should begin to do things for themselves. In its simplest form this was expressed in Suavi's praising of the virtues of work, describing the comforts provided by the material aspects of Western civilization, and explaining why efforts should be made to catch up with European educational advances. This was the subject of Suavi's prologue to the first issue of the *Muhbir*.[14]

At a more advanced level this activism appeared in Suavi's advice to take over from the West the body of knowledge that had enabled it to increase these material benefits. Relying on an Islamic saying that works in this world were a preparation for the next, he stated that this should spur Moslems to devote themselves to the development of industry and that sciences such as mathematics and physics should be studied more intensively. Modern natural sciences, he stated, had no connection with the "theorizings of the ancient Greeks" frowned upon by Islam. Another corollary of this stand was that Ali Suavi thought that economic and commercial enterprises should be taken out of foreigners' hands.[15] This attitude culminated in Ali Suavi's political activism, best expressed in his own

[14] Ali Suavi, "Mukaddime," *Muhbir*, 25 Şaban 1283/January 2, 1867.
[15] *Ibid.*, [?], editorial, *Muhbir*, October 5, 1867, pp. 1-3. A question mark indicates a slight deviation from what would be Suavi's normal style, although the ideas expressed are characteristic of Suavi.

words: "What is this ignominiousness that has befallen us, what is this inability to stir ourselves, what is this sleepiness, what is this effeminateness? Why should it be that the *Frenks* who are not congenitally smarter than we should hold their government to account for state expenditures while we contribute our dues and then do nothing but stupidly stare?"[16] Such "stupid staring" was also an accusation Suavi brought to bear against the ulema, whom he taxed with inactivity in the face of missionary propaganda.[17]

Suavi stated that Islamic law was quite adequate to cope with the modern world wherein all kinds of new economic and social institutions had arisen, such as joint stock companies and factories. All that was needed was to take advantage of the Islamic provision whereby as times changed the law could also be modified—in its application if not in its essentials. The only step that was necessary, according to Suavi, to keep up with the pace of modern social and economic life, was to prepare an "excellent book of *fikh* ['Islamic law'] in a language that everyone would understand."[18] The British had already opened the way, Suavi concluded, by making use of a legal code in India, the compilation of which had been made in the time of the Moghul king Awrangzeb.

A further aspect of Suavi's activism was his patriotism, his attempt to galvanize the Ottomans in a defense of "the fatherland" against Russia, as in the following passage: "Are there no men left in our nation who love their fatherland, their religion, their family? Who care for the defense of their own interests? Will the Turkish people who once made the world tremble accept to be the serfs of the Russians? By no means! Our nation is not as yet dead."[19] Or, as he stated it on another occasion, "Herald it to the world that the Turks are still here." "Proclaim everywhere that the Ottoman Empire cannot disintegrate merely as the result of Greek or Russian hullabaloo.

[16] *Ibid.,* [?] *Muhbir,* December 5, 1867, p. 4.
[17] *Ibid.,* "Adem-i Tesahib-i Din," *Muhbir,* January 13, 1868, pp. 1, 2.
[18] *Ibid.,* editorial, *Muhbir,* August 31, 1867, pp. 1, 2.
[19] *Ibid.,* [?], *Muhbir,* January 27, 1868, p. 3.

... The great *Ulema* have stated it to be a sign of the faithfulness of man and of his keeping his engagements that his cries of sympathy go to his brothers and his love to his fatherland."[20]

It is tempting, in this context, to classify Suavi as the first "Turkist" because of his repeated use of the term "Turk" and because of the attention he gave to the Central Asiatic problem.[21] In fact, however, there were happening in Central Asia events which would have, in any case, directed Suavi's attention to this area. For one, demands for help from Central Asian khans against the Russians had received some publicity at the Porte. Then, too, Russia's Central Asian policy was being discussed in the European press. Suavi did, it is true, speak of Central Asians as "Turks," concluding in his work on the Khanate of Khiva: "To it Russia has sent soldiers and so we wonder what has happened to those Turkish Moslems who were of our religion and our tribe and our family."[22]

Again Suavi spoke of "the Turks, that is to say the Tartars," as the constitutive ethnic element of the Ottoman Empire, adding that, in fact, few of these original Tartars remained because of the mixture of races.[23] Suavi also supported the proposal of an orientalist friend of his by the name of Charles Willis that Ottoman schools should adopt Turkish as a single language of instruction.[24] Furthermore, he had demanded that the codification of Islamic law should also be accompanied by a translation of it into Turkish, but this was more a function of his attempt to make knowledge available to a large audience and simplify *medrese* teachings than part of his Turkism.

Suavi's attitude is made fairly—although not entirely—clear in a piece he wrote in his "Temporarily . . ." at the end of 1870. In this piece Suavi commented:

[20] *Ibid.*, [?], "Keza fi 13 Cemaziyülahir," *Muhbir*, October 26, 1867, p. 4.
[21] *Ibid.*, *Hive* (2nd ed., Istanbul, Asadoryan, 1327), and Ali Suavi, *Le Khiva en Mars 1873* (Paris, Victor Goupy, 1873). For a study of this aspect of Suavi's ideas see Ismail Hami Danişmend, *Ali Suavi'nin Türkçülüğü* (Ankara, 1942).
[22] *Ibid.*, p. 134.
[23] *Ibid.*, "Tefrika," *Muhbir*, August 31, 1867, p. 4.
[24] *Ibid.*, *Muhbir*, January 27, 1868, p. 3.

"Our semi-official gazette, the *Turquie*, states: now the time has come for it; the Porte should follow the example of Italy and Prussia, adopt the cause of nationalism ['*Kavmiyyet*,' textually, 'tribalism'] and assemble all Moslems. First it should make of Egypt a province like that of Edirne.

"Do our ministers realize that the question of nationalities is one special to Europeans and that we do not have a nationalities problem? Nationality questions would cause our ruin. To gather Moslems together could at most be a religious question but not a question of national origin."[25]

In short, it may be stated that Suavi was still too much interested in all of his Islamic brethren to be labeled a "Turkist" although "Turks" were given greater importance in his writings than heretofore.

Suavi's attempt to uplift the people and tailor programs of modernization to their needs was the second aspect of his activism and constituted what we may call his "populism." This stand had two aspects: a positive aspect which expressed itself in new educational ideas and a negative aspect in which Ali Suavi revolted against the privileges of those in power. Ali Suavi was completely set against the traditional methods of teaching as well as the curricula of the religious schools and came out for a thorough modernization of the latter, which he considered too time-consuming, not geared to modern advances, and unsuitable for the education of large numbers. He was also convinced that a simplification of the language was necessary to provide for the intellectual development of "the people."[26] Another facet of the same attitude was that Suavi placed considerable faith in the political wisdom of "the people." Thus, to explanations provided by the Porte that members of an Ottoman national assembly would not have enough education to understand the intricacies of foreign policy, he countered by stating: "The Ottomans, viz. these dense Turks to whom reference is made, say to politicians of

---

[25] Kuntay, *Ali Suavi*, p. 59, quoting *Muvakkaten*, December 15, 1870.
[26] *Ibid.*, "Terk-i Lisan," *Muhbir*, January 18, 1868, p. 1.

this type: such politics, schmolitics [sic] are too subtle for us. If they [the European Great Powers] stop busying themselves with Garibaldi and the Pope and attack you asking why . . . [you established a constitutional assembly], then we shall come to your rescue."[27]

Like Kemal and the rest of the Young Ottomans, throughout his life Suavi's attacks were directed against the ministers of the Porte. Suavi complained, for example, that there were only two types of ministers in the Ottoman Empire—those who only changed portfolios from one ministerial rearrangement to the other and those who kowtowed to the latter. Just as in Kemal's articles, the ministers were taken to task for their opposition to a scheme of representation. But here again the emphasis was different; Suavi's most violent and heartfelt objections were to the humiliation that an Ottoman had to endure when he had business to transact with a governmental officer. Repeatedly he lampooned the flowery circumlocutions with which the ordinary citizen was supposed to address himself to statesmen.[28] "Times [when this type of conduct was prevalent in the world] have changed," said Suavi, adding: "The individual who comes to seek justice is, like the vizier, a man. He is not the slave of the vizier. He does not come to beg for pity."[29] The Şeriat, he stated, gave every man the same right and the representative assembly would provide for the enforcement of this fundamental principle by making it impossible for ministers to drive out of their offices citizens who had important matters to discuss with them.

With all his criticism of ministerial oppression it is significant that Suavi never was able to evolve even as tightly knit a theory of representation as that of Kemal. Suavi's fundamental political theory consisted of a few fundamental principles which may be summarized as follows: God was the seat of political sovereignty; the Şeriat was the instrument whereby

[27] *Ibid.*, "İstanbuldaki Islahat," *Muhbir*, September 28, 1867, p. 3.
[28] *Ibid.*, İstanbuldan fi 18 Kânun-u Evvel," *Muhbir*, January 2, 1868, p. 2.
[29] *Ibid.*, "Sual-Cevap," *Muhbir*, February 6, 1868, p. 4.

this sovereignty was translated from the divine to the human plane; the ulema were the interpreters of this incarnation of God's sovereignty on earth; kings and viziers were only the executors of the interpretive decisions (*"fetvas"*) of the ulema as to the suitableness of basic political acts. This, of course, was a far cry from the emphasis found in later Islamic political theory that the powers of the sultan were, in themselves, important political attributes as well as reflections of God's vicarage on earth. Suavi's views were inspired more by the fundamental statements contained in the Koran and by early Islam than by the political theory of the later jurists. He was, in this sense, a purist, a man going as far back as possible to the original sources of Islam. This purism of Suavi also showed in his conviction that the Islamic state had begun to decline as soon as "matters of state" had been separated from "matters of religion." Suavi like Kemal placed the blame for this separation on the shoulders of the "followers of Çingiz," the Mongols.[30] This was a theme that later also was to be exploited in the *Hürriyet*. As to the ulema, Suavi had to admit that their quality had deteriorated considerably and that therefore using their advice to the extent that Suavi counseled was out of the question.[31] He could, however, maintain at the very same moment that the ulema had deteriorated because the new Ottoman bureaucracy had pushed it into the background.

Insofar as the Islamic canvas on which he embroidered his themes is concerned, one outstanding difference between Ali Suavi and the rest of the Young Ottomans was that while they too exploited Islamic themes, Suavi's attempt to piece together the Islamic background of his arguments is so painstakingly earnest that the impact of his message is lost in the process. Suavi seems either to spend an unnecessary amount of time in the labyrinth of Islamic traditions, precedents, and Koranic dicta or to give way to his raw emotions; in neither case does he build the powerful arguments that Kemal, for example,

---

[30] *Ibid.*, " 'An-naẓar fi'l-maẓālim," *Muhbir*, February 29, 1868, p. 2.
[31] *Ibid.*, "Mevt ul-Ulema," *Muhbir*, January 10, 1868, p. 3.

wove by his controlled use of what were, basically, the same media.

The arguments that Suavi used in defense of representative government—all purportedly based on commands emanating from the body of Islamic law and traditions—were of three kinds: one type took its strength from the institution of *hilf al-Fuzul*, the second was based on the principle of *nazar fi-l mazālim*, and a third went back to the theory of the *shura*.

Hilf al-Fuzul was the name given to an assembly which had gathered before the Prophet Mohammed's mission had become manifest. Mohammed had been one of the participants in this *ad hoc* council assembled to protect the members of all the clans present in Mecca in their transactions with one another. The meeting had culminated in a pledge by the clans gathered that any attempt by the member of one clan to cause damage to the interests of a member of another clan would be jointly redressed by all clans. By the very participation of the Prophet in its deliberations this covenant had become an accepted institution in Islam.[32] To Suavi it meant that there existed in Islam a precedent whereby the rights of a single man were safeguarded by the whole community acting in concert.

The institution of *hilf al-Fuzul* also constituted the theoretical foundation whereby an extra-Şer'i judiciary was accepted in Islam. This so-called "justice of the *mazālim*" was a widespread Islamic practice establishing means for a recourse to justice whenever recourse to the Şeriat, in itself, did not result in the redress of a wrong. Thus, for example, when judges were unable to cope with the situation because of pressure exerted on them, recourse could be had to *mazālim* courts.[33] The exercise of this extraordinary justice was vested in the ruler himself but could be delegated by his provincial or ministerial representative. Normally *mazālim* courts had a collegial composition—on them sat several high dignitaries of the state.

---

[32] Emile Tyan, *Histoire de l'Organisation Judiciaire en Pays d'Islam* (Imprimerie St. Paul, Harissa, 1943), II, 270.

[33] *Ibid.*, pp. 145-147.

Suavi, however, attributed this latter practice to Mongolian influences and stated that it was part of the religious obligation of the sultan to guarantee by his fulfillment of the *mazālim* function that the citizen would be fully protected in his rights vis-à-vis the executive machinery. Since Suavi saw representation as a check on the tyranny of the executive, he considered the normal functioning of the institution of the *mazālim* to be one step toward eliciting the benefits of representative government. Suavi hoped that the reintroduction of the practice of the *mazālim* would, if nothing else, open the eyes of the sultan to the need for a representative assembly.[34]

A third Islamic defense of representative assemblies was justified with the argument that such assemblies had existed in early Islamic times and had been used by the caliph Omar. This was the theory of the *shura*.[35] H. A. R. Gibb's explanation of the origin of this argument clarifies the relevance of such an approach to representative institutions:

"The occasion was the election of the third Caliph, in succession to 'Umar in 644, when (whether on the instructions of 'Umar or not) all the probable candidates for the succession assembled to debate the matter in shūra or committee. Together with this instance, some modern writers have deduced from the references in the historical sources to 'Umar consulting with other Companions (read in the light of the injunction to consultation between the Believers found in the Qur'ān), the existence of something like a regular shūra during his caliphate.

"But there is, in fact, nothing in the texts to justify the suggestion that 'Umar's consultation was more than informal or that there was at Medina any recognized consultative committee, still less a cabinet."[36]

From time to time, Suavi, starting from an accepted

[34] Ali Suavi, " 'An-Nazar Fi'l-Mazālim," *Muhbir*, February 22, 1868, p. 2.

[35] *Ibid.*, "On Dokuz Numarada Emraz-ı Dahiliye-nin Mabadı," *Muhbir*, January 18, 1868, p. 1; also, "Tarik-i Meşveret," *ibid.*, p. 2.

[36] H. A. R. Gibb, "Constitutional Development," *Law in the Middle East*, p. 16.

Islamic premise such as that the primary function of the state was to provide justice, attempted to go on to an exposition of a Western political concept. Such, for example, was his own highly simplified account of the separation of powers, at a time when, under the influence of Young Ottoman ideals, he still was defending it:

"It is common knowledge that the word 'adalet' (justice) is of Arabic origin (it means change in balance). For example it means that if we place one hundred *dirhems* in one side of the scales an equilibrium is established by placing one hundred *dirhems* in the other. A state must necessarily have subjects: well, the state and subjects are like the two sides of a balance. Thus if only the state benefits of protection and subjects do not, there is no justice in the balance of government. In short, subjects will disappear and the state itself come to an end.

"Consequently in European states there is an assembly appointed by the state to protect the rights of the state and to stop those who would trespass on these rights. There also is a representative assembly elected by the people to discuss policies, to control the revenue and expenditures of the state and to protect the population from oppression with regard to taxation and other matters. With one assembly protecting the rights of the state and the other, the rights of the people, the balance of government is naturally a just balance."[37]

The most interesting aspect of Suavi's political theory, however, is his defense of the right of civil disobedience. Three types of Islamic arguments seem to have been used by him to this end. These were: *a*) traditions attributed to the earliest caliphs; *b*) the Koranic obligation imposed by the Prophet on his community to conform to the Good and to avoid evil ways; *c*) arguments taken from later medieval jurists which have to be traced to their source to establish their full significance.

One example of the first type of argument was Suavi's use of a tradition according to which the caliph Omar had requested his community to correct any errors in which they

[37] Ali Suavi, "Meşveret Meclisi Olmadıkça Devlet Yaşamaz," *Muhbir*, February, 6, 1868, p. 3.

might observe him engaging. According to the tradition, on that occasion two of the Prophet's companions, Selman and Bilal, had sworn to correct Omar by the use of their sword, if necessary. Citing the tradition, Suavi continued:

"O ye who desire justice! If you want to go about nodding your heads like snails, tyrants will never allow you to raise your voice. You are slaves.

"If, on the other hand, you take to the sword and show your presence in the field of honor you will stand up against tyrants: you are human beings, you are free.

"O people. How long are you still going to believe that a *Mehdi* shall appear and save you? . . .

"Do you think that the emirs who are in charge and who are free of question and responsibility will abandon what profits they draw out of you and begin to favor you?"[38]

Again, in connection with the same tradition, Suavi went on to say that it established the right of rebellion and continued: "This is truly so. This matter of resistance to oppression which our religion enjoins [*'farz kılıyor'*] is a fundamental political principle which Europeans have only recently discovered after several thousand years of experience."[39]

Suavi went on to state that under these circumstances it took considerable nerve for the Europeans to advise the Moslems to abandon absolutistic practices. The Koranic injunction to refrain from evil and do good was interpreted by Suavi as having granted the right to a group among the believers, the ulema, to redress these wrongs wherever they witnessed them—thus the necessity to protest against oppressive measures.[40]

Finally, Suavi went so far as to broach the subject of Âli Paşa's assassination. This move was justified by reference to the works of the jurists İbn Nudjaim, Dimirdāshi, and al-Zāhidī,

---

[38] *Ibid.*, "Istanbuldan fi 17 Teşrin-i Sâni," *Muhbir*, November 28, 1867, p. 3; *ibid.*, "Istanbuldan Tahrirat fi 15 Ramazan," *Muhbir*, January 27, 1868, p. 3.

[39] *Ibid.*, "Paristen bir Müslüman Mektubu," *Muhbir*, December 25, 1867, p. 3.

[40] *Ibid.*, "Mevt ül-Ulema," *Muhbir*, January 10, 1868, p. 3.

all three of them late medieval Islamic jurists. The significance of Ali Suavi's choice and the relevance of the allegedly favorable comments of these jurists with regard to the right of resistance is obscure.[41]

On the other hand, the historical foundation, as opposed to the doctrinal rationalization of such an attitude, was the following: it had always been to the advantage of the ulema not to relinquish even an iota of the theory about the nomocratic nature of government. If this theory were made effective, the ulema would have stood as interpreters of the divine law where Suavi placed them, i.e., above the *ümera*. Conversely, since a certain amount of doctrinal gnashing of teeth had accompanied the ulema's acceptance of theories of subservience (to the military class, in effect), it was not so difficult for an *âlim* to repudiate or modify it. This was not the case with the higher "official" ulema (*"Ulema-i Rusum"*) who only joined revolts because of fear of losing their life and/or position. Suavi's own outstanding contribution was that he elaborated a new theory of revolt, as well as agitated for it.

The reason for which Kemal, on the other hand, was loath to devise a theory of revolt and engage in it was not due to the Islamic element in his thought. It was due to the fact that Namık Kemal was trained as a bureaucrat, i.e., a recipient of the ideals of the governing class in his own time. Despite his dislike for corporate theories of the state, Namık Kemal was suffused with the idea of service to the state. It was this ideology of service to the state which ultimately had to do with the outlook of the "men of the pen" that lent itself even less than the theories of the ulema to a theory of civil disobedience.

[41] Suavi referred to the "Müçtebi," i.e., the *Mudjtabā*, a commentary of the jurist al-Zāhidī on the *Mukhtaṣar* of Kudūrī. See Bursalı Mehmed Tahir, *Osmanlı Müellifleri*, I, 403; he also mentioned the *an-Nahr al-fā'iḳ* by Ibn Nudjaim. See Brockelmann, *Geschichte der Arabische Literatur* (2nd ed., Leyden, 1949), II, 92, and a jurist by the name of Dimirdāshi of which there apparently were a number. See *ibid.*, pp. 303, 311, *Supplement*, I, 652. See Ali Suavi, "Suavi Efendi tarafından gelen mektup," *Hürriyet*, December 20, 1869, p. 3.

The contrast between the theories of Suavi and the outlook of Kemal do not appear so clearly in his writings in the *Muhbir* as in those of the *Ulûm*. In the first case he was still writing for the Young Ottoman Society and could not inject too much of his own beliefs. Once Suavi separated from the Young Ottomans and began to publish the *Ulûm*, all the doctrinal grudges he was nursing against them rose up.

An interesting aspect of Suavi's relations with the Young Ottomans, as well as a clue to his political beliefs, is that none of the articles in the *Muhbir* in which a fairly sophisticated Western theory of representation appears may safely be attributed to him. All of these pieces bear the imprint of a more refined style than that of Suavi. Most of them too take up themes which reappear in the *Hürriyet*. There thus is a possibility that they might have been written by Kemal in the first place. In fact, this fits in well with Suavi's primary interest in bettering social and educational conditions rather than in working to establish "liberty" in the Ottoman Empire. Already in his articles in *Muhbir* (1) Suavi had given some arresting characterizations of what he thought of liberty as conceived of in Europe: "It is thus clear that freedom (which means that everyone low or highly placed is limited by the law) is a fine thing. But European nations have tried various methods to obtain it and in none of these have they been able to find the middle way. Europeans desire that this justice come from below upward. This is why debates take place in assemblies and finally trickle down to the rabble and cause the troubles that we all see. Too bad! Justice, on the contrary, should come from the top downward. For justice is like an enormous stone which when pushed from above by one single person will fall in motion, while to push it up-grade requires a great many forces. It is reported by Şehristani that even Homer who lived three thousand years ago said the equivalent of the Arabic: 'lā ḥarīfī kesret el-ru'asā' which means in simple Turkish that too many cooks spoil the sauce."[42]

[42] *Ibid.*, "Serbestlik," *Muhbir*, I, 27 Şevval 1283/April 4, 1867, p. 2.

Forced by his association with the Young Ottomans to take up a defense of ideas which, because of their Western origin, catered to "forces coming from the bottom up," Suavi for a time had played along with the Young Ottomans. He went so far along with them as to take up in *Muhbir* (11) a most spirited defense of representation, conceived as a check on the power of ministers. This in itself *could*, indeed, be justified by reference to Islamic precedent and was a matter close to Suavi's heart. But the theory that sovereignty resided in the people and was only delegated to representatives who held it as long as they performed other duties or the opposite Western theory of representation that the representatives of the people realized what the best interests of their electorate were even better than this very electorate, were neither of them theories to which Suavi could subscribe because, indeed, there was no Islamic body of theory to justify them. Following his estrangement from the Young Ottomans, Suavi had therefore reverted to his own earlier approach to the problem of an ideal state, viz., the Islamic attitude that the aim of government was to obtain justice for all members of the community. This was a far cry from the idea of popular sovereignty, and Suavi's attacks on the Turkish ideologues who were consciously or unconsciously injecting theories of popular sovereignty into Turkish political thought were thus quite logical. As for Suavi, he believed that by the mere negative step of doing away with corrupt ministers the Islamic system of justice based on the equality of all before religious law would come back into force. He also was firmly convinced that some form of Islamic direct democracy would ensue from a strict observance of the Şeriat. It is this advocacy of direct democracy by Suavi which has misled many modern Turks into thinking of him as a "democrat."[43]

---

[43] Suavi left no room for doubt on this issue. According to him, true "democracy" was the form of government that provided that whenever regulations were made they would be made by the entire people gathered for this purpose. "Just as in the days of the caliphate one would congregate in the mosques." Ali Suavi, "Demokrasi, Hükûmet-i Halk, Müsavat," *Ulûm*, 15 Safer 1287/May 17, 1870, p. 1099.

The attitude of the British toward the Ottoman Empire during the events of 1876 led Suavi to write an article in which his most fundamental political stand is outlined quite clearly. For one, in 1876 Suavi was not any more convinced that foreign policy matters could be best handled under a parliamentary system. This was due to Suavi's disappointment with British parliamentarism, but more fundamental criticisms of the parliamentary system emerged in the piece in which he criticized the British, showing what had always been his basic beliefs. Thus Suavi asked:

"Can there exist public opinion where there exist a constitution and a cabinet? There used to be the Cabinet of Gladstone-Granville, it was then made to topple by the Disraeli-Derby group, and now Gladstone and Granville are trying in turn to bring about the fall of the latter. Whatever the means necessary to bring this about, they will be used. Should these means harm other states, they still will be used. . . .

"In olden times there existed in Europe neither a Şeriat nor established usages and customs such as morality. Since in those days kings were in power who considered that human life should be spent in obedience to the government and thus caused the depredations of autocracy to bear too heavily on it, one day they [the people] said that they had had enough and elected a council of notables to control state revenue and expenditure.

"Yes, everywhere national assemblies began with this pretext of property. Later 'notables' went under and 'deputies' arose. The mess made by the noble came to an end and the messiness of the lower classes began. The deputies, this or that manufacturer, banker, poet, writer, journalist, grocer, vegetable seller, butcher, doctor and the like held in their hands the fate of thirty to forty thousand of their constituents. The right of 'those present' increased, the right of republic disappeared. Despots increased.

"I am using the word republic here not in the nonsensical sense in which the Europeans use it. I am using it in the sense it has had with us. Just as it was with us in olden times in most places in Europe if there was a matter that needed settling, one peasant, five peasants, ten peasants, that is to say the whole population, would assemble and express their grievances to the government. Who would talk? Men, women, children, everybody would tell what he knew, what he had seen, what he heard. And thus most certainly the matter to be settled would be unraveled. This privilege which I call the 'right of republic' exists no more."[44]

Suavi's later conservatism had found a sociologist of distinction to fasten on in the person of Frederic Le Play. Le Play was one of the early social engineers who also was interested in finding a solution to the problems of the disinherited French masses. He believed too that many problems of social disorganization arose when a population lost its religious faith.[45] Le Play also believed in a strong state, and Suavi's Society of Obedience took its cue from Le Play's ideas.

Suavi's theoretical constructions are mainly of use in bringing out into relief how much less attuned to the current nineteenth-century liberalism he was than was Namık Kemal. Parliamentarianism, the mechanism of representation, popular sovereignty—all of these ideas which stood in the forefront of Kemal's theory had truly Western roots. Whenever a thinker who himself had been an *âlim* attempted to build up a modern political system none of these elements was to be found in the synthesis thus brought about, and one ended with a conception of direct democracy such as that of Suavi. This purely ideological failure, which was the result of new concepts being poured into old Islamic intellectual molds, might well explain

---

[44] *Ibid.*, "Paristen bir Mektup," *Vakit*, September 19, 1876; quoted in Kuntay, *Ali Suavi*, p. 91 *et seq.*

[45] Gottfried Salomon, "Le Play," *Encyclopedia of Social Sciences* (1933), IX, 411, 412. There is a possibility that Ali Suavi's admiration for Le Play may have been inspired by Urquhart (see above, Chapter VII, for Ali Suavi's relations with the latter). Urquhardt praised Le Play for seeking to isolate "those things which are equally necessary under all forms of government." See D. Urquhart, "M. Le Play on the Social Disorganization of France," *Diplomatic Review* (1871), XIX, 165-169.

how the minds of other modernist ulema have worked. It also provides a clue to the reasons for which there have arisen no outstanding advocates of parliamentary government among them, on one hand, and the extent to which they have been able to work in close conjunction with the modern masses, on the other. It is true, of course, that on the surface the transfer of new ideas seems to have been successful sometimes. Suavi's theory of revolt—an attitude at odds with all Islamic traditions—would normally be brought under this category. What is striking about Suavi, however, is that, as he himself reports it, his ideas of social justice and resistance to oppression were family inheritances. Suavi's first clash with administrative authorities at the age of seventeen antedates by far his contact with Western ideas. His idea of social justice was taught to him by his father, a member of a merchant guild; and there is no doubt that it is in the equalitarian folk traditions transmitted through Ottoman guilds that the origin of this aspect of Suavi's thought will have to be traced. In many respects the ease with which the Ottoman capital was aroused by persons like Suavi in times of trouble will have to be sought in the *esprit frondeur* which was the legacy of these same guild traditions, about the influence of which little is known at present.

CHAPTER XIII

Hayreddin Paşa: the Attempt to Compromise

THE political thought of Hayreddin Paşa, who for a short time was grand vizier during the reign of Sultan Abdülhamid,[1] has been described by Engelhardt, the historian of the Tanzimat, as "reproducing exactly the ideas which gained currency in that period of the reign of Abdülaziz, that is to say in the years 1864 to 1868."[2] This, as will appear upon analysis of Hayreddin Paşa's ideas, is not entirely true, but it is certain that these ideas represented the attitude of at least a section of articulate Turkish public opinion toward the problem of reform in the empire. It is probable that the success achieved by this widely popular scheme of reforms was the result of its moderateness and its ability to appeal to the Turks who did not go along all the way with even the limited iconoclasticism of the Young Ottomans. This may also be seen in that one of the ulema who was arrested with Kemal in 1873, but who was somewhat more conservative than Kemal, i.e., Bereketzâde Ismail Hakkı, chose to translate Hayreddin Paşa's main work,[3] the *Reforms Necessary to Moslem States*, during his exile.

Hayreddin Paşa was a Tunisian of Circassian birth at the time when Tunis was still a semiautonomous part of the Ottoman Empire. In his early youth he was sent to France to study military science and after his return to Tunis he occupied several governmental posts. Resigning his function in 1863, he remained in Europe for nine years, entrusted by the Tunisian government with various missions to the courts of Germany, France, England, and Italy. During his stay he published in Arabic his project of reforms for Islamic states. This work was

---

[1] For biographical information about Hayreddin Paşa see Th. Menzel, "Khair al-Din," *Encyclopaedia of Islam*, II, 873, and Mehmet Zeki Pakalın, *Son Sadrazamlar ve Başvekiller* (Istanbul, Ahmet Sait Matbaası, 1944), Vol. 4, p. 324, *et seq.*

[2] Engelhardt, *La Turquie et le Tanzimat*, I, p. 200.

[3] Bereketzâde Ismail Hakkı, *Yad-i Mazi*, Istanbul, 1332/1913-1914, p. 144.

385

translated into French in 1868.[4] Hayreddin Paşa's argument for reform was actually contained in the introduction to the Arabic text, the main bulk of which was a statistical directory of European states meant to indicate the extent to which European states had succeeded in amassing material riches.

Hayreddin Paşa's Arabic text was soon translated into Turkish and attracted considerable attention.[5] The mildly reformist approach of its author, combined with his experience of things European, led Sultan Abdülhamid II to extend to him the invitation to fill the office of grand vizier. This offer was accepted. At the time (1878) Turkey was going through an important crisis and the newly convened national assembly had been dissolved by the sultan. Hayreddin Paşa seemed, therefore, to be the ideal statesman for the situation. Yet within eight months of his establishment in office he resigned because of a conflict that developed between him and the sultan with regard to the role to be played by the prime minister. Hayreddin insisted that the office of prime minister or grand vizier was not that of a certifying agency for the mere will of the sultan.

Hayreddin Paşa's ideas do lead one to the conclusion which Abdülhamid seems to have reached on the basis of Hayreddin's work, namely, that the latter was interested only in a slight modification of the powers wielded by the Ottoman ruler and that his policy had much more in common with basic Islamic conceptions than with those of the Young Ottomans.

As Hayreddin Paşa had been brought up in Tunisia and as he had the opportunity of representing Tunisian interests in Europe, for him the decline of the Ottoman Empire was of interest for all Islamic nations and meant the establishment of European hegemony in lands where Islam had once been powerful. Thus his scheme was a proposal for the rejuvenation

---

[4] Le General Khéreddine, *Réformes Necessaires aux Etats Musulmans* (Paris, Dupont, 1868).

[5] Turkish text: Devletlû Fehametlû Hayrettin Paşa Hazretleri, *Mukaddime-i Akvam el-Masalik fi Marifetu Ahval ül-Memalik* (Dersaadet, Elcevaip, 1296).

of Islamic states in general and was focused on the Ottoman Empire only because the latter had been the leader of Islamic nations for centuries. His preponderantly Islamic approach was indicated both by the title of the book, *Reforms Necessary to Islamic States*, and indirectly by the adverse comments showered on his opus by Namık Kemal, who indicates that the Ottoman Empire had not "sunk so low" as to take counsel from other Islamic states.[6] By such comments Namık Kemal was indicating that although his own schemes of reform started from an Islamic vantage point, his glorification of the Ottoman-Turkish past and achievements was an integral part of his beliefs.

Apart from the title of his work, the content of Hayreddin Paşa's work also pointed to the comparatively undiluted Islamic quality of his proposals. Thus Hayreddin Paşa mentioned two reasons which urged him to write his book: one was to "awaken the patriotism of the ulema and of Moslem statesmen and urge them to collaborate with one another in the intelligent choice of the most efficacious means to ameliorate the state of the Islamic nation";[7] the other was to show "certain Moslems" that European political and social institutions were not contrary to Islamic teachings. To speak of a renewal of the patriotism of the ulema was an absurdity, since the European conception of the *patrie* did not exist in Islam. It is significant of the greater sophistication of Namık Kemal that there is no similar statement about the ulema in his writings. Namık Kemal knew too well the novelty of the notion of fatherland to try to use it in conjunction with the ulema. Again, Hayreddin Paşa believed that the decline of the Islamic states was due to the ulema's lack of concern with politics.[8] In fact, in another passage of his work he described his goal as *"mettre nos ulemas en état de mieux remplir leur role temporel."* No

---

[6] Mithat Cemal Kuntay, *Namık Kemal*, I, 202 f., citing an unpublished letter of Kemal.

[7] Le General Khéreddine, *Réformes Necessaires aux Etats Musulmans* (Paris, Dupont, 1868), p. 7. Hereinafter cited as *Réformes.*

[8] *Ibid.*, p. 5.

similar statement can be found in the works of Kemal, who chose rather to criticize the ignorance of the ulema rather than their lack of "citizenship." This is an indication of the extent to which Namık Kemal had been influenced by the *de facto* separation of state and church which had taken place during the Tanzimat. Finally Hayreddin Paşa was using the word "nation" with the connotation of "religious group," as can be seen by his use of the term "Islamic nation." Namık Kemal, on the other hand, despite the ambiguousness of his "nationalism," used the term "Ottoman nation" consistently enough to make it easy to differentiate his stand from that of Hayreddin Paşa. There were points, however, where Hayreddin Paşa's stand came quite close to that adopted by the Turkish reformists which we have taken up above. Repeating a line exploited by the latter, he declared that the economic subservience of the Islamic nations was due to their imitation of Europeans in consumption patterns without a concomitant establishment of European political institutions, which in reality were the fountainhead of European progress and wealth. The very sight of the people who opposed European liberalism gorging themselves on imported products, on luxury goods of European origin, showed the illogicality of their stand.[9] Hayreddin Paşa characterized this stand as "humiliating, antieconomical and politically destructive."[10]

Proceeding by elimination, Hayreddin Paşa took up for examination all the elements which he believed relevant in an investigation of the sources of European power. Climate, fertility, and racial superiority were all eliminated as irrelevant. Neither could the superiority of the Europeans be attributed to the superiority of their religion, since Christianity separated religion from matters of the state—a remark which showed that as a good Moslem Hayreddin Paşa considered the unity of state and religion to be a factor of strength rather than of weakness. What existed in Europe and the cause of European progress was "liberty." Wealth was only the natu-

[9] *Ibid.*   [10] *Ibid.*

ral consequence of this factor.[11] In short, Hayreddin Paşa equated economic advances with European political liberalism, and spoke of European progress as "the progress achieved by the Europeans with regard to knowledge the development of which is helped by political institutions based on justice and liberty."[12]

Actually, there was nothing in the Islamic creed, according to Hayreddin Paşa, which precluded Islamic states from taking over Western institutions. Indeed, the statement of the Prophet to the effect that science should be sought wherever it existed was indication of the latitude provided in this matter by Islam.[13] Historical example of the tolerant attitude of Islam toward such innovations could be seen in the appropriation by Islam of Greek logical method. Hayreddin Paşa did not investigate, however, the deeper problem as to why Islam had stopped at logic and had not gone farther in its borrowing of Greek attitudes and modes of thought. Hayreddin Paşa's superficial treatment of a tough cultural, philosophical, and historical problem was one which was paralleled in the writings of the Young Ottomans.

Like the Young Ottomans too, Hayreddin Paşa clamored for "justice" and stated, "It is a law of [divine] Providence that justice, good administration and good political institutions be the causes of the increase of the wealth of the population and general well-being and that the opposite bring decadence in all things."[14] Tying in this factor with his own interpretation of the rise of nationalism among the component peoples of the Ottoman Empire, Hayreddin Paşa stated that the disintegration of the empire was due to the fact that the Christian subjects of the Porte, deprived of the most basic benefits of justice by a corrupt judiciary, looked up to European governments for protection. Here again was a strain of thought reminiscent of Sadık Rifat Paşa and Namık Kemal—a way of thinking ultimately traceable to natural-law interpretations of the de-

[11] *Ibid.*, pp. 13, 14, 73.   [12] *Ibid.*, p. 11.
[13] *Ibid.*, p. 9.   [14] *Ibid.*, p. 14.

cline of empire. Hayreddin Paşa, however, attributed his inspiration in the matter to the North African historian Ibn Haldun.

Hayreddin Paşa's suggestions as to the immediate steps to be undertaken to achieve the political advances which he thought basic to the well-being of the Islamic states were to curb the power of the sovereign or, rather, to place it within well-established bounds. Hayreddin Paşa suggested that there were means at the disposal of the Islamic states to achieve such results—the possibilities provided by the institution of the *bai'a* and the Islamic theory of trusteeship. Adopting a line of reasoning already exploited by Kemal, Hayreddin Paşa viewed the *biat* (*bai'a*) as a necessity imposed on the ruler by God to take counsel before engaging in action. He kept in the background the fact that this was an historical development and that in the basic theory of Islam contained in the Koran there was nothing more substantial to rely on in this respect than a vague recommendation to "take counsel." According to Hayreddin Paşa, who saw a much more basic institution in the *Biat*, "[Islam] forbids any individual to act capriciously and in sole accordance with his personal leanings, she orders the protection of the rights of particulars, be they musulmans or not, she recommends the adoption of means and remedies appropriate to times and circumstances. . . . One of the most important prescriptions of this law, from the political point of view, is the obligation to take counsel before acting, imposed by God to his immaculate Prophet. . . . This was ordered to the Prophet only for an eminent reason which was to establish an obligatory rule for all who would follow him."[15]

Hayreddin Paşa concluded, "It is from this most important of measures that result the legitimacy of public acts and the necessity for ourselves to control the latter,"[16] adding, ". . . The citizens upon whom Moslem law imposes this obligation are called to play among us the same part that representative chambers and the press fulfill in Europe."[17] In Islam, repre-

[15] *Ibid.*, p. 15.   [16] *Ibid.*, p. 16.   [17] *Ibid.*, p. 18.

sentative institutions and the press were replaced by "the
direct obligation for sensible and enlightened people in the
nation to oppose themselves to any violation of the law."[18] A
comparison of these two expressions which are used to express
the same thought reveals, however, that Hayreddin Paşa was
encountering a dilemma which had faced Kemal before. In the
first case he spoke of "the citizens" as the controllers of public
acts; in the latter case he had the more able members of the
nation to fulfill this task. In other words, Hayreddin Paşa was
not clear as to the ultimate basis on which this "control" which
he wanted to establish would rest. The classical Islamic theory
had reference to the control of the enlightened members of
the community, but it is probable that Hayreddin Paşa saw
that this conception was not the basis of the European system
on which were founded the "representative chambers" to
which he looked up. However, by speaking of a "control" of
the acts of the sovereign rather than of a sovereign responsible
to the people in terms of a sovereignty which had been transferred from the people to the sovereign, Hayreddin Paşa was
closer to the spirit in which the institution of the *Biat* had been
understood for centuries than was Namık Kemal, who seems
to have thought of the *Biat* as a transfer of sovereignty.

The second theory which, according to Hayreddin Paşa,
pointed the path to be covered by Islamic liberals was the
theory of the delegation of sovereign powers to ministers. As
he stated, "All the authors who have written on this politico-
religious part of our jurisprudence are unanimous in their
interpretation which has the force of law and defend the
thesis that the delegation even of the greatest part of the
powers of the sovereign is not a limitation of sovereignty, but
that it constitutes, on the contrary, one of the sovereign rights
admitted by religion."[19]

All this led Hayreddin Paşa to conclude, "From all that
precedes necessarily follows the legitimacy of the intervention

[18] *Ibid.*   [19] *Ibid.*, p. 25.

of the nation in the sense and the limits of which we have spoken."[20]

Despite the amount of writing that it took Hayreddin Paşa to expose these ideas, it is difficult to extract a clear scheme of government from his work. One thing of which we can be certain is that he had the example of the Ottoman Empire before his eyes when he wrote down his ideas, and that he agreed with Âli Paşa that Turkey was not as yet ripe for the establishment of a national assembly on a nationwide basis. The reasons he gave for his stand were substantially the same as those of Âli Paşa; Hayreddin Paşa expressed his own misgivings as follows: "A certain number of Moslems, in agreement with the non-Moslem subjects of the Empire, finding these reforms to be insufficient, ask for the widest liberty to control the acts of the government. These demands which are requested to be made effective immediately are proffered with a view to the creation of institutions that an assembly composed of members elected by the entire nation would establish and safeguard. . . . Let us be permitted to ask them if they are quite sure that the non-Moslem subjects who demand these same liberties aim at their goal without mental reservations and merit to be trusted fully and completely. According to us there exist indices which allow the supposition that the aim of most of them is to disengage themselves from the rule of the Sublime Porte."[21]

The mention of "a certain number of Moslems" was a disguised reference to the Young Ottomans, and Hayreddin Paşa evidently thought they had gone too far in their proposals. A different sort of qualm was expressed by Hayreddin Paşa when he stated, "Among the tasks of the legislator charged with the founding of institutions is certainly included that of keeping account of the moral state of the masses and of the extent to which they have become recipients of useful knowledge in view of determining the degree of political liberty that can be granted to them and also to find out whether

[20] *Ibid.*, p. 27.   [21] *Ibid.*, pp. 38, 39.

the generalization of its exercise and its extension to all without distinction is indicated or whether political liberty should be granted only to those who find themselves in the special circumstances required for it."[22]

What, then, was Hayreddin Paşa's real goal? The real purpose behind his proposals and the core of his political program comes out in one of his remarks from which one can infer that his aim was the same as that of Reşid Paşa, namely, to establish *"un système immuablement établi,"* as Reşid Paşa had earlier phrased it. Hayreddin Paşa expressed this idea as follows: "Both success and failure in states which do not have political institutions entrusted to the safekeeping of constitutional bodies depend entirely on the character and personal qualities of the sovereign."[23]

Hayreddin Paşa expressed the same thought in a different passage when, in describing the desires of the most honest, competent, and idealistic-minded civil servants, he stated, ". . . [They] like and approve sincerely the system of institutions and prefer the usefulness to liberty, to dignity and to the public good to personal advantages which they could obtain under a system of arbitrary rule."[24]

In short, by proposing in 1868 to establish institutions of a permanent nature to fill in the gap opened by the decomposition of the "old orders" of the Ottoman Empire, by supporting the so-called "system of institutions"—that is, by establishing a stable framework for the activities of the ruler—Hayreddin Paşa was substantially setting forth proposals which Reşid Paşa had already firmly grounded in new institutions.

Hayreddin Paşa's specific proposals concerning the fashion in which governmental activity would be channeled by the institutions he proposed to establish confirm the impression that in substance he wanted to do what Reşid Paşa had already achieved in 1839. In Hayreddin Paşa's own words:

"The examination and the successive use of the means which must remedy to social necessities and contribute, together with

[22] *Ibid.*, pp. 54, 55.   [23] *Ibid.*, p. 24.   [24] *Ibid.*, p. 59.

progress, to the happiness of the nation can only take place by common understanding and by the uniting of one part of the nation composed of enlightened members of the ulema class and of men versed in politics. . . .

"It is thus to statesmen, because of their special knowledge to indicate the need or the ill and to propose the remedies, and it is to the ulema to take into consideration the means indicated by statesmen and to legitimize its application by a healthy and learned interpretation of the law."[25]

In Hayreddin Paşa's scheme the ulema were relegated to the position of legal advisors rather than keepers of the political conscience, and therefore even the special position he accords to the ulema has no special significance. What Hayreddin Paşa did not realize is that by the middle of the nineteenth century the Ottoman Empire was not in need of a strengthening of political institutions but that it needed a system by which those in charge of the institutions created during the Tanzimat would be held accountable to the people. No wonder that Hayreddin Paşa was considered to be incompetent by Namık Kemal, who had seen the system of corruption and irresponsibility evolved by the Ottoman statesmen who considered themselves to be members of a supremely wise elite. No wonder too that Abdülhamid, who was taken in by the mildness of Hayreddin Paşa's approach, realized, when the latter stood up for the use some of the "delegated power" of which he had spoken in his works, that Hayreddin Paşa had independently evolved the same type of theory as Reşid Paşa—a theory which had resulted in the Tanzimat statesmen getting stronger and stronger to the point where they deposed his uncle Abdülaziz.[26]

Hayreddin Paşa's scheme to gather a pool of expert politicians to act as consultants to the sovereign was quite in harmony with the original Islamic conception of the control exercised over political affairs by the "notables." But to this

---

[25] *Ibid.*, p. 49. See also p. 33.

[26] For an interchange of letters between Abdülhamid and Hayreddin Paşa on the subject of ministerial responsibility see Pakalın, *Son Sadrıazamlar ve Başvekiller*, IV, 360 *et seq.*

approach can again be opposed that of Namık Kemal, who, starting from similar Islamic premises, could go so far on his own as to think of the "common" people as an untapped reservoir of statesmanship.[27]

In matters of nationality we have already indicated the stand adopted by Hayreddin Paşa and his use of the word "nation" in the Islamic sense. Yet his mention of such sentiments as "patriotism" is indicative of a certain stiffening of attitude, of a nationalistic recoiling in oneself which is further substantiated by Hayreddin Paşa's accusations that the attempts of the Islamic nations to liberalize their system had been sabotaged by the European powers. Even though Europeans leveled the accusation of backwardness against these nations, they had a natural right to exist as a nation. "Even if it were established that the Moslem people were not mature enough to obtain any degree of political liberty, it must be admitted, nevertheless, that each of them has the natural right to exist as a nation whatever be the form of the government which steers it; one must also admit that, in consequence of the latter, and while not interfering in public affairs, each one of them has, in terms of its being a corporate entity ['association civile'], the right to demand that the administration be organized and regulated so that the functionaries be held responsible for their official acts under the laws."

The political ideas which appear in this paragraph are among those which show the strongest European imprint. In particular, it bears the imprint of such natural-law originators of the idea of nationality as Vattel. It also shows the influence of the theory of nationality. Since, however, the remainder of Hayreddin Paşa's statements do not seem to bear so direct and specific an imprint, it appears probable that Hayreddin Paşa directly appropriated some ideas that he came across in Europe to build up his own theory of national self-determination, a theory for which Islam provided only dubious material.

[27] See Namık Kemal, "Usul-u Meşveret," *Hürriyet*, September 14, 1868, p. 8.

·:۶ CHAPTER XIV 𝑒:·

Conclusions

ONE of the outstanding characteristics of a process of intellectual "modernization" such as we have just surveyed is its complexity. Thus we noticed that not one, but many strands entered into the elaboration of the first systematic—if not entirely consistent—statement of a new political theory by the Young Ottomans. Consequently, the genesis of these theories may be analyzed from a number of vantage points. We may consider them to be the result of institutional change, the product of a psycho-social involvement in traditional values, or the fruits of intellectual "diffusion" or "osmosis." These ideas may also be examined in relation to the reshuffling of elites brought about by the Tanzimat, or viewed as an illustration of changes wrought by a general increase in communications, as they may be taken to be the ultimate products of a certain immanent logic of things. Like the legendary elephant, the thought of the Young Ottomans means different things to different students.

In general, an attempt was made in the preceding pages to point out the various roads from which the corpus of Young Ottoman intellectual productions might be approached. It was also attempted to bring out into the open the mutually contradictory, or antagonistic, nature of some of the sources of inspiration of the Jeune Turquie, to show how larded with conflicting views of man, of society, and of the state was their intellectual inheritance.

Insofar as internal consistency goes, even the best Young Ottoman theoreticians did not cut a particularly impressive figure. This was due to the impossibility of taking over, as they would have liked, the "best" of European political institutions and of placing them on an Islamic substratum.

The major Islamic theory that the Young Ottomans used to create this synthesis was the theory of the *biat* (*bai'a*). Interpreted very liberally, the latter amounted to the ruler's re-membering the symbolic engagement taken at his investiture to account for his actions to the Islamic community. The *Biat*, however, was not a theory of popular sovereignty, for it was unclear as to whether a transfer of sovereignty was involved in the investiture. This was true, in turn, because no precise instrumentality was provided for the repeal of the mandate of the Caliph and because the deferential spirit which had per-vaded Islamic political theory for centuries had placed a pre-mium on obedience. On one hand, the jurists of Islam, while they did not condone tyranny, had not evolved an accepted theory of resistance. On the other, the theory of functionally differentiated orders in the realm, dependent as it was on the unquestioned acceptance of hierarchical relations, was even bleaker on this score. The European theories of responsible government, which the Young Ottomans wanted to use, how-ever, *had* grown around such theories of justified resistance.

This theoretical lacuna, even when established, does not ex-plain why a theory legitimizing revolt would have made the work of the Young Ottomans so much easier. After all, despite such an absence of a theory of justified revolt, revolts had occurred throughout the history of the Ottoman Empire. Could not the Young Ottomans have gone ahead with their protests without such a theory? The answer to this lies in the fact that the Young Ottomans were the first ideologues of the Ottoman Empire. Their medium of action was not the sword but the word. They were dependent for results on the reader-ship of the newspapers they published. But this weapon of the press that they used would have lost much of its force had they had recourse to the traditional fund of Ottoman ideas having regard to the relation between the individual and political authority. The first part of the problem with which they were faced, in other words, was not so much concerned with their own consciences as with the technical question of making effec-tive propaganda. Concentrating their wrath on the bureaucrats of the Porte while protesting their allegiance to the sultan solved this problem.

Insofar as their own consciences were concerned, the difficulty was much less easily overcome. Disliking the Porte did not solve the problem of what they would do if faced with an "evil" sultan. In fact, they were faced by such a sultan. It is in this connection that the close relation between the ability to fall back on a theory of justified resistance and the vitality of a movement of political protest emerges. When Abdülhamid dismissed the Ottoman parliament indefinitely within a year of its establishment, the Young Ottomans, with one exception, did not incite one another to revolt. On the contrary, they accepted administrative posts under his despotic rule.

There is no doubt that this behavior of the Young Ottomans, which has often erroneously been interpreted as a surrender of their ideals, had much more complex roots. It was basically the same type of attitude as had resulted in their earlier tolerance toward Mustafa Fazıl Paşa's contacts with the Porte—a tolerance that one would have expected to last a shorter time than it did. Again, it is the same fundamental outlook that made Namık Kemal establish polite, if not friendly relations with Âli Paşa's offer to enlighten him about the state of affairs in Europe. In all of these situations the actions of the Young Ottomans may be explained in terms of their willingness to sacrifice their ideas to the immediate benefits of the state.

The ideology of loyalty to the state was one which permeated all classes in the Ottoman Empire. In addition, Namık Kemal and his friends were, it should be remembered, former bureaucrats. It is while they were part of the Ottoman administration that they had been fired with the zeal to awaken "the nation." By the same token, however, they were determined to save the Ottoman state. At the end of the war the Young Ottomans did not consider it fair to the state to engage in revolt. It is difficult to separate the point here where traditional ideas with regard to the preservation of the state merge with the patriotism that was one of the major tenets of the Young Ottomans.

The obverse of this *feeling* was the *fact* that there had not developed in the Ottoman Empire the type of intermediate organization between the state and the individual to which a man like Namık Kemal could have pledged his allegiance when circumstances forced him against the wall.

With the ulema, who bore historically conditioned grudges against the employees of the state, the willingness to sacrifice oneself to the *state* was much weaker. The *person heading the state* was much more important.

This alone, of course, did not produce the outburst of Suavi, the only Young Ottoman to have lost his life in an attempted *coup d'état*. Suavi's outlook was fashioned, in addition, by an elusive Populism *cum* folk-tradition-of-violent-assertion which undeniably is one of the most pervasive and also least-known structural component of Ottoman society.

But to come back to the political theory of the Young Ottomans, the corollary of the theory of the *Biat*—the ruler's supposed obligation to consult with his community—was the second Islamic principle advanced by the Young Ottomans in support of responsible government. Yet in Islam this consultation was limited to the "weightier part" of the community. Furthermore, it was a feature of government *for* the people. This was also a feature of medieval Western theories, but since then the idea had arisen in the West of government *by* the people. The Islamic theory was not a theory of this nature. The real point at issue was that the Young Ottomans did not realize that the modern Western theory of representation depended on a belief in the intrinsic worth of the subjective will of the individual. Neither Islamic nor Ottoman consultative practices rested on such a basis.

Paradoxically enough, while the Young Ottomans ran into difficulties because they had no room for atomistic individualism, they also ran into difficulties because they did not dispose of a theory as to the corporate nature of the state. For in some respects liberal thought rested on nonindividualistic conceptions. This is particularly true of the theory of representation. Otto von Gierke traced this theory to Roman conceptions which were taken over in Europe in the Middle Ages, specifically to the Roman theory of corporate personality.[1] This thesis was advanced by Gierke as part of the general theory that the medieval world was on the way to, but never quite achieved, an organic theory of society.

The Roman theory of corporate personality, on the other hand, did take such an organismic view of the activity of social and economic groups. As such it may be considered the fountainhead from which eventually sprang such ideas as that of the Leviathan state, the "Raison d'Etat," and the Rousseauian abstraction of a General Will superior to the will of all. These were the authoritarian products of the Roman theory of corporations. Yet there were other democratic products of the same theory; one of them is the modern theory of representation.

Even though Gierke's main thesis has been challenged,[2] his contention that Western theories of representation could ultimately be traced back to the Roman theory of corporations has not been proved incorrect. And the availability of such a theory, viz., the idea that the community was a whole with a personality different from the sum of component parts, made it much easier to establish a clear-cut distinction between the individual and the body politic, and to create a rationale of representation in the West.

Though traces of the idea of corporate personality can be found in the works of some Islamic political thinkers, Islam did not possess such a theory of corporate personality for the community. The result was that, when Namık Kemal attempted to turn the *Biat* into a theory of representation, he was faced with a difficult task. As a result of the absence of a corporate theory of the state in Islam, the theory of the *Biat* was itself amorphous, half transfer of sovereignty, half con-

---

[1] Otto von Gierke, *The Development of Political Theory* (trans. by Bernard Freyd, New York, W. W. Norton and Co., 1939), p. 241.

[2] Ewart Lewis, "Organic Tendencies in Medieval Political Thought," *American Political Science Review* (October 1938), 32: 849, 876.

sultation with the community. For Kemal to evolve a rationale of representation based on the *Biat* was an almost insuperable task.

Another way of describing the Young Ottoman position would be to say that they opposed the centralizing activities of the state and wanted to establish in Turkey those political institutions which, at an earlier time, had been devised in the West as ideal checks against the encroachments of the state. The philosophy they offered in support of these goals, however, differed from the philosophy of the Western political thinkers who had provided the theory of these politicial institutions, viz., the theory of popular representation and sovereignty. The political philosophy of the Young Ottomans was a pre-Enlightenment philosophy. Its closest affinities were not with eighteenth- but with sixteenth-century Europe. Their ideas were most of all reminiscent of the theories that the defenders of the medieval polity had set forth against the new theory of sovereignty, the arguments they had used against the "progressives" of the sixteenth and seventeenth centuries. Thus the thesis advanced by Sir Thomas Smith in his *De Republica Anglicorum*—that the constitution consisted mainly of courts—paralleled Ziya Paşa's theory about the origin of government in which he made judges the first recipients of political authority. Like the author of the *Vindicae Contra Tyrannos*, the Young Ottomans saw no discrepancy between the theory that the king's power comes from God and the theory that it arose by a contract with the people. Like Sir Edward Coke's, the Young Ottomans' defiance of the existing powers grew out of the fact that they were conservatives. Just as in the case of the author of the *Vindicae*, they did not really develop a workable theory of resistance. But since then Enlightenment political theory, based on much more radical conceptions, had arisen. What the Young Ottomans did not realize was that there existed an organic bond between the political institutions advocated by a philosopher like Locke and the individualistic conceptions which lay behind them.

With respect to the establishment of fundamental freedoms, however, these restrictive aspects of the Islamic element in the thought of the Young Ottomans were counterbalanced by the very benefits of a theory of the state *qua* state which was amorphous. Indeed, Namık Kemal was acting on the strength of this element in Islamic thought when he protested against the idea of a general will. With the adoption of European conceptions of public law, expressing themselves in the anonymity of the administrative institutions created under the Tanzimat, the liberalizing effect of this absence of a conception of the general will in Islam had been lost. Namık Kemal tried to recapture this element of Islamic theory and weave it into his theory of the state.

To the inadequacies of the political theory of the Young Ottomans which have been mentioned to this point should be added a special reference to the intellectual history of the Ottoman Empire, which also ultimately has Islamic roots. That was the failure to devise a system of nature with its own inner dynamic. This factor greatly affected Ottoman intellectual development and placed great obstacles in the way of an empirical science of politics. This influenced the political theory of the Young Ottomans by emphasizing a political system at rest rather than one in motion and gave rise to their contradictory stand with regard to the idea of progress—on one hand praising abstract "progress" and the material advances of Europe and on the other hand looking back wistfully on the harmoniousness of an imaginary, ideal Islamic state.

The foregoing inadequacies in the theories of the Young Ottomans constitute excellent material for a critic of their conceptual schemes. Such critical analysis, engaged in in the present study to pinpoint their ideology as accurately as possible, is, however, beside the point. To dwell on these shortcomings of internal consistency is to be sterile in our appraisal of the Young Ottomans and to lose sight of their very real contributions. For, despite these shortcomings, the Young Ottomans did affect the society in which they were living. This is true both in the short and in the long run. The short run of success of the Young Ottomans consisted in that during their time a constitution was proclaimed, the genesis of which owed something to their propaganda and the substance of which incorporated some of their ideas. The coup which had preceded the proclamation of the constitution and made it possible was, it is true, due to the intervention of the army, but Young Ottoman ideas were also effective in the long run, i.e., the most important result of their propagandistic efforts was not so much the proclamation of the Ottoman constitution as the establishment of the belief that Sultan Abdülhamid had perpetrated a crime in suspending it. It is this belief, which would not have been widely held before the appearance of the Young Ottomans, which fed the underground opposition to the sultan between 1878 and 1908.

That there was such a link between the activities of the opponents of Abdülhamid's autocracy and the earlier Young Ottomans may be gathered from a glimpse at the first of the new series of attempts to make Turkey into a constitutional state after the final disbanding of the Young Ottomans. This was the unsuccessful coup of Aziz Bey. This conspiracy to dethrone Abdülhamid and bring back Sultan Murad to the throne took place in 1878, the same year that Ali Suavi's coup, the last sputter of Young Ottoman activity, failed. The new emphasis on coups to attain political ends marks a substantial change over the reluctance of the majority of the Young Ottomans to sully their hands with such methods, but the link between the two movements may be seen in that at least three members of the Suavi conspiracy were implicated once again in Aziz Bey's plot.

Then too, the most intellectual of the members of this last conspiracy, Ali Şefkati, was able to escape to Europe, where he started to publish the newspaper *Istikbal* ("The Future"). Thus he used one of Kemal's favorite abstractions as a name for a publication which took over where the *Ibret* had stopped. This short-lived organ was the first in a new series which greatly contributed to the undermining of Abdülhamid. Even more effective than this continuity of a tradition of criticism voiced in newspapers published by exiles was the direct influence of the writings of Kemal and Ziya on Turkish public opinion. One of the Turkish ideologists of the twentieth century, Süleyman Nazif (1870-1927), has characterized this effect of Kemal on his own generation by stating, "If we owe our life to God, we owe our entire upbringing to Kemal." Just as in 1876, when Abdülhamid's singlehanded rule came to an end, in 1908 it was the result of action by the military. The latter, however, had shown as early as 1876, during a secret investigation of the contents of their desks, that they were growing up reading Young Ottoman literature.

The impression that nowadays prevails in Turkey that the Young Ottomans were the direct intellectual ancestors of the Turkish Republic thus rests on partly correct foundations, and to cite Namık Kemal as the intellectual mentor of Atatürk is not an entirely erroneous point of view. It is often forgotten, however, that Young Ottoman theories were partly of Islamic origin. In the ideas of the Young Turks this substratum is weaker and it disappears completely in Atatürk. The significant strand to follow, then, in establishing the link between the Young Ottomans, the Young Turks, and Atatürk is the weakening of Islamic content.

Some clue as to what was involved in the later reappraisal of Islamic content may be understood from an analysis of one of the important contributions of the Young Ottomans which has not as yet been enumerated. This was their attitude toward the external world. This most important contribution of the Young Ottomans consisted in an increasing eagerness to *know*, to *study*, to *understand*, with a connection being made between knowledge and survival. Thus arose the Young Ottoman emphasis on education, on the necessity to master all Western governmental, administrative, and financial techniques, on the need to enlighten public opinion. Such knowledge which the Young Ottomans were seeking to keep the empire afloat seems to have differed in at least one essential respect from the knowledge that was pursued at an earlier time within the framework of the traditional Ottoman channels of learning: the drive to acquire knowledge now ran parallel with an ever-increasing awareness of the material substratum of historical change, of the material element in historical and social problems, and ultimately of the material bases of individual happiness. Even Namık Kemal, who thought of the political ideas of the Islamic jurists as basically valid for his own time, could not but state this discovery of the material world in the following terms:

"Let us cast a glance at the intellectual and educational treasurers of the world. In the last two centuries, the product of this knowledge has been a thousand times superior to that of ancient times in content of truth as well as in quantity. . . . And especially when philosophers abandoned abstractions and imaginary things, and established philosophy on experience and rational deduction, civilization began to proceed at an entirely different pace and gait on the road of progress. . . . Those who worked to wrest moral and material advantages by applying knowledge to external [physical] occurrences discovered steam and electricity. Two instrumentalities as productive of beautiful works as the spirit and as quick-moving as imagination were thus created to render service to humanity.

"It is due to steam that men like magicians walk over the sea and fly over the earth. It is due to electrical power that man, as if endowed with supernatural powers, is able to save both from time and space.

"It is due to steam that in countries with a population of twenty-five to thirty million, fifty to sixty million horsepower of steel and copper are unceasingly engaged in satisfying our pleasures and our needs. It is due to electricity that a sick man on this end of the world is able to save his life using the skills of a doctor on the other end of the globe.

"Natural gas appeared and the comfort of humanity was further increased. . . .

"Engineeering has reached the zenith of expectations: through it, continents are separated, seas are united, plots of earth are located in the midst of vast oceans and water found in sandy wastes.

"Economics has given rise to the division of labor. A mediocre artisan is, in his field, ten times as able as an ancient master craftsman. . . .

"Commerce has found an extraordinary welcome. Men richer than a thousand companies establish companies more powerful than states . . . .

"When will we start taking example? . . .

"What we have done does not amount to more than a few superficial changes that newspapers—and that through the efforts of the late Şinasi—were able to bring about in our literature.

"We do not have a single factory. How are arts [and crafts] to prosper in our country?

"We have not been able to establish a single joint-stock company. Is this the way to advance trade?

"Is there a single Ottoman Bank in existence? How do we propose to go about creating wealth?"[3]

The earliest appearance of this interest in the material world may be traced back to the eighteenth century. At that time the discovery that superiority in armaments, methods of warfare, and logistics had led to the victory of European armies began to impress itself with increasing clarity in the minds of Turkish statesmen. But it took approximately a century of intellectual evolution for the admiration of material advances to take place among accepted "operative ideals."

A different facet to the same type of attitude toward the external world was the "activism" of the Young Ottomans, an attitude which, as we have shown, begins to occur as an outright defense of rationality and active control over man's fate some forty years before the Young Ottomans became active. This attitude had existed in embryonic form even

---

[3] Namık Kemal, "İbret," *Namık Kemal ve İbret Gazetesi*, pp. 39-41.

among the earliest Ottoman reformers. The latter, however, were interested in picking up the pieces into which the Ottoman Empire had disintegrated and in building up once more a social and governmental machine identical with the one that had disintegrated ("reform in consonance with the practice of my ancestors"). These men were for action but against innovation. The Young Ottomans were both for action and for innovation. Their desire for innovation, however, was in itself the result of the magnification of the desire for change. It was a "qualitative" change due to a "quantitative" development.

Among the Young Ottomans an activist attitude was expressed in the increasing use of the term *"irade-i cüz'iyye"* ("partial will"). This term was used to denote that sphere of man's actions over which God had only a partial control. It was always associated with urgings to create, to work, to rise up against tyranny, to defend the fatherland. Again, this philosophical development does not seem to have been limited to the Young Ottomans. In its purest form it appears in the form of a revival of the antipredestinarian, Maturidite philosophy in the nineteenth century. It also reappears in the writings of the Egyptian reformer Muhammad Abdu, as well as in the ideas of the Iranian reformer Cemaleddin Afgani.

The Young Ottomans, however, had somewhat of an advantage over their Iranian and Egyptian comodernizers. This advantage consisted in that the spirit of *gazâ*, the underpinning of the Ottoman state, lent itself to an activist ideology. The humiliation of suffering military defeats, of having policy dictated by the European Great Powers, found echoes in the minds of Turks of all walks of life. The Young Ottomans themselves had been urged to action by such considerations in the first place. This was the foundation of Young Ottoman patriotism.

If the activism of the Young Ottomans, which was that part of their theories that was most in tune with the spirit of European modernization, had been allowed to become fused with a smoother conceptual scheme than the one they had to offer, a genuine modernist Islamic synthesis might have resulted. What the Young Ottomans needed was time. In the ten years they were active they had already done considerable work in creating such a synthesis. But the Young Ottomans were never granted the breathing spell they needed to refine their theories. Because he distrusted the alliance between liberal bureaucrats and ulema, Abdülhamid II gave neither an opportunity to regroup. As he persecuted liberals, he also actively encouraged obscurantism in the *medreses*. He turned the latter into refuges for deserters, evaders of military service, and other riffraff. Thus the process of a decrease in sophistication among the ulema, of which Cevdet Paşa had spoken, was compounded.

By the time of the Young Turk coup of 1908, the ulema had been eased into an intellectual limbo. Conversely, of the two elements the Young Ottomans had attempted to fuse— the activist attitude and the Islamic dogma—activism floated to the surface and without deep intellectual underpinning became its own justification. As to the ulema, they never recovered from the blow dealt them by the "defender of the faith," the sultan-caliph.

Authors who died before the passing of the Turkish Law of
Family Names are listed in the alphabetical order of their first
names.

Authors who lived long enough to select a family name appear in
the same order as those included in the preceding category but followed by their new family names in brackets.
All other names are spelled in the order of the last (family)
name.

I. Books

Abdurrahman Sami [Paşa]. *Rumuz ül-Hikem.* Istanbul: Şeyh
Yahya Efendi Matbaası, 1287/1870-1871.

Abdurrahman Şeref. *Tarih-i Devlet-i Osmaniye.* Istanbul: Karabet, 1315/1897-1898. 2 vols.

————. *Tarih Musahabeleri.* Türkiye Cumhuriyeti Maarif Vekâleti Neşriyatından, Aded 10, Istanbul: Matbaa-i Âmire, 1339/
1920-1921.

[Abro Sahak]. *Avrupada Meşhur Ministrolarının Tercüme-i Hallerine dair Risale.* Istanbul: Takvimhane-i Âmire, Şaban, 1271/
1855.

Acollas, Émile. *La Déclaration des Droits de l'Homme de 1793
Commentée.* Paris: A. Chevalier-Moresq, 1885.

Adıvar, Abdülhak Adnan. *Osmanlı Türklerinde İlim.* Istanbul:
Maarif Matbaası, 1943.

Agâh Sırrı, [Levend]. *Türk Dilinde Gelişme ve Sadeleşme Safhaları.* Türk Dil Kurumu, 31. Ankara: Türk Tarih Kurumu
Basımevi, 1949.

Ahmed Cevdet Paşa. *Tarih-i Cevdet.* 2nd ed. Istanbul: Matbaa-i
Osmaniye, 1309/1891-1892. 12 vols.

————. *Tezâkir 1-12.* Ed. by Cavid Baysun, Türk Tarih Kurumu Yayınlarından Seri II, No. 22. Ankara: Türk Tarih
Kurumu Basımevi, 1953.

Ahmed Galib. *Sadullah Paşa yahut Mezardan Nida'.* 1st ed. Istanbul: Matbaa-i Ebüzziya, 1909.

Ahmed Lûtfi. *Mir'at-ı Adalet, Yahud Tarihçe-i Adliye-i Devlet-i*

Osmaniye. Istanbul: Matbaa-i Nişan Berberyan, 1304/1886-1887.

———. *Tarih*. Istanbul: Matbaa-i Âmire-Sabah Matbaası, 1290-1328/1873-1911. 8 vols.

Ahmed Midhat. *Sevda-yı Sây-ü Amel*. Istanbul: n.p., 1296/1879.

———. *Üss-ü Inkilâb*. Istanbul: Matbaa-i Âmire, 1294-1295/1877-1878.

Ahmed Rasim. *Istibdattan Hakimiyet-i Milliyeye*. Istanbul: Vatan Matbaası, 1342/1923. 2 vols.

———. *Matbuat Tarihimize Methal*: İlk Büyük Muharrirlerden Şinasi. Istanbul: Yeni Matbaa, 1927.

Ahmed Refik [Altınay]. *Âlimler ve Sanatkârlar*. Geçmiş Asırlarda Türk Hayatı. Istanbul: Hilmi, 1924.

———. *Hicrî On ikinci Asırda Istanbul Hayatı 1100-1200*. Istanbul: Devlet Matbaası, 1930.

———. *Lâle Devri*. 5th ed. Istanbul: Hilmi Kitaphanesi [*sic*], 1932.

———. *Türkiyede Mülteciler Meselesi*. Istanbul: Matbaa-i Âmire, 1926.

Ahmed Saib. *Tarih-i Sultan Murad-ı Hâmis*. Cairo: Matbaa-i Hindiye, n.d.

———. *Vak'a-yi Sultan Abdülaziz*. Cairo: Matbaa-i Hindiye, 1320 Malî/1904-1905.

Ali [Basiretçi Ali Efendi]. *Istanbulda Yarım Asırlık Vakai-i Mühimme*. Istanbul: Matbaa-i Hüseyin ve Enver, 1325 Malî/1909-1910.

Ali Ekrem [Bulayır]. *Namık Kemal*. Istanbul: Devlet Matbaası, 1932.

Ali Fuad. *Rical-i Mühimme-i Siyasiye*. 2nd ed. Istanbul: Yeni Matbaa, 1928.

Ali Haydar. *Beyan-ı Hakikat*. Istanbul: Matbaa-i Âmire, Muharrem 1293/1876.

[Âli Paşa]. *Réponse à son Altesse Mustafa Fazyl Pacha au Sujet de sa Lettre au Sultan*. Paris: n.p., 1867.

Ali Suavi. *Âli Paşanın Siyaseti*. Istanbul: Asadoryan Matbaası, 1325/1909.

———. *A Propos de l'Hertzégovine*. Paris: n.p., 1875.

———. *Hive*. Istanbul: Artin Asadoryan, 1326 Malî/1910-1911.

————. *Hukuk ül-Şevari'*. Istanbul: Uhuvvet Matbaası, 1324/ 1908.

————. *Kânipaşazâde Ahmed Rifat Beye Yazılan Mektup Sureti.* n.n., n.p., n.d.

————. *Le Khiva en Mars 1873.* Paris-Londres: Imprimerie Victor Goupy, 1873.

Alric, Arthur. *Un Diplomate Ottoman en 1836 (Affaire Churchill).* Traduction annotée de l' "Éclaircissement" ("*Tebsireh*") d'Akif-Pacha, Ministre des Affaires Etrangères de Turquie. Paris: Ernest Leroux, 1892.

Andréossy, General Comte Antoine François. *Constantinople et le Bosphore de Thrace.* 3rd ed. Paris: Duprat, 1841.

[Anhegger, Dr. Robert and Inalcık, Dr. Halil (eds.)]. *Kānūnnāme-i Sultānī ber Müceb-i Örf-i Osmāni: II Mehmed ve Bayezit Devirlerine ait Yasakname ve Kanunnameler.* Türk Tarih Kurumu Yayınları, Seri xi, No. 5, Ankara: Türk Tarih Kurumu Basımevı, 1956.

Anıl, Muallâ (ed.). *Şinasi: Müntahabat-ı Eş'arım.* Istanbul: Ahmet Sait Matbaası, 1945.

Aquinas, St. Thomas. *Selected Political Writings.* Ed. by A. P. d'Entrèvas. Trans. by J. G. Dawson. Oxford: Basil Blackwell, 1954.

Aristarchi bey [Grégoire]. *Législation Ottomane ou Recueuil de Lois, Règlements, Ordonnances et Autres Documents de l'Empire Ottoman.* Constantinople: Freres Nicolaidès, 1873-1888. 7 vols.

Arnold, T. W., and Guillaume, Alfred (eds.). *The Legacy of Islam.* London: Oxford University Press, 1931.

Arnold, Sir Thomas. *The Caliphate.* Oxford: Clarendon Press, 1924.

Arsal, Sadri Maksudi. *Türk Tarihi ve Hukuk: I. İslamiyetten Evvelki Devir.* İstanbul Üniversitesi Yayınlarından No. 336. Istanbul: Ismail Akgün Matbaası, 1947.

Atay, Falih Rıfkı. *Baş Veren bir Inkilâpçı.* Ankara: Doğuş Matbaası, 1954.

Avni, Hüseyin. *Reaya ve Köylü: Feodalite Reayası Bügünkü Köylü Tiplerine Nasıl Tahavvül Etti.* Istanbul: Tan Matbaası, 1941.

Avram Galanti [Bodrumlu]. *Küçük Türk Tetebbüleri.* Vol. 1.

Istanbul Kâğıtçılık ve Matbaacılık Anonim Şirketi, 1341 Malî/ 1925.

Ayad, Dr. Kamil. *Die Geschichte und Gesellschaftslehre Ibn Halduns.* Forschungen zur Geschichte und Gesellschaftslehre 2 Heft. Stuttgart und Berlin: Cotta, 1930.

Ayetullah. *Merhum Ayetullah Efendinin Rüyası yahut Sadrıazam Âli Paşanın Muhakemesi.* Istanbul: Vezir Hanı, 1326 Malî/ 1910-1911.

Azam, Victor. *L'Avénement d'Abdul Aziz: Avenir de l'Empire Ottoman.* Paris: Dentu, 1861.

Babinger, Franz. *Die Geschichtsschreiber der Osmanen und Ihre Werke;* Mit Einem Anhang: Osmanische Zeitrechnungen von Joachim Mayer. Leipzig: Otto Harrassowitz, 1927.

————. *Stambuler Buchwesen in 18 Jahrhundert.* Leipzig: Deutscher Verein für Buchwesen und Schriften, 1919.

Bailey, Frank Edgar. *British Policy and the Turkish Reform Movement:* A Study in Anglo-Turkish Relations, 1826-1853. Harvard Historical Studies, Vol. 51. Cambridge, Mass.: Harvard University Press, 1942.

Baker, James. *Turkey.* New York: Henry Holt, 1877.

Baykal, Ismail Hakkı. *Enderun Mektebi Tarihi.* Istanbul: Halk Basımevi, 1955.

Becker, C. H. *Islamstudien: Vom Werden und Wesen der Islamischen Welt.* Leipzig: Quelle und Meyer, 1932. 2 vols.

Bereketzâde, Ismail Hakkı. *Yâd-ı Mazi.* Istanbul: Tevsi-i Tabaat Matbaası, 1332/1913-1914.

Bianchi, Thomas Xavier. *Khaththy Humaioun* ou Charte Imperiale Ottomane du 18 Fevrier 1856 . . . suivi de notes et d'éxplications. Paris, 1856.

————. *Vocabulaire Français-Turc.* Paris: Everat, 1831.

Birge, John Kingsley. *A Guide to Turkish Area Study.* Washington, D.C.: American Council of Learned Societies, 1949.

————. *The Bektashi Order of Dervishes.* Luzac's Oriental Religion Series, Vol. vII. London: Luzac and Co., 1937.

Birinci Köy ve Kalkınma Kongresi. *Türk Ziraat Tarihine Bir Bakış.* Istanbul: Devlet Basımevı, 1938.

Boué, Ami. *La Turquie d'Europe,* Vol. III. Paris: Arthus Bertrand, 1840.

Brockelmann, Carl. *History of the Islamic Peoples*. London: Routledge, 1952.

Brown, John P. *The Darvishes or Oriental Spiritualism*. Ed. with an introduction by H. A. Rose. London: Oxford University Press, 1927.

Browne, E. G. *The Persian Revolution of 1905-1909*. Cambridge University Press, 1910.

Brunswik, Benoit. *La Succession au Trône de Turquie*. Paris: Amyot, 1872.

————. *La Vérité sur Mithat Pacha*. Paris: Ernest Leroux, 1877.

Bury, Lord Hewart of. *The New Despotism*. London: Ernest Benn, 1929.

Canini, Marco Antonio. *Vingt Ans d'Exil*. Paris: Dramard-Baudry, 1868.

Capoléone, Dr. L. *Une Reponse à M. de Kératry à propos de son ouvrage intitulé Mourad V: prince-sultan-prisonnier d'état*. Constantinople [Istanbul]: n.p., 1878.

Castille, Hypollite. *Rechid-Pacha*. Portraits Politiques et Historiques au Dix-neuvième Siècle. Paris: Ferdinand Sartorius, 1857.

Catalogue de la Bibliothèque du feu Ahmed Vefyk Pacha. Constantinople [Istanbul]: K. Bagdadlian, 1893.

Cemiyet-i Tedrisiye-i İslamiye Salnamesi. Ed. by Cemiyet-i Tedrisiye-i İslamiye. [Istanbul]: n.n., 1332 Malî/1916-1917.

Charmes, Gabriel. *L'Avenir de la Turquie: le Panislamisme*. Paris: Calman-Levy, 1883.

Chertier, Edmond. *Les Réformes en Turquie*. Paris: E. Dentu, 1858.

Chinassi. (See "Şinasi.")

Chumarian, Cricor. *Abregé de la Vie des Plus Illustres Philosophes de l'Antiquité*. Smyrne [sic]: Imprimerie Daveroni et Sogioli, 1854.

Collas, L. B. C. *La Mort d'Abdul Medjid*: Dernier Jour de l'Empire Ottoman. Paris: E. Dentu, 1861.

————. *La Turquie en 1864*. Paris: E. Dentu, 1873.

Collingwood, R. G. *The Idea of Nature*. Oxford: Clarendon Press, 1945.

Comte, Auguste. *Système de Politique Positive ou Traité de Socio-*

logie Instituant la Religion de l'Humanité. Vol. III. Paris: Carillan-Goeury et Dalmont, 1853.

Danişmend, Ismail Hami. *İzahlı Osmanlı Tarihi Kronolojisi.* Türkiye Yayınevi Tarih Serisi Yeni İnceleme ve Telifler No. 1. Vol. IV. Istanbul: Türkiye Yayınevi, 1955.

Davids, Arthur Lumley. *A Grammar of the Turkish Language.* London: Parbury, Allen and Taylor, 1832.

Davison, Roderic H. "Reform in the Ottoman Empire," unpublished Ph.D. thesis. Harvard, 1942.

[de Kay, James E.]. *Sketches of Turkey.* New York: Harper, 1833.

Dérathé, Robert. *Jean-Jacques Rousseau et la Science Politique de son Temps.* Bibliothèque de la Science Politique. Deuxieme Série. Les Grandes Doctrines Politiques. Paris: Presses Universitaires de France, 1950.

Déstrilhes, M. *Confidences sur la Turquie.* 3e. ed. revue et augmentée. Paris: E. Dentu, 1856.

Devvani, Celaleddin [Dawwānī]. *Practical Philosophy of the Muhammadan People* exhibited in its professed connexion with the European so as to render either an introduction to the other, being a translation of *The Akhlak-i Jalaly* the most esteemed work of Middle Asia from the Persian of Fakir Jany Muhammad Asaad. Trans. and notes by W. F. Thompson. London: Allen and Co., 1839.

Dizdaroğlu, Hikmet (ed.). *Şinasi: Hayatı ve Eserleri.* Istanbul: Varlık Yayınevi, 1954.

Djelaleddine, Moustafa. *Les Turcs Anciens et Modernes.* Constantinople: Imprimerie du Courrier d'Orient, 1869.

Douin, G. *Histoire du Règne du Khedive Ismail.* Rome: Institute Poligrafico Dello Stato, 1933. 3 vols.

le Duc, Léouzon. *La Turquie est-elle incapable de Réformes.* Paris: E. Dentu, 1876.

Eichmann, R. *Die Reformen des Osmanischen Reiches*, mit besonderer berücksichtigung des Verhaltnisse der Christen des Orients zur Türkischen Herrschaft. Berlin: Nicolaische Buchhandlung, 1858.

Elliott, Sir Henry. *Some Revolutions and other Diplomatic Experiences.* New York: E. P. Dutton, 1922.

Engelhardt, Edouard. *La Turquie et le Tanzimat*. Paris: Cotillon, 1882-1884. 2 vols.

d'Entrèves, Passerin. *Natural Law*. Oxford: Clarendon Press, 1951.

Erişçi, Lûtfi. *Türkiyede İşçi Sınıfının Tarihi*. Istanbul: Kutulmuş Basimevi, 1951.

[Ertaylan], Ismail Hikmet. *Namık Kemal*. Istanbul: Kanaat Kitabevi, 1931.

————. *Şinasi*. Istanbul: Kanaat Kütüphanesi, 1932.

————. *Türk Edebiyatı Tarihi*. *Ondokuzuncu Asır*. Baku: Azer Neşir, 1925.

————. *Ziya Paşa: Hayatı, Eserleri*. Istanbul: Kanaat Kütüphanesi, 1932.

Esad Efendi [Sahhaflar Şeyhi Zâde]. *Üss-ü Zafer*. 1st ed. Istanbul: n.n., 1243/1827-1828.

Esatlı, Mustafa Ragıp (ed.). *Ölümünden Sonra Rıza Tevfik*. Istanbul: Sinan Matbaası, 1952.

Faik Reşad. *Edib-i Âzam Kemal*. Istanbul: Cihan Matbaası, 1326 Malî/1910.

Farley, J. Lewis. *Modern Turkey*. 2nd ed. London: Hurst and Blackett, 1872.

Fatma Aliye. *Ahmed Cevdet Paşa ve Zamanı*. Istanbul: Kanaat Matbaası, 1332/1913.

Fénelon, François de Salignac de la Mothe. *Oeuvres*. Ed. by Gosselin & Caron. Paris: Lebel, 1820-1830.

Fesch, Paul. *Constantinople aux Derniers Jours d'Abdülhamid*. Paris: Librairie des Sciences Politiques et Sociales Marcel Rivière, 1907.

Finer, Herman. *The Governments of European Powers*. New York: Henry Holt, 1956.

Fontanier, Victor. *Voyage en Orient Entrepris par ordre du gouvernement français*. Paris: Vols. 1 et 2 de 1821 à 1829 (1829); vol. 3 de 1830 à 1833 (1834).

Fontenelle, Bernard le Bovier de. *Nouveau Dialogue des Morts*. Amsterdam: Pierre Mortier, 1701.

Friedrich, Carl J., *Constitutional Government and Democracy*. 2nd ed. Boston: Ginn & Co., 1950.

Gallenga, Antonio. *Two Years of the Eastern Question.* London: S. Tinsley, 1877.

Gardet, Louis. *La Cité Musulmane. Vie Sociale et Politique.* Paris: Librairie Philosophique J. Vrin, 1954.

Gibb, E. J. W. *A History of Ottoman Poetry.* London: Luzac, 1900-1909. 6 vols.

Gibb, H. A. R. *La Structure de La Pensée Religieuse de l'Islam.* Traduit de l'Anglais par Jeanne et Felix Arin. Institut des Hautes Études Marocaines, Notes et Documents, Fascicule VII. Paris: Éditions Larose, 1950.

————, and Bowen, Harold. *Islamic Society and the West: A Study of the Impact of Western Civilization on Moslem Culture in the Near East.* Vol. I, *Islamic Society in the Eighteenth Century.* Parts I and II. London: Oxford University Press for the Royal Institute of International Affairs, 1950-1957.

Gierke, Otto von. *Political Theories of the Middle Age.* Trans. by Frederick William Maitland. Cambridge: The University Press, 1951.

Gough, J. W. *John Locke's Political Philosophy.* Oxford: Clarendon Press, 1950.

Grunebaum, G. E. von. *Medieval Islam.* 2nd ed. Chicago: University of Chicago Press, 1953.

Halil Cemaleddin. *Ecanibin Memalik-i Osmaniyede Haiz oldukları Imtiyazat-ı Adliye.* Istanbul: Hukuk Matbaası, 1331/1913-1914.

Halil Halid. *The Diary of a Turk.* London: A. and C. Black, 1903.

Halil Şerif. *Kudema-i Mulûk-u Mısriye Tarihi.* Kütüphane-i Ebüzziya. Istanbul: Matbaa-i Ebüzziya, 1304/1886-1887.

Hallowell, John H. *Main Currents in Modern Political Thought.* New York: Henry Holt, 1950.

Hammer, J. de [Joseph Freiherr von Hammer-Purgstall]. *Des Osmanischen Reichs Staatsvervassung und Staatsverwaltung.* Vienna: Camesinaschen Buchhandlung, 1815.

————. *Geschichte der Osmanischen Dichtkunst bis auf unsere Zeit.* Pest: Hartleben, 1838. 4 vols.

————. *Histoire de l'Empire Ottoman Depuis son Origine Jusq'à nos Jours.* Ouvrage Puisé aux Sources les Plus Authentiques et Redigé sur des Documens [sic] et des Manuscrits pour la Plupart Inconnus en Europe. Traduit de l'Allemand par J. J. Hellert. Paris: Bellizard, Barthus, Dufour et Lowell, 1835-1843. 18 vols.

Hayreddin. *Vesaik-i Tarihiye ve Siyasiye Tetebbuatı*. Istanbul: Ahmed Ihsan, 1326 Malî/1910-1911. 5 vols.

Hayreddin Paşa. *Mukaddime-i Akvam el-Mesalik fi Marifetu Ahval ül-Memalik*. Trans. by Abdurrahim Efendi. Istanbul: Elcevaib, 1878.

————. [Khéréddin, General]. *Réformes Nécessaires aux États Musulmans*. Paris: Dupont, 1868.

Heidborn, A. *Manuel de Droit Public et Administratif de l'Empire Ottoman*. Leipzig: C. W. Stern, 1908. 2 vols.

Hobbes, Thomas. *Leviathan*. Ed. by Michael Oakeshott. Oxford: Basil Blackwell, 1946.

İbnülemin Mahmud Kemal [İnal]. *Osmanlı Devrinde Son Sadrıazamlar*. Istanbul: Maarif Matbaası, 1940-1953.

————. *Son Asır Türk Şairleri*. Türk Tarih Külliyati Encümeni, Sayi 16. Istanbul: Orhaniye Matbaası, 1930-1942. 12 vols.

————, and Hüseyin Hüsameddin [Yaşar] (eds.). *Evkaf-ı Hümâyun Nezaretinin Tarihçe-i Teşkilâtı ve Nuzzarın Teracim-i Ahvali*. Istanbul: Evkaf-i Islamiye Matbaası, 1330 Malî/ 1914.

Ibrahim Alaettin [Gövsa]. *Türk Meşhurları Ansiklopedisi*. Istanbul: Yedigün Neşriyatı, 1946.

Iğdemir, Uluğ. *Kuleli Vak'ası Hakkında bir Araştırma*. Türk Tarih Kurumu Yayınlarından VII Seri, No. 3. Ankara: Türk Tarih Kurumu Basımevi, 1937.

İnalcik, Halil. *Tanzimat ve Bulgar Meselesi*. Ankara Üniversitesi Dil ve Tarih-Coğrafya Fakültesi Doktora Tezleri Serisi, No. 2. Ankara: Türk Tarih Kurumu, 1943.

İskit, Server N. *Hususî ilk Türkçe Gazetemiz Tercüman-ı Ahval ve Agâh Efendi*. Ankara: Ulus Basımevi, 1937.

————. *Türkiyede Matbuat İdareleri ve Politikaları*. Istanbul: Tan Basımevi, 1943.

————. *Türkiyede Matbuat Rejimleri*. Matbuat Umum Müdürlüğü Neşriyatından, 1939.

İskit, Server N. *Türkiyede Neşriyat Hareketleri Tarihine bir Bakış.* Istanbul: Devlet Basımevi, 1938.

Ismail Habib [Sevük]. *Edebî Yeniliğimiz: Birinci Kısım.* Istanbul: Devlet Matbaası, 1931.

————. *Tanzimattanberi* II: *Edebiyat Tarihi Antolojisi.* Istanbul: Remzi Kitabevi, 1943.

Jorga, N. *Geschichte des Osmanischen Reiches Nach den Quellen Dargestellt.* Allgemeine Staatengeschichte Erste Abteilung: Geschichte der Europaischen Staaten No. 37. Gotha: Freidrich Andreas Perthes, 1908-1913. 5 vols.

Jouannin, J. N., and Van Gaver, Jules. *Turquie.* Paris: Firmin Didot, 1840.

Juchereau de Saint Denys, A. de. *Révolutions de Constantinople.* Paris: Librairie Brissot-Thivars, 1819. 2 vols.

Dr. K. *Errinerungen aus dem Leben des Serdar Ekrem Ömer Pascha.* Sarajevo: 1885.

Kaplan, Mehmet. *Namık Kemal: Hayatı ve Eserleri.* İstanbul Üniversitesi Edebiyat Fakültesi Yayınları, No. 378, Türk Dil ve Edebiyatı Doktora Tezi, No. 1. Istanbul: İbrahim Horoz, 1948.

Karal, Enver Ziya. *Fransa-Mısır ve Osmanlı İmparatorluğu, 1797-1802.* İstanbul Üniversitesi Yayınları, 63, Edebiyat Fakültesi Tarih Semineri VIII. Istanbul: Millî Mecmua Basımevi, 1938.

————. *Osmanlı Tarihi,* V, *Nizam-ı Cedit ve Tanzimat Devirleri 1789-1856.* Türk Tarih Kurumu Yayınları, Series XIII, No. 16s. Ankara: Türk Tarih Kurumu Basımevi, 1947.

————. *Osmanlı Tarihi,* VII, *Islahat Fermanı Devri 1861-1876.* Türk Tarih Kurumu Yayınları, Series XIII, No. 16g. Ankara: Türk Tarih Kurumu Basımevi, 1956.

————. *Selim III'un Hatt-ı Hümayunları.* Türk Tarih Kurumu Yayınları, Series VII, No. 10. Ankara: Türk Tarih Kurumu Basımevi, 1942.

————. *Selim III'un Hat-tı* [sic] *Hümayunları: Nizam-ı Cedit 1789-1807.* Türk Tarih Kurumu Yayınlarından, Series VII, No. 14. Ankara: Türk Tarih Kurumu Basımevi, 1946.

Karatay, Fehmi Ethem. *İstanbul Üniversitesi Türkçe Basmalar*

Alfabe Kataloğu (1729-1928). Istanbul: Osman Yalçın, 1956. 2 vols.

Kaynar, Reşat. *Mustafa Reşit Paşa ve Tanzimat*. Türk Tarih Kurumu Yayınlarından, Series VII, No. 19. Ankara: Türk Tarih Kurumu Basımevi, 1954.

Kératry, Comte E. de. *Mourad V, Prince, Sultan, Prisonnier d'État (1840-1878)*, d'après des témoins de sa vie. Paris: E. Dentu, 1878.

Kern, Fritz. *Kingship and Law in the Middle Ages*. Trans. by S. B. Chrimes. Oxford: Basil Blackwell, 1939. 2 vols.

Khadduri, Majid. *War and Peace in the Law of Islam*. Baltimore: The Johns Hopkins Press, 1955.

Kınalızâde, name used for Alâeddin Ali b. Amrullah. *Ahlâk-ı Alaî*. Egypt: Bulak, 1248/1833.

Kocabaş, Hüseyin. *Ali Suavi Vak'ası Üzerine Verilmiş Fetvâ*. Bursa: Anıt Basımevi, 1949.

[Koçi Bey]. *Koçi Bey Risalesi*: Nizam-i Devlete Dair Göriceli Koçi Beyin Râbi Sultan Murad Han-ı Gaziye Takdim eylediği Risaledir. 1st ed. Istanbul: Matbaa-i Ebüzziya, 1303/1885-1886.

Kohn, Hans. *The Idea of Nationalism*. New York: Macmillan, 1944.

Koprülüzâde, Mehmed Fuad. *Millî Edebiyat Cereyanının İlk Mübeşşirleri*. Istanbul: Devlet Matbaası, 1928.

Koran, The. Emiriyya Edition. Cairo: 1348/1929-1930.

——. *The Qur'an*. Trans. with a critical rearrangement of the Surahs by Richard Bell. Edinburgh: T. and T. Clark, 1937.

Kraelitz-Greifenhorst, Freidrich von. *Die Verfassungsgesetze des Osmanischen Reiches*: übersetzt und mit einer Einleitung versehen. Vienna: Verlag des Forschungsinstituts für Osten und Orient, 1919.

Kuntay, Mithat Cemal. *Namık Kemal*: Devrinin İnsanları ve Olayları Arasında. Vol. I. Istanbul: Maarif Matbaası, 1944; II, 1. Istanbul: Millî Eğitim Basımevi, 1949; II, 2, *ibid.*, 1957.

——. *Sarıklı İhtilalcı Ali Suavi*. Istanbul: Ahmet Halit Kitabevi, 1946.

Kuran, Ahmet Bedevî. *İnkilâp Tarihimiz ve Jön Türkler*. Istanbul: Tan Matbaası, 1945.

Lalande, André (ed.). *Vocabulaire Technique et Critique de la Philosophie*. Paris: Presses Universitaires de France, 1951.

Lammens, H. J. *l'Islam: Croyances et Institutions*. Beyrouth: Imprimerie Catholique, 1925.

Lane-Poole, Stanley. *The Life of the Right Honorable Stratford Canning, Viscount Stratford de Redcliffe*. London: Longmans, Green, 1888. 2 vols.

Layard, Sir A. Henry. *Autobiography and Letters* from his childhood until his appointment as H.M. Ambassador at Madrid. Ed. by William N. Bruce. London: John Murray, 1903. 2 vols.

Levy, Reuben. *A Mirror for Princes, The Qabus Nama by Kai Ka'us Ibn Iskandar of Gurgan*. New York: E. P. Dutton, 1951.

————. *The Social Structure of Islam*. Cambridge: Cambridge University Press, 1957.

Lewis, Ewart. *Medieval Political Ideas*. London: Routledge & Kegan Paul, 1954.

Lindsay, A. D. *The Modern Democratic State*. London: Oxford University Press, 1943.

Locke, John. *Essays on the Law of Nature*. Ed. by W. von Leyden. Oxford: Clarendon Press, 1954.

————. *The Second Treatise of Civil Government and A Letter Concerning Toleration*. Ed. by J. W. Gough. Oxford: Basil Blackwell, 1948.

Lûtfi Paşa, Haci. *Das Asafname des Lutfi Pascha*. Ed., annotated, & trans. by Rudolf Tschudi, Turkishe Bibliothek No. 12. Berlin: Mayer und Muller, 1910.

Lybyer, Albert Howe. *The Government of the Ottoman Empire in the Time of Suleiman the Magnificent*. Cambridge: Harvard University Press, 1913.

MacDonald, Duncan Black. *The Religious Attitude and Life in Islam*. Chicago: The University of Chicago Press, 1909.

MacFarlane, Charles. *Constantinople in 1828*: a residence of sixteen months in the Turkish capital and provinces with an account of the present state of the naval and military power and of the resources of the Ottoman Empire. 2nd ed. London: Saunders and Otley, 1829.

————. *Turkey and Its Destiny*. London: John Murray, 1850.

[Mahmud Celaleddin Paşa]. *Mir'at-i Hakikat: Tarih-i Mahmud*

Celaleddin Paşa. Istanbul: Matbaa-i Osmaniye, 1326-1327/ 1908-1909.

Mardin, Ebül'ulâ. *Medenî Hukuk Cephesinden Ahmed Cevdet Paşa, 1822-1895.* İstanbul Üniversitesi Yayınlarından, No. 275, Hukuk Fakültesi No. 53. Istanbul: Cumhuriyet Matbaası, 1946.

Martin, Kingsley. *French Liberal Thought in the XVIIIth Century.* London: Turnstile Press, 1954.

Mawardi. *El-Ahkam Es-Soulthaniya: Traité de Droit Public Musulman d'Aboul Hasan Ali Ibn Mohammed Ibn Habib el-Mawerdi.* Traduit et annoté par le Comte Leon Ostrorog. Paris: Ernest Leroux, 1901. 2 vols.

Mehmed Esad. *Mir'at-ı Mühendishane-i Berri-i Hümâyun.* Istanbul: Karabet Matbaası, 1316/1898-1899.

Mehmed Memduh. *Esvat-i Sudur.* Izmir: Vilâyet Matbaası, 1328 Malî/1912-1913.

————. *Mir'at-i Şuunat.* Izmir: Ahenk Matbaası, 1328/1912-1913.

[Mehmed Münib] Koca Sekbanbaşı. *Hulâsat ül-Kelâm fi Redd ül-Avam.* Tarih-i Osmanî Encümeni Mecmuası Ilâvesi. Istanbul: Hilâl Matbaası, 1332 Malî/1916-1917.

Mehmed Süreyya. *Sicill-i Osmanî yahut Tezkere-i Meşahîr-i Osmaniye.* Istanbul: Matbaa-i Âmire, 1308-1311/1890-1893.

Mehmed Tahir [Bursalı]. *Osmanlı Müellifleri.* Istanbul: Matbaa-i Âmire, 1333-1342 Malî/1917-1926.

[Meşihat Mektupçuluğu (ed.)]. *İlmiyye Salnamesi.* Istanbul: Matbaa-i Âmire, 1334/1915-1916.

Metternich-Winneberg, Clemens Lothar Wenzel, Fürst von. *Memoires, Documents et Écrits Divers Laissés par le Prince de Metternich Chancellier de Cour et d'État.* Ed. by Prince Richard von Metternich. Part II (1816-1848), Vol. VI. Paris: Plon, 1883.

Michelsen, Edward H. *The Ottoman Empire and Its Resources with Statistical Tables.* London: William Spooner, 1854.

Midhat, Ali Haydar. *Midhat Pacha: sa Vie, son Oeuvre.* Paris: Stock, 1908.

Midhat Paşa. *Bir Dahinin Siyasî Nutukları.* Istanbul: Saadet Kütüphanesi, 1324/1908-1909.

[Midhat Paşa?] *La Turquie Après la Conférence*. Constantinople: Typographie et Litographie Centrales, [*sic*]: n.n., 1877.

——. *Midhat Paşa; Hayat-ı Siyasiyesi, Hidematı, Menfa Hayatı: Tabsira-yı İbret*. Ed. by Ali Haydar Midhat. Istanbul: Hilâl Matbaası, 1325/1909-1910.

Millingen, Frederick. *La Turquie sous le Règne d'Abdul Aziz, 1862* [*sic*] *-1867*. Paris: Lib. Internationale, 1868.

Minkarizâde Dede Efendi. *Siyasetnâme*. Trans. by Şatırzâde Mehmed Arif. Istanbul: n.n., 1275/1858-1859.

Mises, Ludwig von. *La Bureaucratie*. Traduction de Florin et Barbier. Paris: Librairie de Medicis, 1946.

Moltke, Helmuth von. *Briefe über Zustande und Begebenheiten in der Türkei aus den Jahren 1835 bis 1839*. 4th ed. Berlin: Siegfried Miller, 1882.

Mordtmann, A. David. *Anatolien*. Ed. by Franz Babinger. Hanover: Heinz Lafaire, 1925.

[——]. *Stambul und das Moderne Turkenthum: Politische, Sociale und Biographische Bilder von Einem Osmanen*. Leipzig: Dunker und Humbolt, 1877. 2 vols.

Mornet, Daniel, *Les Origines Intéllectuelles de la Revolution Française*. Paris: Armand Colin, 1933.

Mosca, Gaetano. *The Ruling Class*. Ed. by Arthur Livingston. New York: McGraw-Hill Book Co., 1939.

Muhaverat-i Hikemiye: Fransa Hükema-yı Benamından Volter ve Fénelon ve Fontenelle Telifatından. Trans. by Münif Efendi. Istanbul: Ceridehane Matbaası, 1276/1859.

Murad Efendi [Franz von Werner]. *Türkische Skizzen*. 2nd ed. Leipzig: Verlag der Durr'schen Buchhandlund, 1878. 2 vols.

Mustafa Fazıl Paşa. *Bir Eser-i Siyasî*. Istanbul: Zaman Kitaphanesi, 1326/1910.

——. *Lettre Addressée au feu Sultan Abdulaziz par le feu Prince Mustafa Fazıl Pacha (1866)*. Le Caire: A. Costagliola, 1897.

——. *Paristen bir Mektup*. Derssadet: Artin Asadoryan Matbaası, 1910.

Mustafa Necib. *Sultan Selim-i Salis Asrı Vekaüne dair Tarih*. Istanbul: Matbaa-i Âmire, 1280/1863.

Mustafa Reşid Paşa. *Bir Türk Diplomatının Evrak-ı Siyasiyesi*.

Ed. by Mehmed Salaheddin. Istanbul: Alem Matbaası, 1306/ 1888.

———. *Reşid Paşa Merhumun Bazı Âsar-ı Siyasiyesi*. 3rd ed. Kitabhane-i Ebüzziya, Aded 10. Istanbul: Matbaa-i Ebüzziya, 1305/1887.

Nallino, C. A. *Notes on the nature of the "Caliphate" in general and on the alleged "Ottoman Caliphate."* Trans. from the 2nd ed. Rome: Press of the Foreign Office, 1919.

Namık Kemal Antolojisi. Millî Edebiyat Antolojisi Serisinden: 2. Ed. by Ahmet Hamdi Tanpınar. Istanbul: Ahmet Halit, 1942.

Namık Kemal: Hayatı, San'atı, Eserleri. Ed. by Hikmet Dizardoğlu. Istanbul: Varlık Yayınevi, 1954.

Namık Kemal ve İbret Gazetesi. Ed. by Mustafa Nihat Özön. Istanbul: Remzi Kitabevi, 1938.

Namık Kemal. *Makalat-ı Siyasiye ve Edebiye*. Ed. by Ali Ekrem [Bulayır] Külliyat-ı Kemal, Tertip 1, No. 3. Istanbul: Selanik Matbaası, 1327 Malî/1911-1912.

———. *Osmanlı Tarihi*. Külliyat-ı Kemal. İkinci Tertip. Istanbul: Mahmud Bey Matbaası, 1326 Malî/1910-1911.

———. *Renan Müdafaanamesi*. Külliyat-ı Kemal. Birinci Tertip. Istanbul: Mahmud Bey Matbaası, 1326 Malî/1910-1911.

———. *Rüya ve Magosa Mektubu*, Kütüphane-i İçtihad: Aded 13. [Cairo]: Matbaa-i İçtihad, 1908.

———. *Tahrib-i Harabat*. Istanbul: Matbaa-i Ebüzziya, 1303/ 1886.

Noradounghian, Gabriel. *Recueil d'Actes Internationaux de l'Empire Ottoman*, Traités . . . et autres actes relatifs au droit public extérieur de la Turquie. Paris, Leipzig, Neuchatel: 1897-1903.

Onar, Dr. Sıddık Sami. *Idare Hukukunun Umumî Esasları*. Istanbul: Mahmud Bey Matbaası, 1326 Malî/1900-1911.

Oscanyan, C. *The Sultan and his People*. New York: Derby and Jackson, 1857.

Osman Nuri [Ergin]. *Mecelle-i Umûr-u Belediye*. Istanbul: Matbaa-i Osmaniye, 1922. 3 vols.

———. *Türkiye Maarif Tarihi*. İstanbul Mektepleri ve İlim,

Terbiye ve San'at Müesseseleri Dolayisile. Istanbul: Osmanbey Matbaası, 1939-1943. 5 vols.

Özgürel, Mes'ude. *Ziya Paşanın Makaleleri.* İstanbul Üniversitesi Edebiyat Fakültesi Türkoloji Bölümü. Unpublished B.A. thesis. The Institute of Turcology of the University of Istanbul, 1954.

Özön, M. N. (ed.). *Namık Kemal ve İbret Gazetesi.* Istanbul: Remzi Kitabevi, 1938.

―――. *Son Asır Türk Edebiyatı Tarihi.* Istanbul: Maarif Matbaası, 1941 (1st ed., *Muasır Türk Edebiyatı Tarihi, ibid.,* 1934).

―――. *Türkçede Roman Hakkında bir Deneme.* Vol. 1. Istanbul: Remzi Kitabevi [1939?]

Pakalın, Mehmet Zeki. *Son Sadrazamlar ve Başvekiller.* Istanbul: Ahmet Said Matbaası, 1940-1948. 5 vols.

―――. *Tanzimat Maliye Nazırları.* Istanbul: Kanaat Kitabevi, 1940.

Perin, Cevdet. *Tanzimat Edebiyatında Fransız Tesiri.* Istanbul: Pulhan Matbaası, 1946.

Pingaud, Léonce. *Choiseuil Gouffier: La France en Orient sous Louis XVI.* Paris: A. Picard, 1887.

Porter, Sir James. *Turkey: Its History and Progress* (Vol. II by Sir George Larpent). London: Hurst and Blackett, 1854.

Reed, Howard A. "The Destruction of the Janissaries by Mahmud II in June 1826." Unpublished Ph.D. dissertation. Princeton, 1951.

Rolland, Charles. *La Turquie Contemporaine.* Hommes et Choses. Études sur l'Orient. Paris: Pagnerre, 1854.

Rosen, Dr. G. *Geschichte der Türkei von dem Siege der Reform im Jahre 1826 bis zum Pariser Tractat vom Jahre 1856.* Staatengeschichte der neuesten Zeit. Leipzig: Hirzel, 1866. 2 vols.

Rosenthal, E. I. J. *Political Thought in Medieval Islam*: An Introductory Outline. Cambridge: University Press, 1958.

Sabine, George H., *A History of Political Theory.* New York: Henry Holt, 1937.

Sadık Rifat Paşa. *Ahlâk Risalesi.* Istanbul: Matbaa-i Âmire, 1286/1869-1870.

―――. *Müntahabat-ı Âsar.* Istanbul: Tatyos Divitçiyan, 1290/1873-1874.

Said Paşa. *Gazeteci Lisanı.* Istanbul: Sabah Matbaası, 1328/1912.

Şanizâde Ataullah. *Tarih.* Istanbul: Ceride-i Havadis Matbaası, Cemaziyülahir 1284-1291/1867-1875. 4 vols.

[Sarı Mehmed Paşa]. *Ottoman Statecraft: The Book of Counsels for Viziers and Governors, Nasa'ih ul-vuzera ve'l umera of Sarı Mehmet Pasha, the Defterdar.* Trans., introduction, and notes by Walter Livingston Wright. Princeton: Princeton University Press, 1935.

Schlözer, Leopold von. *Das Türkische Heer im neunzehnten Jahrhundert.* Die Reformen bis 1869. Beitrage zur Kenntnis der Türkischen Armee II. Berlin: R. Felix, 1901.

Schopoff, A. *Les Réformes et la Protection des Chrétiens en Turquie (1673-1904).* Paris: Plon-Nourrit, 1904.

Schweiger-Lerchenfeld, Amand Freiherr von. *Serail und Hohe Pforte.* Enthüllungen uber die jüngsten erreignisse in Stambul nach Original-Aufzeichnungen und Dokumenten. Vienna: A. Hartleben, 1879.

Selim Nüzhet [Gerçek]. *Türk Gazeteciliği:* Yüzüncü Yıldönümü Vesilesile. Istanbul: Devlet Matbaası, 1931.

————. *Türk Matbaacılığı.* Istanbul: Ebüzziya, 1928.

————. *Türk Taş Basmacılığı.* Istanbul: Devlet Matbaası, 1939.

Shafer, Boyd. *Nationalism, Myth and Reality.* London: Gollancz, 1955.

Şinasi. *Extraits de Poésies et de Prose Traduit en Vers du Français en Turc.* Constantinople: Imprimerie de la Press d'Orient, 1859.

————. *Müntahabat-ı Tasvir-i Efkâr. Edebiyat.* 2nd ed. Istanbul: Matbaa-i Ebüzziya, 1311/1893-1894.

————. *Müntahabat-ı Tasvir-i Efkâr: İkinci Kısım: Mebahisat-ı Edebiye. Mes'ele-yi Mebhusat-u Anha.* 1st printing. Istanbul: 1303/1885-1886.

————. *Müntahabat-ı Tasvir-i Efkâr: Siyasat.* Cüz I. 1st ed. Istanbul: Matbaa-i Ebüzziya, 1303/1885-1886.

Slade, Sir Adolphus. *Turkey and the Crimean War.* A Narrative of Historical Events. London: Smith and Elder, 1867.

Smith, Wilfrid Cantwell. *Islam in Modern History.* Princeton: Princeton University Press, 1957.

Southgate, Horatio. *Narrative of a Tour through Armenia, Kurdistan, Persia and Mesopotamia.* New York: Appleton, 1840.

Srbik, Heinrich Ritter von. *Metternich, der Staatsman und der Mensch.* Munchen: F. Bruckmann, 1925. 2 vols.

Stern, Bernhard. *Jungtürken und Verschwörer.* Die Innere Lage der Türkei unter Abdul Hamid II. Nach einigen Emittelungen und Mitteilungen Osmanischer Parteiführer. 2nd ed. Leipzig: Bernhard Meyer, 1901.

Süleyman Hüsnü Paşa. *Hiss-i Inkılâb veya Sultan Abdülazizin Hal'i ile Sultan Murad-i Hamisin Cülûsu.* Istanbul: Tanin Matbaası, 1326/1910.

——. *Inkilâp Hissi veya Abdülazizin Tahttan Indirilmesi ile Beşinci Muradın Tahta Çıkarılması.* Ed. by Mediha Gezgin. Istanbul: Berksoy Matbaası, 1953.

——. *Mebani ül-Inşa'.* Istanbul: n.n., 1289-1291/1872-1875.

——. *Süleyman Paşanın Muhakemesi.* Ed. by Sülemanpaşazade Sami. Istanbul: Matbaa-i Askeri, 1327-1328/1911-1912.

Süleyman Nazif. *Iki Dost.* Istanbul: Kanaat Kütüphanesi, 1343/1924-1925.

——. *Namık Kemal.* Istanbul: İkdam Matbaası, 1922.

Tahsin, Hoca. *Esas-i İlm-i Hey'et.* Istanbul: Matbaa-i Safa ve Enver, 1311/1893-1894.

——. *Psikoloji veya İlm-i Ruh.* 2nd ed. Istanbul: Şirket-i Mürettibiye Matbaası, 1310/1892-1893.

Tanpınar, Ahmet Hamdi. *Ondokuzuncu Asır Türk Edebiyatı Tarihi.* Vol. 1, 2nd ed. Istanbul: İbrahim Horoz, 1956.

Tansel, Fevziye Abdullah. *Hususi Mektuplarına göre Namık Kemal ve Abdülhak Hamit.* Ankara: Güneş Matbaası, 1949.

Testa, Ignatz, Baron von. *Recueil des Traités de la Porte Ottomane* avec les puissances etrangères depuis le premier traité conclu en 1536 entre Suleyman I et François I jusqu'a nos jours. Continué par le baron Alfred de Testa et le baron Leopold de Testa, Paris: 1864-1911. 12 vols.

Temperley, Harold. *England and the Near East: The Crimea.* London. Longmans Green and Co., 1936.

Tevfik Nureddin. *Sultan Abdülazizin Hal'i ve İntiharı.* Istanbul: n.n., 1324 Malî/1908-1909.

Toderini, Abbé. *De la Littérature des Turcs.* Trans. by Cournand. Paris: Poinçot, 1789.

Toynbee, Arnold and Kirkwood, Kenneth D. *Turkey*. London: Ernest Benn, 1926.

[Türk Dil Kurumu (ed.)]. *Kutadgu Bilig: Tıpkıbasım*. Istanbul: Alaeddin Kiral, 1942-1943. 3 vols.

Türk Tarih Tetkik Cemiyeti. *Tarih III: Yeni ve Yakın Zamanlar*. Ankara: Maarif Matbaası, 1941.

Ubicini, A. *La Constitution Ottomane du 7 Zilhidjé 1293 (23 Decembre 1876) Expliquée et Annotée par A. Ubicini*. Paris: n.n., 1877.

――――. *La Turquie Actuelle*. Paris: Hachette, 1855.

――――. *Letters on Turkey*. Trans. by Lady Easthope. London: John Murray, 1856. 2 vols.

――――, and de Courteille, Pavet. *État Present de l'Empire Ottoman*. Paris: Librairie Militaire de J. Dumaine, 1876.

Ülgener, Dr. Sabri F. *İktisadî İnhitat Tarihimizin Ahlâk ve Zihniyet Meseleleri*. İstanbul Üniversitesi Yayınlarından No. 480. İktisat Fakültesi, No. 55. Istanbul: Ismail Akgün Matbaası, 1951.

Unat, Faik Reşat. *Hicrî Tarihleri Miladî Tarihe Çevirme Kılavuzu*. Ankara: Maarif Matbaası, 1943.

Urquhart, David. *The Spirit of the East*. London: Henry Colburn, 1838. 2 vols.

Uzunçarşılı, Ismail Hakkı. *Meşhur Rumeli ayanlarından Tirsinili İsmail, Yıllık oğlu Süleyman Ağalar ve Alemdar Mustafa Paşa*. Istanbul: Maarif Matbaası, 1942.

――――. *Midhat Paşa ve Taif Mahkûmları*. Türk Tarih Kurumu Yayınlarından VII Seri, No. 18. Ankara: Türk Tarih Kurumu Basımevi, 1950.

――――. *Midhat ve Rüştü Paşaların Tevkiflerine Dair Vesikalar*. Türk Tarih Kurumu Yayınlarından Seri VIII, No. 13. Ankara: Türk Tarih Kurumu Basımevi, 1946.

――――. *Osmanlı Devletinin Merkez ve Bahriye Teşkilâti*. Türk Tarih Kurumu Yayınları Seri VIII, No. 16. Ankara: Türk Tarih Kurumu Basımevi, 1948.

Vambery, Arminius. *Western Culture in Eastern Lands*. London: John Murray, 1909.

Vandal, Albert. *Une Ambassade Française en Orient sous Louis*

XV. La Mission du Marquis de Villeneuve 1738-1741. 2nd ed. Paris: Plon, 1887.

Vaughan, C. E. (ed.). *The Political Writings of Jean-Jacques Rousseau.* Cambridge: The University Press, 1915. 2 vols.

Volney, Constantin François Chasseboeuf de. *Oeuvres Complètes.* Paris: Firmin Didot, 1943.

Fransiz müelliflerinden, Volney, nam Zatın "Les Ruines de Palmyre" unvaniyle yazmış olduğu makalattan bazı fıkraların tercümesidir. n.p., n.n., 1288/1871-1872.

Voltaire. *Oeuvres.* Paris: Renouard, 1819-1825.

Walsh, R. *A Residence at Constantinople during a period including the Commencement, progress and termination of the Greek and Turkish Revolutions.* London: Frederick Westley, 1836. 2 vols.

Wanda. *Souvenirs Anecdotiques sur la Turquie (1820-1870).* Paris: Firmin Didot, 1884.

Washburn, George. *Fifty Years in Constantinople and Recollections of Robert College.* Boston and New York: Houghton-Mifflin, 1909.

Watt, W. Montgomery. *Free Will and Predestination in Early Islam.* London: Luzac and Co., 1948.

Webster, Sir Charles. *The Foreign Policy of Palmerston.* London: G. Bell and Sons, 1951. 2 vols.

Weill, Georges. *l'Éveil des Nationalités et le Mouvement Libéral, 1815-1848.* Paris: Presses Universitaires de France, 1930.

Willey, Basil. *The Eighteenth Century Background.* New York: Columbia University Press, 1940.

Yazma ve Eski Basma Kitapların Tasnif ve Fişleme Kılavuzu ve Islam Dinî İlimleri Tasnif Cetveli. Istanbul: Maarif Basımevi, 1958.

Yusuf Kâmil Paşa. *Eser-i Kâmil Paşa.* Istanbul: Asır Kitaphanesi, 1308/1890-1891.

———. *Tercüme-ı Telemâk.* Istanbul: Tabhane-i Âmire, 1279/1862.

———. *Tercüme-i Telemâk.* 2nd ed. Istanbul: Tasvir-i Efkâr Gazetehanesi, 1279/1863.

BIBLIOGRAPHY

Zboinski, H. *l'Armée Ottomane*: son organisation actuelle telle qu'elle resulte de l'éxécution de la loi de 1869. Paris: Librairie Militaire J. Dumaine, 1877.

Ziya Paşa. *Cennetmekân Sultan Abdülaziz Han'a 1284 senesinde Londraya Ziyaretinde takdim Eylediği arzuhal*. Istanbul: 1327/ 1911.

———. *Endülüs Tarihi*. Istanbul: Eser Kütüphanesi, 1304/ 1886-1887. 4 vols.

———. *Engizisyon Tarihi*. Istanbul: Matbaa-i Ebüzziya, 1299/ 1881-1882.

———. *Veraset-i Saltanat-i Seniyye*. Istanbul: n.n., 1326 Malî/ 1910.

———. *Zafernâme Şerhi*. n.p., n.n., n.d. Lithography.

II. Articles

Abadan, Dr. Yavuz. "Tanzimat Fermanının Tahlili," *Tanzimat I: Yüzüncü Yildönömü Münasebetile*. Ed. by Maarif Vekâleti. Istanbul: Maarif Matbaası, 1940, pp. 31-58.

Abdülaziz Han, Sultan. "Hatt-ı Hümâyun," *Düstur*, Series 1 (1289-1299/1872-1882), I, 14, 15.

Adıvar, Abdülhak Adnan. "Kınalı-Zâde," *Islâm Ansiklopedisi*, VI (1954), 708-711.

———. "Ali Kuşçu," *Islâm Ansiklopedisi*, I (1941), 321-323.

Ahmed Cevdet Paşa. "Mâruzat," *Tarih-i Osmanî Encümeni Mecmuası* XIV (January 1924), 52, to XVI (July 1927), 220.

Ahmed Lûtfi. "Türkiyede Maarif Teşkilâtı—(1267-1287)," *Türk Tarih Encümeni Mecmuası*, XVI (1927), 302-317.

[Akhisarî]. "Principes de sagesse touchant l'art de gouverner, Usul al-Hikam fi nizam al-'Alam par Rizwan-ben-abd'oulmannan Ac-hissari," trans. by Garcin de Tassy, *Journal Asiatique*, Series I, IV (April 1824), 213-226, 283-290.

Akyüz, Kenan. "Şinasi'nin Fransadaki Öğrenimi ile ilgili bazı belgeler," *Türk Dili*, III (1954), 397-405.

Alberts, Otto. "Der Dichter des Uigurisch-Türkischem Dialekt Geschreibenen Kutadgu Bilig (1069-1070 p. Chr.) ein Schüler des Avicenna," *Archiv für Philosophie, Archiv für Geschichte der Philosophie*, VII (1910), 319-336.

Ali Fuad. "Münif Paşa," *Türk Tarih Encümeni Mecmuası*, I (New Series, 1930), No. 4, 1-16.

————. "Rical-i Tanzimattan Sadık Rifat Paşa," *Türk Tarih Encümeni Mecmuası*, I (New Series, 1929), No. 1, 1-15.

[Anonymous]. "The Late Insurrection in Turkey," *Chambers Journal*, XIII (1860), 193-197.

Antel, Sadrettin Celal. "Tanzimat Maarifi," *Tanzimat I: Yüzüncü Yıldönümü Münasebetile*. Ed. by Maarif Vekâleti. Istanbul: Maarif Matbaası, 1940, pp. 444-462.

Arnold, T. W. "Kashifi," *Encyclopaedia of Islam*, II, 789-790.

Babinger, Franz. "Kınālīzāde," *Encyclopaedia of Islam*, II, 1017.

————. "Niẓām-i Djedid," *Encyclopaedia of Islam*, III, 936.

————. "Pertev," *Encyclopaedia of Islam*, IV, 1066.

Barkan, Ömer Lûtfi. "Kanun Nâme," *Islâm Ansiklopedisi*, VI (1952), 185-195.

Batiman, Burhanettin. "Namık Kemal'in bir Manzumesi ve Alman Idealizmi," [İstanbul Üniversitesi] *Edebiyat Fakültesi Türk Dili ve Edebiyatı Dergisi*, III (1948), 154-161.

Baykal, Bekir Sıtkı. "93 Meşrutiyeti," *Belleten*, VI (1942), 45-83.

Baysun, Cavid. "Mustafa Reşit Paşa," *Tanzimat I: Yüzüncü Yıldönümü Münasebetile*, 723-746.

Belin, A. "Charte des Turcs," *Journal Asiatique*, IX (1840), 5-29.

————. "De l'Instruction Publique et du Mouvement Intellectuel en Orient," *Le Contemporain*, XI (1866), 214-254.

————. "Du régime des Fiefs Militaires dans l'Islamisme, et principalement en Turquie," *Journal Asiatique*, Serie VI, XV (1870), 187-301.

————. "Éssais sur l'histoire économique de la Turquie d'après les écrivains originaux," *Journal Asiatique*, Serie VI, III (1864), 416-489; IV (1864), 242-296, 301-390, 447-530; V (1865), 127-167.

————. "Étude sur la proprieté foncière en pays musulman et spécialement en Turquie (Rite Hanefite)," *Journal Asiatique*, Serie V, XVIII (1861), 390-431, 477-517; XIX (1862), 156-212, 257-358.

————. "Notice sur le premier annuaire impérial de l'Empire

Ottoman . . . (1847)," *Journal Asiatique*, Serie IV, x (1847), 177-207; XI (1848), 1-33, 293-333.

———. "Tableau de la presse périodique et quotidienne à Constantinople en 1864," *Journal Asiatique*, Serie VI, v (1865), 170-174.

Berkes, Niyazi. "Namık Kemal in Fikrî Tekâmülü," *Namık Kemal Hakkında*. Büyük Şairin Yuzüncü Yıl Dönümü Münasebetile Dil ve Tarih-Cografaya Fakültesi Professor ve Doçentleri Tarafından Hazırlanmıştır. Ed. by Dil Tarih-Cografya Fakültesi. Türk Dili ve Edebiyatı Enstitüsü Neşriyatı No. 2. Istanbul: Vakit Matbaası, 1942, pp. 218-249.

Bernhauer, Dr. W. F. A. "Die Türkische Akademie der Wissenschaften Zu Constantinopel," *ZDMG*, VI (1852-II), 273-285.

———. "Hag'i Chalfa's Dusturul-'amel ein Beitrag zur Osmanischen Finanzgeschichte," *ZDMG*, XI (1857), 111-132.

———. "Kogábeg's Abhandlungen Über den Vervall des Osmanischen Staatsgebaudes seit Sultan Suleiman dem Grossen," *ZDMG*, XV (1861), 272-332.

Boran, Dr. B. S. "Namık Kemalin Sosyal Fikirleri," *Namık Kemal Hakkında*. Ed. by Dil ve Tarih-Cografya Fakültesi. Türk Dili ve Edebiyatı Enstitüsü Neşriyatı No. 2. Istanbul: Vakit Matbaası, 1942, pp. 249-278.

Brockelmann, C. "al-Māwardī," *Encyclopaedia of Islam*, III, 416.

Brown, John P. "The Sublime Porte," *Knickerbocker* 38 (1851), pp. 34-41.

Busch. "Aus dem politischen Nachlass des Unterstaatssekretars Dr. Busch," *Deutsche Rundschau*, CXXXVIII (1908), 368-405. Continued with varying titles in CXXXVIII (1909), 203-222, 380-405, and CXXXXI (1909), 12-28, 207-222, 361-379.

Canning, Stratford [Viscount Stratford de Redcliffe]. "Turkey," *Nineteenth Century*, I (1877), 707-728, 729-753.

Carra de Vaux, B. "Akhlāk," *Encyclopaedia of Islam*, L, 231-233.

———. "Al-Fārābī," *Encyclopaedia of Islam*, II, 53-55.

[Cherbuliez]. "l'Angleterre et la Russie en Orient: un page d'histoire contemporaine, 1876-77," *Revue d'Histoire Diplomatique*, x (1896), 65-118, 171-222.

Danon, M. A. "Contribution à l'Histoire des Sultans Osman II et Mustafa," *Journal Asiatique*, Serie XIV (1919), 69-139, 244-310.

Davison, Roderic H. "Turkish attitudes concerning Christian-Muslim equality in the nineteenth century," *The American Historical Review*, XLIX (July 1954), 844-864.

de Boer, T. J. "Aristūtālīs," *Encyclopaedia of Islam*, I, 433-434.

———. "Ibn Sīnā," *Encyclopaedia of Islam*, II, 419-420.

Decei, Aurel. "Fenerliler," *Islâm Ansiklopedisi*, IV (1947), 549-550.

De Salve. "l'Enseignement en Turquie," *Revue des Deux Mondes*. 3rd Series, V (October 15, 1874), 836-841.

d'Éschavannes, E. "Académie des Sciences de Constantinople," *Revue de l'Orient de l'Algérie et des Colonies*, XII (1852), 361-372.

———. "Publications Géographiques en Turquie," *Revue de l'Orient de l'Algérie et des Colonies*, X (1851), 282-283.

Ebüzziya Tevfik. "Farmasonluk," *Mecmua-i Ebüzziya*. 18 Cemaziyülahir 1329/1911, pp. 683-686.

———. "Mahmud Celaleddin Paşanın Mir'at-ı Hakikat'i," *Mecmua-i Ebüzziya*. 1 Cemaziyülevvel 1330/1912, pp. 33-46.

———. "Muhallefat-i Şinasi," *Mecmua-i Ebüzziya*. 8 Şaban 1329/1911, pp. 896-907.

———. "Reşid Paşa Hakkında," *Mecmua-i Ebüzziya*. 18 Zilkade 1329/1911, pp. 97-105.

———. "Rical-i Siyasiye-i Osmaniye," *Mecmua-i Ebüzziya*. 14 Muharrem 1330, p. 353-4 Rebiulevvel 1330, p. 148.

———. "Şinasi ile bir Mülâkatim," *Mecmua-i Ebüzziya*. 1316/1898-1899, 1601-1608. Exact date of publication not indicated.

———. "Şinasinin Eyyam-i Ahire-i Hayatı ve Vefatı," *Mecmua-i Ebüzziya* 23 Receb 1239, pp. 833-841; 1 Şaban 1329, pp. 865-874.

———. "Yeni Osmanlılar," *Yeni Tasvir-i Efkâr*. Istanbul: June 13-25, 1909.

———. "Yeni Osmanlılar Tarihi," *Yeni Tasvir-i Efkâr*. Istanbul: August 28, 1909-January 8, 1911.

———. "Yeni Osmanlıların Sebeb-i Zuhuru," *Yeni Tasvir-i Efkâr*. Istanbul: May 13-June 12, 1909.

————. "Zamanımız tarihine hâdim hatırât," *Mecmua-i Ebüz-ziya.* 9 Rebiülahir 1330/1912, pp. 321-329.

Eckardt, J. T. von. "Islamitische Reformbestrebungen der letzten 100 Jahre," *Deutsche Rundschau,* IV (1900), 39-60.

Elliot, Sir Henry G. "The Death of Abdul Aziz and of Turkish Reform," *Nineteenth Century,* XXIII (1888), 276-296.

Fındıkoğlu, Z. Fahri. "Ahmet Mitat ve bizde Hümanizm," *Cumhuriyet,* December 12, 1944, p. 2.

————. "l'École Ibn Khaldunienne en Turquie," in *Proceedings of the Twenty Second Congress of Orientalists.* Ed. by Zeki Velidi Toğan. Vol. II, Communications. Leiden: E. J. Brill, 1957, pp. 269-277.

————. "Türk Hukuk Tarihinde Namık Kemal," *İstanbul Üniversitesi Hukuk Fakültesi Mecmuası,* VII (1941), 177-223.

Flourens, Gustave. "Sadyk Efendi," *l'Illustration,* LIII (February 27, 1869), 134.

[Fuad Paşa (?)]. "Testament Politique," in *Levant Herald.* Istanbul: September 28, 1869.

————. "The Political Testament of Fuad Pasha," *Nineteenth Century,* LIII (1903), 190-197.

Gautier, Theophile. "La Collection Khalil Bey," *l'Illustration,* LI (11 Janvier 1868), 27.

Gerçek, S. N. "Jön Türk Neşriyatı," *Akşam* (March 19-April 3, 1941).

Gibb, H. A. R. "Constitutional Organization," *Law in the Middle East.* Ed. by Majid Khadduri and Herbert Liebesny. Washington, D.C.: The Middle East Institute, 1955.

————. "Social Reactions in the Muslim World," *Journal of the Royal Central Asian Society* XXI (1934), 541-560.

Goldziher, I[gnatz]. "Aḥmed b. Huḥammed b. Hanbal," *Encyclopaedia of Islam,* I, 188-190.

Gölpınarlı, Abdülbaki. "Namık Kemal'in Şiirleri," *Namık Kemal Hakkında,* pp. 11-77.

Greppi, Comte. "Souvenirs d'un Diplomate Italien à Constantinople, 1861-1866," *Revue d'Histoire Diplomatique,* XXIV (1910), 372-387.

Guillaume, Alfred. "Philosophy and Theology," *The Legacy of*

Islam. Ed. by Sir Thomas Arnold and Alfred Guillaume. London: Oxford University Press, 1931, pp. 239-283.

Haim, Sylvia G. "Islam and the Theory of Arab Nationalism," *Die Welt des Islams,* IV (1955), 124-149.

Hammer-Purgstall, Joseph von, freiherr. "Liste des ouvrages imprimés à Constantinople dans le cours des années 1843 et 1844," *Journal Asiatique,* Series IV, vol. XIII, 253-282.

Horten, M. "Falsafa," *Encyclopaedia of Islam,* II, 48.

Huart, Clement. "Midhat-pacha," *Revue du Monde Musulman,* VIII (1909), 419-430.

Ibnülemin Mahmud Kemal [İnal]. "Hafız Müşfik Efendi," *Türk Tarih Encümeni Mecmuası,* New Series I (1929), 26-39.

————. "Mehmed Emin Bey," *Türk Tarih Encümeni Mecmuası,* New Series I (1930), 33-41.

————. "Meşahir-i Meçhule," *Türk Tarih Encümeni Mecmuası,* New Series II (1928), 37-51.

İnalcik, Halil. "Husrev Paşa," *İslâm Ansiklopedisi,* V (1956), 609-616.

————. "Osmanlı Hukukuna Giriş," *Ankara Üniversitesi Siyasal Bilgiler Fakültesi Dergisi,* XIII (1958), 102-126.

Jäschke, Gotthard. "Die Entwicklung des Osmanischen Verfassungsstaates von den Anfang bis zur Gegenwart," *Die Welt des Islams,* V (1918), 5-56.

Kaplan, Mehmet. "Tanzir-i Telemâk," [*İstanbul Üniversitesi*] *Edebiyat Fakültesi Türk Dili ve Edebiyati Dergisi,* III (November 30, 1948), 1-20.

Köprülü, F. "Âsım," *İslâm Ansiklopedisi,* I (1942), 665-673.

Köprülü, Orhan, F. "Efendi," *İslâm Ansiklopedisi,* IV (1947), 132-133.

————. "Galib Paşa," *İslâm Ansiklopedisi,* IV (1947), 710-714.

Kramers, J. H. "Tanẓīmāt," *Encyclopaedia of Islam,* IV, 656-660.

Kun, T. Halasi. "Ibrahim Müteferrika," *İslâm Ansiklopedisi,* V (1950), 896-900.

Langlois, Victor. "Rechid Pacha et les Réformes en Turquie," *Revue de l'Orient de l'Algerie et des Colonies,* VIII (1858), 1-18.

Laski, H. J. "Bureaucracy," *Encyclopedia of Social Sciences*, III (1935), 70-73.
Lee, Dwight E. "The Origins of Pan-Islamism," *American Historical Review*, XLVII (1942), 278-287.
Leroy-Beaulieu, Anatole. "Les Réformes de la Turquie, la politique Russe et le panslavisme," *Revue des Deux Mondes*. 3rd Series, XVIII (1876), 508-537.
Levy, R. " 'Urf," *Encyclopaedia of Islam*, IV, 1031.
Lewis, Bernard A. "The Concept of an Islamic Republic," *Die Welt Des Islams*, IV (1955), 1-9.
———. "The Impact of the French Revolution on Turkey: Some Notes on the Transmission of Ideas," *Journal of World History*, I (January 1953), 116-135.
Lewis, Ewart. "Organic Tendencies in Medieval Political Thought," *American Political Science Review*, XXXII (October 1938), 849-876.
Lybyer, Albert H. "The Turkish Parliament," *Proceedings of the American Political Science Association* (1910), pp. 65-77.

Macdonald, D. B. "al-Mahdī," *Encyclopaedia of Islam*, III, 111-115.
———. "Idjmāᶜ," *Encyclopaedia of Islam*, II, 448.
———. "Māturīdī," *Encyclopaedia of Islam*, III, 414-415.
Menzel, Th[eodor]. "Kemāl," *Encyclopaedia of Islam*, II, 847-851.
Midhat Paşa. "The Past, Present, and Future of Turkey," *Nineteenth Century*, III (1878), 981-993.
Milev, Nicholas. "Réchid pacha et la réforme Ottomane," *Zeitschrift für Osteuropaische Geschichte*, II (1912), 382-398.
Mohibul Hasan Han. "Medieval Muslim Political Theories of Rebellion Against the State," *Islamic Culture*, XVIII (1944), 36-44.
Mordtmann, J. H. "Ḥusain ᶜAwnī Pasha," *Encyclopaedia of Islam*, II, 342.
Mousnier, Roland. "Les Idées Politiques de Fénelon," *XVIIᵉ Siècle: Revue des Études du XVII Siècle*, I (1949), 190-206.

Namık Kemal. " 'Mes Prisons' Tercümesi Hakkında Kemalin Mülâhazatı," *Mecmua-i Ebüzziya*. 21 Muharrem 1330, pp. 8-

14; 28 Muharrem, pp. 37-43; 5 Safer, pp. 91-94; 12 Safer, pp. 114-119; 26 Safer, pp. 149-153; 4 Rebiülevvel, pp. 169-175 (1911 A.D.).

"Namık Kemal'in İki Mektubu," *Mecmua-i Ebüzziya.* 19 Receb 1330, pp. 14-18; 26 Receb, pp. 39-43; 3 Şaban, pp. 73-81; 10 Şaban, pp. 136-141.

Necib Asım. "Hoca Tahsin," *Türk Tarih Encümeni Mecmuası,* XVII-XVIII (1928), 57-63.

Okandan, Recai Galip. "Âmme hukukumuzda Tanzimat devri," *Tanzimat* I: *Yüzüncü Yıldönümü Münasebetile,* pp. 97-128.

Öz, Tahsin. "Selim III, Mustafa IV ve Mahmut II zamanlarına ait birkaç vesika," *Tarih Vesikaları,* I (June 1941), 20-29.

Prokesch-Osten, Anton Graf. "Ein Beitrag zur Geschichte der Orientalischen Frage, aus dem Nachlass des grafen Prokesch-Osten, K. K. Osterr. Feldzeugmeisters und Botschafter," *Deutsche Revue,* IV (1879), 6-19, 171-188.

――――. "Errinerungen aus den Jahren 1870 und 1871. Aus den hinterlessenen Papiere der K. K. Botschafters Grafen von Prokesch-Osten," *Deutsche Revue,* IV (1880), 11-21.

――――. "Errinerungen aus Konstantinopel aus den Nachlass des Grafen Prokesch Osten, K. K. Botschafter und Feldzeugmeister," *Deutsche Review,* IV (1880), 61-74.

Riza Nur. "Namık Kemal," *Türk Bilik Rövüsü,* II (1936), 912-1601.

Rodkey, F. S. "Views of Palmerston and Metternich on the Eastern Question," *English Historical Review,* XLV (1930), 627-640.

Sami Paşazâde Hüseyin Bey. "Yeni Osmanlılar," *Hadisât-ı Hukukiye ve Tarihiye: Kısm-ı Tarihî* (May 1, 1341/May 14, 1925), II, 18-25.

Santillana, David de. "Law and Society," *The Legacy of Islam.* Ed. by Sir Thomas Arnold and Alfred Guillaume. London: Oxford University Press, 1931, pp. 284-310.

Schacht, Joseph. "Islamic Law," *Encyclopedia of the Social Sciences,* VIII (1935), 344-349.

BIBLIOGRAPHY

——. "Meḥkeme," *Encyclopaedia of Islam.* Supplement (1938), pp. 144-146.

Schlechta-Wssehrd, Ottakar von. "Mitteilungen aus dem Orient über die Neugestifteten Türkischen Gelehrten Verein," *ZDMG*, XVII (1863), 682-684.

Siyavuşgil, Sabri Esat. "Tanzimatın Fransız Efkâr-ı umumiyesinde uyandırdığı akisler," *Tanzimat* I: *Yüzüncü Yıldönümü Münasebetile,* pp. 747-756.

Strothmann, R. "al-Ṭūsī," *Encyclopaedia of Islam,* IV, 980-981.

Sungu, Ihsan. "Galatasaray Lisesinin kuruluşu," *Belleten,* VIII (1944), 315-347.

——. "Mahmud II nin İzzet Molla ve Asâkir-i Mansure Hakkında bir Hattı," *Tarih Vesikalari,* I (1941), 163.

——. "Mekteb-i Maarif-i Adliyyenin Tesisi," *Tarih Vesikalari,* I (1941), 212-225.

Tanpınar, Ahmed Hamdi. "Ahmed Vefik Paşa," *Islâm Ansiklopedisi,* I (1941), 207-210.

Tansel, Fevziye Abdullah. "Akdeniz adalarının elimizden çıkmaması için hususî mektuplarına göre Namık Kemalın mücadele ve ikazları," *Belleten,* XXIII (1949), 479-511.

——. "Arap Harflerinin islahı ve değiştirilmesi hakkında ilk teşebbüsler ve neticeleri (1862-1884)," *Belleten,* XVII (1953), 223-249.

——. "Arif Hikmet Bey," *Islâm Ansiklopedisi,* I (1940), 564-568.

——. "İzzet Molla," *Islâm Ansiklopedisi,* V (1952), 1264-1267.

——. "Muallim Naci ile Recaizâde Ekrem arasındaki münakaşalar ve bu münakaşaların sebeb olduğu edebî hâdiseler," *Türkiyat Mecmuası,* X (1953), 159-200.

——. "Namık Kemal'in Hukukî Fikirleri," *Türk Hukuk Tarihi Dergisi,* I (1941-1942), 51-56.

——. "Namık Kemal'in Midilli de yazdığı manzum ve mensur eserler," *Türkiyat Mecmuası,* XII (1955), 57-90.

——. "Süleyman Hüsnü Paşa ile Namık Kemal'in münasebat ve Muhaberatı," *Türkiyat Mecmuası,* XI (1954), 131-152.

Tarlan, Dr. Ali Nihat. "Tanzimat Edebiyatında Hakikî Müceddit," *Tanzimat Yüzüncü Yıldönümü Münasebetile*, pp. 597-617.

Timur, Hıfzı (ed.). "Türkiyede Abdülmecidin Islahatı Hakkında" [Letters of Prince Metternich to the Austrian Ambassador to the Porte, Baron Sturmer presented by the latter to Reşit Paşa in Turkish translation], *Tanzimat I: Yüzüncü Yıldönümü Münasebetile*, pp. 703-708.

Ülken, Hilmi Ziya. "Tanzimattan Sonra Fikir Hareketleri," *Tanzimat I: Yüzüncü Yıldönümü Münasebetile*, pp. 757-775.

Unat, Faik Reşat. "Şehdi Osman Efendi Sefaretnamesi," *Tarih Vesikaları*, I (1941), 66-80.

————. "Ahmet III Devrine ait bir Islahat Takriri: Muhayyel bir Mülâkatın Zabıtları," *Tarih Vesikaları*, I (1941), 107-121.

Uzunçarşılı, Ismail Hakkı. "Ali Suavi ve Çırağan Sarayı Vak'ası," *Belleten*, VIII (January 1944), 71-118.

————. "Amedî Galib Efendinin Murahhaslığı ve Paristen Gönderdiği Şifreli Mektuplar," *Belleten*, I (1937), 357-363.

————. "Hatt-ı Hümâyun," *Islâm Ansiklopedisi*, V (1950), 373-375.

————. "Namık Kemal'in Abdülhamid'e takdim ettiği arizalarla Ebüzziya Tevfik Bey'e yolladığı bazı mektuplar," *Belleten*, XI (1947), 237-297.

————. "Nizam-i Cedid Ricalinden Valide Sultan Kethüdası Meşhur Yusuf Ağa ve Kethüdazâde Arif Efendi," *Belleten*, XX (1956), 485-525.

————. "Sadrazam Halil Hamid Paşa," *Türkiyat Mecmuası*, V (1936), 216-267.

————. "Selim III 'un Veliaht iken Fransa Kıralı Louis XVI ile muhabereleri," *Belleten*, II (April 1938), 191-250.

————. "Sultan Abdülaziz Vak'asına dair Vak'anüvis Lûtfi Efendinin bir Risalesi," *Belleten*, VII (1943), 349-373.

————. "V. Murad'ı Tekrar Padişah Yapmak Isteyen K. Skaliyeri-Aziz Bey Komitesi," *Belleten*, VIII (April 1944), 245-328.

Uzunçarşılıoğlu, Ismail Hakkı. "Selim III 'un Veliaht. . . ." See Uzunçarşılı, Ismail Hakkı, above.

Valmy, Le Duc de. *La Turquie et l'Europe en 1867*. Paris: Amyot, 1867.

Vambery, Arminius. "Errinerungen an Midhat Pascha," *Deutsche Rundschau*, II (1878), 186-195.

————. "Freiliche Bestrebungen im Moslimischen Asien," *Deutsche Rundschau*, LXXVII (October-December 1893), 63-75.

————. "Vefyk Pasha on Asia and Europe," *Littel's Living Age*, 5th Series, XXIII (1878), 185-188.

Velidedeoğlu, Dr. Hifzı Veldet. "Kanunlaştırma Hareketi ve Tanzimat," *Tanzimat Yüzüncü Yıldönümü Münasebetile*, pp. 139-209.

Vernadsky, George. "Cengiz Han Yasası," *Türk Hukuk Tarihi Dergisi*, I (1941-1942), 106-132.

Weber, Theodor. "Das Gemischte Handelsgericht in der Türkei," *Mitteilungen des Seminars für Orientalischen Sprachen: Westasiatische Studien*, II (1907), 96-165.

Yaltkaya, Şerefeddin. "İlhanîler Devri Idarî Teşkilâtına dair Nasir-ed-dini Tusî'nin bir eseri," *Türk Hukuk ve İktisat Tarihi Mecmuası*, II (1939), 6-16.

Ziya Paşa. "Jean Jacques Rousseau ile 'Emil' i hakkında," *Mecmua-i Ebüzziya* 15 Cemaziülahir 1330/1912, pp. 104-110.

[————]. "Ziya Paşanın Evvan-ı Tıfliyeti hakkında makalesi," *Mecmua-i Ebüzziya* I, 15 Rebiülevvel 1298, 404-409; 1 Rebiülahir 1298, 467-474; 15 Rebiülahir 1298, 484-489.

Index

The names in brackets following proper names are surnames (lâkab). Ottoman personalities were sometimes known by two of their names (i.e., Ahmed Midhat Efendi) and sometimes by only one (i.e., Midhat Paşa). There is no rule here except accepted usage to determine whether one or two names are used in this index.